Development NGOs
and
Labor Unions

Development NGOs
and
Labor Unions

Terms of Engagement

EDITED BY
DEBORAH EADE AND ALAN LEATHER

Kumarian
Press, Inc.

Development NGOs and Labor Unions: Terms of Engagement
Published in 2005 in the United States of America by Kumarian Press, Inc.,
1294 Blue Hills Avenue, Bloomfield, CT 06002 USA

Development NGOs and Labor Unions: Terms of Engagement is based on *Development in Practice* 14, nos. 1 and 2 (February 2004), published by Routledge, Taylor &
Francis, Ltd. *Development in Practice* gratefully acknowledges financial support from
affiliates of Oxfam International. The views expressed in this volume are those of the
individual contributors and not necessarily those of the editor or publisher.

Index by Robert Swanson
Proofread by Beth Richards

The text of this book is set in 10.5/13 Times.

Production and design by Joan Weber Laflamme/jml ediset

Printed in the United States by McNaughton & Gunn, Inc. Text printed with vegetable oil-based ink.

∞ The paper used in this publication meets the minimum requirements of the American National Standard for Information Sciences—Permanence of Paper for printed
Library Materials, ANSI Z39.48–1984.

Library of Congress Cataloging-in-Publication Data

Development NGOs and labor unions : terms of engagement / edited by Deborah
Eade and Alan Leather.
   p. cm.
   Includes bibliographical references and index.
   ISBN 1-56549-196-3 (alk. paper)
   1. Labor unions—Developing countries. 2. Non-governmental organizations—
Developing countries. 3. Developing countries—Economic conditions. 4. Economic
development. I. Eade, Deborah. II. Leather, Alan.
HD6940.7.D48 2005
331.88'09172'4—dc22

                2005002246

14 13 12 11 10 09 08 07 06 05 10 9 8 7 6 5 4 3 2 1 First Printing 2005

Contents

Part 2
Experiences of Union-based NGOs

Part 3
Workers in the Informal and *Maquila* Economies

Part 4
Workplace Codes of Conduct

Part 5
Case Studies

Part 6
Resources

Preface

DEBORAH EADE

Development NGOs and Labor Unions is based on a special issue of the journal *Development in Practice,*[1] whose roots lie deep in the lives of the guest editor, Alan Leather, and myself. Though our professional and political trajectories have taken us in different directions, we share the experience of taking our commitment to labor unionism into our work in development NGOs and of working in and alongside labor unions from a pro-poor and rights-based understanding of development issues. We have often been frustrated by the inability or unwillingness of development agencies to engage with organized labor and by the similar reluctance of labor unions to recognize the positive contributions that development NGOs can make to improving the situation of those who are poor and marginalized. All too often discussions and debates between the two sectors have been marred by antagonism and a touch of arrogance, a dialogue of the deaf rather than a mature conversation. But we have also worked alongside and been inspired by the dedication of people in both sectors, their willingness to fight on in the face of adversity, and their commitment to social and economic justice for all. In his introductory essay Alan charts his personal experience in working toward this vision over the last four decades, moving from the UK labor union movement into the world of international development agencies, back into labor union development-education work, and eventually into the global union federation arena. An inspiration in itself, this experience permits us unique insights into each sector and allows Alan to distill critical lessons for both in standing with the powerless in the fight against injustice.

While there is enormous scope for NGOs and labor unions to support each others' aims—and there have been exemplary cases of such collaboration—relations between the two sectors frequently have been marked by ignorance and suspicion, and sometimes by rivalry or outright hostility. This is hardly surprising. The phenomenal expansion in the number of NGOs operating around the world and their growing international influence have occurred in (and may indeed be a symptom of) a neoliberal political and economic context in which labor unions have experienced overall declines in membership and political influence.[2] In addition, although they may be grappling with similar issues and share many perspectives, unions and NGOs think and work in very different ways. Unions act on the basis of the mandate conferred by their membership, as a result of which they risk becoming overly bureaucratic and slow to react to change. By contrast, in part because they seldom have a single constituency to which they are accountable, NGOs have greater flexibility and can act quickly but may as a result fail to consult or coordinate effectively with other civil society organizations.

Labor unions and NGOs also have had grounds for ideological disagreement. NGOs, for example, may argue that unions do not represent or address the needs of the poorest, most of whom subsist in an informal economy; that their approach to recruitment and mobilization is outdated in today's globalized economy; and that they have a poor record on gender and ethnic equity and the concerns of women workers. For their part, unions have a legitimate concern about the tendency of NGOs to address poverty reduction through informal-economy mechanisms, such as microenterprises or income-generating projects, which often fail to take labor rights fully into account. Nor are NGOs themselves above criticism on issues of gender equity in the workplace, whatever their funding criteria overseas. And very few international NGOs have a glowing record on reflecting ethnic diversity at all levels or on drawing their staff from all social classes. Tensions have arisen when NGOs are seen to have undermined local unions by entering into bilateral dialogue with employers or monitoring codes of conduct. Many NGOs basically ignore labor unions altogether as civil society organizations, while some adopt anti-union policies internally by discouraging or even disallowing their staff to form or join unions.

As the neoliberal agenda continues to erode the rights of workers and their families as enshrined in Article 23 of the 1948 Universal Declaration of Human Rights,[3] and various ILO conventions, in particular those known as the core labor standards,[4] so it becomes imperative that civil society organizations break down the barriers among them in order to keep the rights of poor or otherwise vulnerable people firmly on the international agenda. The gulf between rich and poor has widened enormously in the last thirty years, and employment and access to basic social services are increasingly insecure for most of the human race. There is a pressing need for a concerted voice to challenge the ethos of the market; neither labor unions nor NGOs can afford to go it alone.

In compiling the special journal issue we invited contributions that would help to elucidate some of the underlying tensions between labor unions and NGOs in order to contribute to a greater understanding of the potential sources of conflict and disagreement often afflicting interorganizational relations, and to enhance the scope for constructive and respectful dialogue—and occasionally partnership—between the two sectors.

These papers are organized in this book around five broad but overlapping themes:

- alliances and tensions between labor unions and NGOs
- experiences of union-based NGOs
- workers in the informal and *maquila* economy
- workplace codes of conduct
- specific case studies

ALLIANCES AND TENSIONS

Labor unions and development NGOs can be broadly characterized as value-driven civil society organizations that champion the rights of those who are (or who may potentially be) exploited, oppressed, excluded, or otherwise marginalized. Although NGOs and labor unions are not homogeneous sectors, a goal that many of them would share is that all individuals and communities should play an active role in promoting equitable economic development and in shaping their societies and cultures.

Recent debates about globalization, ILO core labor standards, codes of conduct, and the role of the WTO have placed civil society organizations at the heart of these issues of global governance. While it is to be expected that NGOs and labor unions should pursue diverse strategies and adopt different means of achieving them, it is critical that they each avoid doing so at the expense of the other. There is an urgent need to engage in constructive dialogue and to work together toward a common cause.

Part 1 includes papers that explore some of the generic tensions that affect alliances between labor unions and development NGOs and have to be overcome if collaboration is to be fruitful. Dave Spooner, for example, looks at the different class backgrounds of the two types of organization, the corresponding differences in political and organizational cultures, and the consequent lack of understanding of each other's respective roles and objectives. These tensions came to the fore in recent ILO discussions on the organization of workers in the informal economy, with some NGOs challenging the right or ability of labor unions to represent those not in formal employment. Mark Anner and Peter Evans examine recent attempts to span the double divide between labor unions and NGOs across the North-South socioeconomic cleavage. The promotion first of the North American Free Trade Agreement (NAFTA), and now of the Free Trade Area of the Americas (FTAA, or ALCA in its Spanish acronym), has given new impetus to inter-hemispheric organizing both within specific sectors (notably the apparel export industry) and in relation to more macro issues concerning democratic governance. Sophia Huyer picks up a similar theme in relation to collaboration between Canadian NGOs and labor unions in the face of the challenges posed by NAFTA, illustrating the potential strength but also the inherent weaknesses of such alliances. It is one thing to collaborate on a specific campaign event, but sustaining that collaboration over time is far harder, especially if some partners are stronger and better resourced than others. Tim Connor looks at the involvement of NGOs in promoting the rights of workers through the anti-sweatshop movement, arguing that although the loose networked form of organization has enabled the movement to grow and accommodate a diverse constituency, there will be a need for greater cooperation between such NGOs and labor unions if the movement is to maintain its momentum and achieve any lasting results. Deborah Eade describes the exceptional collaboration between one international development NGO and labor unions in Honduras during the prolonged political violence ravaging Central America in the 1980s. She reflects on the personal and political commitment that often underpinned such relationships at that time, casting development assistance and solidarity as mutually reinforcing rather than at odds with each other. With reference to a project working with immigrant Mexican communities in California, Paul Johnston sets out a mechanism enabling labor unions to establish a semi-autonomous nonprofit "arm" to undertake activities that would be inappropriate or impossible for them to do themselves. Joseph Roman argues that NGOs have tended to focus on race and gender inequalities and to downplay social class as the principal issue to be addressed by working people in general, and in relations between workers in the North and the South in particular.

UNION-BASED NGOS

Many NGOs and foundations around the world have been set up by or have close links with labor unions. Some of these are involved in funding union initiatives in other countries; often, they seek to promote links or twinning arrangements between workers in similar industries or sectors, whether North-South or South-South. In Europe, for instance, Norwegian People's Aid was set up in 1939 by the Norwegian labor movement and is now involved in over four hundred projects in thirty countries. A more recent pioneering example of a labor union–based development initiative is the Steelworkers' Humanity Fund, established in 1985 by the United Steelworkers of Canada on the basis of a weekly contribution of forty cents per member. Since then, a number of similar funds have been set up there, such as the Canadian Auto Workers' Social Justice Fund in 1991, the Canadian Union of Public Employees' Union Aid in 1993, and the Ontario Secondary School Teachers' Federation Humanity Fund in 1996 (Marshall 1997). Solidar, based in Belgium, is an alliance of NGOs, labor unions, and campaigning groups from fifteen countries with links to the social democratic and socialist parties and to the labor union movement. It is active in the fields of social service provision, international cooperation, humanitarian aid, and lifelong learning. The Friedrich Ebert Foundation (FES) in Germany is perhaps one of the most widely known labor-related organizations working in development. Founded in 1925 (and banned under the Nazi regime), FES is committed to promoting the values of social democracy. Its development-cooperation program accounts for half its annual budget and focuses, among other things, on reinforcing free labor unions, supporting democratization, encouraging independent media structures, and promoting peace and respect for human rights. FES also supports research and publications, as well as its own publishing program on labor unionism.

Part 2 describes the work of two such NGOs. Jackie Simpkins outlines The Global Workplace program being run by the UK organization War on Want. This is essentially an umbrella for a range of activities to encourage labor union members in the UK to establish relationships with their counterparts in the South in order that both sides should develop a deeper understanding of how globalization is affecting them, encourage solidarity, and work together as an international force to defend workers' rights. Ken Davis gives an account of the latent tensions and tradeoffs between development NGOs and Union Aid Abroad (formerly Australian People for Health, Education and Development Abroad), and of the sometimes conservative or ill-informed attitudes within the labor movement toward international development. While labor unions may be to the left of the political spectrum, individual members may not immediately see the links between this position and their how they view "competition" from workers in poorer countries. There is therefore a need to educate the union constituency while also defending labor rights at home.

WORKERS IN THE INFORMAL ECONOMY AND ALTERNATIVES TO UNIONIZATION

A point often made by development NGOs and by Southern advocacy organizations such as Focus on the Global South in Thailand or Third World Network in Malaysia is that although millions of workers are unionized, they represent only a fraction of the world's work force. Women and men who are in some form of self-employment or subsistence activity—particularly those in the agricultural sector, who represent upward of 60 percent of the labor force in the South—are not in a position to join a conventional workplace-based union. The same holds true for home-based workers who undertake piecework in some link in the production chain. Within the formal employment sector many workers are prevented from unionizing or choose not to do so. The growth of the informal economy worldwide is cited as further evidence of the waning relevance of labor unions, as is the fact that some 900 million workers are underemployed while a further 150 million are said to be unemployed (Bullard 2000, 32). Hence, it is argued, the formal labor movement cannot represent the interests of most workers. Additional critiques of the representational legitimacy of labor unions are that their leadership tends to be male dominated, and that women are under-represented in the industrial sectors where unions are traditionally concentrated and which are therefore likely to be better protected by labor legislation (ibid., though see World Bank 2003 and note 5 below). Leaving aside the counter-argument that any such legislation has in most cases been fought for by organized labor and that the union movement has no interest in making gains at the expense of workers who are not unionized, some of these concerns are legitimate.

Clearly, the world of work is changing rapidly, particularly in relation to the "flexibilization" of employment and the phenomenon of the "virtual boss."[5] If unions are unable to modernize their own methods of recruiting, mobilizing, and articulating their demands, then the rights of all working people are likely to be still further eroded. Conversely, the presence of strong and effective unions has been found by the World Bank not only to enhance the conditions of unionized workers but also to improve overall economic performance and social stability.[6]

The contributions in Part 3 focus mainly on women workers in the informal and semiformal economy and in the *maquila* industry. Ruth Pearson reports on an action-research approach to map the huge range of home-based employment, in which women predominate, and to explore the potential for establishing sustainable organizations of homeworkers both nationally and internationally. Tracing the production chain that invisibly links women in different parts of an industry is part of the key to such organizing. Marina Prieto and Carolina Quinteros look at the exponential growth in the *maquila* industry in Central America with the cessation of the wars that ripped the region's economy to shreds throughout the 1980s. Focusing on Honduras and Nicaragua, they highlight the tensions between traditional industry-based labor unions and the new proletariat, comprised mainly of young women, many of whom are lone parents or maintaining a family. The old methods of organizing are not only infeasible within the *maquila* (where employers are known to stamp out any attempt to unionize), but they are also unresponsive to the priorities of the female work force. Women's organizations focusing on labor rights and linking up with international anti-sweatshop movements have, by contrast, had greater success, but their relations with the local labor unions have not thrived. Angela Hale from Women Working Worldwide shows how labor unions and NGOs often find themselves around the same table in the wish to improve working conditions in global production and supply chains. Her argument is that although the two types of organization have different ways of working, they have nevertheless proved able to collaborate; building on this collaboration offers the potential to create what she refers to as new forms of labor internationalism.

WORKPLACE CODES OF CONDUCT

The promotion of workplace codes of conduct has been one of the main ways in which NGOs have engaged with labor issues in recent years, whether primarily from a rights-based perspective or as a tangible campaigning goal around which to mobilize public support. There is a strong moral and educational appeal in the argument that consumers bear some of the responsibility for poor working conditions; few would feel comfortable about wearing clothes produced by slave or bonded labor, or eating out-of-season vegetables grown by people who earn too little to feed their own children adequately. There is something obscene about children being denied the right to play and recreation because they are employed in the manufacture of sports equipment. Focusing on cases of extreme exploitation, or where there is a clear link between consumer choices and the oppression of other human beings, can offer NGOs the classic campaigning agenda: a problem with which to identify, a "bad guy" against whom to mobilize, and a tangible solution in the form of a code of conduct.

But in reality neither the picture nor the solutions are so simple. Criticisms of codes of conduct are plentiful. They range from the argument that codes of conduct are mainly cosmetic, designed for public display while business goes on as usual (Utting 2000), to concerns that they divert attention from the need for structural solutions, that is, strong laws and effective enforcement of social clauses. NGOs are also accused of being short-lived in their commitment and perhaps too concerned with profiling themselves, while unions are necessarily in for the long and unglamorous haul. Perhaps the gravest criticism is that the establishment and monitoring of codes of conduct have on occasion allowed NGOs and management to work things out bilaterally, allowing the company to avoid negotiating with employees and their representatives—a criticism that NGOs would rebut by arguing that they focus on industries in which unions are weak or simply nonexistent.

Rainer Braun and Judy Gearhart engage with these tensions head on. They see the underlying issue as being one of differences in the approaches of labor unions and NGOs to political power. The former aim for power and operate within a context of political bargaining and compromise, while the latter need to remain political outsiders if they are to maintain a watchdog role. It is possible to obtain short-term successes, but these will be sustained in the long term only through the self-representation of those directly concerned, in this case the workers. In other words, the litmus test is whether NGO activity facilitates or inhibits this long-term objective. Ronnie D. Lipschutz similarly maintains that the "spillover effects" into the broader society of the host country are ultimately more important than the adoption of codes per se. In his view the real goal is to improve legal, political, and social conditions for workers rather than trying to affect corporate behavior through consumer pressure. Lance Compa has written widely on these and related issues, and we are pleased to reproduce a paper first published in the journal of the International Centre for Trade Union Rights (ICTUR), *International Union Rights*. He recognizes that labor unions and NGOs share the desire to halt abusive behavior by companies and to check corporate power in the global economy. He also acknowledges the real tensions between the two, both over tactics and over their understanding of social justice in the global economy. However, both have more in common with each other than they do with corporations, governments, or with a neoliberal agenda that sees free trade as the way to raise labor standards. In cases where NGOs can act quickly, and given the weak presence of unions in the global assembly line, codes may be a valuable asset. Neil Kearney and Judy Gearhart also look at how workplace codes might help workers to organize, especially in situations where unions are repressed. They focus specifically on a collaborative project between the International Textile, Garment and Leather Workers' Federation and Social Accountability International that aims to help workers to understand how to use codes to their benefit, building on their existing organizational and education strategies.

CASE STUDIES

Part 5 brings together a series of contrasting case studies from around the world. Some illustrate collaboration while others show labor unions and NGOs running almost on parallel tracks; all reveal the critical importance of the wider legal and social framework regulating the activities of both sectors and of the political context more generally. E. Remi Aiyede looks at the role of human rights NGOs in the democratization of Nigeria, emphasizing their alliances with labor unions (which were themselves the target of government repression) in helping to build a wider consensus for change within civil society. Jane Lethbridge gives two detailed examples of NGO and labor union collaboration on issues relating to the health sector: joining in opposition to privatization of the health service in Malaysia, and joining in support for policies and action plans on HIV/AIDS in South Africa. Jonathan Ellis writes about a campaign in the UK to defend the rights of asylum seekers that brought about a unique (and occasionally awkward) alliance among Oxfam GB, the Refugee

Council, and the Transport and General Workers' Union. The campaign was successful in terms of the immediate outcomes, and while it did not lay the ground for long-term collaboration, all parties learned much about the importance of compromise in the interests of alliance-building. Elaheh Rostami Povey compares the role of labor unions and women's NGOs in Iran, where there has to date been very little cross-fertilization between the two sectors. She argues that the women's NGOs have a great deal to offer to the labor movement in terms of greater sensitivity to gender issues and to the specific needs of women workers, while the NGOs would benefit from setting their project-based work within a framework of broader structural change. Satendra Prasad and Darryn Snell turn to the troubled situation of labor unions in three South Pacific countries: Papua New Guinea, the Fiji Islands, and Solomon Islands. The region has undergone significant political and economic turmoil in recent years, and labor unions have had to face the challenge of continuing to stand for a broad social justice agenda, on the one hand, while, on the other, needing to look to their members' immediate interests.

There are many other angles on this issue, and this volume by no means purports to be comprehensive. Nor is it the last word. However, our hope is that these chapters will contribute to greater understanding among the different sectors and types of organization represented here—from labor unions to development NGOs, from labor and human rights organizations to networks of homeworkers, from activist-scholars to union organizers. We hope too that labor unions and development NGOs might also learn from seeing themselves through others' eyes and so be encouraged to step "outside the box" of their own assumptions, self-images, and perspectives and reflect on how they are perceived by one another and by outside observers. Mutual respect depends upon acknowledging and accepting difference rather than trying to impose uniformity, and real collaboration is possible only on the basis of such respect. Conversely, and as many of our contributors show, behavior that is perceived to break rank among progressive civil society organizations will play into the hands of forces that have shown such scant regard for the rights of working people and indifference to the goal of social and economic justice for all. The stakes could not be higher.

NOTES

[1] *Development in Practice* 14, nos. 1 and 2 (February 2004).

[2] The World Bank's website on NGOs, for instance, estimates that there are "between 6,000 and 30,000 national NGOs in developing countries" and that "over 15% of total overseas development aid is channelled through NGOs" (accessed December 12, 2001). The list of NGOs with consultative status at ECOSOC runs to sixty pages of about forty entries apiece—that is one NGO per day for six and a half years or about one NGO per minute for an entire twenty-four-hour day. And that is just the tip of the iceberg.

[3] Article 23 states: "(1) Everyone has the right to work, to free choice of employment, to just and favourable conditions of work and to protection against unemployment. (2) Everyone, without any discrimination, has the right to equal pay for equal work. (3) Everyone who works has the right to just and favourable remuneration ensuring for himself and his family an existence worthy of human dignity, and supplemented, if necessary, by other means of social protection. (4) Everyone has the right to form and to join trade unions for the protection of his interests."

[4] The core labor standards are (1) the right to organize and engage in collective bargaining, (2) the right to equality at work, (3) the abolition of child labor, and (4) the abolition of forced labor. These standards serve as "enabling rights" in that they create conditions that allow access to other important workers' rights. Labor unions have lobbied for the core labor standards to be recognized as internationally accepted guides to a civilized, dignified, and sustainable workplace, regardless of the stage or nature of national development.

[5] A major focus of consumer-based organizations such as the Clean Clothes Campaign and Labour Behind the Label is to trace company mergers and find out who really owns what. Companies often own a range of products, which are marketed under different brand names. A consumer may choose to boycott one product but be unaware that the rival "clean" brand actually belongs to the same company. By the same token, transnational outsourcing means that workers may not even know for whom they are ultimately working.

[6] A report issued in February 2003, based on reviews of over one thousand studies on the effects of unions and collective bargaining, found that in industrialized and developing countries alike, unionized workers earn more, work fewer hours, receive more training, and have longer job tenure on average than do their non-unionized counterparts. Furthermore, wage differentials between skilled and unskilled workers, and between women and men, are lower in unionized settings (World Bank 2003). The clear message is that joining a union is good for workers, and good for the economy—something that labor unions have argued since their inception over a century ago.

Abbreviations and Acronyms

ACFOA	Australian Council for Overseas Aid
ACFTU	All-China Federation of Trade Unions
ACTU	Australian Council of Trade Unions
ADB	Asian Development Bank
AFL-CIO	American Federation of Labor-Congress of Industrial Organizations
ALCA	Free Trade Area of the Americas (the Spanish acronym)
ANC	African National Congress
APHEDA	Australian People for Health, Education and Development Abroad
ART	Alliance for Responsible Trade
ASC/HSA	Alianza Social Continental/Hemispheric Social Alliance
ATTAC	Association for the Taxation of Financial Transactions for the Aid of Citizens
AusAID	Australian government aid agency
BFAWU	Bakers, Food, and Allied Workers' Union (UK)
CARE	Cooperative for American Relief Everywhere
CAW	Canadian Auto Workers
CCC	Clean Clothes Campaign
CD	Campaign for Democracy (Nigeria)
CDHR	Committee for the Defence of Human Rights (Nigeria)
CEP	Communications, Energy, and Paperworkers Union
CHI	Citizens' Health Initiative (Malaysia)

CLC	Canadian Labour Congress
CLO	Civil Liberties Organisation (Nigeria)
CND	Campaign for Nuclear Disarmament
CODEMUH	Honduran Women's Collective
COSATU	Congress of South African Trade Unions
CTM	Mexican Trade Union Confederation
CTUC	Commonwealth Trade Union Council
CUEPACS	Congress of Unions of Employees in the Public and Civil Services
CUPE	Canadian Union of Public Employees
CUT	Central Trade Union Confederation (Brazil)
CWS	Cooperative Wholesale Society (UK)
DFID	Department for International Development
ECOSOC	(United Nations) Economic and Social Council
ETI	Ethical Trading Initiative
ETUC	European Trade Union Confederation
EU	European Union
FES	Friedrich Ebert Stichting
FLP	Fiji Labour Party
FOMCA	Federation of Malaysian Consumer Associations
FLA	Fair Labor Association
FPSA	Fiji Public Service Association
FTA	Free trade agreement
FTAA	Free Trade Area of the Americas
FTUC	Fiji Trade Union Congress
GATS	General Agreement on Trade in Services
GATT	General Agreement on Tariffs
GMB	Britain's General Union
GUF	global union federation
HCA	Health Consumer Alliance (United States)
HSA	*See* ASC/HSA
ICCPR	International Covenant on Civil and Political Rights
ICFTU	International Confederation of Free Trade Unions

ICTUR	International Centre for Trade Union Rights
ICESCR	International Covenant on Economic, Social, and Political Rights
ICHRP	International Council on Human Rights Policy
ILO	International Labour Organization
IMF	International Monetary Fund
INS	Immigration and Naturalization Service (United States)
ITF	International Transport Workers' Federation
ITGLWF	International Textile, Garment, and Leather Workers' Federation
KTV	Municipal Workers' and Employees' Union (Finland)
MEC	María Elena Cuadra (women's movement in Nicaragua)
MFL	Manitoba Federation of Labour
MHW	Mapping Home-based Work
MTUC	Malaysian Trades Union Congress
NAC	National Action Committee on the Status of Women
NAFTA	North American Free Trade Agreement
NDP	New Democratic Party (Canada)
NGO	Nongovernmental organization
NLC	National Labor Committee
OECD	Organisation for Economic Co-operation and Development
OGB	Oxfam GB
ORIT	Organización Regional Interamericana de Trabajadores
PAC	Pan African Congress
PLO	Palestine Liberation Organization
PNG	Papua New Guinea
PNGTUC	Papua New Guinea Trade Unions' Congress
PSI	Public Services International
REBRIP	Brazilian Network for People's Integration (Rede Brasileira pela Integração dos Povos

SA8000	Social Accountability 8000
SAI	Social Accountability International
SDL	United Fiji Party
SEWA	Self-Employed Women's Association (India)
SICTU	Solomon Islands Council of Trade Unions
SiD	Danish General Workers' Union
SILP	Solomon Islands Labour Party
SINUW	Solomon Islands National Union of Workers
SMO	Social movement organization
T&G	Transport and General Workers' Union (UK)
TAC	Treatment Action Campaign (South Africa)
TGWU	Transport and General Workers' Union (UK)
TNC	Transnational corporation
TUIREG	Trade Union International Research and Education Group
UDHR	Universal Declaration of Human Rights
UFW	United Farm Workers
UNDP	United Nations Development Programme
UNITE	Union of Needletrades, Industrial, and Textile Employees
USAID	US Agency for International Development
USAS	United Students against Sweatshops
US/LEAP	US Labor Education in the Americas Project
WHO	World Health Organization
WIEGO	Women in Informal Employment Globalizing and Organizing
WRC	Workers' Rights Consortium
WTO	World Trade Organization
WWW	Women Working Worldwide

One

Labor Union and NGO Relations in Development and Social Justice

ALAN LEATHER

In this chapter I concentrate on the evolution of relationships between labor unions and NGOs that have developed in the field of development and social justice. In so doing, I explore how these relationships started, how they functioned, and what the outcomes have been. Most of the reference points are drawn from my experience working for *both* labor unions and NGOs in the UK and other parts of the world over the last forty years.

As a young labor union activist and printing apprentice in the late 1950s and early 1960s, I became very concerned about international injustices. Much of this concern was rooted in my labor union experience— the workplace discussions, labor union education programs, and the books and newspapers that were passed around the workplace. For example, the father of the chapel (shop steward) in my first workplace gave me Trevor Huddleston's book *Naught for Your Comfort* (Huddleston 1956). The effect on my fifteen-year-old self of reading about life in Sophiatown, a South African township near Johannesburg, has never left me. "Jacob Ledwaba had been arrested for being out after curfew and without a pass. On Saturday morning he came home. He told his wife he had been kicked in the stomach in the cells and that he was in so much pain that he couldn't go to work." This was an everyday occurrence in Sophiatown.

My reaction to this and other instances of tyranny and inequity was to go and do something practical—but despite labor union concern with international injustice and a long tradition of international solidarity, there wasn't much a labor union could offer a young activist in terms of

1

hands-on involvement. I therefore moved toward the cause of NGOs such as Oxfam,[1] the Campaign for Nuclear Disarmament (CND), and the Anti-Apartheid movement. At Easter in the late 1950s we marched with CND from Aldermaston, the UK government's Nuclear Research Establishment, to London. We carried tins of powdered milk as a symbol of food for the hungry in a world where vast resources were being spent on the arms race.

It seemed quite natural for a wide range of progressive organizations, labor unions, political parties, peace groups, churches, and development NGOs to be marching together against a threat to global peace and against the global injustices of poverty and colonialism. Only recently in London have demonstrations against the Iraq war surpassed the CND marches of the 1960s in terms of numbers of protesters on the streets.

By the age of eighteen I had decided to apply to Voluntary Service Overseas. The projects available did not (and probably still don't) place volunteers with labor movement organizations, but there is nonetheless enormous scope for labor unions to work with international volunteer-sending agencies, and I took part in discussions in the 1970s about placing volunteers with labor movement organizations. This was not just in terms of North-South exchanges but also South-South and South-North, a different vision of volunteering that was the founding spirit behind UN Volunteers, for example, and many smaller agencies. The strengthening of labor unions has never been seen as a developmental goal, but I have recently learned that in order to promote HIV/AIDS prevention in the workplace, UN Volunteers may now be placed with labor as well as employer organizations in selected African countries.

As a volunteer I was fortunate to find myself in Lusaka, Northern Rhodesia (now Zambia), where I became involved with refugees from apartheid South Africa, many of whom had fled from the townships so vividly described by Huddleston. This was the time when the first African National Congress (ANC) and Pan African Congress (PAC) offices were being opened in Lusaka, and despite the colonial administration's connivance with the South African authorities, there was an opportunity to do something on the ground.

When I returned to the UK in the mid-1960s I eventually took a job with Oxfam. I worked in one of the London offices in the Trade Union and Cooperatives Department. The department had two main objectives—to work with the UK cooperative movement on building a consumer cooperative movement in Botswana, and to raise money from UK labor unions to support projects in the Third World. There were also strong links between the Cooperative Wholesale Society (CWS) and the unions, and many UK labor unionists were members of the CWS as well as being the major users of its different commercial services. I can still remember the Leather family dividend number. Oxfam's links with the cooperative movement were well developed before I joined, and part of my job was to fundraise with CWS groups in different parts of the country. The CWS had underwritten the project and, in consultation with Oxfam's Africa Field Office, had sent experts in consumer cooperative development to Botswana to train local cooperators.

The labor union work, however, was still at an early stage, and we were responsible for making contact with labor union head offices to open up fundraising possibilities by offering specific projects for sponsorship, based on the idea of twinning a union with a project in the same line of work as the union members. Oxfam helped the unions to raise the money by providing materials and speakers for union meetings. The initiative was well received as fitting into the tradition of international solidarity, though the projects—usually involving some form of training for young people—were more likely to be run by a church mission than a labor union.

Reflecting on it today, I find it interesting that, from Oxfam's perspective, the relationship was simply based on fundraising, and indeed the unions saw it this way as well. Neither side saw the other as a potential ally to fight world poverty in political or strategic terms, for example, through joint campaigning, or even to extend the educational opportunities offered by the fundraising. It was still about using the starving child to move hearts, and never mind using the head to link that child to issues of exploitation and inequality that labor unionists understand so well.

The labor unions, for their part, also saw Oxfam as a fundraising organization and supported Oxfam projects without getting involved in a broader international strategy to challenge the causes of poverty. Many of the same labor unions were members of international labor union federations—now known as global union federations (GUFs)—and even these organizations took until the 1990s to make it a priority to raise the awareness among their affiliates about the workings of the international system and to take steps to challenge it.

My stay in the Trade Union and Cooperatives Department was rather short-lived because of differences of opinion over strategy, but it gave me insights into some of the internal workings of Oxfam. Labor unions were organizations outside the experience of most of the staff at Oxfam's headquarters in Oxford, which was unsurprising given the class base of

Oxfam at the time. There was no staff union until the 1980s, and even then the initiative initially met considerable resistance from senior management. The Trade Union and Cooperatives Department lasted a few years longer than I did but was never a central activity. Without the support of then-director Leslie Kirkley it would not have existed, though there have been labor union liaison staff based in Oxfam for periods of time since then. Even today, I don't believe that an active labor union leader sits on or has ever been invited to join Oxfam's board of trustees, although there is room for the great and the good from most other walks of life.

Oxfam's labor union links in the 1960s should be seen in the context of an important difference of opinion at the time over the organization's involvement in "political" movements for change. The loudest arguments were between the fundraisers and the campaigners for social justice. The fundraisers did not want Oxfam's image to be tarnished by pictures of young Oxfam supporters taking part in CND demonstrations or associating with anti-establishment organizations such as labor unions. One irony of this debate was that Oxfam's leadership at the time was strongly linked to the Quakers, who in turn were very active in CND. Fundraising needs versus campaigning work—complicated by UK law and the role of the Charity Commission—has been an ongoing dilemma, one that has obviously influenced the relationship between Oxfam (and other similar organizations in the UK) and labor unions, and, more broadly, one that has also constrained the role of development NGOs in taking political action.[2]

I should also like to reflect briefly on Oxfam's involvement with social movements and political action in other parts of the world, as I experienced it when working for Oxfam in India. In 1967 I went to work on a famine-relief project in Bihar State, NE India. This was primarily a feeding program organized in cooperation with the state government and CARE. Famine had followed the failure of the monsoon rains in 1966, leaving thirty million landless laborers and small farmers without any income. The feeding program was a success in that it focused on the most vulnerable—children and nursing mothers.

I returned to India after a six-month break to work on a rural development project in the same area. The project was a joint Oxfam program with Sarva Seva Sangh, the main Gandhian organization for social and economic development. It provided irrigation and agricultural know-how to small farmers to enable them to cope with the problems of irregular rainfall. There was a strong social-reform aspect to the project in terms of the *Gramdan* (village council) approach to village development. This was based on the idea of each village establishing a council that would take responsibility for running village affairs, including the pooling of land so that there was no social exclusion. This was the first time that Oxfam had become involved in this type of social movement. Most of the organization's previous assistance in India had been directed toward mission-run welfare and training projects, the increasing of food production through support for hybrid crop production, and refugee relief.

Working with a movement for social change such as Sarva Seva Sangh raised major questions for Oxfam, as any change process meant getting involved with politics on the local, district, and possibly state levels. Challenging the rural status quo—as the Oxfam project did by providing employment for laborers on their own land when they were wanted by the landlords for work on theirs—caused enormous problems. As many of the laborers were bonded to the landlords, their not reporting for work when called was interpreted as a strike. Local Gandhian social workers eventually sorted out the conflict, but it was clear that Oxfam could have been blamed for causing social unrest. This highlights another fundamental dilemma: one of the key ways of helping the poor and marginalized is to support the organizations they set up to improve their situation, which often involves challenging the local power structure. At the same time, such support can threaten the ability of an external NGO, in this case Oxfam, to continue functioning in the country. This helps explain Oxfam's reluctance, for many years, to form alliances with labor union organizations in the South.

On returning to the UK after this period in India I decided to use my international experience in labor union education and took a job teaching development studies at Ruskin College, Oxford, which has close links with labor unions. While working with a group of students in 1976 on the impact of the international economy on UK workers, we decided to develop an audiovisual presentation that would explore this relationship and to show it at a fringe event at the Trade Union Congress in Brighton. This led to the formation of the Trade Union International Research and Education Group (TUIREG), an NGO whose aim was to create awareness of the impact of the international economy on the UK workplace, and vice versa, through labor union education programs. In many respects the aim was to create awareness among rank-and-file activists and shop stewards about how the world works. It was clear that an increasing number of jobs in the UK were dependent on the global economy, but there was little discussion within labor unions about the policy implications. The main area of activity during the first years of TUIREG's existence was to explore the ways in which multinational companies operated internationally.

TUIREG could be described as a service NGO for the labor union movement. However, despite its name and its base at Ruskin, labor unions took time to be convinced that TUIREG could offer useful input in labor union education. Initially, labor unions were suspicious of a message that was critical of global capitalism. This seemed too political, even for labor unions!

Over the next few years several unions recognized TUIREG's educational role, and there was a constant demand for work. Once the unions concerned had commissioned TUIREG, staff members were given a free hand to develop course materials and programs. A study that TUIREG undertook in the late 1970s with the European Trade Union Confederation showed little ongoing educational activity that strategically examined the international economy. There were, however, international solidarity activities around major causes such as Chile, South Africa, and Nicaragua, and some links between labor unions and the NGOs that were taking up these causes. It was, however, still an effort to link these issues to national or international economic policies and global trends in trade and investment.

In order to spread TUIREG's funding base, it was necessary to approach other organizations for support. In the UK these included Oxfam, Christian Aid, and various foundations. Initial approaches to Oxfam in the early 1980s received a sympathetic hearing but did not produce any tangible support. Christian Aid did respond positively and remained a TUIREG partner for many years. Later, Oxfam also provided funding. TUIREG was also obliged to undertake an increasing amount of commissioned work. This included the production of audiovisual education materials, educational programs for international labor unions and the International Labour Organization (ILO), and projects in developing countries for individual labor unions. To some extent this changed the original conception of the organization, although much of the experience gained from working in different developing countries was used in the UK-based education work.

I have concentrated on TUIREG because of firsthand experience of its activities,[3] but it is important to recognize that there were other NGOs in the UK and elsewhere in Europe that were working with labor unions on international issues with varying degrees of success. One example worth considering is War on Want, which had strong labor movement links when it was started in the early 1950s; for a long time, however, it did not develop this alliance. The late 1970s witnessed a resurgence in the agency's interest in labor unions through the work of Don Thomson who, with Rodney Larson, wrote a book for War on Want entitled *Where Were You, Brother? An Account of Trade Union Imperialism* (Thomson and Larson 1978). The book was highly critical of certain aspects of national and international labor union activity. Its publication created a major furor, and War on Want came to be regarded with great suspicion by large parts of the labor union establishment. This, in turn, had implications for labor union relations with other development NGOs in the UK, and to some extent at an international level.

TUIREG entered new territory in the 1980s by starting to work for some of the GUFs. For the most part the federations had little experience working with NGOs. The organization that used TUIREG's services the most was Public Services International (PSI), representing public service workers worldwide. PSI employed TUIREG to develop information and education materials, especially video programs, and to run education and training programs, mainly in West Africa.

I joined PSI in 1987 as its education officer. Apart from using TUIREG in a service or consultancy role, PSI had few links with NGOs, but as it began to develop its policies on gender equality and public-service reforms, including privatization, the organization became aware of the increasing number of NGOs working in the same areas.

An initial reaction—not only on the part of PSI but quite commonly among labor unions—was to see these NGOs as competitors who had moved into a field of activity that should have been theirs. Issues of particular concern related to the extent to which such organizations represented the view of their "membership" in a democratic way, as NGOs tend to talk about "speaking for" or "on behalf of" the members of the groups they support but do not have an explicit mandate to do so. At the same time, the unions had to recognize that on many issues they had been slow to react.

Since the mid-1990s there has been a marked change in the relationship between PSI and NGOs. This has come about because of the recognition that in major policy campaigns where PSI is trying to influence the functioning of international bodies such as the WTO, it is impossible to be effective without forming alliances with like-minded organizations. One of the best examples is the World Is Not for Sale Campaign, an international alliance of 150 organizations. One central aspect of this alliance is the fact that there is a shared objective, though at the same time the organizations involved have been ready to recognize the value of one another's points of view—and increasing efforts are made to reflect a range of views in joint position statements. For example, as the only labor organization in the alliance, PSI policies have on the whole been accepted by the others because there is an understanding and appreciation of the workers' perspective and the importance of including it. This mutual trust has taken a long time to build, and many links have come about because of the impact of globalization and the ensuing social injustice and exclusion.

A study made of the eleven GUFs dealing with NGOs in the late 1990s showed that a wide variety of relationships exist. Some, like PSI, have close and growing relations, while one or two remain suspicious of contacts of this sort. There are many unresolved concerns, such as the role of NGOs with relation to the ILO, where it is important that the special role of labor unions is maintained.

In conclusion, what we need to hold on to are two key realities: first, there are issues of such significance to civil society, including workers and their organizations, that the only way to tackle them is through the broadest possible coalitions; second, imbalances in the distribution of power and resources are so great that all those who wish to oppose such injustice and stand with the powerless must celebrate their differences and use their diversity in a many-stranded alliance for change.

NOTES

[1] Known at the time as OXFAM, the organization later changed its name to Oxfam UK and Ireland, and more recently to Oxfam GB.

[2] This tension was by no means peculiar to Oxfam. Most development NGOs in the UK are registered as charities and so come under the scrutiny of the Charity Commission, which is charged with investigating allegations of involvement in activities not permitted under this legislation. Any advocacy, campaigning, lobbying, or research activities conducted or supported had to be directly related to the organization's charitable purpose and be "non-political." Campaigning and human rights organizations such as Amnesty International UK and World Development Movement have long called for reform of the UK Charity Law, which is based on a four-hundred-year-old statute. In July 2003 the government set out a broader definition of charitable purposes to include a range of "purposes beneficial to the community" (Home Office 2003).

[3] For current information about TUIREG, see its website.

Part 1

Alliances and Tensions between Labor Unions and NGOs

TWO

Labor Unions and NGOs

The Need for Cooperation

DAVE SPOONER

THE BASIS FOR COOPERATION

Both labor unions and NGOs are major global actors in civil society. NGOs are organizations that are voluntary, independent, not-for-profit, and not self-serving in aims and related values. Labor unions may be said to be self-serving insofar as they are membership organizations with a primary responsibility to protect and advance the interests of their members. Nevertheless, although unions are concerned primarily with conditions in employment and the workplace, they have always had broader social and political concerns over a wide range of national and international issues.

Some would argue that there has been a partial retreat of the labor movement, and in particular labor unions, from this broader social and political commitment in recent decades, creating a vacuum that has been filled by the growth of NGOs (see, for example, Gallin 2000a and 2002). Others, such as Annie Watson of the Commonwealth Trade Union Council, would argue that the trend has been in the opposite direction, as evidenced by labor union campaigns on human rights, women's rights, and participation in pro-democracy movements and alliances on the debt issue (see Spooner 2000, appendix). Historically, labor unions have argued that a consistent defense of their members' interests demands a long-term struggle for a social and political context at national and international levels that is favorable to the well-being of people and society as

11

a whole. They legitimately claim to be serving the interests of society in general, as do NGOs, in acting on the desire to advance and improve the human condition.

INTERNATIONAL DEVELOPMENT

Many unions in industrialized countries are engaged in international development activities. In many cases they are financially supported through their government's international development agencies, providing support for labor union education and organization programs in developing countries. They are often organized through international labor union federations—the industrial sector–based GUFs or the federations of national labor union centers, notably the International Confederation of Free Trade Unions (ICFTU), for example. Other development programs are organized bilaterally between some of the larger national union organizations and counterpart organizations in developing countries, such as those undertaken by UNISON in the UK, the Danish General Workers' Union (SiD), or Bondgenoten FNV in the Netherlands.

In some countries, unions are active members of the national platforms of NGOs engaged in international development, such as SiD, the Commonwealth Trade Union Council, the LO/FTF Council in Denmark, and the metalworkers' and municipal workers' unions in Finland. Internationally, these unions are concerned primarily with supporting the development of the labor union movement in developing countries, either bilaterally or through international union federations, as well as with promoting campaigns on workers' rights, child labor, HIV/AIDS, women's development, health, the informal economy, and so on.

In addition to labor unions, international development programs are also undertaken by specialist organizations established by or with the labor movement. These would include the workers' aid organizations such as Norwegian People's Aid, the Olof Palme International Centre in Sweden, ISCOD in Spain, and War on Want and One World Action in the UK, represented internationally through Solidar (formerly International Workers' Aid); and workers' education organizations such as the British and Nordic Workers' Education Associations, labor union education departments and institutions, and labor service NGOs in developing countries, represented internationally through the International Federation of Workers' Education Associations. The member organizations of these networks vary widely in size, structure, and capacity, ranging from national organizations with a multi-million dollar turnover to small organizations with an annual budget of less than US$25,000.

HUMAN RIGHTS

Human rights have always been a central concern of the labor union movement. Apart from reasons of ideological principle, labor unions simply cannot function in an environment where human and democratic rights are not safeguarded (for example, in highly repressive dictatorships or in police states) except in the form of illegal cadre groups or proto-unions.

Labor unions, as clandestine organizations when necessary and public ones wherever possible, are often at the forefront of critical battles for democracy. In South Africa, for example, the campaign against apartheid was rigorously supported by labor unions—both inside and outside the country. The strength of the internal democratic labor union movement, itself the product of massive popular protest in the 1970s and 1980s, was a crucial factor in the eventual emergence of a democratic South Africa (see, among others, Marx 1992). In China, workers attempting to form genuine democratic labor unions—notably the Beijing Workers' Autonomous Federation—were at the forefront of the democracy campaign in 1989, culminating in the Tiananmen Square massacre. Despite the massacre and the consistent repression of subsequent attempts to organize democratic labor union activity, labor unionists continue to risk their lives by demanding democratic reform (see, for example, "China Labour Bulletin," online). There are numerous further examples, both historic and contemporary, including, among others, Spain, Poland, Hungary, Czechoslovakia, Indonesia, South Africa, Brazil, Korea, Zambia, and Zimbabwe. The history of democratic development in Britain, for example, is inextricably linked with the growth and development of the labor union movement.

More broadly, all "normal" labor union concerns are in fact human rights issues, starting with the most elementary: the right of unions to exist. Restrictions on the right to freedom of association, the right to strike, and labor union recognition are infringements of fundamental human rights. In recent years the international labor union movement has explicitly recognized the importance of basic workers' rights—human rights—as a "line in the sand" from which no retreat is possible. These "core labor standards" are encapsulated in the *ILO Declaration of Fundamental Principles and Rights at Work.*[1]

SPECIFIC AREAS OF COMMON CONCERN

There are numerous specific points of contact between labor unions and NGOs. Some are highly specialized, related to the industrial and employment sectors represented or to the particular needs of workers in union membership. Nevertheless, it is possible to consider a limited range of commonly shared agenda items within the broad scope of core labor standards, which may have a more general potential for the development of NGO and labor union partnerships.

Defense and organization of workers in sectors of employment with traditionally low levels of union organization. In sectors of employment (waged or otherwise) where labor union organization is traditionally very difficult, national and international unions, by necessity, seek alliances and cooperation with NGOs. This includes specific sectors of employment such as garment manufacturing, construction, agriculture, and subsistence farming; and particularly vulnerable groups of workers, such as young women, migrant workers, ethnic minorities, and so on.

Defense and organization of workers in countries and regions facing state or para-state repression of labor union organization. In countries where labor unions have historically been forced underground, it has frequently been NGOs that have provided a basis for organizing and defending workers. There are vivid examples from Korea (up to the late 1980s), the Philippines (under Marcos), Indonesia (to the present day), and South Africa (in the early 1970s).

Campaigns for the inclusion of core labor standards in international trade agreements. In recent years unions and NGOs have worked side by side to lobby governments and intergovernmental institutions for the inclusion of basic workers' rights in international trade agreements (so-called social clauses).

Campaigns to ensure that employers, particularly transnational corporations (TNCs), respect and adhere to core labor standards. With slow progress being achieved in the incorporation of workers' rights into trade agreements through intergovernmental lobbying and negotiation, unions and NGOs are engaged in a range of initiatives to ensure that employers respect those rights. These include negotiations between GUFs, sometimes in alliance with NGOs (see, for example, IUF 2001) and international employers to enshrine workers' rights in signed and verifiable agreements reached through collective bargaining, known as International Framework Agreements. Where these are not possible or appropriate, unions and NGOs increasingly work together in the development of codes of conduct that employers can sign up to, without necessarily forcing the employer to the negotiating table with union representatives.[2]

Protection of workers in the informal sector. Of particular interest is the interaction of unions and NGOs over the defense and organization of workers in the so-called informal economy. In the past the informal economy was regarded as a marginal or temporary phenomenon that was bound to wither away and die with modern industrial growth, as illegal activity with which the labor union movement should have no contact, or as a conspiracy of employers to undermine the rights and conditions of organized workers. This has changed dramatically in recent years as unions in both industrialized and developing countries are increasingly aware of the need to reach, support, and organize workers in the informal economy. Inevitably, this has brought national and international unions in contact with a wide range of NGOs for whom the informal economy is of central interest, whether from an international development, gender, environment, or human rights perspective. Debates on the informal economy provide a good illustration of key issues in the labor union–NGO relationship.

OBSTACLES TO COLLABORATION

These key areas of common concern, in addition to the general issues of democracy and civil society, represent important points of contact between labor unions and NGOs of different types. It is therefore not surprising that such cooperation should indeed take place. What is surprising is that there is not far more of it and that it is not a general and permanent feature of the activities of either unions or NGOs. To understand the reasons for this, and to appreciate where tensions in labor union–NGO relations may arise, it is necessary to examine some of the main obstacles to effective collaboration.

Diversity of the Labor Union Agenda

It would be a mistake to view the labor union movement agenda as homogeneous or undifferentiated, despite strong historical and cultural commonalities. Unions have very different needs for cooperation with NGOs. Unions representing agricultural workers, for example, often face problems of a poor organizational base, low levels of unionization, countless numbers of people working in little more than subsistence conditions, prevalence of child labor, poor levels of education and literacy, difficult communications, and so on. Under these conditions, national or international union organizers have much to gain from alliances and partnerships with NGOs—building campaigns for protective legislation, working alongside organizations representing rural communities, organizing and lobbying for basic education, health, and development programs, and so forth.

In contrast, unions representing workers in the automotive manufacturing sector, or segments of the transport sector, such as civil aviation, for example, generally work with comparatively large and well-organized workplaces, with relatively skilled work forces, high levels of unionization, and a highly developed sense of the global economy in which they work. Pay rates are generally higher, reflected in the relative wealth of the national and international unions that represent workers in these sectors. Partnerships with NGOs are less essential for the day-to-day activities of these unions, although their industrial strength often places individual unions in the front line in defense of the union movement as a whole in the face of state repression. This is what led to alliances with human rights organizations in South Korea, South Africa, and Brazil, for example. The range of approaches, priorities, policies, and traditions of the GUFs when working alongside NGOs—reflecting industrial circumstances—provides a crude indication of this diversity.

National Centers and Individual Unions

It is also important to understand the differences in approach between confederations of national labor union centers—ICFTU, ETUC (European Trade Union Confederation), CTUC (Commonwealth Trade Union Council), and so on—and federations of individual national unions (for instance, UNISON in the UK, the Canadian Auto Workers, the GUFs). National union centers, by and large, are bodies established to represent workers to government and intergovernmental organizations on broad economic, industrial, and social policy, whereas the "industrial" union structures deal with employers over wages and conditions, collective bargaining, and union coordination. The profile of NGOs that work with national centers is thus somewhat different from those that work with industrial unions—although there are obvious points of overlap.

North and South, East and West

Many people involved in NGOs, and some in the labor union movement itself, identify North-South and East-West differences between unions as particularly important. But while there are, of course, huge differences in the relative resources available to unions, there are frequent overgeneralizations of "poor South" and "rich North."

Among the most sensitive North-South and East-West problems between unions are financial donor-recipient relationships, much like those faced within and between NGOs. There are examples of financial support from unions in the North resulting in their counterparts in the South becoming "client" unions dependent on external finance. There are examples, particularly in the Cold War period, of such relations being deliberately fostered. More typically, however, client-patron relations emerge from ill-conceived, badly designed, or insensitively managed acts of solidarity. On the other hand, Northern unions play an essential role in supporting national or regional organizations of unions in the South, gaining access to government funds, and managing sometimes large-scale programs of development assistance without which these union organizations would be substantially weakened.

European or Global?

In some European unions (including some in Central and Eastern Europe), *international* is virtually synonymous with *European.* Over the last decade or more, contact and cooperation among European unions have expanded considerably, but anecdotal evidence suggests that, for some unions at least, non-European activity has possibly decreased. This is, of course, the result of the growing influence and importance of European Union (EU) institutions and of the ETUC, along with its industrial structures, which have provided substantial resources to encourage cooperation within Europe. It has been further encouraged by the expansion of the EU to include countries of the former communist bloc, and by the important role of Western European unions in supporting democratic labor union development.

Coupled with the institutional independence of the ETUC from the ICFTU, the development of a "Europeanist" agenda often creates considerable problems for global federations, which are keen to avoid diverging international priorities. The rise of "Europeanism" is also partly the result of settlement (or decline in fashion) in the "big" international solidarity campaigns that galvanized considerable labor union support in the 1980s, such as the anti-apartheid movement. As a result, some NGOs claim it has become more difficult to attract European labor union support for activities in developing countries.

"Undemocratic" Labor Unions

Despite the labor union movement's overall commitment to representative and accountable democracy, there are clearly some examples of unions that are not representative of the standards to which the international movement would aspire, nor are they accountable to their members for these standards. Some are simply not recognized as "genuine" unions by the bulk of the international labor union movement, as represented by the ICFTU, for example. NGOs working in countries or areas where such unions are active or influential may understandably be reluctant to consider labor unions reliable partners in development in light of such experiences; indeed, they may draw the conclusion that the labor union movement as a whole is not to be trusted.

Foremost among these "undemocratic" unions are *state-controlled unions*, particularly those established in communist one-party states as one of the "mass organizations" of the ruling party. They were (and are) entirely controlled by the state, and in many cases were created after genuine labor unions, along with other independent civil society organizations, were destroyed. Their function is to assist the state in administering and controlling the work force. When called upon, some participate in the repression of workers attempting to develop forms of independent unions. In the countries of the former Soviet Union these institutions collapsed together with the regime, but they continue to thrive in surviving one-party communist states, for instance, the All-China Federation of Trade Unions (ACFTU) in China. Other examples can be found in Vietnam, Laos, Cuba, and North Korea. In other countries that may not be communist but display certain authoritarian tendencies, such as Indonesia, Syria, Iraq, and Iran, union federations are tightly controlled by the state as well.

It is important to distinguish between unions that are fully state controlled, such as those mentioned above, and a larger number of union organizations that, while not directly answerable to the state, are nevertheless supportive of the government, even when it advocates policies that are clearly restrictive of labor union rights. Some within the NGO community (and indeed within unions) confuse the two and assume that government friendly automatically means government controlled. Reality is far more untidy, with a spectrum of union-state relations that range from state corruption to democratically determined policies that reflect the views—or fears—of union members.

Aside from state-controlled unions there are numerous examples of workplace or company-wide unions *under the control of employers*. These can be organizations specifically created by employers in an attempt to break unions or preempt their formation. They can also be unions that have been brought under the control of employers through inducements to leaders, intimidation of members, or—in some cases—outright corruption and election rigging. The most vivid example of such corporatist unions is the *solidarismo* movement in Central America (Levitsky and Lapp 1992).

Finally, there are unions where *organized crime* has gained a foothold. Serious and sometimes bloody battles have been fought by labor unionists in a number of countries, most famously in the United States, in order to clear their organizations of racketeers and mafia. These cases are often highly publicized but, without seeking to minimize the problem, overstated. In 1978, for example, the US Justice Department declared that the number of local unions controlled by organized crime amounted to three hundred out of a total of seventy-five thousand (AP 1978). Since then there have been strenuous efforts to eliminate organized crime from the labor movement, and although pockets still survive, it is considerably weaker than it was twenty years ago.

More common are examples of unions autocratically controlled by individuals, cliques, or even families who manipulate union funds, procedures, and elections to ensure a monopoly and continuity of power. These could be, for example, individual lawyers developing their commercial practice through legal representation of workers in a number of workplaces (a widespread practice, for example, in the Philippines, due to the peculiarities of labor law), or small cliques of union leaders who take financial advantage of exploitative employment practices (notoriously within the shipping industry, for example). The problem is generally more common in developing countries, where the sheer weight of poverty exacerbates the temptation of union leaders to maintain their income by ensuring continuity of office through corruption or intimidation.

Nevertheless, it is again easy to overstate instances of undemocratic or unrepresentative labor unionism—whether the result of state or employer control, organized crime, or corruption. Those with experience and knowledge of the international labor union movement strenuously deny that such examples (with the exception of China) represent more than a very small fraction of unions worldwide.

GENDER EQUITY

Like all other social movements, labor unions vary in the extent to which they are responsive to and representative of the needs of women workers. Many national and international unions give high priority to the need to encourage women to take up positions of leadership, to reform organizational structures and cultures to be inclusive of women, and to conduct campaigns and education programs designed to overcome sexism within unions. Nevertheless, there are undoubtedly some unions that continue to be almost entirely dominated by a male leadership, even in some of the industries and countries where the work force is overwhelmingly female. The relative failure of some unions adequately to address issues faced by women workers creates friction with certain NGOs, particularly those created specifically to support international development programs with women. Some NGOs—Women Working Worldwide, for example—have been established partly because of the perceived failure of unions to address the concerns of women workers (see Chapter 13 in this volume). Gender sensitivities and insensitivities are particularly heightened in relation to the informal economy, which is generally a far larger source of employment for women than for men in the developing world, and where organizations led by women—notably the Self-Employed Women's Association (SEWA) in India—are at the forefront of informal economy workers' representation.

CULTURE, DEMOCRACY, AND CLASS

Whether or not an NGO can easily cooperate with labor union organizations does not depend on its size, its structure, or its organizational form. It does not even depend on its function, especially where distinctions of function are not clear cut. Some NGOs will work on several issues at once; many issues are interconnected. It is difficult to promote sustainable development without at the same time seeking to advance human rights, education, equality, and environment issues, all of which are also labor union issues. Far more important are questions related to the governance and management of NGOs and labor unions, which include issues of transparency, accountability, management, evaluation and monitoring, information sharing, networking, and alliance building. Behind these lie important differences in culture and class perspectives that may lead to certain tensions.

The Cultural Gap

Many NGOs, particularly those with a religious background, originated in a nineteenth-century culture of charitable work and philanthropy. Whether dedicated to political action and advocacy (for example, the abolition of slavery and child labor, or support of universal suffrage), or to charity and welfare, these organizations were initiated and led by the middle and upper classes. Labor unions and the labor movement generally organized at the same time but on rather different principles. No one invented labor unions. Workers spontaneously combined because they realized that they could not improve their situation as individuals but only by acting together on the basis of solidarity. Inevitably, some within the industrial and political labor movement regarded the middle-class "NGOs" of the time with distrust and hostility. Nevertheless, there was considerable cooperation and alliance between middle-class reformers and labor unions.

From the end of the nineteenth century to the Second World War the labor movement built up networks of its own "NGOs" (covering welfare, education, sports, and leisure activities in virtually all areas of social life). These were meant to form a counter-culture of labor, together with the labor unions, cooperatives, and the political labor parties, to create "a new society within the shell of the old" (Gallin 2000b).

In the period after the Second World War, and particularly in recent decades, dramatic world developments seriously affected the relationship between the labor movement and NGOs. The Cold War, decolonization, the emergence of the so-called Third World, the growth of globalization, and the radicalization of part of the middle classes (in the student movement, the women's movement, in churches influenced by liberation theology, and so on) led many in the NGO community to adopt a radical agenda for social change. This did not necessarily lead, however, to a closer relationship with the labor unions. On the contrary, unions were now perceived by many of their middle-class critics as conservative, bureaucratic institutions unable or even unwilling to advance their members' and society's true interests. Several politically radical NGOs even became interested in organizing workers outside the labor union framework in supposedly more democratic forms, thus deliberately entering into direct conflict with labor unions. A dismissive and hostile attitude toward labor unions continues to exist in some NGOs, reciprocated by deep suspicion from some labor union organizations.

Nonetheless, a more positive perception of labor unions has developed in many NGOs. In recent years unions have proved themselves to be irreplaceable in the fight for progressive social change in difficult circumstances (Brazil, South Africa, South Korea, Poland). They have increasingly become the targets of repression and of anti–labor union campaigns, in industrialized as well as developing countries, and have therefore come to be perceived as "underdogs" rather than as part of the establishment. At the same time, confronted with worsening conditions and the accelerating impact of globalization, a growing number of labor unions, including international labor union federations, increasingly recognizes the importance of developing good relationships with NGOs, especially where the latter are clearly having a strong international impact (for example, in the environmental movement).

There are two reasons for this. First, on a practical level, many unions—particularly GUFs—face problems of capacity in mounting additional international campaigns or education programs. Trusted NGOs, those with a proven track record of delivery and respect for labor union democratic principles, can provide a useful "subcontracting" role in delivering grant-aided projects without having to increase the core costs of the commissioning unions themselves. Second, there has been, in effect, a failure of the international labor union movement to convince intergovernmental institutions (particularly the WTO) of the need formally to recognize their responsibilities to uphold basic workers' rights. Unions have therefore been encouraged to seek alliances with broader social movements, including NGOs, with overlapping agendas for campaigning and lobbying activities.

Governance and Democracy

For more than a century the labor union movement had developed its own culture of representative democracy. While examples of autocratically run and bureaucratic labor unions, some well known, exist in many countries, it remains true that the labor union movement as a whole is far and away the most democratic institution in every society and certainly the only major democratic international movement worldwide.

All labor unions have a clearly defined constituency—their members—to whom the leadership is accountable. All labor unions have a leadership elected at regular intervals by representative governing bodies (such as a congress). This leadership may lose the next election and is sometimes subject to recall. Union accounts are usually audited and available to the scrutiny of the membership and the general public. The consequences of union policy are immediately felt by the membership (for example, in the form of good or bad results of collective bargaining), and monitoring and evaluating takes place constantly, at the workplace to start with and more formally through frequent meetings of elected governing bodies.

In a democratic (that is, typical) labor union, members are the "citizens" of their organization. By contrast, there are few NGOs with a membership that has a sense of "citizenship" and ownership of the organization. In many cases NGOs are perceived by unions to have a self-appointed and coopted leadership, with no accountability to a constituency other than public opinion and funding agencies.

For such reasons, relations between trades unions and NGOs in general can be problematic, even when the motivations on either side are not in doubt. The first questions that labor unions are likely to ask are about the credentials and legitimacy of their potential NGO partners: Who elected you? To whom are you accountable? Who finances you and why?

This need not be interpreted as a form of rejection before the discussion has even started. The questions are genuine. Labor unions need to be sure that their partners are reliable. With limited resources and under constant pressure from employers and sometimes from governments, many unions lead precarious and dangerous lives and cannot afford to make mistakes. In some cases the record of an NGO will speak for itself and establish credibility. In other cases credibility remains to be demonstrated through action and experience.

Representation and Advocacy

Many labor unionists, at least in private, retain a deep skepticism of or hostility toward NGOs. The middle- or upper-class origins of NGO activists or staff members, especially in the UK context, are vividly obvious to working-class union representatives. Their apparent shared confidence and social and cultural affinity with the "enemy" (corporate or governmental) and their frequently displayed academic training can easily create distrust and animosity among unions. NGOs may be perceived as being populated by "posh" people, perhaps with private incomes and no experience or understanding of the realities faced by working-class communities, whether in inner-city London or on the streets of Manila.

The frequent ability of NGOs to gain a high media profile for their campaigns can also be intensely irritating to unions, which by and large receive hostile or nonexistent press coverage. Newspaper headlines featuring an NGO campaign on a particular example of workers' exploitation, for example, can be exasperating for those unions that may have been campaigning for many years on the same subject but have never broken through media indifference. There is an underlying suspicion that such NGO proficiency at media management and public relations is based more on dinner party networking and shared class background than on good research and journalism—or the force of argument.

Labor unions deeply resent any organization or individual purporting to represent workers' interests—whether to employers, governments, or the media—unless it has a democratic mandate from unions or other recognized structures of the labor movement to do so (notably cooperatives). There is, of course, a distinction between "representation" and "advocacy." But NGO actions that step over that dividing line are almost certain to be met with hostility.

This is particularly sensitive in circumstances where workers are not organized or where unions are too weak to be effective. There is a history of NGOs, outraged with the levels of exploitation, poverty, or denial of human rights faced by unorganized workers in specific circumstances, tempted to step beyond providing assistance through media campaigns or development programs and take it upon themselves to represent the workers to employers, governments, or other agencies. Understandably, perhaps, such NGOs are motivated by the fear that if they do not represent the workers' interests, nobody else will.

Unions, however, are based on the fundamental principle that workers can only be represented by their own democratically accountable organizations. Where workers are not organized, it is the responsibility of the labor union movement to do so. Where union organization is not possible (for a variety of reasons) or has yet to be achieved, national and international unions reserve the right to speak on the workers' behalf—particularly when facing governments and intergovernmental organizations such as the ILO. NGOs, normally accountable to no one apart from themselves and their donors, and frequently led by members of the upper or middle classes, can cause major problems when they assume the role of speaking on behalf of workers; in some cases they may even deflect or thwart genuine union organization efforts.

UNIONS, NGOS,
AND THE INFORMAL-ECONOMY DEBATE

> The issue of NGO relations frequently crops up when the subject of labor union efforts to organize the informal sector is mentioned. Indeed, NGOs obtain considerable funds earmarked for the informal sector. They also find it much easier to obtain cooperation from informal workers since they address the immediate concerns of these workers. . . . Trade unions and NGOs have entered into a sort of competitive relationship, which often turns out in NGOs' favour. . . . It is essential for trade unions [says trade unionist Christine Nathan] "to recapture lost territory. This has become even more important in light of the fact that the number of informal workers is constantly increasing." (Locmant 2001)

In June 2002 the International Labour Conference held a special discussion on the informal economy (see International Labour Conference 2002). Debates and discussions within the labor union movement, and between labor unions and NGOs, leading up to and during the ILO discussion revealed and illustrated many of the points of tension between the two. Many unions and NGOs were involved in these discussions, but perhaps the crucial debates were broadly between the ICFTU, its secretariat in Brussels, and the ICFTU Task Force on Informal and Unprotected Work (established after its Congress in 2000) on the one hand, and those participating in Women in Informal Employment Globalizing and Organizing (WIEGO), on the other.

WIEGO, based at Harvard University, was established in 1997 as a "coalition of institutions and individuals concerned with improving the status of women in the economy's informal sector" (see WIEGO 2002). It was created from the conviction that

> Women workers—particularly those from low-income households—are concentrated in the informal sector. Although the

informal sector contributes to both poverty alleviation and economic growth, it remains largely invisible in official statistics and policies. Thus WIEGO strives to improve the status of the informal sector through compiling better statistics, conducting research and developing programs and policies. (WIEGO 2001)

Financially supported by the Ford Foundation and Rockefeller Foundation, WIEGO's core activity is undertaken through five program areas: urban policy, global markets and trade liberalization, social protection for informal economy workers, statistics, and, most important in the context of this discussion, the organization and representation of informal economy workers.

Although WIEGO would certainly be described as an NGO, its board contains academics and researchers, ILO and World Bank personnel, NGO activists, and labor unionists. At the heart of WIEGO, and its inspiration, is SEWA—itself a labor union as well as a women's organization, a cooperative, and many other things besides—along with StreetNet and HomeNet, the international networks of street vendors and market workers and homeworkers, respectively.

The "Informal Economy" as a Trojan Horse?

The debate at the International Labour Conference was dominated from the outset by the question of whether there should be a discussion on the informal economy at all. The term itself was (and remains) highly problematic for the labor union movement, only slightly less unpalatable than the term *informal sector:*

> The use of the term "informal sector", as the ILO is now employing it, must be countered. The word "sector" is misleading because it is confused with the use of the same word to indicate an area of economic activity. The word "informal" is misleading because it is a euphemism and because it does not suggest what the work or workers being described have in common. (ICFTU 2001, 2)

Underlying these concerns is a fear that "informality," as a form of economic activity in itself, could become almost acceptable, when in fact it is a description of workers who are "insufficiently protected by law and excluded from various forms of social protection" (ICFTU 2001, 3).

Still less acceptable is the notion that the informal economy should be actively promoted as part of a development strategy. From the union perspective the problem is thus not that government(s) fail to recognize and uphold workers' rights and welfare, but rather that they intend to remove obstacles to the further development of an informal economy. In other words the unions, as represented by the ICFTU, feared that the informal-economy discussion was a Trojan horse, concealing an employer's (and neoliberal government's) agenda of weakening labor standards: if the informal economy cannot be formalized to bring it into compliance with internationally agreed standards, then the standards themselves must be amended (that is, weakened) to accommodate the informal economy. Much of the ICFTU's efforts were therefore concerned with shifting the discussion entirely away from the informal economy and back toward the main concern that "workers in a wide variety of occupations lack legal and social protection and an effective representative voice. The many different forms that this lack of protection takes need to be clearly identified so they can be specifically addressed" (ICFTU 2001, 2). It is therefore not surprising that WIEGO should have found itself at variance with the ICFTU (WIEGO 2002).

The ICFTU questions the commonality of informal-economy workers, pointing out that "all workers are workers" (all agricultural workers are agricultural workers, all transport workers are transport workers, and so on); it is simply that some of these workers are unprotected by law, are deprived of their rights, and so on (Justice 2002). The commonality (and therefore solidarity) is in the industry or the occupation, not in workers' relation to the law. In contrast, WIEGO seeks to highlight the commonality of workers in the informal economy and, in essence, argues that while they need organization and representation in particular industries or sectors of employment, they also need organization and representation specific to their position as unprotected and unregistered workers (WIEGO 2002). At one stage during the run-up to the ILO discussion, the WIEGO Organisation and Representation Working Party proposed the creation of a new international federation of unions and associations representing informal-economy workers. This was fiercely resisted by the ICFTU and some of the GUFs, who argued that it was dangerous to abandon "a sectoral approach [that is, metalworkers, food workers, transport workers, and so on] to organising and representing workers," and that such a federation might "promote divisions between 'formal' and 'informal' workers at the national and even international level" (ICFTU 2001, 2).

Some union leaders, representing workers in countries or industries where the informal economy is more prevalent, are more sympathetic, however. They recognize that despite policies and frequent discussions to address the growing problem of informal work, their own unions simply do not have the capacity—when their slim resources may be by necessity allocated elsewhere—seriously to undertake the task of organizing informal-economy workers. To these leaders an organization working in partnership with labor unions but specifically dedicated to assist the organization of these workers—nationally or internationally—would be welcomed.

This reflects a broader dilemma in union-NGO relations. Unions are democratically bound to represent the interests and priorities of their members, while—in the eyes of the ILO at least—they represent the interests of *all* workers, some or most of whom are not members of a union at all. The International Transport Workers' Federation (ITF), for example, recognizes that there is a responsibility and need to organize the many thousands of workers in the informal transport economy (in some parts of the world, the vast majority of transport workers), but maintains that the day-to-day priorities of its members in formal employment must and should take precedence. Responding to the world crisis in civil aviation after the 9/11 attack on the World Trade Towers or coordinating solidarity with the West Coast dockworkers' strike in the United States cannot, however, be put on hold while they organize half a million minibus drivers scattered across towns and cities throughout Africa, for instance (see the ITF website).

An NGO, on the other hand, can choose which themes, sectors, or locations it wants to concentrate on without reference to the priorities determined by a membership; it can therefore respond to issues that generate particular ethical or political interest. Or, indeed, it can also respond to the fluctuating priorities of funding agencies. It is this freedom to act independently of specific constituencies of members that enables NGOs to concentrate on informal-economy workers and, if there is mutual respect for the work of labor unions, this can lead to fruitful partnerships with unions that lack the capacity to do so. The ITF, for example, "notes the efforts of NGOs and other community organisations to assist the organisation of informal workers and supports any such efforts which are carried out in full cooperation with the trade union movement" (ITF Congress 2002).

REPRESENTATION
OF INFORMAL-ECONOMY WORKERS

Tensions between unions and NGOs are underpinned by labor union nervousness about arguments being developed within the ILO and elsewhere that call for the revision of the tripartite nature of the ILO itself. The ILO is constructed to represent the three "stakeholders" in labor standards and legislation: governments, employers, and labor unions. Labor unions have, in effect, exclusive rights to represent the interests of workers. Some within the ILO argue that the rise of NGOs in recent years, and the expansion of their representation within other intergovernmental institutions and events, should be reflected within the ILO. Thus the ILO would become "quadripartite," with NGOs as the fourth actor with a seat at the table.

This is fiercely resisted by most in the international labor union movement, and many regard any NGO engagement in the ILO as a dangerous step toward the dilution of labor union influence. For instance, the ICFTU 2000 Congress declared:

> Trade unions should extend their activities with NGOs on areas of common agreement, such as human and trade union rights, equality and gender issues, development, health and the environment, as a means of furthering trade union goals and enriching public debate. Joint activities with NGOs are expected to expand as trade union centres, regional organisations and ITSs become more familiar with this way of working. . . . *[But] any moves to weaken tripartite social dialogue, for example through the establishment of "quadripartism" should be rejected.* (ICFTU 2000, emphasis added)

This is not simply the labor union movement attempting to defend its turf to the exclusion of NGOs. There is concern that a growing number of so-called NGOs are in effect employers' organizations, supported financially and/or staffed by TNCs or employers' associations. Other NGOs are signing partnership arrangements with employers, which has led to unions expressing particular alarm about those involved in social auditing of employment practices.

If NGOs were allowed seats at the table, it would not just weaken labor union representation but could shift the fundamental historic balance between capital and labor at the ILO. Therefore, any suggestion that NGOs could "represent" the interests of informal-economy workers is fundamentally opposed by the unions, who sense a potentially dangerous precedent for ILO reorganization.

On the other hand, it was widely argued—by many within the ILO Workers' Group, among others—that leaving the representation of informal-economy workers to (male) delegates of union organizations with no democratic mandate from informal-economy workers themselves would be indefensible. A relatively small but increasing number of unions, particularly from developing countries, is successfully organizing informal-economy workers. There is considerable variety in the organizational models in evidence, including new informal-economy unions sponsored by national centers (for example, in Mozambique), direct recruitment of informal-economy workers into individual unions (for example, in Ghana), alliance building with "associations" of informal-economy workers (as in Zambia), and new unions of women workers (as in South Africa). The best-established and most celebrated organization is SEWA, representing over 300,000 women employed in the informal economy. SEWA is a union—although it had to overcome considerable suspicion and hostility from some labor unionists to be accepted and recognized as such.

Most, if not all, of these union organizations work with NGOs. They are all clearly identifiable as unions: with democratic accountability to mass membership, affiliation to national and international labor union structures, and so on. Yet they exhibit many characteristics associated with NGOs and are perceived by many more traditional unions as belonging to the "NGO culture." Because of the legal and economic position of the workers concerned, their particular vulnerability, the nature of the workplace (the streets, the home, the land), and so on, the organizing agenda for such unions frequently requires alliances with NGOs, and the adoption or adaptation of NGO organizational tactics.

There are sufficient numbers of unions, parts of unions, associations (not necessarily affiliated to the labor union movement), and other democratic organizations representing informal-economy workers to talk about the development of an international movement of informal-economy workers. Compared to the labor union movement itself, however—which has well-established democratic structures; organizational rules; procedures and criteria for membership; and so on—this movement of informal-economy workers is as yet ill-defined, with a variety of regional and international focal points, a multitude of democratic (and less than democratic) organizational forms, and a wide range of philosophical and political traditions. It currently consists of a set of overlapping alliances, platforms, federations, and networks.

This emerging international movement was well represented among the workers' group participants in the ILO discussion, some as formal delegates within national labor union center delegations, and others as observers from global union federations or ILO-accredited NGOs. Some of the tensions described above were reported to be very evident in workers' group caucus meetings.

The ILO discussion will almost certainly not lead to new formal conventions or major new ILO initiatives on the informal economy, per se, given the insurmountable problems of definition and universal application. It is possible, however, that specific existing conventions or recommendations may be strengthened or modified as a result—referring to specific groups of workers facing specific conditions. On the other hand, the debates in and around the formal ILO event within and between unions and those NGOs aligned with the workers' group may prove to be a major turning point in union-NGO relations—at least in relation to the informal economy. There are subsequent signs of national and international unions strengthening their organizing efforts in the informal economy and displaying a greater willingness to work in partnership with some of the NGOs concerned. There are also signs of a greater understanding among the NGOs themselves of union concerns and of recognition of the unique status of the labor union movement in workers' organization and representation.

NOTES

[1] For more information, see the Caux Round Table, "ILO Declaration of Fundamental Principles and Rights at Work." Available online at the cauxroundtable.org website.

[2] The Clean Clothes Campaign is a leading example of union-NGO cooperation, developing codes of conduct for the garment and sportswear industry, together with an independent monitoring system.

Three

Building Bridges across a Double Divide

*Alliances between US
and Latin American Labor and NGOs*

MARK ANNER AND PETER EVANS

INTRODUCTION

The North-South divide, specifically between the United States and Latin America, has always riven the labor union movement. Workers in the South have, with justification, accused workers in the North of being protectionist and allowing their unions to become instruments of the reactionary foreign policies of their governments. Workers in the South have also been susceptible to nationalist appeals that have led them to support local elites at the expense of solidarity with their fellow workers in other countries. In the United States, especially during the Vietnam War, a dramatic divide came about between the conservative national union leadership on the one hand and progressive social movement organizations (SMOs) and NGOs on the other. In the South, labor unionists have often been unwilling to give space on the workers' movement agenda to the interests of women, informal-sector workers, and marginalized minority groups.

The perversions of Cold War union practices have been well documented, with writers quick to point out the contradictions between the rhetoric of solidarity and union practices. For example, Åke Wedin (1991), in describing the pattern of US and German union policies in Latin

America, provocatively titled his book *International Trade Union "Solidarity" and Its Victims*, while Beth Sims (1992) wrote in detail about AFL-CIO activities in Latin America in her book *Workers of the World Undermined*. Nor did Southern unionists always set their priorities along strong international ties with their Northern counterparts. During import substitution industrialization, many Latin American unions developed a corporatist ideology that made a harmonious relationship with the state rather than class confrontation a priority (Collier and Collier 1991; Murillo 2001; Zapata 1993).

These old problems have not disappeared. Even in some highly globalized sectors, domestic labor strategies often take priority over international solidarity (Gentile 2002). And in cases where labor transnationalism is prevalent, weaker Southern actors find that their Northern counterparts tend to dominate campaign strategies and agendas (Anner 2001). Northern union protectionism remains a concern (Seidman 2001). Nor is business unionism, which deals solely and exclusively with workplace issues, a dead letter (Dreiling 2001). Nonetheless, economic and political shifts from the 1970s to the 1990s have modified many old patterns. During the 1970s and 1980s, Latin American unions fought dictatorships and developed close ties to popular organizations that persist today (see, for example, Moreira Alves 1984). Analyzing recent trends in the United States, Voss and Sherman (2000) note how the decline of labor's power there has engendered a shift from bureaucratic conservatism to social movement unionism. Labor unions are also building links to other social movements, albeit with some difficulty. Most notably, labor joined environmental groups and others in the protests in Seattle against the WTO (Smith 2001). Internationally, regional trade pacts such as the North American Free Trade Agreement (NAFTA) and international trade institutions such as the WTO have created an incentive for labor to organize across borders (Cook 1997; O'Brien et al. 2000). In some cases where products are made in low-wage countries and sold in high-wage countries, the ties among "workers of the world" are being replaced by "workers and consumer activists of the world." Growing labor-rights campaigns focus on brand-name images (Anner 2002). Combined, these trends create conditions for what Evans (2000) refers to as "counter-hegemonic globalisation."

Global neoliberalism has presented traditional labor unionism with the prospect of extinction if it cannot confront globally organized employers with global counter-organization. The aggressive ideological unions of the emerging markets of Latin America are essential allies. At the same time, eroding union densities, deteriorating working conditions, and the growth of the informal economy cannot be reversed by formal-sector workers acting alone. Social movement unionism, in the practical as well as the ideological sense, must include whole communities, especially women's organizations, if it is to succeed.

We focus here on the United States and Latin America both because the double divide has been particularly debilitating in the Americas and because the Western hemisphere has become the site of a series of innovative efforts. We focus specifically on two complexes of activity. The first we call the basic rights complex. This complex consists of a collection of diverse and differentiated organizations that work in concert to improve the balance of power that workers confront as they struggle to gain basic rights in oppressive, labor-intensive industries in Latin America. Specifically, we explore the set of organizations that is popularly known as the anti-sweatshop movement. The basic rights complex is more than a transnational network, although it is that as well. It is a complex in which the distinctively different capacities of the organizations involved are integrated in a way that gives the assembly much more effectiveness than the sum of its individual parts.

The second complex also entails a dense set of organizational alliances, but its goals are more political and substantially removed from the shop floor. This is the coalition of labor organizations and NGOs that are trying to defend democratic governance in the hemisphere against the antidemocratic threat posed by the neoliberal governance model embedded in the FTAA (Free Trade Area of the Americas, also known by its Spanish acronym, ALCA). The most obvious organizational embodiment of this coalition is the alliance of alliances called the Alianza Social Continental or Hemispheric Social Alliance (ASC/HSA).

Analyzing these two very different cases together conveys a sense of the range of actions that new North-South and labor-NGO alliances are undertaking. It illustrates the strengths and accomplishments of the new initiatives bridging the double divide. It also illustrates the challenges that these new constructions continue to confront. Part of the response to these continuing challenges must, of course, be to develop a more sophisticated understanding of the complicated political and organizational dynamics that sustain (or undercut) these efforts. We offer this analysis as a first step toward such an understanding. Despite the difficulties, we find that in several important cases labor is shifting its strategies, and that shift involves broad coalitions and stronger North-South ties. Future relief from the rise in inequality and job insecurity and the decline in real wages, as well as from the unraveling social peace and the destruction of ecological resources, will depend in part on how successful these emerging labor and NGO complexes and alliances become.

ORGANIZATIONAL COMPLEXITIES OF SECURING BASIC RIGHTS

Securing basic rights in the global South depends first of all on the determination, skill, and militancy of workers engaged in local struggles, but the economic power of employers and the repressive role of local governments create overwhelming odds against even the most militant and creative local campaigns. The right structure of connections to the global political economy can help. More specifically, an organizational complex has grown up over the last ten to fifteen years that, when fully engaged, does seem to improve the odds. It involves at least three elements. Ideologically, as Margaret Keck and Katherine Sikkink (1998) suggest, success requires a set of clear, compelling normative ideas combined with an equally clear causal logic connecting normative evaluation to the possibility of action. Economically, it requires a "commodity chain" that links workers and consumers to gain leverage over companies. Making this work means constructing a complex matrix of organizations playing a variety of roles that work synergistically. Labor-NGO alliances that operate across the North-South divide are at the heart of this organizational matrix.[1]

The Kukdong case is one of the best illustrations of how the matrix can come together. On September 21, 2001, the first-ever collective bargaining agreement between an independent union and a Mexican *maquiladora* manufacturing apparel was signed by SITEMEX on behalf of the four hundred workers at the Kukdong (renamed Mexmode) *maquiladora* in Atlixco, Mexico.[2] This led to an agreement in April 2002 to increase wages and benefits significantly. A wide array of labor organizations and NGOs were involved in this victory, including the Workers' Support Center in Mexico, United Students against Sweatshops (USAS), the AFL-CIO, and the Canadian Labour Congress. Solidarity groups included the US Labor Education in the Americas Project (US/LEAP), the Campaign for Labor Rights, Global Exchange, Sweatshop Watch, the European Clean Clothes Campaign, the Korean House for International Solidarity, and the Maquila Solidarity Network.

This list of groups gives a hint of the organizational complexities involved in winning the basic right to organize, but really understanding this victory requires a more thorough analysis of the evolution and interaction of the organizations involved. The potential role of traditional labor unions like UNITE[3] is a good place to start.[4]

In the 1970s, UNITE's predecessor unions watched their membership dwindle as the flow of apparel and textile production to the global South accelerated. The natural response was to try to stem the tide by pushing "Made in America" labels and imposing import restrictions. By the time UNITE was formed in the mid-1990s, it was no longer possible to prevent the hemorrhaging of jobs or of union membership by trying to insulate the US market from imports. Even the new Democratic administration, which was relatively sympathetic to labor, opposed import restrictions. At the same time, UNITE's members in the garment trades within the United States increasingly were emigrants from the same countries to which the work was being relocated, and therefore they identified with workers in the global South. It made sense to shift to a strategy built around solidarity with workers there who were trying to organize.

The need to have greater flexibility and legitimacy as UNITE and other US unions struggled to overcome their protectionist past led to involving a variety of NGOs and SMOs. Some labor solidarity groups such as the National Labor Committee (NLC) had already been actively involved in international anti-sweatshop campaigns since the early 1990s. The NLC was formed in 1980 by unionists who were concerned about US government policy in Central America. In the 1990s, as civil wars in Central America ended, the NLC changed its focus to the gross violation of labor rights in the region's booming export processing zones. Other US NGOs, such as the US Guatemala Labor Education Project (later US/ LEAP), became involved in the anti-sweatshop movement. One of its first major anti-sweatshop campaigns involved workers producing for Phillips-Van Heusen in Guatemala. The anti-sweatshop movement also spread to Canada, where activists formed the Maquila Solidarity Network, while Europeans formed the Clean Clothes Campaign, which has its headquarters in the Netherlands.

Southern actors were generally receptive to forming alliances with these Northern solidarity groups. In Central America the violent and systematic violation of labor rights in the region during the 1980s had left unions weak and fragmented. Unionists found that traditional organizing strategies were not working in the booming global apparel industry. For example, from June 1995 to June 1996 a wave of organizing drives in the Salvadoran *maquila* sector resulted in two plants closing and 5,044 people being fired. In the end, only three hundred workers were successfully organized. Similar problems occurred in the Dominican Republic, Guatemala, Honduras, and Nicaragua, where traditional organizing led to mass dismissals and subsequent blacklisting of all workers involved in trying to form unions. Unionists learned that local organizing was much easier when pressure could be put on the brand-name apparel companies, and to do so, workers needed allies in the countries where these products were sold.

In addition to building alliances with groups in the North, these Southern unions developed alliances with local civil society organizations. In the 1980s many Southern unions had learned that it took strong social alliances to democratize their countries. They grew accustomed to working with women's groups, human rights organizations, and progressive sectors of the church to achieve their goals. In the 1990s, with the boom in export processing zones, the violent abuse of human rights in the apparel sector made these rights a concern for religious and human rights groups. On average, 80 percent of the work force was female, and some of the most common rights abuses included sexual harassment, the firing of pregnant women, and denial of maternity leave; gaining these rights thus became an issue for women's groups too. As a result, Southern labor and non-labor groups had an interest in forming an alliance to address the sweatshop problem.

By the late 1990s Northern students supplied yet another key link in the coalition. The students provided greater legitimacy to the movement and replaced the stereotypical animosities of "patriotic hardhats" versus "long-haired, anti-American students." Student activists wanted to help the labor movement fight sweatshop conditions that violated basic human dignity. The character of the "commodity chain" connecting the students and the sweatshops actually gave students power to change working conditions. As large institutional buyers, universities could influence producing companies, and collectively their advantage was substantial. In the summer of 1997 some of these student activists ended up doing internships at UNITE. Interaction with UNITE staff helped students think about how they could turn outrage into an effective campaign to change working conditions. Over the course of the next few years a national network of campus organizations was built and the USAS, which has had affiliates on 180 different campuses, emerged as a major force in the anti-sweatshop movement (Featherstone and USAS 2002).

The combination of North-South and union-NGO alliances produced several successful campaigns in the 1990s and early 2000s, including the Kukdong case in Mexico, mentioned above. The movement also successfully organized workers and improved conditions in several plants in the Dominican Republic and in the Kimi plant in Honduras, the Phillips-Van Heusen plant in Guatemala, and the Mandarin plant in El Salvador. However, in several cases the victories were short-lived. In Kimi and Van Heusen, after the unions won recognition and negotiated contracts, the plants closed down. This highlighted the difficulty in sustaining achievements in such a highly mobile industry. One answer was to press for industry-wide standards and monitoring. An early effort to do this resulted in the Fair Labor Association (FLA). But unions, USAS, and NGOs like the NLC and US/LEAP considered the FLA inadequate.[5] Consequently, in 1999 the Workers' Rights Consortium (WRC) was set up, supported by funds provided from logo royalties received by what came to be 100 affiliated universities, to provide thorough, credible assessments of cases where there was evidence of violations. In the Kukdong case the WRC's authoritative reports were crucial in giving broad credibility to the workers' battle for a union.

The American Center for International Labor Solidarity, known as the Solidarity Center, provides another organizational element, as it is an auxiliary to the labor union movement. The top leadership of the AFL-CIO dominates its board of trustees, and the AFL-CIO also contributes small but crucial amounts of funding. At the same time, the Solidarity Center has substantial government funding. It competes for grants from USAID as an NGO and gets a yearly core grant from the National Endowment for Democracy. With an annual core project budget of over US$20 million, its resources exceed those of USAS, the WRC, and the smaller labor NGOs put together. It can afford to maintain a network of twenty-eight offices, with a total full-time staff of about 160 people, in all regions of the global South (and transitional economies). While accepting US government money limits the ability of the Solidarity Center staff to work as international labor organizers, the center adds a whole new level of organizational resources that ultimately redound to the benefit of the less politically encumbered actors in the basic rights complex.[6] In the Kukdong case, for example, the Solidarity Center's Mexico office was an invaluable resource.

This whole organizational matrix is knit together by a set of internationally oriented labor activists, some of them inside the labor movement, some in the NGO world, many shifting back and forth between the two. The importance of network connections among these activists makes the basic rights complex appear similar to the transnational advocacy networks of Keck and Sikkink (1998), but the fact that the complex is rooted in the labor movement gives the structure a different flavor. Unlike the transnational advocacy networks, which are, in theory at least, made up of organizations whose reason for being is to defend "principled ideas or values," the organizational matrix of the basic rights complex also includes organizations that are directly accountable to (that is, elected by) a constituency with immediate interests grounded in the everyday struggles of hard political realities for livelihood and dignity, as well as long-term and ideological interests.

The fact that the basic rights complex is able to integrate principled ideas and values with everyday interests is arguably its most exciting characteristic, both practically and theoretically. How is this circle squared? First, the key role of activists for whom the pursuit of long-term political and normative goals is intrinsically satisfying in itself needs to be acknowledged. Even more interesting, however, is the logic of organizational relations—a logic that forces groups and leaders to adopt a broad vision, even those whose natural tendencies might be to pursue their own interests in a more pedestrian, immediate way.

Drawing a schematic version of the relations between UNITE and the rest of the basic rights complex is the easiest way to make this point. UNITE's core mission must be to serve its members' interests and to organize new members. Helping textile and apparel workers in the global South in their efforts to organize and to win better working conditions, while obviously in the long-run interest of UNITE's members, is unlikely to have any obvious direct impact on its members' own fights. The idea that UNITE is interested in having workers in the global South get organized because it will somehow lead to bringing the jobs back to the United States is implausible, both historically and theoretically. Indeed, a simple model of UNITE might predict that it should continue to mount protectionist battles, no matter how quixotic such efforts might be in reality.[7] What is fascinating and much more difficult to explain is why UNITE is quietly expending its precious organizational resources to help unions in places like Guatemala, Indonesia, and Mexico.

The answer lies in the larger ideological character of organizing in the contemporary United States. Although UNITE's members are likely to identify with the workers whose struggles they are supporting, there is more going on here than just sympathy and values. Contemporary labor unions are rarely in a position to win gains for their members by shutting down production. Strikes still play a key role, but unless they are embedded in a strategic campaign they are unlikely to succeed. In the apparel industry the best way of attacking employers is to attack their brand image; the most strategic point at which to attack these images is the inhumane conditions under which their goods are produced, especially in the global South. It is an ideological battle, not just an economic one. In this ideological battle scrappy little unions in the South are key allies, helping to build links among UNITE, Northern NGOs, and organized rich-country consumers while at the same time furthering their own local struggles in the South. The nature of the battle with US employers, which must be fought in terms of ideas and images as much as with picket lines, makes the basic rights complex central to the immediate interests of UNITE's members.

None of this is to say that labor unions, NGOs, and SMOs have discovered a sure-fire ideological and organizational formula. The basic ideological logic is robust, but the organizational ties necessary to make it work require constant creative renovation. For example, new USAS activists could easily view the established WRC leadership as insufficiently responsive to the concerns of their campus base. Conversely, the WRC may feel that USAS (or UNITE) is pushing them too far in the direction of advocacy when its function is to produce credible assessments. UNITE will always be suspected of putting the interests of its members above those of workers in the global South. Tensions are also common within the South, and between North and South. Southern unions often accuse Southern SMOs, particularly women's groups, of attempting to usurp their role as organizers. Women's groups have responded that male-dominated unions are often insensitive to the needs of female workers in the apparel sector, where the vast majority of the workers are women, and therefore women's groups have a right to attend to this sector.[8] On the North-South axis, Southern unionists have at times felt that their Northern allies have pursued targets and established demands without fully consulting them. The very nature of the organizational matrix means that it must continually be renegotiated and trust continuously reestablished. At the same time, tensions within the complex can help bring about innovation, generating new organizations and new relationships that will extend success.

Viewed as a whole, the ideological and organizational matrix of the basic rights complex provides an exciting model of how alliances with NGOs and SMOs can facilitate North-South labor alliances and how the combination can help give labor (and ordinary citizens) leverage against the naturally non-egalitarian thrust of global neoliberalism. It is not, however, the only model. As discussed below, the ideological and organizational matrix of the global governance complex, exemplified by the current hemisphere-wide fight against the FTAA, illustrates a very different model.

DEFENDING DEMOCRATIC GOVERNANCE: THE FIGHT AGAINST THE FTAA

The complex of alliances that has been constructed around workers' rights enables workers to draw on the reservoir of support among consumers and NGO activists that flows from the ideological legitimacy of the quest for workers' dignity and decent working conditions. For labor-NGO alliances to have a broader impact on politics and policy, they must be able to cohere around shared goals that go beyond labor's immediate interests. Without a strategy for building more democratic forms of economic governance, nationally and globally, shop-floor struggles are at best a finger in the dike. The current union-NGO alliance that has coalesced around opposition to the FTAA demonstrates the possibility of broader alliances built around the larger issue of democratizing economic governance.

The degree of political change represented by the alliance against the FTAA is especially striking when compared with the character of hemispheric trade politics a decade ago at the time the fight over NAFTA began. The labor politics of NAFTA initially fell into a traditional mold of job geography. North American labor unionists decried the likelihood of job loss in the United States, and the official Mexican Trade Union Confederation (CTM) wholeheartedly supported the treaty. NGO involvement, which focused primarily around environmental issues, found some tactical support from US labor but little sympathy from Mexican labor.[9] There were really three "sides" to the struggle—labor in the United States, NGOs based primarily in the United States, and labor in Mexico—with agendas that conflicted more than they complemented one another. A decade has not erased the concerns of workers in either the United States or Mexico over the effects that trade politics will have on their jobs— whether it is jobs leaving the United States for Mexico or jobs leaving Mexico for China—but these concerns are now embedded in a very different political panorama.

The fight over NAFTA, and then the experience of living under the neoliberal economic regime reinforced by NAFTA, changed labor union perspectives on both sides of the border. Experience with neoliberal reforms confirmed the suspicions of some progressive Mexican labor unionists that nationalist strategies built around corporatist ties with Mexican parties were unlikely to improve their wages and working conditions.[10] At the same time, US labor unionists came to realize that building cooperative ties with their Mexican counterparts was not only possible but the only way to increase their bargaining power in the face of the almost universal commitment of US politicians to a corporate-dominated model of global economic governance. Most important, living with NAFTA helped create a new understanding of what trade agreements were really about.

NAFTA's Chapter 11 and the tribunals instituted under the provisions of its "Investor-State Dispute Mechanism" dramatized the fact that neoliberal trade agreements are as much or more about replacing democratic governance procedures with corporate-dominated economic governance than they are about facilitating the flow of goods between countries. The experience with NAFTA has made it clear that if the FTAA process is allowed to run its course, an "economic constitution" for the hemisphere will be created in a way that contravenes the kind of democratic constitutional process that all of the participating governments supposedly espouse. It will produce instead economic governance in which unelected international corporate lawyers are given the power to decide which economic rules are valid, domestically as well as internationally.

One crystallization of this learning process was the April 2001 declaration by ORIT (Organización Regional Interamericana de Trabajadores) against the FTAA. This document emphasized the FTAA's undemocratic character and underlined the central importance of preserving the basic rights of all workers, regardless of what country they were working in or what their legal status was. It was not an "anti-globalization" document but rather advocated "a progressive version of economic globalization" that entailed the "globalization of human, economic, social, labor, cultural, and political rights" but rejected "confining democracy, participation, and legitimacy to the domestic sphere while technocracies, in the name of States and national interests, negotiate away the rights of the large majorities, exclusively favoring small privileged groups." In this document the reasons why the hemispheric labor movement opposed the FTAA paralleled those of NGOs and social movement organizations. In fact, this ideological correspondence had been reflected by the ASC/HSA transnational organizational alliance, which grew out of the Joint Declaration of Unions and NGOs following a 1997 ministerial meeting in Belo Horizonte, Brazil, and was officially constituted in 1999.

Building the organizational alliances that form the foundation of ASC/HSA was not an easy task. It marks the first time that ORIT has agreed to establish a structure to coordinate strategies and actions with NGOs. Nor was ideological consensus automatic. ORIT at first preferred a "free trade with a labor rights clause" approach, while NGOs were quick to take the "anti-globalization/No to the FTAA" stance (De la Cueva 2000). The shared position of opposing the FTAA while developing an alternative model of regional integration required lengthy discussions among unions and NGOs. Perhaps the most important factor motivating the formation of ASC/HSA was labor's realization that it did not have the power to defeat the FTAA alone. Broad social alliances became a political necessity.

ASC/HSA is a coalition of coalitions. Most of its members are umbrella organizations, each of which represents a coalition of NGOs or labor organizations. For example, the US member is the Alliance for Responsible Trade (ART), itself a coalition of NGOs and labor groups.[11] REBRIP, the Brazilian Network for People's Integration (Rede Brasileira pela Integração dos Povos), is likewise an alliance of labor and NGO groups. While ASC/HSA has not been able to find local labor-NGO alliances of the ART/REBRIP sort to work with in every country, it always tries to involve the labor movement in its activities, even when local labor-NGO alliances are not well developed. Thus in Ecuador, where labor-NGO alliances remain weak and the indigenous peoples' organization (Confederación de Nacionalidades Indígenas del Ecuador) played a leading role in organizing ASC/HSA actions around the November 2002 FTAA ministerial meeting in Quito, labor was still involved.[12]

Making sure that the countries of the South play a central organizational role has been even more important to ASC/HSA's strategic thinking than the focus on labor-NGO alliances. Its secretariat was first lodged with the Mexican Action Network on Free Trade but has now moved to REBRIP in Brazil with Kjeld Jakobsen, the international affair's director of the CUT (Central Trade Union Confederation), serving as the executive secretary. Seven of the twelve members on the Operations Committee represent organizations from Latin America and the Caribbean.[13] ORIT's representative, Victor Báez, is from Paraguay. Two representatives are from

Canada and one from the United States, with a general Women's Committee rounding out the dozen. (Also from the South is the Women's Committee representative, Miosotis Rivas Peña, from the Dominican Republic.) Spanish is the organization's de facto working language, and steering committee meetings move up and down the hemisphere along with FTAA ministerial meetings.

ASC/HSA has its limitations. While ORIT is participating actively in ASC/HSA, several of ORIT's largest members—such as CTM/Mexico, CGT/Argentina, CTV/Venezuela, and Força Sindical/Brazil—are not. Indeed, according to one source, ASC/HSA has managed to articulate labor-NGO alliances fully and effectively in only four or five of the thirty-four countries in the Americas. The most active ASC/HSA chapters are in Brazil, Canada, Peru, and the United States.[14] ASC/HSA activities tend to focus on organizing parallel peoples' summits and protests at presidential summits and ministerial meetings: Belo Horizonte 1997, Santiago 1998, Quebec 2001, and so on. Ensuring that an alternative voice is heard at these events is one of ASC/HSA's greatest contributions, but this event-focused strategy has its limitations. Gathering activists from throughout the Americas is costly. Moreover, ASC/HSA would greatly benefit if more members were to work actively to influence their governments in between the big summit events.

Yet despite ASC/HSA's limitations, unions and NGOs have made important progress since the first Presidential Summit for Free Trade was held in Miami in 1994. Sarah Anderson writes: "There is no comparable network on globalization in any other region in the world" (2001, 26). ASC/HSA not only bridges the double divide but is exactly the kind of broad-based conglomeration of civil society groups that one would hope would be involved in any process of creating an economic constitution.[15] While ASC/HSA cannot yet claim to be sufficiently representative to legitimize imposing its own version of an "economic constitution" for the hemisphere, it has at least as good a claim as the opaque technocratic process that is currently under way. Its "Alternative for the Americas" document not only parallels the official draft version of the FTAA but in fact provides a more detailed policy analysis to back up its positions than does the publicly available FTAA draft. Equally important, ASC/HSA has been trying to involve ordinary citizens in the debate over its alternative vision through public meetings and a series of referenda. Ballot or petition campaigns are currently under way in Canada, El Salvador, Mexico, and Peru. Brazilian organizers have already completed an impressive referendum on the FTAA in which 10 million people participated.

ASC/HSA is a solid demonstration that a North-South, labor-NGO alliance can generate a positive political agenda with respect to governance issues. The question that remains is whether this sort of broad political agenda can generate sufficient mobilization among rank-and-file union members and ordinary citizens at the community level to make a political difference. Unlike the basic rights complex, which can focus on concrete attacks on the dignity of identifiable individuals, ASC/HSA must convince ordinary people that a set of relatively abstract governance changes constitutes a threat to principles they hold dear.

VARIATIONS AND FUTURE CHALLENGES

Many other examples of bridging the double divide could be added to the two that we have explored here. Some of the most exciting labor-NGO campaigns focus on specific companies or sectors. For example, banana-sector unionists in Central America and in the Andean region joined forces with international organizations such as US/LEAP and the International Union of Foodworkers to force the Chiquita brand to accept a framework agreement that guaranteed respect for labor rights, recognition of international labor standards, and a commitment to improve working conditions.[16] In Brazil, with strong local community support and international pressure, workers at the Rio Tinto mine in Paracatu were able to strengthen their union and make important gains in a new enterprise agreement. The effort was part of a sustained global network of Rio Tinto unions that coordinates information exchange, provides training, and organizes transnational campaigns.

Brazil is also home to an innovative NGO-union alliance organized by the Social Observatory, which was formed in 1997 by CUT/Brazil in coordination with several Brazilian labor research institutes.[17] The purpose of the Social Observatory is to research and analyze the conduct of multinational and national companies with respect to core ILO labor-rights standards. The Social Observatory has worked closely with foreign labor centers and received financial support from them, including the AFL-CIO, FNV of the Netherlands, DGB of Germany, LO-Norway, and SASK-Finland. It provides unions and companies with detailed studies on the conduct of multinationals. The unions and companies then discuss the findings and possible solutions. Should the company decline to cooperate, a union may use the findings to organize an international campaign to pressure the company to rectify any problems that the research detects. This strategy has begun to show positive results in several cases. For example, at the Danish Hartmann/Mapol factory in Brazil, reports by the Social Observatory documenting labor-rights violations led to a visit by Danish unionists, and then to productive collective bargaining between the local union and the company.

Like the basic rights complex and the ASC/HSA movement for democratic economic governance, TNC-based campaigns are difficult organizational constructions, fraught with potential conflicts, sustained only on the basis of continuous imaginative reinvention, and always vulnerable to the evaporation of the scarce material and organizational resources that nurture them. Maintaining organizational innovations is always a challenge, and maintaining them in the face of powerful economic and political interests is even more daunting.

Efforts to bridge the double divide are even more fundamentally challenged by the way in which global neoliberalism is shifting the nature of work and employment. Perhaps the biggest single challenge facing the kinds of organizational efforts we have been describing here is how to incorporate informal-sector workers. None of the campaigns we have discussed really addresses this problem. For the informal sector, it is hard to see how transnational corporate connections can be leveraged in the way that the anti-sweatshop movement works for apparel workers. The benefits of corporate campaigns are often limited to workers with jobs in multinational companies and their subcontractors. Yet a very large percentage of Latin Americans work in the informal sector, and even in the United States the process of informalization is expanding rapidly. Broad coalitions like ASC/HSA must find ways of incorporating informal-sector workers if they are to be politically effective.

Contemplating the problem of informal-sector workers demonstrates how much further reconstruction of North-South, labor-NGO alliances still has to go. But in no way does it negate the accomplishments that have been described here. If UNITE members can be convinced that realizing their own economic interests depends on building alliances with relatively small unions in the global South, and a labor union confederation like ORIT can leave its traditional anti-communist past behind to build alliances with environmentalists and community groups across the hemisphere, it would be a grave error to set limits on what organizational leaps the next generation of hemispheric organizers might be able to take.

NOTES

[1] For an analysis of earlier efforts in which success varied, in part depending on the degree to which the full range of elements described here was present, see Anner 2002.

[2] A *maquiladora* is a small factory run by a foreign company, to which it exports its products.

[3] The Union of Needletrades, Industrial and Textile Employees (UNITE), was formed in 1995 by the merger of the International Ladies' Garment Workers' Union and the Amalgamated Clothing and Textile Workers' Union.

[4] Another important traditional trade element in the organizational matrix, which we do not have the space to discuss here, is the Global Union Federations (GUFs, formerly known as International Trade Secretariats). For example, the apparel sector GUF, the International Textile, Garment and Leather Workers' Federation took over with an organizing project of its own in Central America when UNITE decided that it did not have the resources to remain directly involved in organizing.

[5] The FLA's role in the evolution of this complex is an intriguing story that we cannot pursue here. On the one hand, had it not been for the opposition of USAS and UNITE, the FLA could have ended up succumbing to its corporate constituency and letting apparel companies off the hook by providing easy certification. On the other, the FLA's prior existence, sanctioned by both government and business (as well as respected NGOs like the International Labor Rights Foundation), legitimized the whole idea of monitoring and, ironically, may have made universities more comfortable signing onto the Workers' Rights Consortium (WRC).

[6] The Solidarity Center's largest source of funds is the US government, through core grants from the National Endowment for Democracy and USAID—with the unfortunate consequence of evoking memories of the political role of its predecessor, the American Institute of Free Labor Development. The Institute was accused, especially in Latin America, of playing an auxiliary role in repressing militant labor unionists that the US government considered too left wing, and it never escaped suspicions of historical ties to the Central Intelligence Agency (cf. Ancel 2000; Carew 1998; Scipes 2000). This historical reputation is a burden that the new generation of Solidarity Center staff works hard to surmount.

[7] It is hardly surprising that UNITE's political repertoire still includes activities that could be labeled protectionist. For example, faced with a desperate constituency of textile workers in the south of the United States with no hope of finding jobs to replace their disappearing textile jobs, Bruce Raynor, UNITE's president, became a founding member of the American Textile Trade Action Coalition, a union-business lobby group formed in April 2002. The coalition has lobbied against providing greater market access to textiles from Central America,

the Caribbean, and Andean countries (Rogers 2002). Likewise, after the 9/11 attacks on the World Trade Center, UNITE shifted attention from its newly launched Global Justice for Garment Workers campaign to a Buy New York campaign that supports New York City garment workers (Featherstone and USAS 2002).

[8] The most notorious conflict between a union and a women's group involved the Federación Nacional de Sindicatos Textil, Vestuario, Piel y Calzado and the Movimiento de Mujeres Trabajadores y Desempleadas "Maria Elena Cuadra" in Nicaragua.

[9] While environmental NGOs were the most prominent, other kinds of NGOs were also involved, including family-farm groups and policy organizations like Development Gap and the Institute for Policy Studies.

[10] To be sure, this experience has still not persuaded the leadership of the CTM to join a hemispheric alliance against free trade.

[11] Founded in 1991 at the very beginning of the battles over NAFTA, ART was also a very early example of labor-NGO collaboration. It brought the AFL-CIO together with think-tank NGOs like the Institute for Policy Studies, environmental groups like Friends of the Earth, and traditional NGOs like the American Friends Service Committee (AFSC).

[12] Among other activities, the ASC/HSA action provided an opportunity for the Noboa Banana workers, who were confronting a powerful and violent local plantation owner in their struggle to form a union, to highlight their case at a workshop that was attended by several hundred people.

[13] This is the committee that oversees ASC/HSA's activities between the meetings of the organization's governing council, in which forty networks of organizations are represented.

[14] Mexico has a very active NGO movement that is part of ASC/HSA, but except for the Frente Auténtico del Trabajo and the Unión Nacional de Trabajadores, organized labor in Mexico is not participating. Chile also has active NGO participation, but the Chilean CUT labor center has expressed skepticism about ASC/HSA. In Uruguay the unions have been active in ASC/HSA, while in Argentina, the non-ORIT labor center Central de los Trabajadores Argentinos has been active.

[15] The contrast between ASC/HSA's efforts to involve a full range of civil society groups and the way in which such groups (with the obvious exception of the Business Forum of the Americas) have been carefully kept at bay by the official FTAA process is stark. A Committee of Government Representatives on the Participation of Civil Society was finally created as part of the official process in 1998 (after ministerial meetings had been taking place for three years). The committee's efforts, however, consisted essentially of opening up a suggestion box. Korzeniewicz and Smith summarize the results of this effort as follows: "The fact that the FTAA's civil society committee's final report contained none of the substantive recommendations put forward by the CSOs [civil society organizations] was seen by both 'insiders' and 'outsiders' as a slap in

the face" (2000, 10). More recent official efforts to increase participation have also been superficial.

[16] For more information, go to the usleap.org website.

[17] Centro de Estudos de Cultura Contemporánea, Departamento Inter-sindical de Estudos Sócios Económicos, and Rede Inter-Universitária de Estudos e Pesquisas sobre o Trabalho.

Four

Challenging Relations

*A Labor-NGO Coalition to Oppose the Canada-US and
North American Free Trade Agreements, 1985–1993*

SOPHIA HUYER

INTRODUCTION

In 1987–88 a national debate erupted in Canada on the desirability of
entering into a free trade agreement with the United States. Characterized by an unusually high level of passion and militancy for a discussion
on economic policy, it was reminiscent of the 1911 trade debates that
brought down the Liberal government of Wilfrid Laurier "in a wave of
nationalist, protectionist and emotional sentiment" (Hart 1994, 56). However, the parameters for the 1988 debate were different, both national
and international. Although Canada had previously participated in negotiations on the General Agreement on Tariffs and Trade (GATT), it was
not until the intention to negotiate a Canada-US Free Trade Agreement
(FTA) was announced that a debate not only about the agreement's economic viability but also about the effects of regional integration on Canadian culture, society, and national sovereignty entered Canadian public discourse. The 1988 debate was called "one of the most significant
policy initiatives in the life of the Canadian nation" (Doern and Tomlin
1991, 2), in that the decision to negotiate a free trade agreement involved
a redefinition of Canada's relationship with the United States.

The range of the comprehensive bilateral agreement signed in 1987
extended far beyond the parameters of previous sectoral trade agreements
or negotiations (Hart 1994). In the March 1985 announcement of its intent

to negotiate a free trade agreement with the United States, the Conservative government made a sharp break with Liberal policies of the past to chart a new economic path based on closer economic ties with the United States and establishing a Canada that was "open for business." This was and remains a sensitive issue for Canadians, ever mindful of the "sleeping elephant" south of the border, and it prompted concerns about the wider implications to Canadian national and political sovereignty, control over investment (and jobs), environmental protection and natural resource management, social programs, and cultural survival.[1]

In the course of initiating trade talks with the United States, the Conservative government of Brian Mulroney set in motion economic policies and trends that were to touch on some of the fundamental perceptions of Canadian nationhood and identity (Doern and Tomlin 1991) and marked the first (regional) phase of Canada's introduction to economic globalization.

One of the most prominent groups opposed to the FTA—and later to the North American Free Trade Agreement (NAFTA)—was the Pro-Canada Network, which coordinated a coalition of popular-sector groups and social movements, including representatives from labor, the women's movement, churches, the environmental movement, and cultural and social justice groups. It intended to defeat the FTA by mobilizing member organizations and their constituents and mounting a campaign to sway public opinion. The primary strategy was to force a general election on the trade issue with the intention of defeating the Conservative government in favor of a Liberal or New Democratic Party (NDP) government, which the coalition believed would block the FTA.[2] When the Conservative government was reelected in 1987, the Pro-Canada Network continued in a new phase, whose legacy of cross-sectoral collaboration in Canada continues to this day.

The active and equal participation of labor was seen by many members as one of the significant and new characteristics of this coalition, ushering in new possibilities for activism in Canada. One observer argued that labor participation in the Pro-Canada Network augured the development of a "common front" against the neoliberal economic agenda of the 1980s. In this view the process "may well have gone further and faster in Canada than in any other OECD country . . . [to the point where] it becomes more difficult to say where the labour movement stops and the other progressive social movements begin" (Robinson 1994, 5).

Although it seems clear that labor and NGOs experienced a beneficial and productive relationship during the campaigns against free trade, the argument that a seamless relationship developed bears closer examination. Despite what was in many ways a positive collaboration, the relationship between labor organizations and NGOs in the coalition was faced with several challenges, including the following:

- Difficulty in reconciling approaches and goals among members were resolved with varying degrees of success.
- There were mixed views among labor unions about participating in the coalition. Even within those unions that did join, dissent was expressed concerning the value of popular-sector collaboration.
- Relations with other groups, including women's and environmental groups, were at times confrontational.
- Differences in structure, decision making, and leadership styles between unions and the other groups in the coalition caused tension.
- The relationship of labor with the NDP was uncertain.
- Issues of representation and accountability arose.

EMERGING LABOR-NGO COLLABORATION AGAINST FREE TRADE: THE BACKGROUND

In December 1985 the Confederation of Canadian Unions and the National Action Committee on the Status of Women (NAC) organized a meeting of labor, women's, agricultural, social service, church, university, and cultural groups opposed to the FTA. This group became the core of the Ontario-based Coalition Against Free Trade (Salutin 1989; Bashevkin 1989). The following year it organized two hugely successful and well-attended cultural events in Toronto, the Free Trade Revues.

Other groups organized separate campaigns. The introductory autumn 1986 issue of *The Moment*, a newsletter produced by the Jesuit Center for Peace and Justice, focused on an analysis of the implications of the FTA. On September 11, 1986, Shirley Carr, president of the Canadian Labor Congress (CLC), announced a "'massive campaign across this country, into every community' to speak to every government and 'every group of people we can talk to' on free trade" (Carr 1986). On the same day a prominent Canadian nationalist, Mel Hurtig, told the US Congress that Canadian and US opponents of the deal were likely to "torpedo" the bilateral talks (Lewington 1986).

One notable event was Dialogue '86 in January of that year, organized by the CLC in response to a government conference convened in March

1985 to consult businesses, individuals, and social groups on the question of free trade. For the popular-sector groups that attended, Dialogue '86 marked a new era of collaboration. Many groups developed new working relationships during the course of the conference and the organizing meetings leading up to it. For example, discussions between Marjorie Cohen of NAC and Leo Gerrard of the Steelworkers' Union led to a supplementary conference session led by Cohen on women and trade. This event marked the beginning of cooperation between NAC and labor on free trade.

A further series of trade-related meetings and conferences convened in the next year or so increased momentum toward a coordinated position among diverse sectors on trade and economic policies. GATT-fly, a church-based NGO, organized several important consultations and conferences, notably the Ecumenical Conference on Free Trade, Self-reliance and Economic Justice, held from February 26 to March 1, 1987, and attended by over eighty participants from church, labor, farm, women's, business, and anti-poverty groups. Participants recall the excitement and synergy generated at this meeting as the moment when a cross-sectoral and cross-regional social movement on Canadian economic issues was said to have crystallized (Clarke 1999; Dillon 1999; Turk 1999).

All these activities culminated in the Canada Summit held in April 1987, where up to one hundred representatives of the thirty-two national organizations that attended, including the CLC, NAC, the National Farmers' Union, and the Ecumenical Coalition for Economic Justice, agreed to work together in a formalized coalition to oppose free trade. A call for an election to allow the people of Canada to decide on a free trade agreement with the United States was contained in the Canada Summit Declaration as a common-denominator platform around which all the groups present believed they could mobilize their respective memberships. The event was marked by a march to Parliament Hill, where the declaration was taped to the doors of Parliament (Canada Summit 1987).

The assessment of the FTA and NAFTA by Ian Robinson, an anti–free trade researcher with strong ties to the Canadian labor movement, provides a summary of the concerns expressed by opponents of the anti–free trade lobby. The Mulroney agenda was seen to "free" corporations from investment restraints that limited development "conducive to the wider public interest," and to promote international capital mobility that would reduce the ability of states to tax and regulate capital, and by extension provide social programs and national-level development programs. In sum, the trade agenda was seen as a strategy to "substantially increase the power of capital vis-à-vis governments, unions, and other NGOs that are relatively immobile and primarily national in organization and focus" (Robinson 1994, 6).

The role of the Pro-Canada Network as first articulated was to support the ongoing activities of its members against free trade: to facilitate information sharing, to formalize links among members, to improve intercommunication, and to help members develop and compare concerns, analyses, and strategic priorities. However, once the FTA was completed and signed on October 3, 1987, the role of the network was to become more active. It developed a collective analysis and critique of the agreement, and it coordinated a series of actions across the country whose purpose was to generate public opposition to the FTA and force the ruling Conservatives to call an election before it was implemented (Clarke 1999).

THE ROLE OF LABOR IN THE PRO-CANADA NETWORK

The participation of labor groups was considered one of the achievements of the anti–free trade coalition, and also one of its defining characteristics. The Canadian Auto Workers (CAW), the CLC, the National Union of Provincial Government Employees, the Canadian Union of Public Employees (CUPE), the United Steelworkers of America, and several other unions were founding members of the Pro-Canada Network. Tony Clarke, founding member and chair of the network from 1987 to 1993, considers that the work to mobilize the labor membership in collaboration with other popular-sector groups was a new and important characteristic of the coalition—labor had never before participated in a social-sector coalition to the same extent (Clarke 1999).

Labor brought several strengths to the coalition: comparatively large financial resources, active members, a long tradition of organizing, and regional offices across the country. These resources were an enormous boost to the coalition, but they also far outweighed the resources of other members, so that the real or perceived domination of labor was a constant issue of concern in decision making and resource mobilization. Additional problems derived from difficulty in reconciling the hierarchical and institution-based structures of labor with the consensus-oriented and ad hoc decision-making styles of other popular-sector groups. As a result, although the unions were strongly supportive of and involved in both the FTA and NAFTA opposition campaigns, the degree and nature of collaboration that developed between labor and other popular-sector groups was viewed with mixed reactions on both sides.

The labor "contradiction," or differing views within labor on the value of NGO collaboration, is clearly expressed in a nationwide survey of participants in the anti-FTA campaign by the magazine *Canadian Dimension* in 1989. On the one hand, it was noted that labor was "clearly at the forefront of the fight against free trade" (Gonick and Silver 1989, 8), providing intellectual and political leadership, working cooperatively in many parts of the country with regional-level coalitions, and in many cases demonstrating an "exemplary" level of activity and resource commitment to the campaign. Contributions by labor included publication by the CUPE in *Facts on Free Trade* (1988) of the FTA analysis developed by the Pro-Canada Network. One of the successes of the opposition campaign, a cartoon booklet entitled *What's the Big Deal?*, included as an insert in a national newspaper, was funded primarily by the CAW. The CLC provided a credit card during the campaign to facilitate travel to events by Pro-Canada Network leaders (Turk 1999). Union leaders played a high-profile public role in opposition to free trade. Other contributions included participation in public debates and panels by labor leaders and financial contributions to local and regional activities.

However, according to survey results, the labor record was disappointing to many of its NGO partners. Labor groups generally tended to remain separate from regional and local coalitions, and sometimes even worked against them, either by failing to coordinate with other groups or by attempting to dominate or supersede other initiatives. For example, the Manitoba Federation of Labour (MFL) treated the Manitoba Coalition Against Free Trade as a sub-affiliate of the MFL, dominating meetings and subcommittees and driving away other union affiliates. Eventually, a unilateral decision was made by the MFL to fold the Coalition on the grounds that it was inactive. When the Coalition was reestablished, the MFL set up a rival group, which had the effect of diverting energy and activists. Yet once the 1987 election campaign began it withdrew entirely from anti–free trade activities in order to work in the political campaigns of the NDP. This was upsetting to many: "By insisting on occupying and monopolizing the leadership role, while at the same time being incapable of delivering on it, the MFL stood in the way of an effective fight-back campaign" (Gonick and Silver 1989, 8). Similar complaints were made at the time about the Ontario Coalition Against Free Trade, which was seen by many to be dominated by labor and to promote little diversity of participation and approach (Barndt 1998). The British

Columbia Federation of Labour identified free trade as an election issue, but carried out "token" coalition work and failed to mobilize its membership (Gonick and Silver 1989).

Coalition members were also disappointed by the priority labor groups accorded their alliance with the NDP. As the actions of the MFL indicate, union relations with the NDP generally took precedence over work with coalitions during the anti-FTA fight. Many union activists withdrew from coalition work when the election campaign began and concomitantly withdrew from anti–free trade work when the NDP decided to stress other election issues. Many voices in labor considered coalition work to be a drain on resources and less directly productive than direct campaign support for the NDP. The result was that while some activists blamed the 1988 election loss partially on labor, the fact that the coalitions could not be counted on to provide strong electoral support to the NDP was a sore point with some labor members (Dillon 1999; Turk 1999). After the 1988 election this situation began to change to a certain extent, partly as a result of labor's reevaluation of its relation to the NDP after the disappointments of the election campaign and labor's perception that the NDP had ignored its union supporters in its election strategy (White 1988).

The split personality displayed by labor during the anti-FTA campaign reflects internal conflicts taking place at the time. Writing in 1997, Swartz and Albo referred to a split among Canadian workers on attitudes to free trade in general. In their view the argument that free trade would threaten Canadian jobs held appeal only for those parts of the labor force not dependent on trade with the United States. That is, they argued, forest and steel product workers would be more amenable to a trade agreement in the face of increasing US protectionism, while public-sector workers, dependent on government funding, were more concerned about the possible risk of job cuts (see Swartz and Albo 1987).

Other observers analyzed the labor split differently. Union participation in coalitions such as the Pro-Canada Network is seen as the product of a social unionism approach that "emphasises unions being active in social and political struggles on a broad range of issues in coalition with other social movement groups" (Howlett 1996, 9). Reference is made to "right" and "left" unionism in the North American labor movement. Right unionism (also known as business unionism) focuses strictly on the employment situation of its members: more jobs, higher wages, better working conditions. The left approach, or social unionism, acknowledges the effects on its members of broader societal and employment issues, such as health care, education, militarization, and so on (Turk 1999).

By the time of the anti-NAFTA campaign (1992–94) the idea of working with coalitions was more generally accepted within the labor movement. The election in 1992 of Bob White, a supporter of coalition work, as president of the CLC was seen to reinforce a labor commitment to the Pro-Canada Network, while those unions not interested in broader coalition work had by that time left the field to the pro-coalition or pro-community unions (Turk 1999). However, debate on the issue continued. In a November 1993 comment at an Action Canada Network Assembly, White outlined four labor positions vis-à-vis collaborative work:

- support of coalitional work with popular-sector organisations;
- support of collaboration with the NDP;
- support of a mixture of both; or
- support of neither. (Action Canada Network 1993)

LEADERSHIP STYLE AND PROCESS

Leadership became a contentious issue within the coalition in different ways, both among leaders and among the broader membership. The Pro-Canada Network was set up as a network of national organizations.[3] Each organization sent one or more representatives and in the early high-profile days of the coalition, often the very high-level representatives participated. The executive committee was made up of representatives or leaders of the key member organizations, in which labor played a high-profile role.

Several members have observed that there was at times a struggle between labor representatives and other network leaders concerning who would represent it in the public eye. Certain labor leaders considered that the strength of their membership and contributions gave them the right to direct and represent the network in public. This tendency by Shirley Carr (president of the CLC from 1986 to 1992) was resisted on the grounds that the network would be publicly identified as a labor coalition, reinforcing an already existing tendency by the media to conflate labor leaders and the labor agenda with those of the Pro-Canada Network. The network often found itself choosing between the high profile that a labor leader would provide—but which delegated non-labor representatives to the periphery—and the lower media profile of other Network spokespersons who might be more representative of the broader coalition.

In the course of the anti-FTA and NAFTA campaigns the major campaign activities consisted of a focus on high-profile people like Bob White, president of the CAW; Marjorie Cohen, president of NAC; Shirley Carr, president of the CLC; and Maude Barlow, who gave speeches, participated on panels, gave press conferences, and engaged in televised debates. This approach fostered the perception within the Pro-Canada Network that it operated in a top-down manner, directed by a small coterie of national leaders working together.

For members of NGOs used to working with flatter hierarchical structures and decision-making processes, the prominence of union leadership detracted from democratic, effective operation. Judy Rebick of NAC recalls that in the "early, high-power days of the coalition, decisions were made not in open debates, but through behind the scenes negotiations with major players"—the CLC (a major donor) especially (Rebick 1998). In order to follow up on decisions made at a Network meeting, the CLC representative discussed the decision with his or her superior. If the superior required changes, the representative revised the decision with Clarke and other Network leaders. Writes Rebick: "Perhaps Tony felt he had to work that way, but I saw it as negative coalition building" (Rebick 1998).

For many members the focus on individual leadership was not only a hindrance to their experience of the coalition but an obstacle to building the popular movement they envisioned. Discussion at the June 1990 assembly on the meaning of social solidarity concluded that "solidarity is often fragile. . . . In order to achieve true solidarity, differences and problems, political and personal, must be named and addressed" (Pro-Canada Network 1990, 3). References to conflict and distrust among sectors appear repeatedly throughout the document, including "fear of group members of coalition gaining dominance," "difficulties in getting popular and union groups to work together because of distrust and prejudices about each other," and fear of losing control of priorities and agenda in view of the situation that "often the same people are involved again and again [in Network events and planning]" (ibid., 8, 3). Strategies articulated by workshop participants to redress these problems focused on "building a common vision *collectively*, with joint planning and strategy, and exploring various models of decision making (specifically forms of consensus decision making)" (ibid., 5, emphasis added). Although these comments were acknowledged by the leadership at the time, follow through was inconsistent.

Another difficulty emerged, which exacerbated labor-NGO tensions concerning the internal and public focus on leaders. The Pro-Canada

Network found itself increasingly caught in a cycle of dependence on the funds of national organizations (primarily labor), which in turn led to dependence on their leaders' approval of the network agenda and increased dissatisfaction among its members. Although by their very participation in the network, national representatives demonstrated support for the idea of a cross-national and cross-sectoral coalition, leaders nevertheless remained accountable to their own constituencies. By the time of the anti-NAFTA campaign, labor funding to Pro-Canada Network activities tended to be "directed." For example, support provided by the CLC for the October 26, 1991, National Day of Action for "strengthening the work of provincial or regional coalitions" was tied to participation in CLC-defined and CLC-coordinated national initiatives; regular reporting to the CLC by the regional network groups was also required (Action Canada Network 1991, 1).

Some regional members felt that lack of financial support for regional training and networking was a matter of will or the result of central decisions to focus on media events and targets rather than on regional coalition building (Silver 1999). Some coalitions were able to continue their work effectively, but many others were not. This situation militated against ongoing creative activity in the coalitions, which in turn reduced the vibrancy of the network outside Ottawa. As the regional coalitions declined, the newly renamed Action Canada Network was in less and less of a position to help them. Regional coalitions perceived themselves to be less integrated into decision making, the entire Network experienced increasing financial stress, and by the early 1990s overall resources had decreased to such an extent that the central office was scarcely able to function properly, and only so long as the minimal staff was willing to work for low wages.

RELATIONS WITH WOMEN'S GROUPS AND ENVIRONMENTAL GROUPS

Specific tensions existed to varying degrees between labor and two major sectors represented in the network, namely, women's groups and environmental groups.

The Network's Relationship with Women's Groups

NAC representatives Marjorie Cohen and Judy Rebick were both critical of what they considered an "absolutely" (Cohen 1999) male-dominated operating structure during the FTA campaign.[4] The alliance between labor and women was difficult in the early days. References are made to "knock-down drag-outs" taking place between representatives of NAC and labor. Cohen recalls that representatives of the CLC "wanted the women to knuckle under. I wasn't representing NAC simply to say, 'and women too'" (ibid.). Part of the difficulty arose from differences in approach between feminists and leftists, as remarked upon by Cohen and Rebick. According to Rebick (1998), many of the women in the network came from the labor or socialist world, so their approach was almost entirely political. Furthermore, they were accustomed to working in a male-dominated process and context. Feminist members used to working in the predominantly social, grassroots context of women's issues felt they were in an alien world of strict process, rigid hierarchy, and even sexism.

Cohen's experience of the Pro-Canada Network from 1986 to 1988 was slightly different. She is recognized by many leader-participants as having been a strong leader and was in fact co-chair of the network's precursor and influential member Ontario Coalition Against Free Trade. She concurs with Clarke that strong women leaders kept women's issues front and center in the network, and Cohen's high-media and public-speaking profile contributed a great deal to anti-FTA momentum. But while Cohen felt that network members were receptive to the raising of women's issues, she states firmly that they were not receptive to women taking direction in the organization (Cohen 1999).

Some unions, namely, the CAW and the Steelworkers, were more supportive, and in the end the coalition provided a venue for social and labor groups to work out power dynamics and address sexism. According to Cohen and Rebick, the coalition experience became a successful educational opportunity: labor and women's groups now enjoy a more collaborative working relationship, one that was resolved to a great extent in the network. Peggy Nash of the CAW corroborates, stating that the network experience taught the CAW the importance of on-the-ground action and collaboration (Nash 1998; Cohen 1999; Rebick 1998).

The Network's Relationship with Environmental Groups

Statements by participating environmental groups indicate that the network did not effectively integrate environmental groups or environmental issues into its rhetoric, approach, or structure. A Greenpeace representative stated at the April 1991 Action Canada Network Assembly that the "environmental movement has not been integrated yet" (Action Canada Network 1991). Michelle Swenarchuk, the Canadian Environmental Law Association representative in the network, recalls that she "pleaded with them repeatedly" to integrate environmental concerns and work with the many environmental groups they could tap into. But this did not occur, in her view, because the leaders, as "fundamentally left economists," were neither open to nor capable of broadening their perspective to incorporate a substantive environmental analysis. She contends that the same was true of Common Frontiers, a subgroup of the network that focused on anti-NAFTA networking with groups in the United States and Mexico, in which she was a key member from 1991. In her opinion a strong environmental perspective was not integrated into North American anti–free trade or anti-globalization networking until 1998—the culmination of many years of work (Swenarchuk 1999).

INTERNATIONAL LABOR SOLIDARITY

Another substantive effect on labor of its collaboration with Canadian NGOs was an expansion of international activities and solidarity networks. Several unions had come into the coalition with preexisting international links—although several observers commented that labor links in Mexico, for example, tended to be with pro-government labor organizations such as the Confederación de Trabajadores Mexicanos, and that more progressive Mexican partners in the form of the independent labor federation Frente Auténtico del Trabajo and Cuauhtémoc Cárdenas' Partido de la Revolución Democrática were initiated through the network (Traynor 1999). In October 1990 CAW representatives made a tour of *maquiladoras* in Mexico, where they had an opportunity to develop solidarity connections with Mexican workers in the auto, airline, and fisheries sectors (Seymour and Wohlfarth 1990, 7).

The Canadian Steelworkers showed an early commitment to international networking. The Steelworkers' Humanity Fund, set up in 1985 as a direct response to famine in Ethiopia, became active in the early 1990s. Where relations with Latin American groups are concerned, the Steelworkers initially worked primarily through Common Frontiers on opposition to NAFTA. At a January 1991 Common Frontiers forum in Ottawa, Hugh Mackenzie, research director of the Steelworkers, commented that the Canadian economy had been changed by the FTA to such an extent that nothing would be accomplished by repealing the agreements.

Instead, his view was that it was important to work for a less vulnerable economic structure and that strategic alliances with Mexican groups were "really important. If we can help Mexicans and see Mexicans fighting on these issues, it helps Canadians see how much we gave up, and that there is a chance to do something else" (Common Frontiers 1991, 15). By 1994 the Steelworkers had expanded their agenda to South America. Projects included mining exchanges in Chile (Marshall 1999); collaborations with NGOs and labor organizations on economic integration in the Americas; and tri-regional research in Africa, Latin America, and Canada on local community-based organizations and responses to economic restructuring. At this time the CAW also expanded links to metal workers in Brazil. Upon taking the leadership of the CLC, Bob White had been encouraged by Common Frontiers to expand links to other groups in South America (EAI 1992; White 1999).

The nature of labor's international networking was also affected. When the Hemispheric Social Alliance (HSA) emerged in response to the FTAA negotiations in the mid-1990s, union members of Common Frontiers began to recognize a different kind of benefit to their members of this kind of international work, moving away from a paternalism based on a simplistic relationship of transferring funds to what was termed a new dynamic of mutual cooperation and respect around building positive social responses to the trade liberalization process.[5] In the view of one union worker, "the qualitatively different relationships and alliances in various sectors [built around the FTAA campaign] are interesting and exciting, providing building blocks to future work" (Marshall 1999).

An example of this is found in the experience of the Steelworkers, who had been developing links with compatriot unions in South America. According to one representative, the Steelworkers and other unions have found that the globalization of industry necessitates the coordination of strategy, position, and actions with counterparts in other parts of the world facing the same corporate owners. When a Brazilian multinational steel company bought out Manitoba Rolling Mills and Curtis Steel in Canada, existing links among the labor groups in both countries helped the unions respond to this new situation. Canadian labor organizations making up the Labor International Development Committee find that there is value in supporting the strengthening and empowerment of union membership in other parts of the world. These groups take the view that work in literacy, housing, and training in labor negotiations not only strengthens their partners but builds the counteractive strength of unions in a globalized world and contributes to upward harmonization of labor capacity and standards—all of which benefit the Canadian unions as well (Marshall 1998; 1999).

Other international exchanges of experience and expertise, which began in the anti-NAFTA campaign, continue to varying degrees. The Mexican Frente Auténtico del Trabajo and the Organización Regional Interamericana de Trabajadores (ORIT), both large Latin American organizations, are well established, active, and innovative in many of their actions. The experience of ORIT, which as a labor body has institutional status in Mercosur (South American common market) as well as the greater operational opportunities that exist for influence and input into that specific trade regime, informed the goals of the FTAA advocacy. Bob White has also commented on the expansion of networking engaged in by the CLC and its members, both through Common Frontiers and through other international labor links such as ORIT and the ICFTU (White 1999).[6]

CONCLUSION

The collaboration between labor and NGOs during the anti-FTA and anti-NAFTA campaigns was seen as an exciting new era in popular-sector organizing in Canada. At the same time, difficulties arose in working out the nature and process of that collaboration. Labor unions are large, highly organized, centralized, and bureaucratic systems that cannot easily intersect with more informally structured and much smaller popular organizations. That the labor movement is a coalition in itself, with its own internal set of debates, politics, and conflicts, meant that resolving the contradictions in the relationship between labor and the rest of the network was a constant characteristic of the coalition.

The feminist, environmental, and anti-racist analyses of other groups at times came into conflict with what was seen as a predominantly political and economic perspective of labor, further complicated by the situation that many union members, especially auto workers, are now solidly middle class. This problematized the belief that the unions speak for the disenfranchised and marginalized—who, in the Canadian coalition, were more closely tied to the National Action Committee on the Status of Women and anti-poverty groups.

Resource and funding issues were a particular strain, in that the comparatively resource-rich unions were seen as having a disproportionate influence in the coalition and forcing a particular style of leadership and decision making on their non-labor partners.

On the other hand, union members also had to account to their membership for union money that was spent in work only indirectly related to union goals and programs (Action Canada Network 1995) and to adjust to a membership structure and decision-making process that was not only foreign but seemingly less organized as well. Bob White, a strong supporter of coalition work with NGOs, found coalitional work with NGOs difficult at times, the NGO processes "very different from the CAW" (White 1999). Nevertheless, although labor-NGO collaboration had existed to a certain extent before the Pro-Canada Network, it became more solid and intense during the campaigns against the FTA and NAFTA. The legacy of this work is substantial: labor groups continue to collaborate with NGOs and other popular-sector groups today, albeit in smaller and shorter-term coalitions, such as the coalition on child poverty in Canada. In addition, collaboration between several labor unions and NGOs continued in Common Frontiers, a network that grew out of the experience gained in confronting the free trade agenda.[7] It emerged out of a recognition that for opposition to trade liberalization to be most effective, it needs to reach across borders. Common Frontiers helped to initiate and participated in a tri-national network of anti-NAFTA groups from Mexico and the United States. It is now part of the HSA, which was formed in Brazil in 1997 for the purpose of "building a broad-based movement throughout the hemisphere to confront the current economic model and corporate rule" (HSA, n.d.).

Activities in which Canadian groups have participated have included joint preparations for the November 1999 FTAA Trade Ministerial Americas Civil Society Forum, held in Toronto, and the Quebec Summit of the Americas in April 2001, held parallel to an FTAA Ministerial Meeting in Quebec City. Jointly developed documents were submitted to the FTAA body, and several were presented to the Toronto meeting, preparations for which also included a wide range of public information and protest events organized by groups including the Labor Council of Toronto and York Region, the Metro Network for Social Justice, and Common Frontiers, among others (Marshall 1999). More recently, in October 2002, the Quito Encuentro and Days of Continental Resistance to the FTAA were timed to coincide with the seventh Ministerial Summit of the FTAA held November 1–3, 2002.

Despite the strong presence of NAC leaders Cohen and Rebick in the earlier coalition days, gender is not a strong component of the Canadian contribution to the international coalition. NAC no longer participates actively in Common Frontiers, and several members consider it difficult to "find" a gender approach to trade liberalization. According to Judith Marshall of the Canadian Steelworkers, this stems from the political and bargaining context of the hemispheric negotiations, since by definition these are about the ability of corporations to make profitable investments in other countries. This leaves little room for social issues generally, let alone gender ones. On the other hand, one of the approaches of the current phase of continental networking is to question the fundamental assumptions of the FTAA in terms of jobs, poverty, and exclusion, which is where gender politics can find an entry point. Accordingly, then, in Marshall's view, the gender network of the hemispheric advocacy is less visible and organized than the poverty network, which is made up almost entirely of women (Marshall 1999). However, the most recent critique of the FTAA, "The FTAA Unveiled," includes a chapter on gender in the agreement, contributed by the US Network on Gender and Trade (HSA 2003).

While promoting the FTAA has been a priority for US president George W. Bush, popular opposition to "free trade" schemes seems to be very strong. This is supported by the election of leftist governments in several Latin American countries, including Brazil, where in a recent plebiscite 98 percent of the population voted against the agreement. Venezuela's left-populist government refuses to commit itself to the 2005 target date, and even trade proponents in Latin America are expressing doubts about the FTAA. "We have reservations about demands from the northern countries to dismantle protectionist measures, especially in agriculture, while we do not observe that happening in those countries," Ecuadorian Foreign Minister Heinz Moeller is quoted as saying in a Common Frontiers report culled from articles appearing in the *New York Times* and the *Financial Times*. As a result, US trade representative Robert Zoellick has admitted that the FTAA could collapse (Common Frontiers, 1999).

The HSA experience and the strong popular opposition to the FTAA are part of what Marshall has called a new kind of benefit to Steelworkers members: gaining a larger perspective, both internationally and with other sectors. She sees a new dynamic of mutual cooperation and respect that "gives one optimism" about building positive social responses to the trade liberalization process. In her view, however much the FTAA repeats NAFTA, "the qualitatively different relationships and alliances in various sectors is interesting and exciting, providing building blocks to future work" (Marshall 1999). And while all potential for conflict may not be completely resolved, it seems that labor and NGOs in Canada are continuing to develop new and positive forms of interaction.

NOTES

[1] Prime Minister Trudeau first used the metaphor of the mouse beside a sleeping elephant to refer to the political, cultural, and economic aspects of Canada-US relations. The mouse needs to be alert in order not to be crushed when the elephant rolls over.

[2] When the Liberals eventually gained power in 1993, they in fact contradicted their earlier rhetoric and confirmed NAFTA. For a detailed history of the politics and campaigns around the Canada-US Free Trade Agreement and NAFTA, see Huyer (2000, chap. 3).

[3] Later renamed the Action Canada Network.

[4] Cohen and Rebick represented NAC in the coalition from 1985 to 1987 and from 1990 to 1993, respectively.

[5] The FTAA (Free Trade Area of the Americas) was seen as an expansion of NAFTA into South America, and negotiations began soon after the passage of NAFTA.

[6] See Huyer (2001) on the collaboration of the ICFTU with business- and social-sector groups to block the MAI (Multilateral Agreement on Investments) during White's tenure as president.

[7] Members of Common Frontiers include the umbrella NGO network the Canadian Council for International Cooperation; Canadian Auto Workers; Canadian Environmental Law Association; Canadian Federation of Students; Canadian Labor Congress; Canadian Union of Public Employees; Communications, Energy and Paperworkers Union of Canada; Council of Canadians; Canadian Ecumenical Justice Initiatives; Maquila Solidarity Network; Oxfam Canada; Rights and Democracy; Sierra Club of Canada; Steelworkers' Humanity Fund; United Church of Canada—Latin American and Caribbean Division; and Réseau Québécois sur l'Intégration Continentale.

Five

Time to Scale Up Cooperation?

Labor Unions, NGOs,
and the International Anti-sweatshop Movement

TIM CONNOR

BACKGROUND

In October 1999 labor unions and NGOs involved in the anti-sweatshop movement received a surprising proposal from Philip Knight, the CEO of Nike. Knight's company had been a key target of the movement, and his letter expressed frustration that the company's attempts to engage individual organizations in bilateral dialogue had been "episodic" and "repetitive" and had not allowed "progress or mutual understanding." He proposed that groups involved in the campaign select "a core team of individuals you designate as representative of your collective interests" and indicated that the company's vice-president for corporate responsibility would work with that group.[1] After much discussion the majority of the campaign organizations decided against accepting this proposal. In bilateral negotiations Nike had indicated very little interest in agreeing to some of the campaigners' core demands, and they were concerned that establishing a structure for the proposed new talks would use up a lot of time while achieving little. While this may well have been the right decision, Knight's proposal highlights a key issue for the movement. At the international scale it has a loose, networked form of organization that has proved well suited to spreading awareness of and generating protest activity focused on labor abuses in the production networks of particular transnational corporations (TNCs). The negative side of maintaining this loose structure is that labor unions and NGOs have so far been unable to offer Nike and other companies an adequate incentive to respond positively to their proposals for improving respect for workers' rights. Arguably, their ability to do so would be substantially enhanced if they could establish broad agreement on a mechanism for giving some credit to companies who make progress in this area. While they are a long way from establishing the depth of international cooperation necessary to develop such a mechanism, the existence of broad and mutually beneficial alliances between unions and NGOs in particular countries suggests that the task is at least worth attempting.

THE PROBLEM OF CAPITAL MOBILITY

The international labor union movement is going through a difficult and challenging time, with unions experiencing falling membership across the industrialized world and struggling to gain a foothold in industrializing countries (Wills 1998, 113). The problem is particularly pronounced in industries such as apparel that require low-skilled labor and low levels of capital investment. The international garment industry is characterized by complex and fluid networks of production. Contracting and subcontracting are common, and homeworkers form a significant part of the industry's global work force. This structure allows production to be shifted relatively easily from organized work sites to nonunion ones, and from states that respect and enforce the right of workers to freedom of association to states that do not. This makes it very difficult for workers to assert their union rights, since any attempt to take industrial action could result in production moving from their work site to other parts of the production network, putting their jobs in danger. The belief that increasing capital mobility will inevitably continue the global decline in labor union power has been described as "something of an orthodoxy in much academic debate and political commentary about the future of labor organization" (Wills 1998, 112).

In the context of the debate about the best way to go forward, one option that has been promoted is for unions to link with other civil society organizations in joint international campaigns (Wells 1998c, 24; Wills 1998, 119). The hope is that by working together they might mobilize sufficient numbers of people to persuade companies and governments to respect workers' rights. The international anti-sweatshop movement—a series of interconnecting international networks of NGOs and unions campaigning to end labor abuses in the production networks of TNCs operating in particular industries[2]—presents a useful case study of this kind of cooperation.[3]

ANATOMY OF A SOCIAL MOVEMENT

While anti-sweatshop campaigns have a long history, the current phase of international activity began to gather momentum in the early 1990s.[4] The sizes, constituencies, geographical locations, and political orientations of the labor unions and NGOs involved vary considerably. On the labor union side the campaign has included not only the relevant International Trade Secretariat, the International Textile, Garment and Leather Workers' Federation (ITGLWF) and its affiliates, but also small unaffiliated unions in industrializing countries, some with only a couple of hundred members.[5] NGOs that have had some involvement in the movement have varied in size from major development organizations such as Christian Aid in the UK and Development and Peace in Canada, to medium-sized labor-rights groups with a dozen or so staff, such as the Urban Community Mission in Indonesia and the Asia Monitor Resource Centre in Hong Kong, to small volunteer organizations essentially made up of one or two people, including Thuyen Nguyen's Vietnam Labor Watch and Jeff Ballinger's Press For Change, both based in the United States.[6] It is difficult to estimate exactly how many organizations participate in the international movement, but they certainly number in the hundreds.[7]

For much of the 1990s the impetus for most of the research and campaign activity that involved international cooperation came from organizations based in industrialized countries, but it is becoming more common for unions and NGOs based in the South to take the initiative, and for organizations based in the North to respond with support. Representatives of garment unions from many Southern countries, including Lesotho, South Africa, the Philippines, and Indonesia, participated in the March 2001 Clean Clothes Campaign's strategy meeting in Barcelona.[8] In May 2001 the Lesotho Clothing And Allied Workers' Union called on groups who had participated in the Barcelona meeting to support their campaign to persuade the US government to make access to the US market under the African Growth and Opportunity Act dependent on the Lesotho government's enforcement of its labor laws.[9] At the request of the Federasi Serikat Pekerja Tekstil, Sandang Dan Kulit union in Indonesia, Oxfam Community Aid Abroad and other NGOs are still seeking to persuade Nike to ensure that workers from the PT Doson factory receive their full legal entitlements after the factory closed in October 2002. Under the umbrella of its current "Make Trade Fair" campaign, Oxfam International will work on women workers' rights in trading chains by adding its support to a number of campaign initiatives based in Africa, Asia, and Latin America, as well as some countries in the North.

A LOOSE, NETWORKED FORM OF ORGANIZATION

A variety of organizational forms operate across the movement. Internally, the more established labor unions and larger NGOs, such as those unions affiliated with the ITGLWF and the various member organizations of Oxfam International, tend to have hierarchical decision-making structures and formal processes for international cooperation. Other groups operate differently. The Clean Clothes Campaign's European Secretariat in Amsterdam, for example, makes decisions by consensus. At the global level there is a loose, networked structure that is common in broad social movements (Gerlach 2001; della Porta and Diani 1999). Such movements are rarely hierarchically or bureaucratically structured. They commonly exhibit a more flexible and mobile form and tend not to have a single leader or group of leaders with power to make decisions that bind others. Instead, they have "multiple, often temporary, and sometimes competing leaders or centers of influence," and are "composed of many diverse groups, which grow and die, divide and fuse, proliferate and contract" (Gerlach 2001, 289–90). Participants in these movements are drawn together by common elements in their value systems and political understandings, and hence by a shared belief in narratives that problematize particular social phenomena. They do not share allegiance to a particular organizational form or to a particular strategy for action (Keck and Sikkink 1998, 5; della Porta and Diani 1999, 27, 53; Arquilla and Ronfeldt 2001, 323).

This loose form of organization has many advantages. In the context of the anti-sweatshop movement it has facilitated innovation and adaptive learning. There has not been an expectation that campaigners must seek approval from all other movement participants before taking action. This has freed individuals and organizations to experiment with new and potentially risky campaign activities without waiting for the approval of a slow-moving bureaucracy and without endangering the movement as a whole. Other participants have been able to distance themselves from tactics with which they disagree or which prove counterproductive and to copy those that prove effective (Gerlach 2001). Email and other relatively new information technologies have increased the effectiveness of this form of organization by enhancing campaigners' ability to learn from, and respond to, each other's experiments. Key campaigners are linked by numerous email lists through which they receive the latest reports on factory conditions, on meetings with particular corporations, and on the success or otherwise of campaign initiatives. Future strategies are also discussed on these lists, or at least flagged and then debated more intensely by email among subsets of actors with higher levels of trust. Through participation in these lists such organizations have gained an understanding of the other groups involved and of the dynamics of the movement itself. This has allowed them to engage with other groups in particular activities without risking their reputation by being identified with everything done in the name of the wider movement. It has also allowed particular organizations and individuals to develop specialized roles, so that some are relied on for their expertise in health and safety, others for their knowledge of working conditions in the production networks of particular companies, and still others for their skills in attracting the interest of journalists.

WHAT HAS BEEN ACHIEVED?

The movement has had significant success in raising public awareness of labor abuses. Since 1996 the campaign against the sportswear company Nike has generated more than one thousand newspaper articles a year linking the company's name to allegations of sweatshop conditions.[10] More than 350,000 people have signed petitions calling on Nike to allow independent factory monitoring,[11] and there have been hundreds of demonstrations against the company in North America, Australia, Europe, and East Asia.[12] In the United States a growing student anti-sweatshop network called United Students against Sweatshops (USAS) has established branches on over two hundred campuses and has persuaded over one hundred universities to join the Workers' Rights Consortium, an organization governed by unions, students, and sympathetic academics that investigates whether clothes bearing university logos are being produced in accordance with core international labor standards (Featherstone and Henwood 2001).

Unfortunately, the students' success in turning activist pressure into progressive policy change is the exception rather than the norm, and the students' impact has been limited to a relatively narrow section of the US garment market. Over the long term most organizations involved in the movement aim to persuade states to put in place legislated regulatory regimes that ensure that workers' rights, particularly their right to freedom of association, are respected. Many also put pressure on corporations to commit to a broadly agreed-upon set of labor rights and to cooperate with credible unions and NGOs to establish systems of independent monitoring to ensure that those rights are respected.[13] For most of these groups codes of conduct and other voluntary forms of regulation are not seen as an alternative to legislation but as a step toward it.[14]

Both of these goals remain elusive. Few organizations involved in the movement would claim to have yet had a positive impact on government regulation, and so far progress with voluntary initiatives has been limited.[15] Many companies have established their own codes of conduct, but in the great majority of cases these have been nothing more than public-relations tools, commonly avoiding key issues such as living wages and union rights, and lacking any kind of enforcement mechanism.[16] Some companies have established programs to implement their codes and monitor their effectiveness. There is at least anecdotal evidence[17] that this monitoring can result in some improvements in health and safety conditions and increased compliance with some local laws in factories in the first tier of the supply chain.[18] There is, however, very little evidence of its improving respect for workers' union rights, which is a key priority of the movement. Several multi-stakeholder initiatives involving representatives from both unions and NGOs have become established, including the Ethical Trading Initiative in the UK, the Fair Wear Foundation in the Netherlands, the No Sweatshop Label in Australia, and Social Accountability International. The ITGLWF has also sought to persuade a number of companies to sign international framework agreements with the union. Thus far, however, only a relatively small number of companies have been willing to participate in such programs, and, as a rule, the more rigorous they are the less companies are involved (Utting 2001).

TIME TO SCALE UP COOPERATION?

Notwithstanding the advantages listed above of a loose, relatively unstructured form of organization, arguably a lack of broad global agreement on what companies should do is undermining the ability of unions and NGOs to persuade companies to respond positively to any of their proposed solutions. More specifically, the lack of an extensively endorsed process by which companies can be recognized—in however limited a fashion—for making gradual, systemic progress gives them little incentive to do so. It is not that policy questions have not been debated at the international level. Since at least 1995 there have been numerous international conferences, meetings, and email discussions considering the merits of various ways of institutionalizing cooperation among companies, unions, and NGOs to oversee systems monitoring factory conditions.[19] However, those multi-stakeholder initiatives that have been established reflect negotiated agreements between particular sets of unions and NGOs and particular sets of companies. They lack the support or endorsement of the wider movement, and some have drawn vigorous criticism from other unions and NGOs.[20] Hence, companies currently have no guarantee that participation in any multi-stakeholder initiative will improve their reputation. Indeed, to the extent that an initiative requires greater transparency, such participation may well increase criticism, since other activists thereby gain access to much more information regarding labor abuses in a given company's supply networks.

Agreement on some kind of scale by which the progress of companies can be measured would also increase the movement's ability to mobilize supportive consumers and investors to reward companies that are making some progress—and to focus activist pressure on companies that are not. Much more research is needed into the extent to which consumers and investors are interested in this kind of action, but the constant phone calls and emails that anti-sweatshop campaigners receive along the lines of "what brand of clothes should I buy?" suggest that interest would be considerable. Arguably, part of the reason that stories of sweatshop abuses generate strong feelings is the challenge they present to the identity of their audience—consumers who might otherwise regard themselves as respectful of the dignity and welfare of others find themselves implicated in a system of exploitation. But unless campaigners can successfully promote credible means by which consumers can bring their actions in line with their self-image by helping to solve the problem, the campaign runs the danger of ending in apathy rather than activism.[21]

BUILDING TRUST

In order to establish credibility, such a system would need extensive international support from established unions and reputable human rights organizations.[22] These organizations would need to agree, or at least reach a compromise position, on a number of controversial questions. Detailing these issues and considering how they might be resolved goes beyond the scope of this essay, as do practical questions regarding how such cooperation and negotiation might be organized.[23] It is, however, worth considering the current extent and nature of cooperation between unions and NGOs involved in the movement in order to consider whether global cooperation is feasible.

While the quality of cooperation varies considerably across geographical contexts, it is not difficult to find examples of strained relationships. As representatives of democratic organizations that derive their legitimacy from their membership, many union leaders have been wary of lending their credibility to a movement involving NGOs, whose mandate to work on labor issues is far from clear. In Indonesia, for example, many union leaders are concerned that labor-rights NGOs are taking over roles that properly belong to democratic workers' organizations. In at least two recent cases a new union that had become established as a result of education work conducted by a labor-rights NGO has severed relations with that NGO on the grounds that the leader of the NGO was attempting to control the union.[24]

Many unions have also been concerned that NGOs might bilaterally negotiate agreements with companies that benefit the companies' public image but fail to protect workers' rights effectively.[25] This fear was inflamed in November 1998 when the US NGOs involved in the Fair Labor Association (FLA) finalized an agreement on factory monitoring with participating companies against the will and behind the back of UNITE, the US clothing union that had been involved in negotiations regarding the FLA since 1996. Although the FLA's code of conduct affirmed workers' right to form unions, UNITE believed that the proposed monitoring program would not adequately protect that right. The NGOs' decision understandably caused considerable animosity between those NGOs and US unions and reinforced union concern about cooperation with NGOs.[26] On the NGO side there has been disappointment that a number of US unions have not been interested in cooperating with the broader NGO movement. In a March 2001 interview Jeff Ballinger acknowledged that the AFL-CIO had funded research and campaign work by a particular NGO, the National Labor Committee, and that the AFL-CIO's Solidarity Centers play an important role in funding unions in the South and in facilitating communications between such unions and Northern campaigners. Nevertheless, he was frustrated that many US unions had not made more of the opportunity that the anti-sweatshop movement presented to "reach a lot of people who are not normally sympathetic to unions."[27] He noted, for example, that he had tried without success over many years to interest the US teachers' union in the campaign targeting Nike.

In other countries, experiences of cooperation have been more positive. A number of umbrella organizations have developed, representing national alliances or networks of unions and NGOs. These include the eleven Clean Clothes Campaigns in Europe and India and the FairWear campaign in Australia. In these countries a considerable amount of work has gone into building trust, and in most cases it has resulted in relatively close working relationships. In an October 2001 meeting of the Clean Clothes Campaign, unions and NGOs from several European countries reflected on their experience of working together. While some areas of concern were identified, the overall assessment was very positive.[28] Union representatives noted that cooperating with NGOs had allowed them to reach a broader audience and had significantly increased their ability to put pressure on companies to take account of workers' rights. At the international level, the ITGLWF has also indicated its willingness to coordinate campaigns with NGOs. In January 2002 the union organized a meeting in Singapore with representatives of workers from Taiwan, Indonesia, and Vietnam to discuss the possibility of negotiating an international framework agreement with the Pou Chen Corporation.[29] NGO and academic participants in the anti-sweatshop movement were invited in order to consider the viability of a joint campaign to persuade Pou Chen to sign such an agreement.

CONCLUSION

Given that in many countries the level of trust between unions and NGOs involved in the anti-sweatshop movement is still relatively low, it may well be utopian to hope for effective coordination of policy assessments at the international level. In the absence of such coordination, however, it is difficult to see how the movement's considerable success in building awareness of—and generating protest activity against—labor-rights abuses can be effectively leveraged to persuade TNCs to reform their practices substantially. The number of institutions claiming to ensure that participating companies are acting ethically is likely to divide and confuse consumers, activists, and investors, and there is a danger that interest in the issue will decline due to the lack of a clear direction forward.

Fortunately, at the national level there are examples that suggest that when unions and NGOs put adequate time and resources into establishing cooperation, then the potential to establish close and productive working relationships is considerable. Whether such cooperation is achievable on a global scale remains to be tested, but the potential benefits make the attempt well worthwhile.

NOTES

[1] Dated October 5, 1999, the letter was addressed "To all the signatories of the Clean Clothes Campaign's open letter." A month earlier, human rights organizations, unions, and academic researchers from fifteen countries had sent an open letter to Knight. Representatives of the Clean Clothes Campaign had delivered that letter at Nike's annual shareholders' meeting in Hilversum in September 1999.

[2] Although industries such as toys and cut flowers have also received campaigners' attention, for the purposes of this essay I focus on campaigns against companies operating in the clothing and footwear industry.

[3] I have been involved in this movement since 1995 as coordinator of Oxfam Community Aid Abroad's NikeWatch campaign.

[4] In 1991 the Clean Clothes Campaign was founded in the Netherlands as a European network of unions and NGOs working on the issue. That same year US labor activist Jeff Ballinger initiated the Nike campaign in Indonesia. In 1992 the National Labor Committee managed to generate significant media coverage in the United States of working conditions in factories in El Salvador and Honduras.

[5] An example of such a union is Persatuan Buruh Indonesia/PBI (Indonesian Labour Union) based in Serang in West Java, Indonesia.

[6] As far as NGOs are concerned, it is necessary to be clear about which organizations are considered to be part of the movement, because in a number of cases targeted corporations have funded sympathetic NGOs to work with them on labor issues in a manner that fits the companies' priorities and objectives rather than those of organizations involved in the campaign. For example, Nike has funded the International Youth Foundation to establish the Global Alliance for Workers and Communities, an organization that runs development programs in some Nike contract factories. For the purposes of this essay I use the term *NGO* to refer to nonprofit organizations that have participated in public criticism of targeted corporations and that do not receive funding from those corporations.

[7] The Clean Clothes Campaign runs an email list for representatives of unions and NGOs supportive of the campaign that has over two hundred members. I coordinate a confidential discussion list for unions and NGOs involved in the campaign targeting Nike that has representatives from over fifty organizations.

[8] In this essay I use the terms *South* or *Southern* to refer to countries with relatively low average per capita incomes and with economies that are either largely non-industrial or else in the process of industrialization. Similarly, I use the terms *Northern* or *North* to refer to industrialized countries.

[9] I received a letter dated May 31, 2001, from Willy Mats'eo, national coordinator of the Lesotho Clothing And Allied Workers' Union, to this effect.

[10] These statistics were generated by conducting "all publications" searches on the Dow Jones Interactive Media Database on July 4, 2001. I searched for articles containing the word *Nike* within sixty words of a reference to factories, workers, or labor, as well as within sixty words of a reference to sweatshops, exploitation, abuse, or wages. The exact search phrase was "Nike near60 (factory or factories or worker or workers or labor or labour) near60 (sweatshop or sweatshops or exploit$ or abus$ or wage$ or strike or hour or child)." The search phrase was applied only in English, not in other languages. I also reviewed a sample of articles from each year in order to estimate the percentage of articles picked up by the search that did not relate to sweatshop allegations against Nike. Note that this is a relatively blunt measuring instrument because many newspapers are not listed on the database.

[11] This includes over 200,000 signatures collected by the Canadian Catholic Organization for Development and Peace and over 100,000 collected by the Belgian Clean Clothes Campaign.

[12] In 1996 and 1997 the US organization Campaign for Labor Rights used email to organize three "days of action" against Nike, the most successful of which resulted in demonstrations on the same day in over ninety cities in twelve countries. Nike has also become a key target of the broader movement protesting neoliberal globalization. This movement, both documented and inspired by books such as Naomi Klein's *No Logo* (2000), has become much more visible since the demonstrations at the Seattle meeting of the WTO in 1999. Its adoption of Nike as a key target has substantially increased the level of protest activity focusing on that company.

[13] There is a relatively standard list of labor rights that are included in codes that have the broad support of unions and human rights groups. These include the "Clean Clothes Campaign Code of Labour Practices for the Apparel Industry Including Sportswear," the International Confederation of Free Trade Unions' "Model Code of Conduct," and the Ethical Trading Initiative's "Base Code."

[14] The strategy guiding Oxfam Community Aid Abroad's work on the NikeWatch campaign has been that if, through consumer and activist pressure, enough corporations can be persuaded to become involved in effective independent monitoring, then those corporations will want others to be held to the same standard and hence may support effective state regulation.

[15] One possible exception to this is the FairWear campaign in New South Wales, Australia, which has been working to enhance respect for the rights of homeworkers in that state. In 2002, in response to lobbying from FairWear and the Textile, Clothing and Footwear Union of Australia, the Labor government

introduced a package of policy and legislative changes that responded positively to many of the campaigners' demands.

[16] A US Department of Labor Study of the codes of forty-two US companies found that "most of the codes . . . do not contain detailed provisions for monitoring and implementation, and many of these companies do not have a reliable monitoring system in place." The same study found that many corporate respondents "did not know whether workers were aware of the existence of their codes" (US Department of Labor 1996).

[17] Areas of improved compliance relate primarily to health and safety provisions, hours of work, and the payment of a legal minimum wage. I have found this, for example, when researching conditions in sport-shoe factories producing for Nike in Indonesia (see Connor 2002). In an email dated October 29, 2002, Ineke Zeldenrust of the European Secretariat Office of the Clean Clothes Campaign indicated that in her research in India and Pakistan, companies, auditors, labor unions, and NGOs had all reported that company-controlled monitoring systems were at least improving compliance with legal requirements in these particular areas.

[18] That is, in factories with which brand-name companies have direct contracts, as opposed to subcontractors.

[19] See, for example, the history of the Clean Clothes Campaign network's debates regarding codes of conduct, summarized on the cleanclothes.org website.

[20] See, for example, Labour Rights in China (1999).

[21] Research into this has been minimal, but a 2001 survey into the effect of Oxfam Community Aid Abroad's NikeWatch campaign on attitudes among University of Queensland students suggests that, in Australia at least, anti-sweatshop activists have been much more effective in raising awareness of labor abuses than in inspiring confidence that they can be brought to an end. The survey was of 185 first-year social science students at the University of Queensland. Over 75 percent of the respondents indicated that they were "incensed" at worker exploitation, and over 80 percent reported that it made them "frustrated and angry." But a higher proportion, 85.8 percent, agreed with the suggestion that "trying to improve poor labour practices is more trouble than it is worth." This unpublished survey was conducted by Scott Bretton and Lotte ten Hacken as a final-year research project for their social science degrees at the University of Queensland.

[22] It would be neither necessary nor desirable for all organizations involved in the movement to endorse such a system of assessment; it is useful for any strategy to be subject to rigorous critique.

[23] These issues are currently being debated by email and in various meetings by organizations involved in the international movement.

[24] Twenty-four international NGOs with links to both organizations have had to choose between them or to maintain careful and separate relationships with each.

[25] Union sensitivity to the dangers of NGOs undermining their role has also led to differences of opinion regarding what sort of factory-monitoring programs

should be demanded of companies. Whereas a number of NGOs involved in the campaign have argued that corporations should allow local nonprofit human rights groups to monitor factory conditions, many union leaders are concerned that such groups might undermine unions in factories that have them or act in place of them in factories that do not.

[26] Interestingly, in April 2002 the FLA announced a number of improvements in its factory-monitoring program.

[27] Research interview with Jeffrey Ballinger, director of Press For Change, March 5, 2001.

[28] On the union side, areas of concern regarded the instability of NGOs and the need for NGOs to establish their legitimacy through democratic and transparent structures. On the NGO side, it was suggested that labor unions could do more to educate and mobilize their membership to take action on sweatshop issues, and it was reported as well that in some countries NGOs find it difficult to persuade labor unions to prioritize issues of gender inequality.

[29] Pou Chen is the world's largest sport-shoe manufacturer and a major supplier to Nike, Reebok, and Adidas.

Six

International NGOs and Unions in the South

Worlds Apart or Allies in the Struggle?

DEBORAH EADE

In the early 1980s support for labor unions started to become a signifi-cant component of Oxfam GB's (OGB) programs in various parts of the world, notably Central America and South Africa.[1] The unprecedented rise in this area of funding, particularly in such politically charged re-gions, gave rise to a 1983 policy guideline stressing that support for the organizational development or internal workings of labor unions could be given only if it could be demonstrated that doing so would have a significant impact on "the relief of poverty, distress, and suffering," the legal definition of OGB's charitable purpose.[2]

In practice, of course, this was a thin line to tread: no organization, whether labor union, faith-based agency, or NGO, can have any impact on poverty if it has no office infrastructure, no financial security, no legal status, no paid staff, and a dispersed and poorly informed membership. In the 1980s this was pretty much the situation for many of those pro-gressive labor unions and rural workers' organizations throughout Cen-tral America that were critical of government policy or that simply got on the wrong side of the powers that be.[3] In addition, labor unions in the region are often company based, which obviously limits their potential membership. Furthermore, each time a company relocates, merges, or opens up under a new name, the process of registering the union goes back to square one. For the very small labor unions and for most rural

83

workers' unions, revenue from dues is barely sufficient to affiliate to a labor federation or pay for one more person to attend the occasional training event, let alone sustain a strike fund; yet without joining forces, these unions cannot hope to do more than simply survive.

A still more fundamental issue in the context of interpreting the policy guideline to separate the internal workings from its specific activities is that a union's raison d'être is in a sense to evangelize or proselytize—to recruit more members, to promote the rights of working people, to lobby for inclusive social and economic policies, and to win public opinion to its cause—though of course its authority and influence depend on looking after the needs of existing members. By definition, a person who has a job in the context of high under- and unemployment is not one of "the poorest of the poor"; improving conditions for a relatively (albeit only marginally) privileged work force is seldom the prime contribution that labor unions make to reducing poverty. But to the extent that they can retain "the vision of social-movement unionism" and develop the capacity to "[assert] broad-based national interests" (Frundt 2002, 43) through representing the needs and rights of *all* working people and their families, unions are politically better placed than most NGOs or other civil society organizations to influence government policies in favor of the majority. And a popular movement that does not include organized labor is a lopsided platform upon which to shape public opinion and social policy.

In the 1980s the situation in Central America had become so polarized that any organizations that were working to relieve poverty, distress, and suffering were under attack precisely because of what they were trying to do. Simply assisting those who were poor and marginalized to improve their lot was perceived as stirring up social unrest; actually supporting organizations of such people was regarded as subversive. In such a context "development work led inexorably to confrontation with powerful forces . . . implacably opposed to change" (Thompson 1996, 327). If politics abhors a vacuum, the importance of creating and maintaining the space for free expression becomes paramount; popular organizations that can in some way take up the causes of those who are denied a voice and stand up for the right to dissent play a fundamental role in defending that space.

This essay first sketches out the regional context of the 1980s against which OGB's increasing focus on support for popular organizations in Honduras took place. It then looks at the nature of the support given at this time. Despite the evident gulf between unions (membership-based and sometimes militant organizations representing working-class interests) and international development NGOs (whose employees tend to be middle-class professionals), a relationship of mutual respect and trust developed between OGB and certain Honduran unions over these years. The loyalties and personal friendships established during that period have endured over time and distance. The chance to revisit Honduras in October 2002 was an opportunity for me to retrace the steps leading to this phase in OGB's history and to invite some of the labor union and rural workers' leaders of that era to share reflections on what that experience had meant both for us as individuals and for our respective organizations. The essay ends with some personal thoughts on how aid workers' personal convictions interact with their agency's position on ideologically charged issues such as labor unionism or feminism in ways that can inhibit or enhance the quality of relationships established with their Southern counterparts.

THE REGIONAL CRISIS

If the 1980s is the "lost decade" for development, then for Central America it was a period in which development was not simply arrested but went into reverse. The region was wracked by armed conflict. In Nicaragua the US-sponsored Contra were fighting a war of terror against the civilian population, designed to destabilize and eventually topple the Sandinista government. In El Salvador the US-backed regime was engaged in a brutal war against the FMLN guerrilla movement and any civilians thought to support it; one-fifth of the population became displaced or was forced out of the country. In Guatemala a counter-insurgency war was being waged against the armed opposition movement, the URNG, but in practice was aimed at crushing the majority indigenous population and at destroying its culture and way of life (Alecio 1995). The neighboring countries of Belize, Costa Rica, Honduras, and Mexico all suffered the consequences of the regional conflict, directly and indirectly. All became unwilling hosts to refugees, and all came under diplomatic and economic pressure to support the Reagan administration's "fight against communism." But only Honduras was assigned a military role in this strategy. Its borders with El Salvador, Guatemala, and Nicaragua made it a critical geopolitical playground for those forces determined to crush any efforts to bring about social transformation at either the national or the regional level.

Honduras had no democratic traditions to speak of, having effectively been since the early 1900s in the thrall of two US banana companies—United Fruit and Standard Fruit—and ruled by a succession of unrepresentative governments, both military and civilian (see, for example, Meza 1982; Salomón 1989; Selser 1983). It was said to be one of the four poorest and least developed countries in the Western hemisphere, along with Bolivia, Haiti, and Paraguay. Whatever its rating, the country's social indices were (and remain) woeful: grossly unequal distribution of land and economic resources; high adult illiteracy; low life expectancy; and much of the country all but incommunicado, with a deficient road network, public transport that scarcely penetrated the rural areas, and the country's only railway serving the banana companies on the north coast. The judicial system was deeply flawed, and the security forces often colluded with the criminal brutality of large landowners—the 1975 massacre at Los Horcones being a vivid example. Throughout the twentieth century there were popular uprisings, culminating in the 1954 general strike, and high-profile land seizures were organized by rural workers well into the late 1970s (Meza 1982). Influenced by liberation theology, some priests and lay-preachers were also encouraging peasant communities to stand up for their rights, and several rural workers' organizations had their roots in the Catholic Church. But Honduras was less sharply polarized than its neighboring countries, so, despite occasional rumblings, the population was by no means on the brink of revolution.

Social discontent was, however, to become louder and more widespread in the 1980s as the humiliating implications of the government's compliance with the Reagan administration became clear. A huge US military base was established in Palmerola, between the capital, Tegucigalpa, and San Pedro Sula, the country's industrial center. The Contra moved freely in the departments bordering Nicaragua, establishing bases and infiltrating Miskito refugee camps in the remote eastern department of Gracias a Dios. A "regional" training center for Salvadoran military officers was established in the north, notwithstanding the objections of the Honduran military; Salvadoran armed forces would make frequent incursions into Honduran territory during operations in FMLN-controlled areas in the bordering departments of Chalatenango and Morazón. In return, the government of Honduras received millions of dollars in US military and economic assistance and hardware, including helicopters and other combat equipment. To be sure, this was rather less than the US$1 million a day said to be received by the government of El Salvador at one stage, but for a country not at war, this military buildup was extraordinary (Oseguera de Ochoa 1987; Selser 1983).

Opposition began to take the shape of (modest) public demonstrations, fly-posting and leaflets, and a veritable frenzy of courses run by church-based groups and popular organizations in an effort to persuade Hondurans to repudiate compliance with US policy toward Central America and to explain that the Salvadoran refugees were not the "terrorists" that government and US spokespersons made them out to be. A human rights committee was set up initially to investigate a small but significant number of political disappearances (Americas Watch 1989) and later to train paralegals how to recognize and document the growing incidence of human rights abuses. Peace groups and women's organizations were formed to protest the financial and social costs of militarization, including the rise in prostitution and sexually transmitted diseases in the vicinity of Palmerola. And for good measure, small armed groups carried out a couple of spectacular operations, including an attack on the country's strongman General Alvarez Martínez.

These events conspired to turn Honduras into a "national security state," with the military and secret police protecting the country against internal as well as external enemies (Americas Watch 1989). The "low-intensity" warfare favored at the time was calculated to sow distrust and fear as well as routing out "unpatriotic elements." One poster that appeared from one day to the next all over the capital featured a "dirty dozen" of popular leaders and human rights activists under the heading: "Know these traitors for what they are—subversive scum." This was tantamount to a death warrant. Most of these individuals worked in legitimate organizations funded by a range of European and North American NGOs. Then there were radio and television slots telling audiences how to spot a terrorist—apparently they wore spectacles and beards, read a lot, and could be heard typing late at night. Laughable, maybe, but a frightened and credulous public was being told that to stem the revolutionary tide sweeping through Central America it was their patriotic duty to inform the police of any suspects. And indeed, there were dawn raids, shoot outs, and much-publicized "discoveries" of arms caches designed to prove that "the reds were under the beds."

Having worked in Mexico and Central America since 1982, and as the OGB representative responsible for developing the Honduras program from 1984 to 1991, I know all too well the difficulties faced by any organization that challenged the government during the 1980s. Although the repression was less extensive and efficient than in El Salvador or Guatemala, it is perhaps the one occasion where the aid agency jargon "target group" is appropriate. Social organizations and their leaders were singled out for attack, and many were forced underground or into exile, or were subject to arbitrary arrest. A number of Honduran union officials were

assassinated. Union organizers and members were threatened. NGO representatives were also suspect: a Nicaraguan visa in one's passport was
likely to lead to unpleasant questioning by migration officials. Surveillance was both overt and insidious. Minor informants *(orejas)* were encouraged to pass on scraps of detail—hotel cleaners, for instance, might
go through one's personal effects, or the telephone operator would note
calls made to and from one's room. This was scarcely a context in which
trust and openness could flourish.

How were unions to conduct even their normal business in such a
climate of fear and repression? And how could international NGOs support them and their work without courting undue risk for either party?
And yet then, more than ever, it was critical that the Honduran popular
movement remain strong and cohesive—abandoning such courageous
people at this juncture would make a reprehensible mockery of partnership. Without their public voice it seemed that there was nothing to prevent Honduras from becoming the launching pad for all-out war. In such
circumstances how could one distinguish between supporting the activities of a union as these related to the alleviation of poverty and suffering,
while stopping short of anything that might be construed as political or
having to do with its internal workings? For instance, the unions were
"protagonists" (Posas n.d.a, 82) in resolving a major constitutional crisis
affecting the country in 1985. To do this, the various labor and rural
workers' unions and federations needed to spend long hours working out
their own ideological and strategic differences in order to present a coherent proposal to the National Congress, the president, and the Supreme
Court. For some, this required unpaid time off from work. For others, it
meant the expense of traveling to and staying in the capital. This was an
excellent example of broad-based advocacy that transcended the interests of the individual unions. But was it essentially to do with their internal affairs, and hence off limits? Or was it a discrete and time-bound
activity that could qualify for grant funding? There was and is no simple
answer to this question.

UNIONS MOVE CENTER STAGE

A quick look at the figures gives an idea of how the nature of OGB's
Central America program shifted as the region became dominated by war
and political violence from 1980. Until about 1981, apart from emergency

relief relating, for example, to major earthquakes in Managua (1972) and Guatemala (1976), regional expenditure was largely either welfarist *(asistencialista)*, including support to orphanages and the like, or centered on agricultural cooperatives and health programs, especially among indigenous communities in Guatemala, Nicaragua, and southern Mexico. From 1982 humanitarian relief for refugees and displaced persons became the main focus in El Salvador and Guatemala, and assistance to Salvadoran refugees accounted for a significant percentage of funding in Honduras. But from fiscal year 1983–84 onward, support for popular (what today would be called civil society) organizations—organizations of rural workers and peasant farmers, labor unions, and their respective federations, as opposed to grassroots or community groups—grew rapidly, rising in Honduras from zero in 1982–83 to GB£100,000 in the following year. Although the amounts fluctuated, they averaged an annual GB£62,000 between 1984 and 1991. The percentage of this funding going to labor unions as distinct from rural workers' organizations in Honduras shifted significantly over this period. In 1982–83 it represented 15 percent of the total dedicated to popular organizations. By the year 1986–87 this had risen to 44 percent, peaking at 50 percent of the GB£120,000 allocated to such organizations the following year.[4] This situation was not to last, however. Already by 1993–94 direct funding for Honduran labor unions was down to GB£7,130, representing 26 percent of a much reduced allocation for unions overall. This had dwindled to a symbolic GB£1,270 by 1995–96, representing only 0.4 percent of the budget for Honduras, with total support for trade and rural workers' unions accounting for less than 5 percent of the program that year.[5] The rise and fall of funding for unions in OGB's Honduras program is a phenomenon worth examining.

Support for popular organizations was at its greatest when the regional conflicts were at their most acute—and when the popular movements in El Salvador and Honduras were pushing hardest for negotiated political settlements rather than military solutions. The OGB regional team at the time felt that it was vital to support this objective in ways that would encourage the movements to be as peaceful, broad based, and nonpartisan as possible. To forge a movement that could unite different sectors called for the participating organizations to overcome old rivalries and suspicions and build on each other's strengths: unions, in particular, had experience in mobilizing, organizing, and leadership, as well as in negotiation. Thus OGB began to engage with labor unions and to step up support for rural workers' unions, as well as to fund some women's and peace groups, and human rights organizations that formed part of the popular movement.

In concrete terms OGB's funding was principally for popular education, which would include training in "political literacy" and organizational skills increasingly linked, in the rural organizations, to adult literacy programs. In the case of labor unions, many of which represented professionals such as teachers and civil servants as well as industrial and other public service workers, the emphasis was on improving the analytical skills of the membership and developing middle-level leaders, as well as the staple fare of courses on collective bargaining, health and safety, and workers' rights under the labor code.[6] Support was also given to help unions to develop their understanding of emerging issues. For instance, a 1987 grant to one federation was to conduct research into the situation of women workers, at a time when the *maquila* was first being established in the country's northern belt. (The researcher, Zoila América Madrid, is now a leading light in the women's organizations supporting *maquila* workers described in Chapter 12 in this volume.) Another was for a study on *solidarismo*, an anti-union movement that spread through Central America from the mid-1980s, with particular effect in Costa Rica. Based on an ideology of solidarity and harmony among workers and employers, as opposed to class conflict, *solidarismo* gave rise to workplace-based associations that revoked the right to strike, collective contracts, and other rights for which unions had fought (Hernández 1991). The world's three largest banana companies—Chiquita (United Fruit), Dole, and Fresh Del Monte—actively promoted *solidarista* associations to replace unions in their plantations (Frundt 2002, 11).

Something that all parties were very clear about, however, was that there was no core funding for recurrent office costs or salaries for union office-bearers—these had to be met through existing resources. This was in part to limit organizational dependency on external funding (though, of course, other donors were free to apply quite different criteria to this issue) but mainly to avoid distorting leaders' accountability to the rank-and-file membership.

TEN YEARS ON

The Honduras I returned to in October 2002 was in some respects a very different one from the country I had last visited ten years earlier. One remarkable difference was that instead of the military police who were so much in evidence throughout the 1980s and early 1990s, the capital was awash with heavily armed private security guards—a grotesque microcosm of how the public sector had been retrenched, restructured, and outsourced, and how very insecure ordinary citizens still felt.

The rural sector was in deep trouble. Small but significant advances that had been tolerated (though not actively promoted) under the auspices of the agrarian reform law had been rolled back. Landowners were returning to reclaim their title to once idle lands that had been recuperated by peasant organizations years before. The full impact of Hurricane Mitch had been felt nationwide but had badly hit the large plantations of banana, sugar cane, and African palm in the northern departments. Some agricultural cooperatives from the reform sector were selling up, and ever more rural households were looking for jobs in the *maquila* sector or trying to emigrate to the United States (Swanger 2003; Pérez Sáinz 1999). Coffee producers had temporarily benefited from crop failures in Brazil, but, as elsewhere in Latin America, the proposed Free Trade Area of the Americas (ALCA in its Spanish acronym) will favor agro-export production that is usually in the hands of large landowners (beef or strawberries, for instance) and not the small farmers or subsistence sector. Latin American self-reliance on staple foods is simply not part of the plan. Honduras is now well on the way to becoming a predominantly urban country, but one without the infrastructure to support large conurbations.

There were also more positive developments, of course. At the height of the repression one hesitated to enter the single bookstore in Tegucigalpa selling anything that might pass for political analysis or social commentary. Now it is a thriving concern, and although most books are beyond the purse of many Hondurans, they are no longer seen as seditious propaganda. Interestingly, however, although a spate of books and monographs on the Honduran labor movement had been published in the 1980s (mainly uncontroversial historical accounts hinging on the 1954 general strike), nothing newer was on the shelves. The director of the publishing house that owned the bookstore—who had headed the Central American human rights commission in Costa Rica in the mid-1980s—explained that the labor movement had been dealt a severe blow by privatization and the rise of the *maquila* industry, irrespective of its own shortcomings. The 1990s, therefore, was not a positive phase in the movement's history and as yet nobody had been motivated to write about it.

This demoralization in terms of the movement was in contrast to the dramatic change in the roles of various union leaders with whom I had worked at a time when their lives were on the line. Two are leading figures in the Bloque Popular, a broad-front alternative to the traditional Liberal and National parties. The former director of the internationally acclaimed literacy program run by a rural workers' union represents the Bloque Popular in Congress, and her deputy had long headed the country's most progressive labor union federation. The former general secretary of the national cooperatives union is now a big player in the worldwide agricultural workers' movement, La Via Campesina. One of the infamous "dirty dozen" had even shown up as a senior diplomat in one of the Honduran embassies in Europe!

Despite their own success at moving from opposition to constructive engagement, however, the picture these labor activists painted was bleak. The financial and organizational mainstay of the labor movement had been the large public sector unions. That had all changed in the 1990s with Central America's enthusiastic embrace of neoliberal policies. The standard neoliberal package does not need rehearsal here. What is more remarkable is the speed and intensity of the country's transformation from producer of bananas and coffee into a giant *maquila* or assembly plant. Central American textile and apparel shipments to the United States jumped from US$500 million in 1986 to US$6.5 billion by 2000, with over one-third of this trade from Honduras alone (Frundt 2002, 14). The *maquila* sector is notoriously hostile to any effort to organize its work force. In any case, the way the assembly industries are structured, with extensive subcontracting and homeworking, makes it hard to negotiate agreements on labor rights and working conditions, and harder still to ensure that they are respected. As the Honduran journalist Manuel Torres put it, workers in the *maquila* are dealing with a "virtual boss" and often do not even know which brand(s) they are producing.

I was aware that some observers now consider labor unions to be at best irrelevant and at worst outdated, exclusive, bureaucratic, and *machista*—in short, an obstacle to development. Bullard (2000) pretty much says it all. I had also heard some NGO representatives say that the investment in popular education among trade and rural workers' unions had been money down the drain. I knew, too, that Honduran unions had fared no better than others in organizing workers in the *maquila* sector. But I had also attended a public debate (again, inconceivable in the past) on ALCA in which the union representative from the Bloque Popular, which opposes the treaty, was criticized by the business sector speaker for being inflexible and unrealistic; more was to be gained by compromise with the United States, including the adoption of the US dollar as national currency, than by total resistance. A fair point from a narrow commercial perspective, but the Bloque Popular's monograph on ALCA had sold out even before the debate got under way—the union speaker may not have had a state-of-the-art PowerPoint presentation, but he certainly had the upper hand in terms of bringing ordinary citizens on board.

REFLECTIONS

Looking back at the 1980s, and contrasting the present with the past, what were the lessons that former and current union leaders were willing to share with me, an NGO representative who had accompanied them through those difficult times?

General Perceptions of NGOs

The labor unions supported by OGB had never worked directly with international NGOs before the agency approached them in 1982, though the rural workers' unions had a fair amount of prior experience. Before that, they had occasionally participated in courses organized by a local popular education center, which in turn received funds for these activities from a range of European and North American NGOs. As the repression heightened, this center became the main interlocutor for the NGOs, almost none of which had staff based in the region. Such dependence on an intermediary organization became increasingly unsatisfactory, both for the popular organizations and for the international NGOs. Gradually, these NGOs started to fund the rural workers' organizations to undertake their own educational activities, but apparently none except OGB approached the labor unions except, perhaps, to get their perspective on the situation. Apart from occasional funding from labor-based NGOs such as Norwegian People's Aid or the Friedrich Ebert Foundation, the labor unions we supported have received no NGO grants since that period.

In their personal and/or political capacity, some union leaders had also been involved in human rights work; for example, two individuals served on the board of a small NGO set up to provide humanitarian assistance to the victims of repression and their families—for instance, helping the family of an assassinated union leader to leave the country. And several had frequent dealings with the rural workers' organizations in the popular movement and doubtless compared notes with them.

Their perceptions of international NGOs were obviously colored by these experiences. In their view:

- NGOs have always preferred the rural sector, though they do not necessarily support rural workers' unions. In general, their anti-poverty focus leads them to *asistencialista* interventions, which tend to have a depoliticizing impact. With or without ALCA, the Honduran population is increasingly urban, and this will pose very different challenges to NGOs' ways of working.
- International NGOs hop from one thing to another and seldom set down deep roots. In a comment echoed by many (for example, Ardón 1999, 62–67; Biekart 1999), international NGO interest in Central America during the 1980s was governed more by a wish to act as a counter force to the US position than by a lasting commitment to social transformation in the region. This "instrumentalization" was particularly true in the case of Honduras, given its geopolitical importance. Once the conflicts were over, attention (and funds) moved elsewhere.
- NGOs seldom take a long-term or strategic view, and they shape their engagement around projects rather than processes. Nor do they generally engage with their local counterparts' strategies but tend rather to impose their own. This "projectization" of NGO relations with local counterparts impedes rather than facilitates political dialogue.
- The focus on *projects* can also distort relations between a union's leaders (who negotiate and report on grant funding) and the rank-and-file members. For instance, if the members no longer perceive an NGO-funded activity as a high priority, the leaders should have the authority to reallocate the resources to where they are needed. But NGOs expect "their" projects to be implemented or the funds returned—not an attractive option. In practice, this encourages local "partners" to tell the donors what they want to hear rather than feeling free to report truthfully on the situation.
- External funding of any kind tends to introduce inappropriate or asymmetrical forms of accountability; it fosters corruption by centralizing power in the individuals charged with fundraising or public relations (see also Posas n.d.b, 46).
- While grant funding is welcome, it should not be at any price. The rural workers' organizations were heavily reliant upon international NGO funding because the revenue from membership dues was so

limited. Labor unions valued their relative autonomy and had not sought to compromise it.

What Had Unions Learned from Working with NGOs?

Far more important than the small amounts of money was the quality of the relationship between union and NGO representatives, and in particular the question of mutual trust and honesty. The unions very much appreciated that NGO staff were not immune from security problems, and that visiting their offices—let alone funding their work—entailed risks for those individuals as well as for the agencies. Specific lessons or learning points included the following:

- Dealing with the same NGO staff over many years allowed a proper relationship to develop. This gave unions an insight into debates on international cooperation that they would not otherwise have had, and which proved increasingly valuable after those individuals had moved on.
- Concerns about short-term projects aside, the experience of applying for funds and then running and reporting on projects helped unions to improve their own organizational and administrative skills and gave them some access to the language and mindsets of aid agencies.
- While the membership of many unions had dropped, most of the workers who had been in training programs were still active community or union organizers ten years later. In terms of quality of impact, they looked to this kind of indicator rather than to numbers, especially given that public sector retrenchment had been so extensive.
- Receiving support from an international NGO enabled them to tap into other experiences both in Central America and more widely. Given their isolation at that time, the opportunity for dialogue, rather than simply negotiating project funding, was much appreciated.

The learning process was far from one way. Our own analysis of the situation in Honduras benefited from the insights and perspectives of organizations of rural workers and labor unions, and our understanding of how to bring about social change was immeasurably enriched by our many conversations. We witnessed at close hand the difficulties of building a democratic popular movement in a society that was profoundly undemocratic and *machista*. We shared the frustrations of trying to synchronize project funding with social processes, and there were certainly times when the two were out of gear. Trust does not come with the mere fact of working for an international NGO; perhaps one of the most enduring lessons for our regional team was to understand that gaining the trust of people who are trying to change their world is both a privilege and a responsibility.

NGOS AND UNIONS: A WORLD OF DIFFERENCE

International NGOs are seldom unionized, and NGOs in the South probably less so. This has to do with the many factors described in Chapter 2 in this volume. Most NGOs do not have working-class roots (though individuals may), and many depend as much or more on volunteers as on paid staff. Social attitudes toward unions are also ambivalent, particularly in relation to the "caring professions" such as teachers, nurses, and social workers, whose vocational calling is thought to override material interests. Similarly, it is often assumed that people working in the voluntary sector, including international NGOs, are willing (and able!) to work long hours for low salaries. The fact that strikes are referred to in the UK as "industrial action" speaks volumes. Strikes and picket lines are associated with militant factory workers, not with the professions. In the UK, with the onslaught on labor unions by the Thatcher government and the gradual decline in union membership, public attitudes toward unions have shifted since the 1970s from sympathy to hostility to indifference.[7]

With or without a union, pay and conditions vary among international NGOs, but the private sector is not the benchmark. Staff representatives may negotiate salaries and press for reasonable terms and conditions, but this will be done through discussion rather than confrontation. The arguments are well expressed by the then director of OGB when the UK staff opted to unionize in the mid-1980s. Management and trustees, he said, were willing to endorse this, provided that the activities of the union were based on "acceptance of Oxfam's traditional approach to pay, use of volunteers, unity of purpose and collaboration between all staff in whatever position, strikes and involvement in other organizational disputes, and so on."[8] In essence, then, there was to be no difference between a union and a staff association.

Why is this relevant? One reason is that an NGO's policies concerning the representation of its own work force are bound to influence the way its staff engage with labor unions in other countries. My colleague Ines Smyth writes candidly about this in the context of feminism. Noting that "most people in Oxfam seem to be more comfortable to speak of 'gender and development' (GAD) than of feminism," she suggests that

> Oxfam staff perceive a dominant non-feminist stance in the organisation, and conform to it by opting for the less confrontational language of 'gender' and 'women'. I have confirmed that proposals employing controversial language are re-phrased and toned down in order to secure approval for funding. How often this self-censorship goes further than merely the choice of wording and affects the actual choice of partner organisations or project activities probably depends on a variety of factors. But this phenomenon will certainly have a profound impact on the nature of Oxfam's work. (Smyth 1999, 135)

Similarly, if an NGO is ambivalent about or hostile to the unionization of its own staff, then its employees are likely to project these attitudes in their work. The choice of whether to engage with organized labor in the South is not just a question of "who represents the poor," as it is sometimes portrayed. NGOs know very well that poverty will not be eradicated simply by multiplying the number of grassroots projects but depends on complementary action at a policy level of the kind that the labor movement is often able to carry out. It is also a question of the importance attached to organizing for political rather than simple poverty-reduction ends—and this is where development NGOs risk distorting relations with local organizations by looking at them through their own lens. For instance, it is easy to view rural workers' unions as directly addressing poverty—which indeed they may be. But they define themselves primarily as representative organizations, not as anti-poverty groups. By the same token, labor unions may be perceived as being concerned only with protecting the interests of their members, though many would advocate for the interests and rights of all working people both now and in the future.

Looking from the Inside out

Some consider that "objectivity" in development and humanitarian work depends on aid workers' capacity to divest themselves of all political opinions or personal convictions. As a feminist, I believe on the contrary that the personal and the political are inseparable and inevitably inform (though not necessarily determine) our professional judgments. Since international aid is inescapably about politics, aid workers' political convictions and experience matter a great deal. This is not to imply a crude link between what individuals believe and whom they talk with or how they allocate funds. But inside knowledge of a given issue really does make a difference not only to the individual's own understanding but also to how others perceive that individual. Those with a technical background will obviously and unavoidably bring that knowledge and understanding to every aspect of their work. Similarly, being a feminist and labor union member affected my engagement with unions and other counterparts in Central America, and theirs with me. Being frank about one's personal convictions and concerns, and able if necessary to distinguish between these and the agency's policy positions on these matters, seems to me an essential first step in evening up the asymmetrical nature of the relationship between a donor agency and those who receive its funds. It doesn't do away with the power dynamics, to be sure (Rowlands 2003, 6), but it does help to move the relationship beyond the charitable outsider coming in to lend a hand toward a genuine dialogue about the issues in question.

A brief anecdote serves as an illustration. There came a point when I had to tell local counterparts that I would eventually be leaving Central America and returning to the UK. The leaders of the union federation in Honduras asked why I should want to go, given my commitment to the region. I explained that our contracts were of fixed duration and that mine had already been renewed a couple of times, that I wanted to have children but that international staff didn't have guaranteed maternity leave, and that, no, I didn't have a job lined up back home—I would have to try my luck.[9] Their response—quite immediate and completely genuine— bowled me over: that our labor conditions were out of order; that after so many years of service our contacts should automatically be open ended; that maternity leave was a right regardless of contractual status, as a matter of nondiscrimination on the basis of sex; and so on. Not only this, but they also offered to come and advise our shop stewards on how to get a better deal for international staff and vowed to send a petition to the bosses. Fortunately, I dissuaded them, explaining that we didn't have paid union representatives or shop stewards, just colleagues volunteering their own time, and that direct action on their part would be counterproductive.

Worlds apart, maybe. But this episode has stayed with me now for over a decade, and the sincerity of this expression of solidarity with the situation of relatively privileged aid workers continues to move and humble me. It also confirms my belief that, in the ultimate analysis, one of the most important impacts that aid workers can have is as go-betweens linking the two worlds—North and South; international agency and local organization—helping each to understand the other a little better so that collaboration is based on true respect for our differences and a lasting appreciation of what brings us together.

ACKNOWLEDGMENTS

This essay has been inspired by the experience of working alongside rural workers and labor unions in Honduras. I am especially grateful to the *compañeros* who so generously made time to meet again in October 2002, among them Rafael Alegría, Isolda Arita, Doris Gutiérrez, Héctor Hernández, Martín Enamorado, Ayax Irias, Zoila América Madrid, Carlos H. Reyes, Ma Esther Ruíz, and Hermilo Soto. My deepest thanks go to Lourdes Aguilar, who made it all possible. Chris Jackson and Martha Thompson made valuable comments on earlier drafts. The usual disclaimers apply. Likewise, the views expressed herein are not to be attributed in any manner to OGB.

NOTES

[1] The regional office for Mexico and Central America moved from Guatemala to Mexico City in 1980, for security reasons, and channeled humanitarian assistance through Central American aid agencies based in Mexico. However, this essay refers only to direct in-country funding in the region, principally Honduras.

[2] For a detailed discussion of the policy and related issues, see Eade and Williams 1995, 349–53, 397–400.

[3] As elsewhere, Central American unions were divided along ideological or sectarian grounds, to say nothing of personal animosities and rivalries (Posas n.d.a, 46). Broadly speaking, the more conservative unions and their federations enjoyed legal status and could therefore open bank accounts and go about their normal business. The more progressive unions were denied legal status and viewed by some as subversive.

[4] Though significant for OGB, these amounts are dwarfed by the international support during this period for conservative or overtly anticommunist labor unions. According to Frundt, "US government contributions in the 1980s and 1990s to isthmus labor organizations and related development programs totalled

more than 3 billion dollars" (2002, 29–30). European labor federations also sent "substantial monies to independent confederations as an antidote to North American subversion of bona fide trade-union activity." It is now recognized that such levels of funding effectively inhibited the development of autonomous local movements.

[5] Although funding for trade and rural workers' unions in Honduras declined, OGB began to commit funds to activities relating to women workers in the *maquila* sector in the San Pedro Sula area and to programs for women's legal rights. Such work accounted for approximately 15 percent of the country program in the fiscal year 1994–95.

[6] The rural organizations funded by OGB from fiscal year 1983–84 include Unión Nacional de Cooperativas Populares de Honduras, Federación Hondureña de Mujeres Campesinas, Frente de Unidad Nacional Campesino de Honduras, and Unión Nacional de Campesinos Auténticos del Campo Hondureño. These were later amalgamated into the Central Nacional de Trabajadores del Campo, which became our main counterpart within the popular movement. The labor union federations supported by OGB were Federación Unitaria de Trabajadores de Honduras and, to a lesser extent, Federación Independiente de Trabajadores de Honduras. Individual unions received small one-off grants, like the staff union of the agrarian institute and some of the unions of part-time and contract workers on the sugar-cane plantations. The nature of these individual unions shows the sometimes arbitrary distinction between rural workers and labor unions in Honduras, particularly in view of high seasonal migration to the plantations.

[7] Although the labor union movement was born in Britain, such attitudes are peculiarly Anglo-Saxon. Elsewhere in Western Europe organized labor forms an integral part of society, and unions play a central role in the political economy.

[8] Director's Report to the Executive, September 20, 1984.

[9] Until the EC Directive on Fixed Term Work was transposed into UK law as Fixed Term Employees (Prevention of Less Favourable Treatment) Regulations in October 2002, employers had no obligation to offer work after a fixed-term contract or to allow paid maternity leave to such employees. Back in the mid-1980s it was argued that maternity leave was irrelevant as "a woman with a baby couldn't really do a field job"!

Seven

Organizing Citizenship at Local 890's Citizenship Project

Unleashing Innovation through an Affiliate Organization

PAUL JOHNSTON

INTRODUCTION

As low-waged immigrant workers became a focus of new efforts by the AFL-CIO to organize the unorganized at the turn of the twenty-first century, US labor unions changed their approach to immigrant issues. While in the past most unions and AFL-CIO leadership sought to limit immigrants' access to US labor markets, now much of labor, including by 2001 the top leadership of the AFL-CIO, had aligned itself with advocates for immigrants to embrace amnesty or "legalization."[1]

Thus the stage is currently set for local unions to develop immigrant rights programs that not only respond to their members' needs but also to involve unorganized workers and the larger community. This is an opportune time not only for immigrants, who confront a turbulent and often hostile policy environment, but also for labor organizations that have as yet failed to make significant breakthroughs in organizing new members to counter the long-term decline in their membership.

But although support for this agenda is broad in principle, unions are not well prepared to respond to the challenge of organizing unorganized immigrant workers (Bronfenbrenner 2001; Fletcher and Hurd 2000). Most unions lack staff who are familiar with issues facing immigrants, and many lack the language and other skills necessary to gain access to immigrant social networks. The main obstacle, however, is union organization it-self.

US labor unions are organized around a well-defined set of practices associated with the collective bargaining system. Initiatives like organizing unorganized workers or setting up immigrant rights programs threaten resources already devoted to collective bargaining. Such initiatives conflict with their relationships with their own union members, who are more familiar to them. These initiatives require a radical shift in orientation toward organizing a social movement. Consequently, observers have noted that "changing to organize" (the catchphrase employed by US unions today) frequently portends catastrophic crisis, which involves importing new leaders from other social movements and coercing members as demanded from above (Voss and Sherman 2000). This offers little hope for those unions that have as yet avoided catastrophe, and it is dismal news indeed for those who believe that union power depends on the development of union democracy (Parker and Gruelle 1999; Offe 1985).

Also in recent years a new "industry" of organizations dedicated to immigrant needs has emerged in the United States. These organizations emerged in waves, many as products of the amnesty movement of the late 1980s, and even more as a result of the naturalization movement of the late 1990s.[2] The organizations vary in form, including membership-based mutual-aid groups, conventional nonprofit service agencies, policy-advocacy groups, and community-based immigrant workers' rights centers.

How to best help immigrants poses significant challenges. To be sure, local unions could rely on their own staff resources to operate an immigrant rights program. Those resources are already stretched, however, between the demands of collective bargaining and those of internal and external organizing. And the few local unions that can dedicate significant support to such programs through membership dues are unlikely to sustain that commitment as other priorities intrude.

On the other hand, even labor-friendly nonprofit agencies tend to be outsiders to the labor movement. Union leaders are unlikely to invest confidence or resources in such organizations. And nonprofit organizations are typically less accountable either to their clients or to their organizational partners than to their funders. They are also subject to powerful pressures toward ways of working that produce passive and individualized clients, rather than fostering the networks of leadership and mutual aid that are essential to reviving the labor movement (Lipsky 1980; DiMaggio and Powell 1991).

Over the past decade international unions and the AFL-CIO itself have tried several times to set up affiliate immigrant or workers' rights centers.[3] But although these central bodies have access to far more resources than do local unions, even these efforts have by and large been unable to sustain themselves. Over the past decade, moreover, immigrant and other social movements have produced a new network of active community-based immigrants' and workers' rights organizations. These have remained, however, largely detached from existing labor organizations. It is easier, it appears, to set up an entirely autonomous project than to wrestle with the organizational problems studied here.

This study examines these problems through the Citizenship Project, a community-based immigrant and workers' rights center located in a storefront office that belongs to Teamsters Local 890 in Salinas, California. The project serves as the main resource for the rights of Mexican immigrants in the rural valleys of coastal central California. Oriented by a radical vision of citizenship that includes an expansive approach to unionism, this organization propels the union beyond the boundaries of its existing bargaining units.

Some other local unions also offer immigration and naturalization assistance to their members, and a great many local unions are currently seeking to launch more ambitious projects in the United States. Surprisingly, though, as of early 2002 the Citizenship Project was the only project of its kind in the entire country—a community-based project for organizing immigrants and workers, serving "the whole community," and sponsored by a conventional local AFL-CIO union.

The Citizenship Project suggests, in brief, that an affiliate organization strategy can unleash innovative potential while sidestepping certain barriers to change and can tap external resources while sustaining a necessary balance of autonomy and accountability. It also suggests that "citizenship" may serve as a radical and expansive agenda for social change. It can imply distinctive methods of organizing—"citizenship work," in the language of the project. With reference to the Citizen Project, this essay shows that organizational partnerships between labor unions and community-based immigrant organizations may help unions to innovate, acquire new resources, and deepen their relationship with immigrant communities, while avoiding certain obstructions to change and escaping coercive measures imposed from above.

THE CASE OF THE CITIZENSHIP PROJECT

Teamsters Local 890, the Citizenship Project's parent organization, is based in California's fertile Salinas River Valley. Both organizations are based in the city of Salinas. Along with a large population of migrant workers in the fresh-vegetable agricultural and food-processing industries, both organizations move with the harvest between the rural coastal valleys and the rural Imperial Valley to the south and east, on the Mexican border. For over fifty years, since millions of Mexican agricultural workers or *braceros* came in to replace the Anglo Dust Bowl refugees of the 1930s, these connected regions have been linked to Mexico by a chain of migration that has produced, over time, one of the highest concentrations of Mexican-born residents in California.[4]

This is Steinbeck country, characterized by deep inequalities between those who own and manage the land and those who work it, and long controlled by conservative agribusiness interests with little or no tolerance for labor organizing. Since the end of the *bracero* program in the early 1960s, "people with papers"—legal immigrants, US-born children of undocumented immigrants, and participants in the amnesty programs of the 1980s—have moved steadily out of the fields and into jobs in food-processing plants or urban areas, while the farm-labor force itself has been replenished by undocumented arrivals from Mexico. As a result, the patterns of power and inequality described in Steinbeck's novels of an earlier era have been overlaid, deepened, and reinforced by differences in citizenship status (Thomas 1985; Wells 1995).

Local 890 is the largest union in the region. Its jurisdiction traditionally includes the Teamsters' truck drivers and related workers, but over 90 percent of the union's members work in the fresh-vegetable industry that dominates the region's economy. These include some four thousand agricultural workers, often undocumented, and around five thousand workers in packing sheds and other food-processing plants, mostly of Mexican origin and of mixed citizenship status (undocumented, legal resident, or naturalized US citizen).

Historical Roots

Local 890 was famously involved in the jurisdictional battle between the Teamsters and the United Farm Workers (UFW) that first erupted in the Salinas Valley when, following its grape strike victory in 1970, the farm workers' movement exploded into the rest of California's agriculture. That battle began with a general strike in the Salinas Valley by immigrant agricultural workers demanding the right to vote in order to determine for themselves which union would represent them. Many Mexican and Chicano Teamsters, themselves farm workers and former farm workers, were inspired by the UFW and supported that union despite their own union's role in the labor war taking place in the fields.

Also starting in the 1970s a movement for racial justice, union democracy, and stronger representation surfaced among the Mexican immigrants, who had by then replaced Italians as the overwhelming majority of members in the Teamsters' food-processing unions. Independent of the better-known Teamsters for a Democratic Union, this movement produced a network of cannery-worker committees. In an election in 1985 (and with the quiet assistance of the UFW), a coalition led by shop stewards involved in the cannery-workers' movement won leadership in Local 890 on a platform that included opposition to organizing in the fields. Thus, over the past few decades the local was transformed by democratic upheavals both in the larger work force and within the union itself.[5]

Then came the passage of California's Proposition 187 in 1994, which targeted undocumented immigrants, unleashed a wave of anti-immigrant policy measures throughout the United States, and triggered the naturalization movement that swept through immigrant communities across the country in the mid-1990s. By that time, most of Local 890's members were legal, permanent US residents, some having acquired that status in the amnesty period five years before, but most were already long-term legal residents who had not chosen to naturalize in earlier years. Now, following the November passage of Proposition 187 and the election of a Republican Congress pledged to roll back immigrant rights, their interest in acquiring US citizenship surged. Early in 1995, responding to the emergence of that naturalization movement, the leaders of Local 890 launched the Citizenship Project.

This brief background suggests historical reasons why this union, unlike others with large numbers of immigrant members, produced and sustained support for such a project. This agenda both responded to the union's own interests and was consistent with the legacy of its past. Local 890's leaders are almost all first- or second-generation Mexican immigrants. They faced the surge of interest in naturalization among themselves, in their families, and among the members of their union. They anticipated that by responding positively they would strengthen their own political standing in those ranks. They owed their own positions, moreover, to a democratic process within their own organization. Their values and aspirations had been shaped by decades of struggle for democratic labor rights, first in the farm workers' movement and then in the Teamsters union.[6]

Unleashing Innovation

The original goals of Local 890 leaders and members who launched the Citizenship Project were to help members and their families become US citizens and active participants in public life, and the original methods were modeled on other naturalization assistance programs. Gradually, as events led them to broaden their constituency and deepen their conception of citizenship, their goals would evolve and their methods would rapidly change. The learning process reflected here was brought about by the repeated emergence of new problems, by continuous self-assessment, and by the organization's openness to initiatives from volunteer workers.

The group began by forming a nonprofit corporation with tax-exempt status (501c3) that could receive grant funding to hire staff. By mid-1995 it had obtained enough funding to take on a person with skills in nonprofit administration and social services and to give her a desk in the union office. She learned about eligibility rules and application procedures for naturalization, and she began to make appointments with union members and their families to complete naturalization packets in a manner similar to that of other naturalization-assistance projects.

During this first year I entered into an action-research process in partnership with the union and the project. Late in 1995 we conducted a self-assessment. We observed that if we used conventional methods for providing immigration and naturalization assistance, we would be able to help only a small number of those in need of our support. We also confronted a contradiction between these methods and the founders' goal of helping union members become active participants in public life. This self-assessment promoted the decision to shift the project's methods of work from "client processing" (our term for treating participants as passive recipients of services) to "organizing methods" (our term for treating people as competent, active co-producers of services, providing services through networks of volunteers, and linking services to campaigns in defense of people's rights).

Now naturalization assistance would be approached not as a service to clients but through campaigns that recruited, trained, and supported networks of workplace and community volunteers and that tied naturalization to the cause of community self-defense. Looking forward to the time when the votes of new citizens might change the region's political landscape, the group decided to give this campaign a name in Spanish: ¡VOTE! Over the next two years, over one thousand immigrant community volunteers (and a few nonimmigrant supporters) would help over ten thousand eligible immigrants to complete their applications for citizenship.

The new campaign strategy inspired interest among progressive foundations. Additional funding became available, and the project hired more organizers. The project moved into an abandoned building belonging to the union, around the corner from the union office. Volunteers helped to clear out trash, paint a sign, and do other tasks to produce a storefront organizing center.

Throughout its history the Citizenship Project would mark its development by similar self-assessments and decisions to innovate. In early August 1996, for example, President Bill Clinton announced an election-season decision to adopt Republican proposals to exclude long-term legal permanent resident aliens from all federally funded public assistance and to abolish open-ended welfare entitlement for all poor families. Clinton's embrace of welfare and immigration reform created panic among very poor, elderly, and disabled immigrants dependent on Medicare and Supplemental Social Security. For them, naturalization thus became critically important. (While the new law gave them one year to become US citizens, the Immigration and Naturalization Service [INS] was taking an average of two years to process a valid application for US citizenship.) Confronted by the question of how to respond, the Teamsters on the project's board decided to change the project's target population to include the whole immigrant community. They also decided to shift priorities away from union members and to emphasize help for the most vulnerable immigrant groups. As a result, the Teamsters' union and its Citizenship Project emerged as the region's main resource for the elderly, the disabled, and the very poor immigrant families during the painful and uncertainty-filled year following August 1996.

Another early self-assessment produced the recognition that immigrant work forces and families include people in (and moving through) a variety of different citizenship statuses. The group soon recognized that an emphasis on naturalization was not enough. Rather, it decided to develop programs and campaigns responding to the interrelated needs and interests of undocumented immigrants, on one hand, and new citizens, on the other. Later, responding to strong pressure from funders and other influences (discussed below) to adopt more conventional methods of client processing, another such assessment helped the organization steer itself back toward its early emphasis on volunteer activism.

It is worth noting that staff members are not directly supervised. A sociologist (myself), who is nominally director (although present only one day a week), "stimulates and facilitates" mainly by asking questions and draws on this involvement for his own learning. These methods gave rise to several self-assessments, described above, which helped shape the organization's development.

A variety of important innovations emerged, however, not from such planned interventions but rather through volunteers' responses to immediate needs and opportunities. Among the first important innovations produced by volunteer activists was the Escuela de Libertad (Freedom School), which grew out of a self-organized study group among female farm workers in late 1996. In its origins in the citizenship movement, its reliance on volunteer teachers (especially youth volunteers), its approach to learning about citizenship through active political participation, and even its name, this school resembles the freedom schools that were created during the campaign for civil rights in the US South.

Then, in 1998, responding to a surge of gang violence that took the life of a young man associated with the project, participants began to pay more attention to support for young volunteers, mostly between the ages of ten and sixteen. They discovered that immigrant youth volunteers— long a strong force in the project—had themselves already produced a vigorous although informal immigrant youth community service and leadership program. Youth volunteers and their parents formalized this project as Jóvenes en Acción (Youth in Action) in 1999, and that group continued to volunteer in the office, teach in the Freedom School, register voters, and help with union organizing while also developing its own advocacy agenda and cultural programs.

By 2000 the demand for a political voice had intensified. New citizens were shedding passive attitudes toward school authorities. Recall movements and other election campaigns erupted among parents in school districts and local residents in city council races. In response, the project launched a political club called ¡VOTE!, which embraced immigrants in a variety of citizenship statuses. Over the next two years some twenty ¡VOTE! members were elected to local office. And late in 2001 in the south Salinas Valley, newly elected Latino officials, unionists, and youth-activist residents launched yet another political club called Alianza para un Mañana Mejor (Alliance for a Better Tomorrow).

Other project activities are union-related work (discussed below); a four-year campaign for educational rights for undocumented youth; a new campaign for youth employment rights; and an array of cultural activities including a mural, a youth theater group, and several radio projects. The project worked with the UFW and the Teamsters' unions to conduct amnesty hearings in Salinas in 2000 and to defend recently arrived indigenous *Triqui* migrants from southern Mexico from an ethnically targeted INS raid in the town of Greenfield in 2001.

As the project responded to the needs of immigrants in a variety of citizenship statuses, it became a vehicle for advocacy and political engagement by the Mexican immigrant communities in the region both with Mexican and with US public institutions. Thus, touring activists and elected officials from Mexico increasingly approached their constituents in the Salinas Valley through the Citizenship Project. Similarly, the Mexican consulate in San José to the north relies on the project for help in extending its services to the region. In 2000, when a cross-border movement emerged among ex-*braceros*, the Citizenship Project naturally became the base for a Salinas Valley ex-*bracero* organization set up to challenge the treatment of cross-border workers by both the US and the Mexican governments.

Citizenship Work

During these years the project's networks of volunteers responded to a barrage of attacks on the rights of immigrants—state propositions abolishing bilingual education and affirmative action, employers' efforts to slash immigrant workers' wages and eliminate their rights, and so on— and also moved onto the offensive in campaigns for goals like educational rights for undocumented youngsters. In the process they developed a concept of citizenship involving a wide array of rights—rights that belong to people of *all* countries, not only of the United States—and requiring education and organization to exercise and defend those rights. *La ciudadanía*, in the language of the movement, *es más que papeles* (citizenship is more than [identity] papers).

Through a difficult learning process, and often in conflict with funders and with legal and educational professionals, the project's volunteers developed an approach to "citizenship work," which they identified with principles of active citizenship:

- Provide rights-related assistance through campaigns that emphasize a passionate commitment to social justice and "responsibility for our community."
- Recruit, train, and rely on volunteer activists interested in learning how to help family members and co-workers on issues related to the exercise—or the denial—of basic rights (for example, how to immigrate, how to become naturalized, how to vote, how to deal with employment discrimination against undocumented youth, and how to understand wage and overtime law). Assume that volunteers are intelligent, capable, often highly skilled, interested in learning, and willing to work selflessly if asked.
- Constitute groups by assembling circles of activist volunteers and posing questions about what is to be done. In the discussion and decision making that follow, a gathering of volunteers becomes a group able to make decisions and act together.
- Help these leaders to conduct broader campaigns and large-scale events within their own constituency. Typically, because of our partnership with the labor movement, these campaigns target strategically selected groups of organized and unorganized workers.

In general, organizations (and admittedly, the Citizenship Project as well) often treat volunteers as "helpers" for trained staff. Volunteers are given simple tasks but do not participate in decision making. Assistance in exercising rights is provided exclusively by trained staff as a "service." Information is provided to larger groups en masse by individual experts speaking in meetings to a passive audience.

Staff of the Citizenship Project became more adept at helping groups to form, organize mutual self-help, make decisions, and act together. The project also spawned a growing network of grassroots organizations with various degrees of autonomy. As a result, it would now be accurate to describe the project as a support system for a network that includes the union, the project itself, the set of grassroots organizations that project organizers have generated, and a larger network of partner organizations— other unions, the central labor council, schools, churches, and some local government agencies—all of which rely on the project for assistance in responding to the needs of immigrants.

Organizational Structure

Although the leaders, staff, and active members of Local 890 have been deeply involved throughout its history, the project was launched as a new organization, and the innovations that shaped its development occurred within that more flexible new organizational "space." These years of development have produced a project that is both semi-autonomous from (or loosely coupled to) and closely connected to the union. This organizational structure is relevant because, as researchers have long observed, networks and loosely coupled systems within and between organizations improve the performance and adaptability of organizations facing complex and changing tasks (Weick 1976; Powell 1990).

Founded by the Teamsters with an initial focus on Teamster members, the project's board originally consisted only of union members (most of them immigrant low-wage female workers). Eight years later, although the Teamsters continue to lead the board, most board members are not Teamsters but are elected to represent the grassroots groups sponsored by the project.

The project is staffed by a team of organizers with paralegal and other skills, recruited from the Mexican Chicano community, and a grant writer-administrator. The author serves as part-time director. Key volunteers—mostly immigrants who emerged as leaders through the citizenship work described above—also play important leadership roles in the various groups sponsored by the project. While the union's staff of business agents and organizers remains all male, the Citizenship Project staff consists of five women and two men.[7]

Figure 7–1 presents the project's organizational structure. It depicts not a single organization but a network—portrayed, moreover, as part of a larger network of overlapping and often mutually supportive groups. This network includes different forms of organization; in addition to the union, the 501c3 (nonprofit tax-exempt status) Citizenship Project, and unincorporated groups like the Jóvenes en Acción or the ex-*braceros*, it includes an affiliated 501c4 (nonprofit but not tax-exempt status) corporation (¡VOTE!) and two political action committees. The Citizenship Project can receive tax-exempt funding but is limited in its policy advocacy work and cannot support candidates for election; by contrast, ¡VOTE! cannot receive tax-exempt grants but can advocate without restriction and can operate political action committees that support candidates.[8] While the 501c3 project is governed by a conventional self-elected corporate board, the 501c4 has an elected board. It thus provides a political arena for organizing citizenship within the project.

As this pattern of organization emerged at the Citizenship Project, the union's structure and operation remained more or less unchanged except

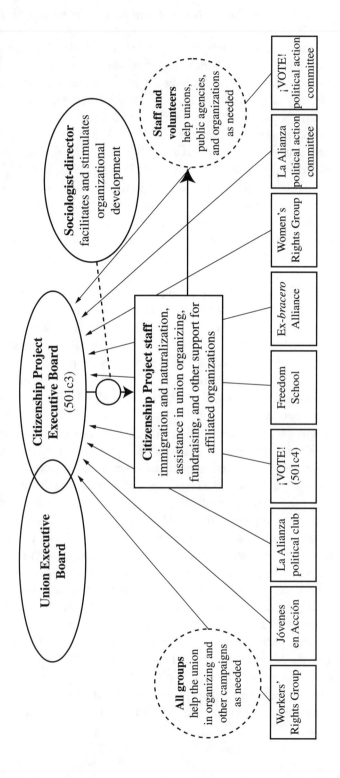

Figure 7–1. The Citizenship Project: A Labor/Community Network of Partner Organizations

Sociologist-director
facilitates and stimulates organizational development

Staff and volunteers
help unions, public agencies, and organizations as needed

Citizenship Project Executive Board
(501c3)

Union Executive Board

Citizenship Project staff
immigration and naturalization, assistance in union organizing, fundraising, and other support for affiliated organizations

All groups
help the union in organizing and other campaigns as needed

Workers' Rights Group

Jóvenes en Acción

La Alianza political club

¡VOTE! (501c4)

Freedom School

Ex-*bracero* Alliance

Women's Rights Group

La Alianza political action committee

¡VOTE! political action committee

during strikes or in other times of crisis. Yet, even in such times, the local displayed the same appreciation for political processes and commitment to democratic methods that had brought the project to life. This pattern of stability in periods of change suggests that the affiliate-organization strategy represented by the Citizenship Project—or more precisely, the formation of a new organization overlapping with the old—may be an effective way to respond to the widely recognized problem that change tends to pose in long-established unions. Most recently, in response to the challenges of organizing unorganized workers, the union has entered into a struggle to change its own internal culture. If successful, this change is likely to lead to further changes in the relationship between the organizations.

Such hybrid or overlapping organizations always carry potential for conflict and raise concerns about control. For example, the project's transition from a wholly union-owned program to a broader community-based organization with more limited union control depended heavily on project staff and union leaders maintaining a relationship of trust, and especially on the union's belief that the project was and would remain an asset to its organization. Also, successful partnership between an international union and a local one, both with vigorous internal political dynamics, has required project staff to be studiously uninvolved in internal union politics.

Because every local union is its own political universe, union leaders' political concerns are inevitably aroused by the prospect of launching a new project, especially one that is organizationally distinct from the union itself. Union leaders are unlikely to embrace a new initiative unless they see it not only as a useful resource for the union but also as accountable to themselves, responsive to their direction, and valuable to their own political standing. These concerns may lessen with a clear understanding of nonprofit organizational structure, through which union leaders can lead a policy-setting board that may also include nonunion members. The founders initially saw the Citizenship Project as an organizational resource that would remain accountable to them even if they lost power in subsequent elections—and so it has remained. With visible improvements in the union's reputation growing out of the project's work in the larger community, with repeated proof of the project's loyalty to the union cause, and with the founders' own repeated success in union elections, concerns about control have not come to the surface.

Project Finances

Power and control depend on patterns of funding as well as on political processes and formal organizational structure. The experience of the Citizenship Project demonstrates a fairly obvious rule: the greater the percentage of funding from a single source, the greater the power of that source over the organization. Unions are unlikely, however, to be able to sustain large amounts of support for a prolonged period of time.

Because few large sources of funding—whether unions or foundations or other organizations—last forever, projects that depend principally on a single source of support are unlikely to survive. A familiar finding in organizational research (Thompson 1967) is that multiple smaller sources of support have a number of merits, even if they place greater fundraising demands on staff. Such smaller contributions leave an organization less subject to external control, more financially secure, less vulnerable to the loss of any one source, better able to sustain programs that union leaders may consider less essential (for example, projects to develop leadership among youth), and more likely to survive when union priorities shift (as they inevitably do).

Over its first eight years the project's budget grew rapidly to nearly US$400,000 in 1997, declined to around US$250,000 a year by 2000, and dipped to US$200,000 with the onset of the recession in 2003. Over the entire period expenditures totalled over US$2.2 million. Where did this support come from, and what were its consequences for the organization?

Little cash support came from the union or other labor sources. The local union provided free office space and phone service, but beyond that was able to contribute only around US$1,000 each year to the project. Occasional contributions from the international union totalled US$40,000 over the eight-year period, while smaller contributions from other unions amounted to less than US$5,000. Over US$2 million came from sources outside the labor movement.

High revenues between 1997 and 1999 were due to a single large grant. In late 1996, responding to a new immigration law that excluded all noncitizens from federally funded social services, billionaire financier George Soros gave US$50 million over two years to support naturalization programs in the United States. Because the project had launched a successful volunteer-based program over a year earlier, it was well positioned to receive its regional share of that support through a northern California consortium of projects.

This single large grant was a mixed blessing. It put power over the project in the hands of a relatively conservative community foundation (which served as a conduit for the grant), and it was accompanied by cumbersome data-gathering requirements imposed by "experts" three levels of bureaucracy away from the point where services were delivered. During the period of support from this large grant, the project moved away from the organizing methods described above and closer to the conventional model of a service agency. Only with great difficulty did the organization move back from that brink over the next several years.

If this large grant is excluded, it appears that the project's normal revenue has been around US$250,000 a year. Figure 7–2 displays the average income from different sources that might be expected, based on this experience, to produce a normal Citizenship Project budget.

Figure 7–2. Revenue Sources
for a US$250,000 Citizenship Project Budget

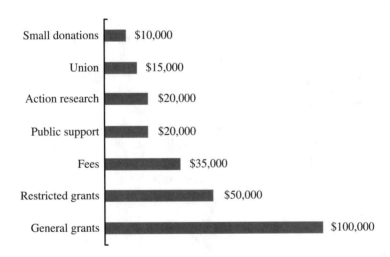

Small donations flow from small contributions by those who benefit from the project; occasional contributions from other unions, groups, businesses, and individuals in the immigrant community; and an annual fundraising event. Union support to the project is expected to be greater than historically has been the case because of the new climate of labor movement interest in immigrant rights. Local unions interested in developing their own immigrant rights projects should receive seed money from their international unions. And certainly, if a union-sponsored project seeks support from other sources, it will be essential for the union to show some commitment of its own by contributing resources to the effort. Revenue from action research stems from the project's partnership with the author, a university-based researcher. Virtually any such project—and especially projects using innovative methods—can be of interest to social and policy researchers and so can get support from research-related funding sources. Fees are produced by immigration and naturalization services (and some public jurisdictions are also willing to provide funds for naturalization assistance). Most of the fees that the Citizenship Project takes in are for very low-cost help in completing immigration packets.

Few public agencies and few mainstream foundations are likely to support union organizing, advocacy for the rights of immigrants, or progressive social change. Some, however, will provide more restricted support to a variety of projects that is limited in scope if these projects are seen as responding to an urgent public need. All of the public support and a significant part of the grant support summarized in Figure 7–2 come from diverse streams of funding associated with such needs: naturalization assistance, youth development, adult education, immigration assistance to victims of spousal abuse, and so on.

Finally, the most important source of support for an organization like the Citizenship Project consists of small- to medium-sized grants (US$5,000–50,000) from progressive foundations interested in immigrant rights, economic justice, expanded democracy, or social justice more generally. These organizations are also unlikely to provide direct support to unions, and most are unlikely to support projects that serve only union members. So not only the project's nonprofit (501c3) status but also its involvement with the broader work force and community are essential for getting such support.

Mutual Involvement

Throughout its history the local union's support for the project remained constant, while the involvement of the members themselves and the staff in project campaigns and with related groups varied over time. While the project became increasingly visible within the communities in the region, it remained identified with the union. Through the project the union led campaigns against INS raids, against anti-immigrant propositions, and in favor of election rights and youth rights, and it worked in ways similar to those of the project. As a result, while it remained focused on the problems associated with collective bargaining, the union also assumed a larger role and acquired an expanded identity in the broader community.

At the same time, the Citizenship Project was constantly drawn into workplace struggles. Volunteers began to learn about and demand enforcement of widely disregarded wage-and-hour laws, and Citizenship Project contacts among unorganized workers became organizing opportunities for the union. Most project staff and many volunteers were themselves current or former grassroots activists at their workplaces, and so the project frequently found itself participating in picket lines, strikes, and other protest actions.

The union's organizing staff works from the same storefront facility where the Citizenship Project is located, and the project's staff and volunteers play an active part in union organizing campaigns. Copies of over twelve thousand naturalization packets retained by the project include information regarding the applicants' current and former employers and so offer useful leads to workplace contacts already served by a union-sponsored project. Project staff and volunteers also have provided a ready force of volunteer organizers for making house visits, securing leaflet pickup points, and assisting in other activities. The union also has relied on the project for strike support and other assistance in major battles over contracts.

In July 1999, for example, a strike erupted among Local 890 members at Basic Vegetable Products, a large garlic and onion dehydration plant fifty miles south of Salinas in King City. A month later the company "permanently replaced" the strikers, and the union settled in for a long battle. Over a year later that battle became even more daunting when, after the sale of the company to the giant ConAgra Corporation, that company embraced the previous owner's agenda of pay and benefit cuts and the permanent replacement of strikers.

During two years of all-out support for the Basic Vegetable strike, project staff and volunteers organized community support, conducted research, produced and printed strike literature, helped operate a food pantry for strikers, helped distribute strike benefits, and so on. The project hired two Basic Vegetable strikers to organize community support and do "citizenship work" in the south Salinas Valley. And with funds from a dollar-a-week "solidarity assessment," raised from union members through worksite votes, ¡VOTE! employed five more Basic Vegetable strikers, who fanned out across the state and later the country to wage a corporate campaign against Basic Vegetable and subsequently against the ConAgra Corporation. The union's successful conduct of the Basic Vegetable strike demonstrated the power of political processes, broadly defined, to outflank the overwhelming economic power of employers (Johnston 2003).

In the aftermath of the Basic Vegetable strike, both the union's development and the project's self-assessment continued. While the project's semi-detached relationship vis-à-vis the union had permitted it to develop an "organizing culture" without challenging the union's long-established "servicing culture" of client processing and collective bargaining, it left those routines in place. The proximity and daily interaction of two such different organizations at times led to conflicts over shared resources (such as the use of the union hall) and to a more generalized sense of alienation between the two groups.

Very recently, moreover, declining employment in the food-processing industry combined with the union's failure to make significant breakthroughs in organizing led to new financial problems and staff layoffs at Local 890. This intensified intergroup tensions, as some union staff questioned the loyalty of project staff and asked why the union should devote its scarce resources to the project. The project responded by making support for union organizing efforts its highest priority. Since then, union leaders' own self-assessment led them to conclude that, in order to organize successfully, their organization needed to change to adopt organizing methods similar in some respects to those employed by the project. These developments may lead both to more significant change within the union and to closer integration of the work of the two organizations.

CONCLUSION:
LESSONS FROM THE CITIZENSHIP PROJECT

As suggested by the union's recent recognition of its own need for organizational change, the affiliate-organization strategy cannot by itself produce a renewal of the culture of social movement within unions. Rather, it can permit activists to sidestep confrontation with entrenched interests and institutionalized ways of working, while building a bridge between union and community.

In these circumstances the experience described in this article suggests that neither full autonomy nor full union control would serve such a project well. Especially in the case of a union with an organizational culture that is less movement oriented, the relationship requires both separation and attachment, careful management of inevitable tensions, and constant efforts to maintain a foundation of mutual trust.

It does appear from the case of the Citizenship Project, however, that launching a new organization overlapping the old—that is, an organization that penetrates both the old union and the larger unorganized work force—can help jump start innovation. Such new beginnings can win support within existing unions to the extent that they bring new resources, appeal to the interests of union leaders, and draw upon and identify themselves with the legacy of the past in the union's "community of memory." Also, reliance on many partners and multiple small funding sources can increase the organization's autonomy and chances of survival. Organizations are most likely to survive, innovate, and perform well when they are responsible for their own fate.

It also appears that organizing methods that rely on the leadership of activist volunteers for the delivery of "rights-related services" can produce networks of mutual self-help. To the extent that organizers involve activist volunteers in decision making, they can trigger the formation of new groups. These methods of citizenship work are relevant not only to immigrant rights, but also to the rights of workers, tenants, and other similar groups. And if such campaigns and organization-building efforts are sponsored by labor unions and target work forces—organized and unorganized—they can also lay the foundations for union organizing.

Given that both the revival of the labor movement and civic development in immigrant communities depend in part on many emerging grassroots organizations, the sprouting of new groups under the Citizenship Project's nonprofit umbrella is particularly significant. Because of the project's tax-exempt status, its capacity to serve as an employer, its organizational know-how, its hospitable meeting spaces, its printing facilities, and so on, obstacles to its organizational survival were much reduced. Some international unions, labor councils, and labor centers already operate 501c3 affiliate organizations to reinforce their own resources. By also serving as 501c3 support centers for their own constituencies of local unions, they may create a more fertile environment for forming immigrant rights programs and other innovative projects based in local unions.

At the time of writing (2002–3) we are observing a broad surge of interest on the part of unionists in establishing local immigrant-rights projects. If our experience with a variety of unions in California and with Teamsters locals around the country is taken as an indication, then hundreds of local unions are interested in such initiatives. It is unlikely,

however, that many of these local unions will have the capacity (or acquire partners with the capacity) to raise funds that approach even
the modest annual budget of the Citizenship Project. If the affiliate-
organization strategy is to bear fruit, two developments appear to be necessary. First, a greater flow of foundation support is indispensable—and
is likely only if foundations that are interested in civic engagement, naturalization, immigrant rights, and economic justice respond to the current
opportunity to promote the development of union-sponsored immigrant-
rights projects. Second, it will be essential to develop and document much
less expensive immigrant rights and organizing projects. Tentatively, we
believe that a single 501c3 support center with two staff members may
be able to sponsor a large network of local union-based projects with as
little as one volunteer coordinator. This is the current frontier of program
development for labor-based immigrant rights.

ACKNOWLEDGMENTS

I helped to develop the Citizenship Project in 1995 and currently serve as its
director. My brother Mike Johnston is a business agent at Teamsters Local 890
and also was actively involved in founding the project. This personal relationship certainly helped the relations between the two organizations. I am indebted
to the members and leaders of both organizations for the learning opportunities
our collaboration afforded me. This article benefited from helpful editorial comments by Katie Quan, Claire Van Zevern, and the peer reviewer of *Development
in Practice*. The study was conducted with support from the Center for Labor
Research and Education at the Institute for Industrial Relations at the University
of California, Berkeley, and is part of a larger study of the relationship between
labor movements and the emergence of citizenship among Mexican immigrants
in California that the Institute supports.

NOTES

[1] Upon the retirement of AFL-CIO president Lane Kirkland in 1995 an internal power struggle led to the emergence of a new leadership committed to
more aggressive organizing. Early setbacks in the United Farm Workers' strawberry campaign, which did not emphasize the defense of immigrant rights, convinced key strategists that greater emphasis on immigrant rights was essential
for success in future organizing efforts.

[2] In the late 1980s, 2.7 million immigrants, mostly of Mexican origin, applied for legal residency under the 1986 Immigration Reform and Control Act.

Starting in 1995, amid a barrage of attacks on immigrant rights, record numbers of legal residents, both amnesty recipients and long-term legal residents, applied for US citizenship.

[3] A partial list includes the Workplace Project in Long Island, New York; the Latino Workers' Center, Chinese Staff and Workers' Association, and Workers' Awaaz in New York; the Tenants' and Workers' Support Committee in Alexandria, Virginia; the Korean Immigrant Workers' Association in Los Angeles; the Asian Immigrant Women's Advocates in Oakland, California; the Workers' Organizing Committee in Portland, Oregon; La Mujer Obrera in El Paso, Texas; the Immigrant Workers' Resource Center in Boston; the Mississippi Workers' Rights Project in Oxford, Mississippi; and the Coalition of Immokalee Workers in Immokalee, Florida. Among AFL-CIO unions, the UFW and UNITE (garment workers) have both operated service centers, although UFW service centers have recently been closed throughout California. UNITE's immigration program complemented the union's innovative justice centers, but those centers closed in the early 1990s. The AFL-CIO–sponsored California Immigrant Workers' Association operated immigrant rights and organizing projects in the early 1990s, as did the ambitious regional organizing project LA MAP; neither of those programs, however, was sustained past the mid-1990s.

[4] Two of the four counties in the state with the highest percentage of Hispanic population are Monterey (48 percent) and San Benito (47 percent) on the central coast; Imperial County on the Mexican border has by far the highest percentage (72 percent), according to the 2000 US census.

[5] It is interesting to note that in the mid-1980s, the relatively decentralized Teamsters international union tolerated a democratic transition at Local 890 that some more centralized international unions might well have suppressed.

[6] Bacharach et al. (2001) argue convincingly that new logic of labor action must tap into unions' "community of memory." Past struggles for inclusion by African American workers and other immigrant groups may help some unions tie initiatives for immigrant rights to the legacy of their own past.

[7] Four more female volunteers and one male volunteer also receive "social justice leadership" stipends. As discussed elsewhere, women play a distinctive and central role in the process of citizenship development described here (Johnston 2001).

[8] This strategy is outlined in Schadler (1998).

Eight

The Labor Union Solution or the NGO Problem?

The Fight for Global Labor Rights

JOSEPH ROMÁN

Labor rights are a contentious issue within contemporary social justice movements. Different organizations have different responses when asked about the topic. What are "core labor rights"? Should they exist? What is their purpose? Who benefits? These are the difficult questions that need to be answered. Particularly perplexing, however, is that movements of a more progressive politics, namely labor unions and NGOs, vehemently disagree over how to achieve the same goals. Numerous NGOs lob accusations of protectionism, economic nationalism, and rent-seeking against labor union efforts to push for the inclusion of labor rights in trade agreements. In response, labor unions accuse NGOs of exposing workers in developing countries to exploitation by transnational corporate juggernauts.[1] Fortunately, for all the bad news stories existing between NGOs and labor unions, there are just as many good ones (Waterman 1993).

But there is an urgent matter that needs to be addressed by NGOs over the issue of labor rights. While many NGOs seek to create a more just and sustainable global economy, they often make a glaring oversight in terms of labor rights: class relations. In particular, our concern lies with those NGOs that seek to pursue the alleviation of racial and gender inequalities while simultaneously ignoring the dynamics of class subordination in a world characterized by free-market capitalism. Labor unions are one of the few movements that are by definition dedicated to dissolving

123

Joseph Román

class inequalities, especially among workers in both the North and South. Until NGOs rethink their omission of class from their priorities, labor unions are the only agency capable of pushing forward an agenda centered on labor rights.

THE NECESSITY OF CLASS

A neoclassical perspective on the relationship between capital and labor suggests that a mutually beneficial tradeoff exists between the two parties. Employers pay workers to do a job; in return, workers receive a wage to pay for basic necessities. If employees do not like the conditions of work or wages provided by the employer, they are free to look elsewhere. And if employers want to keep their employees, they must provide competitive pay and conditions of work or risk losing them to a company that does.

Unfortunately, the world is not as simple as this picture suggests. The relationship between capital and labor is increasingly taking on a coercive nature, as workers in the North are compelled to compete with workers in the South. Northern workers may look back fondly on the postwar era following World War II, when competition between workers was less than it is today. Jobs were plentiful, labor unions were strong, production was, for the most part, geared toward the domestic market, and workers of one nation were not pitted against workers of another. However, the economic crisis of the 1970s saw a profit squeeze. Workers were the inevitable victims of this situation. Capital's move toward outsourcing and the internationalization of production meant that workers, especially unskilled workers in the North, saw their world crumbling around them. Of course, states themselves also promoted the internationalization of production and placed labor in a position of extreme subordination. For instance, though it is clear that national experiences vary widely, attacks on the welfare state helped to deregulate labor markets in many countries.

As Kim Moody points out, only certain types of industries have moved to the South, most of which are labor intensive, that is, they require low-skilled labor (Moody 1988, 51–66). But if capital can move, it will. And move it does! So workers must work harder and faster while capital reaps the fruits of their labor. Indeed, William Blake's satanic mills have made a comeback since the economic crisis of the 1970s. The clothing industry uses sweatshop labor, and the factories of major multinational manufacturers located in the South skimp on health and safety. Labor has entered the twenty-first century in an even more subordinate position than it was in during the previous century.

Under capitalist relations of production, labor is treated as property, to be used, abused, or thrown away as employers deem fit. Though not everyone would agree, in my view it is this fundamental inequality that needs to be challenged. Joan W. Scott, for instance, believes that class is not the only way to analyze inequality and that, among other things, race and gender are more useful categories of discussion (Scott 2000). But such arguments disconnect individuals' experiences from the wider world of capitalist relations. The fact remains that, under capitalism, most people will have to work for someone else in order to have access to the basic necessities of life. In this sense we can say that at no other time in history has the world seen more working-class people than it has today. Ellen Meiksins Wood puts it best when she writes:

> The concept of class as *relationship* and process stresses that objective relations to the means of production are significant insofar as they establish antagonisms and generate conflicts and struggles; that these conflicts and struggles shape social experience "in class ways," even when they do not express themselves in class consciousness and clearly visible forma-tions; and that over time we can discern how these relation-ships impose their logic, their pattern, on social processes. (Wood 1982, 50)

People are exploited, in both the literal and the Marxist senses, for the pursuit of profit. Given that it is unlikely that the relationship between capital and labor will ever be an equal one, understanding this dynamic is central to understanding the need for global labor rights.

THINKING ABOUT CORE LABOR STANDARDS

What constitute core labor rights? Core labor rights are the subject of contention, but they only become so if they are overanalyzed. Breaking things down to the most basic of human needs is perhaps the best way of arriving at an answer to the question. So-called core labor rights consist of three main factors, as described below.[2]

The Right to a Living Wage

This is the most basic core labor right, though one that is not even acknowledged in advanced capitalist countries. Whether by choice or by force, the number of people required to sell their labor in order to survive is increasing every day. More often than not, once this choice is made, there is no turning back for these individuals. And since people sell their labor to gain the necessities of life, their wages should adequately reflect this.

The Right to a Safe and Healthy Working Environment

A majority of people will spend a good portion of their lives working for someone else. But during periods of recession employers are tempted to cut corners and make the work environment less safe and workers thus more prone to injury or disease. This will be done, of course, in the name of maintaining a profit margin sufficient to prevent the firm from going under. However, health and safety standards may also be violated during an economic boom, as when, for instance, production cannot keep up with demand, so employers put pressure on workers to meet rising production targets. Another possibility is that workers themselves consciously abrogate health and safety standards in order to satisfy the demands made by management, even when the latter emphasizes the importance of health and safety.

Regardless of the situation, a worker's labor power is worthless if the worker is sick or maimed. For the employer, an injured employee working at a less than optimal pace prevents the further extraction of surplus value. While the argument may go that workers can turn to governments for help, only in a few countries do workers actually have access to adequate help once they become physically unable to work. Unfortunately, even these programs are coming under attack, making it increasingly difficult for workers to be eligible to benefit from them.[3] And even if a worker is not immediately forced out of the labor market because of illness or injury, ailments may creep up many years after being in contact with a dangerous substance or being positioned in a poorly designed workstation. Two ailments that illustrate this are asbestosis and carpal tunnel syndrome, respectively.

All of this adds up to the question of quality of life. Should human beings be forced into accepting poor working conditions? Clearly not. After all, in a free market people have little choice but to sell their labor power and therefore have the basic human right to be employed in a safe and healthy workplace. Without this protection workers risk becoming nothing more than commodities that are disposed of once they have out-lived their usefulness.

The Right to Be Free from Discriminatory Labor Practices

This right seems rather straightforward: one's ethnicity or sex should not affect one's chance of getting a job. Even though many countries have made great strides in ending this kind of discrimination, this right goes far deeper. Securing employment can, in fact, depend on one's sex or ethnicity, and such employment is often in industries with awful working conditions. For example, Mexican agribusinesses often choose indigenous women to harvest pesticide-drenched crops earmarked for export to the lucrative US and Canadian markets. The pay is poor, and working condi-tions are far from ideal. Racist and sexist ideology is used to justify the use of such labor, as well as to perpetuate the misery of this segment of the working class (Martínez-Salazar 1999).[4]

Many industries justify poor treatment of their workers by denigrat-ing their skills because they are women from specific ethnic backgrounds. Roxana Ng's discussion of the Toronto garment industry illustrates this point: "For instance, sewing is seen to be a woman's skill; it is paid less than the work done by cutters in garment production" (Ng 1998, 23). For manufacturers, being a cutter equates with being male, and as such, a cutter deserves to be paid more than a woman who has a "magical incli-nation" to sew. One can also see the outsourcing of labor-intensive pro-duction processes to East Asia in this light. Apparently, East Asian hands are nimble and can more adeptly put together whatever gadget or part rich Northern consumers have an appetite for. And let us not forget that East Asians are somehow more inclined to accept authority and an overly rigorous work schedule than Europeans, who have supposedly been spoiled by their welfare states and strong labor unions.[5]

LABOR UNIONS VERSUS NGOS: THE FIGHT FOR LABOR RIGHTS

Why should labor unions be the agents for advancing labor rights? Why not look to NGOs to solve the problem? It would be unfair to say that labor unions should not be the obvious organization to reduce the gap between what owners and workers make, and the suggestion that labor unions are inert is largely based on the US experience of labor unionism during capitalism's golden age. US unionism should not be the model for realizing the call "Workers of the world, unite!" The central federation of US labor, the American Federation of Labor-Congress of Industrial Organizations (AFL-CIO), for many years did more to tear than mend the quilt of labor internationalism. Witness the willingness of the AFL-CIO in assisting the US government during the Cold War to help only those unions in communist countries that were resolved to introduce "American-style" democracy: liberal democracy combined with free markets, albeit the latter much more important than the former (Sims 1992). But what was even more damaging was the AFL-CIO's steadfast determination to rid itself of communists and socialists during that time, which effectively dashed any hopes that the world's leading industrial nation would develop a robust and radical labor movement.

What is even sadder about this experience is that US workers themselves were left on the outside looking in during this period. Refusing to put resources into organizing, US unions limited their activities to obtaining better wages, benefits, and working conditions for their members. Not surprisingly, large segments of the working class were left out and became alienated from the labor movement, most notably the black and female proletariat, since most of the gains being won for US workers during the boom period were for white males. Nevertheless, despite the gains won, US unions were willing to engage in concession bargaining when the economy eventually turned sour in the late 1970s and early 1980s. The legacy of this policy has left labor union members in a desperate position, as employers' bargaining power vis-à-vis their employees has never been stronger (Moody 1988).

Fortunately, labor unionism of the old AFL-CIO type is not the only model available to the world. Labor unions and their leadership are beginning to realize—and in some cases, had already done so—that a large segment of the working class has been excluded from the benefits that unionization brings. A veritable epiphany has even occurred whereby labor unions see that it is not only the local that matters but also the global (Munck 1999). Nowhere is this more evident than in North America.

Despite the existence of a labor side agreement in the North American Free Trade Agreement (NAFTA), high-wage workers in the United States and Canada feel threatened by Mexico's large supply of cheap labor. It is therefore conceivable that labor could have gone into its shell and begun an offensive campaign demonizing the Mexican working class. Although some of this did occur, many labor unions chose the road of international solidarity instead (Wells 1998a). Looking to the Canadian labor movement, prominent unions such as the Canadian Auto Workers (CAW) and the Communications, Energy, and Paperworkers Union (CEP) have forged transnational links with their counterparts in the United States and Mexico in order to lift, among other things, wages for Mexican workers (Wells 1998b, 6–9). Such activities are vitally important. Gerard Greenfield, a labor activist and researcher working in East and Southeast Asia, suggests that labor union activity is the only way to ensure that the obligations set out by social clauses are met; social clauses are only as effective as they are followed (Greenfield 1998, 187).

Could NGOs have achieved similar results? NGOs are useful in that they are able to bring attention to specific issues, but that is all they can do. Clearly, labor unions and NGOs would like to see infra-subsistence wage levels disappear. Yet it is important to think through the structure of NGOs and labor unions when it comes to achieving the right to a living wage. One of the problems is that NGOs tend to be focused on a single issue. Of course, one may argue that the labor internationalism displayed by the CAW and CEP are narrow in focus, in that the CAW focused on the auto industry in Mexico and the CEP would also focus on industries its membership occupies. However, as I will discuss below, NGOs tend to focus on one single actor within a given industry.

The Case of Sweatshop Labor

Let us take the example of sweatshop labor. NGOs and labor unions alike have been active in the fight to raise the wages of workers in industries that are likely to depend upon sweatshop labor. Such industries are notorious for the following: refusing to pay workers a living wage, exposing workers to dangerous working conditions, and creating a gendered and "racialized" work force. Labor union efforts to stamp out this blight have extended beyond what NGOs have sought by demanding that governments produce codes of conduct; on the other hand, NGOs will focus on an issue until it is resolved. More important, though, is that an issue taken up by an NGO can have the effect of "hogging" the spotlight (Bob 2002). A case in point is Nike's shifting of production to countries like China, Indonesia, and Thailand once factories in South Korea and Taiwan became unionized. In response, a joint campaign was launched by labor unions and NGOs (Cavanagh 1997, 39–40). But while the spotlight was shining on Nike, where was the NGO pressure on other shoe companies to increase their wages? And where are the NGOs when it comes to ensuring that the promises made by shoe companies and other industries employing sweatshop labor are in fact kept?

Discussing corporate strategies to justify sweatshop labor, Andrew Ross writes:

> Pitting First World against Third World workers has been a highly serviceable corporate strategy. It drives down wages on both sides, and allows business to portray labor rights advocates as domestic protectionists bent on depriving maquila workers of their industrial wage ticket out of poverty. (Ross 1997, 25)

Unlike what NGOs are able to do, the Union of Needletrades, Industrial, and Textile Employees (UNITE)—a diverse union in its own right—has expanded its campaign to all companies using sweatshop labor, not just a select few. Indeed, numerous campaigns by UNITE persuaded the US government to crack down on sweatshop labor within and outside US borders as the Department of Labor produced a list of companies aspiring to rid themselves of this barbaric work regime (Ross 1997, 28–29), and the union continues to press for workers' rights in sweatshop industries despite the battles already won.

This is not to deride NGOs' activities in trying to make the working world more humane for workers. NGO campaigns and strategies certainly do help bring attention to issues that would otherwise be ignored. But any organization that gets capital to agree to a set of terms and then disappears or becomes a shell of its former self does a disservice to workers, especially those who continue to lack real protection from employers' whims. Even when labor standards are present in trade agreements, what is to stop employers from ignoring their obligations? What if labor standards are not even present?

This last point is particularly relevant given that the main body overseeing international trade, the WTO, does not see labor rights as a matter within its purview (Howse 1999). It is, therefore, important to explore the increased importance of labor unions and to consider why NGOs should let this battle belong to them.

A LIBERAL TRADE REGIME:
WHAT DIRECTION SHOULD LABOR TAKE?

As the supranational institution charged with setting out the rules for free trade, the WTO is not shy in proclaiming that its chief purpose is to facilitate freer trade among nations; labor rights are not within its purview (WTO 1999). So what direction should labor take? As I have discussed above, NGOs' activities are too narrow in their focus—though this in and of itself does not make their work any less important. But since the WTO is intent on creating a worldwide trade regime exclusive of labor rights, the task of labor unions in achieving even an iota of social justice for workers has become ever more difficult; especially as the state has been capital's very willing partner in making laissez-faire capitalism a global reality. That globalization nullifies the role of the state is largely a myth. International trade agreements and the liberalization of finance since the end of the Cold War have been created by states, not by transnational corporations.

But let us not forget one of the contradictions embedded in a liberal trade regime, namely, that despite capital's international nature, its factories must be located within national jurisdictions. This potentially offers great opportunities for labor unions to advance labor rights in a global economy. Class struggles occur in numerous places but most visibly at the level of the workplace. Labor history shows that workers have had to fight against employers in order to gain proper recognition as human beings. Moreover, the historical function of labor unions has also been to give workers an identity that can denounce the unequal relationship between workers and owners (Catalano 1999, 27–31).

David Harvey suggests that struggles on the shop floor in an international trade regime devoid of labor rights are made even more difficult as a result of the mobility of capital—making the realization of working-class identities at the factory level also harder to achieve. He goes on to suggest that labor must take its fight to the international level (Harvey 1998, 70–72). But this logic is flawed. Consider the following scenario. Say a company decides to move from Country A to Country B because labor unions are nonexistent there. Unionized workers left in Country A then decide to help organize workers in Country B, and succeed. In response, the company swiftly moves to Country C, where conditions are much more favorable to capital. However, capital movements such as this are not as simple as Harvey suggests. Relocating fixed capital is not as easy as relocating portfolio capital. The costs a company incurs in moving machinery and in building a new plant in a labor-unfriendly zone may well outweigh the benefits.

Pondering this point, then, the task for labor unions should be to challenge capital's quintessential basis of power: absolute control over the means of production; in other words, to introduce democracy into the economic realm. Even if economic democracy is limited to the activity of workers bargaining with employers on such issues as wages and working conditions, this is at least a start, given that workers in the South—and increasingly in the North—lack workplace protection.[6]

Perhaps the most pressing matter for labor union activity in many developing countries is the repression that workers face. Are NGOs rather than labor unions the organizations that workers should be looking to in countries lacking labor rights? The answer is no, because NGOs tend to be based on identity politics more than on class politics (della Porta and Diani 1999, 87–109), and this in turn obscures the greater reality at hand, namely, capital's dominance and control over the labor process.

Further compounding the problem is the fact that worldwide attention given to causes in developing countries often largely depends on the activity of NGOs in developed countries (Bob 2002), although labor unions show a greater capacity to lift labor standards than NGOs do.[7] Again, it is important to look at labor union activities in the NAFTA countries. Close links have been developed among US, Canadian, and Mexican unions. Information is exchanged about labor laws, working conditions, and other issues related to labor. More significant than the exchange of information is the show of solidarity among these unions. Acts of defiance have occurred on all sides of the borders of NAFTA countries in response to what rank-and-file unionists feel are injustices to their fellow workers (Carr 1996).

What this activity points to is that the power of capital must be challenged at the shop-floor level. Whether or not governments are complacent about abuses on the part of capital toward workers, labor unions must confront the very idea that, in a capitalist economy, workers should succumb to the bourgeoisie's control over the means of production. Historically, this has never been the case in developed countries, where workers organized labor unions in order to challenge employers' divine rule in the workplace. Of course, the danger always exists that labor union leadership can become isolated from the rank and file and so become an arm of capital. But as workers' rebellions in Europe's industrial centers during the late 1960s and throughout the 1970s showed, members' feelings of alienation will eventually boil over, resulting in serious consequences for a labor union leadership that is perceived as an extension of capital (Gorz 1999, 10). Similar scenes were seen during the late 1990s in East Asia. Alongside student protests, workers' demonstrations erupted in Indonesia against the Suharto regime, which took a hardline approach to labor union activity. And in South Korea, where workers are no longer prohibited from forming or joining a union, rank-and-file workers came out against the main South Korean labor union body, the Korean Confederation of Trade Unions, after the union had endorsed the IMF's plans to "rescue" South Korea from total economic ruin in the aftermath of the economic crisis that swept East Asia in 1998 (McNally 1998, 149–50).

As this discussion shows, workers are quite capable of organizing, protesting, and acting in defiance of the status quo without any outside help. There is no reason to assume that outside forces are needed, even in countries where internal dissent is frowned upon. Indonesian workers have fought for their labor rights, as have South Koreans, much as Americans, Canadians, Germans, and Italians have done. These class struggles may take various forms. The means used will always be different, as are the ends (Arrighi 1990, 36–37), though this should not be taken as an endorsement of the post-modern ethic, which would in fact be a disservice to the struggles that workers are facing worldwide.

Suggesting that workers in different countries have different needs would seem to entail a rejection of those core labor rights outlined earlier in this essay. Journalist Barbara Ehrenreich pointed out, based on her experiment of masquerading as a low-wage worker in the United States, that employers often justify the poor treatment of workers on the basis that they are women or of a different ethnic background—a clear sign of a gendered and "racialized" labor market, which is something that should not exist (Ehrenreich 2001). Yet, diverse as the workers encountered by Ehrenreich were, all were well aware that their basic needs were not being met. Regardless of gender, ethnicity, or race, workers do have common needs: adequate food, shelter, and clothing. Because workers have no choice but to reproduce themselves through market exchanges—selling their labor power for a wage—labor unions are the only vehicle capable of fighting for labor rights in a trading regime that deprives workers of these rights.

CONCLUSION:
FORGING A NEW PATH
FOR LABOR UNIONS AND NGOS

The argument made in this essay is based on the idea that class is the key starting point in understanding the fundamentally unequal relationship between labor and capital. Capitalism's logic of continuous growth requires capitalists to squeeze workers whenever possible in order to maximize profits. But while labor remains local, capital has gone global. So too have labor union and NGO activities. But their respective activities have taken rather different forms. NGOs tend to focus only on one issue until it has been resolved, while labor unions try to remain as vigilant as possible across a wider spectrum of labor issues. Where workers have been aggrieved, transnational solidarity has been spawned more often by workers than by NGOs.

While labor unions are, in my view, the agency most capable of pushing forward the agenda of global labor rights in a world that does not see them as paramount, the question arises: can NGOs and labor unions work together? The answer is quite simple—of course they can! The outcry against sweatshop labor was a joint effort by labor unions and NGOs. But much more can be done through mutual collaboration by both sides.

NGOs need to accept the fact that class, not race or gender, is the basis of exploitation in the global economy. Capital's justification for exploiting segments of the working class on the basis of race or gender masks the essence of capitalism's squeezing of the working classes. Why pay a working man more when you can pay a working woman less?

For their part, labor unions should move beyond their focus on supplying better wages and working conditions for workers. The fight for labor rights is only a starting point. How soon this fight will be won (or lost) is unknown. Labor unions should start thinking beyond getting a piece of the economic pie for workers. The labor movement should contemplate a program to emancipate workers from capitalism. Often, this will mean aligning itself with NGOs railing against capitalism's excesses. Ultimately, however, class remains the basis of inequality in a world dominated by capitalist relations. The exclusion of labor rights from the WTO shows whose side the state is on. But until NGOs rectify their general disregard for class, labor unions will remain alone in their fight for labor rights.

NOTES

[1] This is not to suggest that these attitudes pervade all NGOs or labor unions but simply to offer a general sense of the disagreements hovering over the labor rights debate between the two parties.

[2] By no means am I suggesting that these three areas are the only labor rights that workers should enjoy, for there are a great many other areas that need to be seriously addressed. For reasons of space, I have narrowed these down to what I believe are the three most basic and fundamental rights that workers should have.

[3] A prime example is in the Canadian province of Ontario, where changes enacted by the neoliberal Progressive Conservatives to provincial labor standards have put the burden of proof on the employee to show that he or she has been injured on the job. Of course, the layers of bureaucracy that workers must go through in every country to obtain what should be rightfully theirs can also discourage them from seeking compensation for employers' disregard of health and safety standards.

[4] Much of this ideology is conditioned by Mexico's history as a Spanish colony. Egla Martínez-Salazar (1999) emphasizes that Mexico's indigenous peoples are seen as being naturally consigned to poverty by the Mexican state, not to mention its elites, because they lack the "Europeanness" of Mexico's colonizers.

[5] Indeed, this was at the heart of the Asian values debate of the 1990s. Authoritarian governments in East Asia justified poor treatment of their workers and an iron-fisted attitude toward workers' dissent by insisting that "This is the way things are done in Asia." Workers' protests over the IMF's structural adjustment policies in East Asia after the 1998 economic meltdown show otherwise.

[6] While some countries might spell out employers' legal obligations to employees, laws are only effective if they are enforced. Mexico is a perfect example of labor laws that are strong on paper but end up having an almost nonexistent impact on employees because they are not enforced.

[7] Although many NGOs in developing countries attempt to bring attention to the plight of workers, these calls often go unheeded because NGOs in developed countries show relatively little interest in them. While child labor has been a favorite cause in the North, very little is said about the inhumane working conditions endured by workers harvesting crops—though, ironically, such workers exist in developed countries too.

Part 2

Experiences of Union-based NGOs

Nine

The Global Workplace

Challenging the Race to the Bottom

JACKIE SIMPKINS

WAR ON WANT—FIGHTING GLOBAL POVERTY

In February 1951, publisher Victor Gollancz wrote a letter to the *Guardian* that called for a negotiated end to the Korean War and the creation of an international fund "to turn swords into ploughshares." All those in support were to send a postcard to Gollancz with the simple word *yes.* He received over four thousand replies.[1] The Association for World Peace was formed, and it quickly commissioned Harold Wilson and others to write a plan for world development under the title War on Want in 1952. Since that time, War on Want has been a movement of people fighting world poverty.

Harold Wilson, one of our founders, created a government Ministry for Overseas Development with Barbara Castle, an early patron, as its first minister. War on Want was at the forefront of many of the debates on so-called third-world issues. One of the first campaign aims of the War on Want was to mobilize the British people in support of persuading the UK government to allocate 1 percent of GDP to development programs overseas.

In 1961 War on Want noted that debt would become a central issue in the future, warning of the need to reduce the proportion of loans in our aid in order to avoid trouble in future years. Throughout the 1970s and 1980s War on Want campaigned for workers' rights on tea plantations, supported Southern African liberation movements, and developed ground-breaking campaigns on the role of women in the developing world. In developing a response to globalization in the 1990s, War on Want put workers' rights at the center of its campaigns and explored innovative ideas such as the Tobin Tax to ensure that the benefits of globalization might be shared equally.

War on Want's first flyer stated: "Transcending all our immediate problems, this gap between the rich and the poor of the earth is the supreme challenge of the next fifty years." In the twenty-first century, in a world in which the United States and Europe spend US$17 billion a year on pet food, while 1.2 billion people live on less than US$1 a day, it is clear that a lot more remains to be done.[2]

GLOBALIZATION–RISING TO THE CHALLENGE

> The danger is that globalisation can come to mean only the
> free flow of goods and finance. . . . The concern for the com-
> mon good . . . [and] international solidarity . . . [are] in dan-
> ger of being lost.[3]

The experience of the last fifty years has also shown that globalization has the potential to bring many benefits. The greatest tragedy is that the benefits are not distributed equally, either within or among countries.

The labor union movement has a great tradition of international solidarity. However, because of the challenges of globalization there has been a strong backlash of protectionism and xenophobia. There is a view in the UK, for instance, that British jobs are undermined by the low wages of developing countries. Such a view undermines efforts by government and other agencies to alleviate world poverty.

The 2001 Labour Force Survey shows that labor union membership in the UK numbered 7.5 million in 2001. This figure, which represents 27 percent of total employment, includes unions that are not affiliated to the Trades Union Congress. It is fair to say that there has been a considerable decline in labor union membership since the 1980s—probably as much as 40 percent. Multiple factors—not just political—affect this figure. For example, the nature of work has changed, with a move away from manufacturing to the service industries and a more "flexible" work force. Since 1997, however, membership has stabilized and the number of workplace recognition agreements has risen. Consequently, it is anticipated that there will be a real upturn in numbers over the next few years.

In the developing and the developed world alike, labor unions may be a valuable and progressive part of civil society. Their democratic processes make their leaders and activists important advocates within society. Recruiting them into the campaign against world poverty therefore gives a vital boost to our messages and helps to influence and educate the UK population as a whole. Labor unions are invited to affiliate to War on Want at the national and local levels, giving them a democratic role in policies and activities. Most major national unions and many local groups affiliate. War on Want has senior union officers and lay officials serving on the governing Council of Management. It is from this body, but also through less formal dealings with labor union officers, that the need for a development education project emerged.

As a small charity based in London, it may seem that War on Want's work can only ever be a drop in the ocean. However, globalization has given us new tools such as computers and the Internet, which allow us to keep in contact with partners overseas and to work together to ensure that the voices of the poor and powerless are heard. It also means that we can strengthen our links with other campaigners around the world, making international solidarity more powerful than ever. Our supporters in the UK labor union and labor movement know that there is now an even greater need for people to work more closely with one another to confront the inequities of globalization, and they keep alive our tradition of solidarity.

A NEW PARTNERSHIP
BETWEEN NGOS AND LABOR UNIONS

There are some who question the legitimacy of NGOs. Critics have argued, for example, that they distort the democratic process. In Britain, for instance, we have an elected government that should make decisions unhindered by a minority represented by NGOs—if the majority of voters are not interested in world poverty, then so be it. The lack of internal democracy within many NGOs merely serves to underline their lack of legitimacy. Those who support the need for a strong NGO base, however, argue that the electoral system usually delivers a one-party government on just over 40 percent of the vote. In a truly "liberal" democracy, minority views should be protected (War on Want 2001).

Proponents of NGOs, on the other hand, claim that their role in raising public awareness and understanding is crucial to the democratic process.

People might not *think* they have an interest in international trade—until they see the conditions of child laborers in sweatshops in the developing world. It is the NGOs, not the political parties, that are bringing these kinds of issues to public attention. In short, NGOs try to compensate for the deficiencies in our representative democracy.

The change of government in the UK in 1997 was undoubtedly a watershed in a previously unremarkable relationship between the Department for International Development (DFID), formerly the Overseas Development Administration, and the labor union movement. The change from a Conservative to a (New) Labour administration elevated the importance of labor unions both in the North and the South as legitimate arenas for highlighting workers' rights as key to getting people out of poverty. Labor unions, as democratic and accountable organizations, are seen as somehow more legitimate than NGOs. However, many of the arguments applied to the NGO movement can also be applied to the labor union movement at an international level. Even overtly good intentions might be deceptive. It could be argued that although labor unions in the developed world take an apparently honorable position on child labor, for instance, this may be based more on concerns about the level of employment and wages "locally" than on an ethical commitment. Groups based in the developing world are not immune from this critique. Workers in Bangladesh, for example, might be involved in a "race to the bottom" (not that those affected necessarily know they are in this so-called race) with workers in China or Vietnam, as firms search around for the most conducive (usually cheapest) labor market. Where unions exist, it is in their interest to be seen to be fighting for improvements in their members' terms and working conditions rather than concentrating on an even bigger picture.

It was against this backdrop that War on Want sought funding for the Global Workplace project. It came from recognition that there is much to be done in terms of raising awareness about development issues among grassroots labor unionists. The funding was secured from DFID's Development Awareness Fund. The project recognizes the influential role of labor unions and their activists within civil society in the UK and further recognizes that in the global economy the strategies adopted by labor unions in the UK can influence working conditions and poverty in the developing world. War on Want's unique position as an NGO with strong roots in the labor movement and its accountable structure have enabled us to link our campaigns and partners in the South with the labor union movement in the North. This funding has meant that War on Want has been able to increase the breadth and depth of its labor union campaigning work. It has also provided a platform for issues relevant to a younger generation of activists to find their way onto the agenda of the labor union movement, which has otherwise found it difficult to recruit young people coming into new working environments where labor unions have no history of organizing.

Many labor unions in the UK, large and small, are already involved in international work. Some, like UNISON, the public service union, have dedicated international departments. Other unions work through the Global Union Federations (formerly known as International Trade Secretariats), while others affiliate to NGOs such as War on Want and support their campaigns, projects, and other initiatives. Joe Marino, general secretary of the Bakers, Food and Allied Workers' Union (BFAWU) says that "the need to support comrades throughout the world is central to our work. 'An injury to one is an injury to all' is not a concept that stops at the Channel" (War on Want 2001, chap. 2).

THE GLOBAL WORKPLACE
PROJECT

A key objective of the program is to build a network of activists across a number of labor unions who will act as advocates for international development within their own unions. If the program is successful, it is these activists who will put pressure on their labor union institutions for greater institutional commitment to international development and globalization issues, and to "mainstream" this work with other existing activities. Initiated in July 2000, the aim is to build grassroots support and pressure for international development. The project has already built on this bottom-up approach with the building blocks of intra-union regional international committees now in place.

There are a number of elements to this program:

- education
- Global Workers' Forums
- mini-campaigns
- pensions
- website

Education

Educating people in the workplace, and in the context of work, exposes them most clearly to the integration of the global economy and the mutual dependence linking developed and developing countries in the contemporary world. As part of the Global Workplace, War on Want has developed an education unit and associated manual that aim to equip grassroots labor unionists with a range of practical skills and knowledge about international development issues. By educating a large cross-section of the whole movement, not *just* key national officers, this project challenges crude and xenophobic attitudes. Labor unionists are encouraged to develop negotiating strategies that take greater account of the needs of workers in the developing world and to advocate the adoption of core labor standards.

The education unit is designed to be integrated into existing labor union training courses. It does not assume any technical level of knowledge about globalization. The course element can be used at varying levels of complexity, allowing students to explore the issue further if they so choose. The manual that accompanies the course can also be used as a stand-alone reference point. It is anticipated that it will provide information that is both factual and thought provoking for those who are interested in global issues but are not participating in a training course.

The long-term objective is to get international development integrated into the mainstream training programs of all labor unions. By highlighting the similarities rather than the differences in the workplace, it is anticipated that this will help activists to campaign on behalf of workers in other parts of the world. One clear example of this is demonstrated by asking activists to draw up a code of conduct for an employer and then looking at what they would change for workers in Bangladesh rather than the UK. The answer is, invariably, "nothing."

Global Workers' Forums

Another integral part of the program entails organizing a Global Workers' Forum every six months. Over an eighteen-month period we organized such forums in Bangladesh, Ecuador, Haiti, and South Africa. The purpose of these events is to take workers from the UK to meet workers from the same industry, or if possible the same company, in the developing world.

Global Workers' Forums are aimed at grassroots labor union activists in the UK. By taking activists to a similar sector or employer abroad, the forums aim to:

- Develop the participants' understanding of globalization on the industry in which they work, most notably on workers in both the developed and developing world.
- Formulate ideas for a global workers' response to the globalization process.
- Make contacts that will lead to permanent links as a starting point for global action.
- Act as multipliers both in informing and in activating others members of their labor union locally, regionally, and nationally.
- Assist in developing War on Want's strategy on how the global economy affects poverty alleviation.

The forums have been a great success and have enabled those activists who have participated in them to establish working groups within their regions, where they had not previously existed. It is anticipated that this will develop into a multi-union initiative operating at the regional level, thus allowing for as much access as possible to those who are interested in taking an active role. The unions that have participated so far include Britain's general union, the GMB; the Transport and General Workers' Union (T&G); the Union of Shop, Distributive, and Allied Workers; the National Union of Knitwear, Footwear, and Apparel Trades; and UNISON. The participants have all worked in the same or related industries as the partners they were visiting.

For example, activists from the retail sector visited FENACLE, a partner of the small UK NGO Banana Link. FENACLE is a labor union that is working hard to organize banana plantation workers in Ecuador. Bananas epitomize the "race to the bottom" in terms of labor standards and workers' rights. Bananas are the biggest-selling single food items in UK supermarkets, and price competition is fierce. In the banana supply chain the greatest profit is made in the North. Since their return to the UK, the delegates who visited FENACLE have been working inside their unions to take action and to lobby the UK supermarkets as well as the producers in Ecuador to effect change for the workers at the other end of the supply chain. Most of the delegates have managed to get media coverage not only in their union but also in their local and community press, thus reaching an even wider audience.

Another delegation went from the UK to South Africa as part of a water workers' forum and produced tangible benefits, such as the twinning of the UNISON Yorkshire Water Branch with the Central Johannesburg Water Workers' branch of the South African Municipal Workers' Union. These unions represent workers working for the same multinational company, Suez Lyonnaise. The delegates have had extensive coverage in their labor union journal and a video currently in production will be available for use by union branches.

Mini-campaigns

As with any "charitable cause," individual activists are likely to be attracted to wider issues of international development through campaigns on specific issues. War on Want has a great deal of experience organizing such campaigns. As part of the Global Workplace project, War on Want has committed itself to run at least one such thematic campaign each year. The campaigns have been activity based, with an opportunity for labor unionists to take part. This may be by letter writing, attending a meeting or conference, or joining an e-discussion group. Those who become actively involved will be added to the activist database. Undeniably, this is a recruiting tool for War on Want, but it is hoped that these activists will also become advocates within their unions.

The specific campaigns tend to be topical, so it is often difficult to decide their exact content in advance. They have included issues such as child labor, labor union rights in Colombia (see Box 9–1), and "Sweatships" (working conditions for Southern workers on luxury cruise ships can be as bad as those in sweatshop factories). Care has to be taken to ensure that campaigns do not breach the DFID guideline of direct lobbying of the UK government or of international organizations in which the UK is a member, or of lobbying for or against individuals, companies, or institutions.

Pensions

A generation ago most people in the UK didn't have a pension. Today, pensions are big business. Over twenty million people in the country now have a personal pension, around ten million of them in occupational schemes run through the workplace.

Pension funds control huge amounts of money. For example, the total assets of UK pension funds amount to more than US$1.3 trillion. Over

Box 9–1. Case Study of a War on Want Campaign–Colombia

"Labor union leaders are suffering a humanitarian crisis," says the Colombian labor union federation (CUT).

Colombia is one of the most unequal societies on earth: 3 percent of the population owns 70 percent of the land. It is also one of the most dangerous countries in the world in which to be a trade unionist. In the last decade 1,535 people have been killed as a result of their involvement in labor union activity—more than in the rest of the world combined. Trade union activists are assassinated, forced into exile, kidnapped, harassed, and sacked, while peaceful demonstrations are sabotaged.

The trade union movement is one of the principal victims of Colombia's internal conflict, and the situation is getting worse: according to the International Labour Organization (ILO), of 213 labor unionists murdered worldwide in 2002, 184 were Colombian; members of teaching and other public-sector unions are especially targeted. It is no coincidence that these sectors are also those targeted for government spending cuts, privatization, restrictions on employment rights, and redundancies. These trade unions have been particularly active in organizing protests against such measures, believing the latter would throw vast sections of society into utter desperation.

War on Want's campaign began because of the recognition that unionists in Colombia need practical solidarity from workers across the world. Without such support the union movement and the fight for a better society face catastrophe in Colombia. Unions in Colombia often link up with social movements to defend human rights. Every year over three thousand activists and leaders from social movements—including community groups, peasant associations, black and indigenous groups, and organizations of displaced people—are the victims of political assassinations. Fighting for trade union rights has an impact on the lives of people throughout Colombia.

War on Want works with the human rights department of the Colombian trade union federation. Three thousand members of that union have been killed since its formation in 1987. In the UK, War on Want has facilitated action by encouraging trade unions to become actively involved with organizations such as the Colombia Solidarity Campaign and Justice for Colombia, which support human rights in Colombia.

half this sum is invested in the UK stock market and US$455 billion is invested in UK companies. So pension funds effectively own part of many large multinational companies. As pension-fund holders, ordinary people—many of them labor union members—have a right to express their views on how these companies behave, both in the UK and through global supply chains.

Since 1997, most occupational pension-fund holders have been directly represented by employee-nominated trustees, who have a responsibility to ensure that the fund maximizes returns. Recently, however, pension holders have begun to realize that seeking the best rate of return is not incompatible with "socially responsible investment"—taking into account the impact of investments on society, the environment, and human rights.

The War on Want Invest in Freedom campaign now offers an alternative approach to the traditional idea of ethical investment, more open to ordinary members of occupational schemes. Pension funds can adopt a strategy of "engagement" and use their shares to influence companies. Pension holders are entitled to ask fund trustees to act on their behalf, and trustees can then instruct the fund managers, who make day-to-day decisions about holding shares, to press companies for certain things like workers' rights. The Invest in Freedom campaign is based on the understanding that pension holders should take an interest in working conditions across the globe and ensure that their money is not being used to encourage poor labor standards.

There is growing evidence to suggest that socially responsible companies get better returns. Labor unions have argued for many years that workers who have decent employment conditions are more productive and that companies that protect their workers are less susceptible to negative campaigns. By joining War on Want's Invest in Freedom campaign, pension-fund holders can now make sure that by campaigning to improve labor standards across the world, their pensions can work for the world's poorest people as well as for themselves.

The union response has reflected both the importance and relevance of the campaign, which has been endorsed by the Associated Society of Locomotive Engineers and Firemen; the Broadcasting, Entertainment, Cinematograph, and Theatre Union; BFAWU; GMB; T&G; and UNISON. Meanwhile, the Communication Workers' Union, which represents members in two of the largest pension funds in the UK (BT and Royal Mail), will be running the campaign in conjunction with War on Want and will target all 300,000 of its members.

Global Workplace Website

The ultimate expression of a globalized world is the Internet; having a virtual presence to raise awareness and activity around the global economy is now essential. The Global Workplace website—www.globalworkplace.org—aims to be a point of inspiration for labor unionists who want a wider understanding of the global economy and its impact on workers and to give some direction to the ubiquitous question, "But what can I do about it?" Beyond War on Want's own attempts at further internationalizing grassroots layers of the labor union movement—with links to our own website—the site is also a portal for the work of labor unions and activists themselves. It is anticipated that the website will develop as an "information point" and become self-sustaining. Ultimately, it should include concrete examples; for instance, talking not just about the theory of twinning union branches but detailing the practice or providing not just a set of teaching materials but also feedback and examples of where and how successfully they have been used.

In terms of materials, the Internet allows a much more cost-effective use and delivery of diverse background materials, such as a video of our Global Workers' Forum in South Africa or interviews with unionists facing danger in Colombia. The links to War on Want's own site—www.waronwant.org—will become just one of many links to international campaigns on workers' rights.

OTHER STRATEGIES

In order to further strengthen the case for international work, efforts have been made to influence and to work directly with individual labor union members through their union journals and through workplace meetings.

Most labor unions meet annually for their decision-making conferences. The rest meet biennially. By having a presence at these conferences, War on Want makes direct contact with the leading labor union activists and officers from major unions. Having a presence also allows direct engagement with key people in the union movement, giving an opportunity to recruit them directly at some level into the campaign against world poverty. Fringe meetings and other events at conferences allow another opportunity for delegates to engage with the issues. We aim to have overseas or relevant speakers to make the global issues more local. Conferences also provide an opportunity to monitor the success of the project in terms of the number of international motions on the agenda and the number of other international organizations exhibiting and arranging fringe events.

It is anticipated that there will also be indirect beneficiaries of the Global Workplace project. Workers in the developing world will benefit when labor unionists in the UK are better equipped to take their needs into account during negotiations. A wider understanding in the UK of issues such as core labor standards will lead to greater implementation of such standards in developing countries—whether through consumer action, shareholder action, or lobbying. DFID and other agencies working in international development will benefit from greater support from the labor union movement of the campaign against world poverty.

CONCLUSIONS

The Global Workplace is a bold, multifaceted initiative aimed at increasing awareness of international development issues among grassroots labor unionists—a group of people who are almost by definition "active." Support for the project has come from the UK government's recognition that workers' rights are essential if globalization is to deliver for the many and not just for the few. As democratic organizations, labor unions are widely regarded as the best means of delivering this global message. As a fully accountable organization, War on Want is well placed to answer those critics who challenge the legitimacy of NGOs in general. Some labor unions already have an integral international structure, while others have only limited resources; through the Global Workplace project, War on Want hopes to be in a position to act as a facilitator for union action.

As discussed here, the Global Workplace project is aimed primarily at raising awareness among grassroots labor unionists. However, War on Want would not have been able to do this if there had not already been a history of good relations with many labor union headquarters. It is clear that to be truly effective, pressure for action needs to be both bottom up and top down.

Labor unions are moving into a new era, and a new generation of labor union leaders is emerging with a clear vision of the importance and relevance of internationalism in a global economy where there are very few workers who are unaffected by the tumultuous changes that are taking place. War on Want's campaigns and projects are well placed to work alongside them. The need for internationalism on the labor union agenda is not just about representing current labor union members but is also a means of rejuvenating the union movement. Workers' rights issues are on the agenda of young people, and it is essential that the movement capture their dynamism and show that it has relevance for them as potential labor union members.

NOTES

[1] For a detailed history, see the waronwant.org website.

[2] See Water Supply and Sanitation Collaborative Council, available online at the wsscc.org website (accessed December 5, 2003).

[3] Nelson Mandela, 2000 Labour Party Conference, Brighton, UK, September 24–28.

Ten

Working at the Intersection

A Story from Australia

KEN DAVIS

GENESIS

On June 6, 1982, the Israeli army invaded Lebanon following the attempted assassination of Israeli Ambassador Argov in London. Dubbed Operation Peace for Galilee, the invasion progressed rapidly. By June 18 the Palestine Liberation Organization (PLO) forces in the western part of the capital had been surrounded. A ceasefire, mediated by US Envoy Philip Habib, resulted in the PLO evacuation of Beirut on September 1. On September 11, Israeli Defense Minister Ariel Sharon stated that two thousand terrorists remained in the Palestinian refugee camps in Beirut. On September 15, the day after the assassination of Phalangist militia leader and Lebanese President-elect Bashir Jemayel, the Israeli army occupied West Beirut, encircling and sealing the UN-administered refugee camps of Sabra and Shatila. On September 16 the Lebanese Christian Phalange militia entered the camps. Over the following days they killed between eight hundred and thirty-five hundred (according to various Israeli estimates) unarmed and unprotected women, children, and old men.[1] Israel's 1983 Commission of Inquiry, chaired by Yitzhak Kahan, declared that Sharon, as minister of defense, bore personal responsibility.

In 1982 Helen McCue, an Australian nurse, was working for WHO in the Middle East. Horrified that the international organizations could allow this crime to take place, Helen resigned and turned up unasked to offer her services as a volunteer with the Palestinian Red Crescent in the camps in Beirut. On the border of the Shatila camp, in the Gaza hospital, where health workers had been killed, she met Olfat Mahmoud, a nurse who had survived the massacre.[2] At an awards ceremony in 2001 Helen described her experience thus:

> Along with Palestinian health workers we lived in one of the bombed out hospitals in the camp. We were better off than most of the refugees but still there was no electricity, no lighting, no heating and as it was winter it was absolutely freezing. On 5 March 1983, I was in bed, fully dressed in all the clothes I could muster, lying on a mattress on a cement floor and listening to the BBC world news on my small precious transistor radio. Bob Hawke's voice came over celebrating a Labor victory in Australia.[3] Ironically in a way, at that moment I knew that I had to go home to broaden the base of support for Palestinians and to somehow set up an organisation, based in the union movement. I felt that we were such a wealthy country and that as workers we had skills and knowledge to share, not only with Palestinians, but with workers across the world. I felt too that through such work we would be able to make our contribution to global justice and world peace. At that time I knew that justice for the Palestinians was then, and would continue to be, one of the central issues in determining world peace. For over two decades now I can say that I have been witness, tragically, to the deterioration of the physical, psychological, social and cultural wellbeing of four million Palestinian refugees. (McCue 2001)

The vision of a new Australian aid agency was thus born in the squalor and misery of the Palestinian refugee camps in Beirut in March 1983, initially a conspiracy of nurses. Also assisting in the camps were some foreign workers, among them volunteers from the labor union movement in Norway, and from Norwegian People's Aid, established as a labor movement–based humanitarian organization in 1940.

CRAFTING AN AUSTRALIAN LABOR UNION RESPONSE

Helen left for home on one of the last planes to carry the foreign aid workers who were being forced out of Beirut. In October 1983 she approached the leader of the Australian Council of Trade Unions (ACTU), Cliff Dolan, who, like Helen, was a Catholic with a strong sense of international social justice. Within twenty minutes he had agreed to support the establishment of a new labor union–based international humanitarian organization, the Australian People for Health, Education and Development Abroad (APHEDA). In November the ACTU executive endorsed this.

> In January 1984 we held our inaugural meeting and . . . APHEDA was named and formally established. Having put in some ground work with what was then the Australian International Development Aid Bureau (AIDAB), and with Bill Hayden as Foreign Minister, by February 1984 we received two government grants: one of AUS$30,000 for health worker support in Eritrea and the second of AUS$250,000 to train Palestinian health workers.[4] (McCue 2001)

APHEDA (which resonates with *benefit* in Arabic) is now called Union Aid Abroad. Initially the founders wanted to emphasize that the organization was concerned with broad issues of humanitarian aid and advocacy for human rights and social justice and so took a name like Norwegian People's Aid, albeit somewhat less elegant.

In addition to being chartered as the ACTU's international aid agency and granted core funding equivalent to four cents a year for each of the two million unionists, APHEDA joined up each union as a contributing member: 22 unions in 1985, 100 unions in 1987, and 190 unions by 1991. This number decreased radically as union amalgamations streamlined the Australian labor movement in the early 1990s. Now all unions bar the Shop Distributive and Allied Employees' Association are members.

Five of the nine Management Committee members are appointed by the ACTU executive, while the remaining four are elected by union and individual members. Maintaining a gender balance and, more important, a political balance between the left and right factions of the Australian labor union movement has been a hard-won success. All unions in Australia are part of the ACTU, whose member unions may or may not be affiliated with the Australian Labor Party, but who span the political spectrum from conservative, to post-social democrat and post-communist, to the Greens.

Unlike other international labor movement or socialist party–based agencies, such as Germany's Friedrich Ebert Stiftung, which build unions, undertake research and political education, and provide development aid,

APHEDA was set up with a "neutral" name for the purpose of humanitarian development assistance on behalf of the Australian organized working class.

PRACTICAL SOLIDARITY

Even from the start, while Helen was observing the Norwegians and other labor union aid workers, the focus was on providing resources for local training rather than providing relief directly. Retraining, upgrading, and empowering local workers had to be the central strategy, even during crises. At the time, however, few aid agencies or donor-country departments regarded training as a valid developmental activity.

The early ethos of APHEDA was that of solidarity with national liberation struggles, and partnerships—under the guidance of national liberation leaderships—that maximized the transfer of resources from Australia. From the first days APHEDA gave priority to projects for women and refugees. This was feasible, given the political space opened up in the wake of the opposition of the Australian labor movement to the US war in Vietnam. APHEDA's original motivations in national liberation struggles have meant that, as a relatively small aid agency, it has emphasized noninterference, self-determination, and decision making by autonomous implementing partner organizations.

Soon after an office was established in Sydney's grand but dilapidated nineteenth-century Trades Hall, representatives of national liberation movements and isolated socialist countries were brought to APHEDA by labor unionists, including the health minister of Vietnam, and Eddie Funde, the new regional representative of the African National Congress (ANC). The representative of the Eritreans also came, and though the independence struggle was opposed by much of the left, APHEDA began assisting. José Ramos-Horta, then in exile from East Timor, came to APHEDA, but at that stage there was little scope to help. Later the Kanak independence struggle in the French colony of New Caledonia was able to get substantial assistance from APHEDA for projects such as indigenous health.

APHEDA found it difficult to link with other European or North American labor union aid organizations, not wanting to be completely under the sway of union leaders' decisions or the policies of the international labor union structures, and aware that Cold War divisions then affected the international labor movement deeply. Also, APHEDA was regarded as too much an NGO because, unlike its European counterparts, its early partners were rarely labor unions in low-income countries, but rather community-based organizations, official mass organizations, or provincial government departments.

APHEDA was able to win large amounts of funding from Australian Labor governments for projects that furthered in a humanitarian way the national liberation struggles. But APHEDA did not cultivate good relations with all parts of the NGO aid sector in Australia and was not a member (until the early 1990s) of the 100–member Australian Council for Overseas Aid (ACFOA), which Helen regarded as too conservative and standoffish toward the ANC and Palestinians, among others.

There have also been some generational tensions among aid agencies. Some, like the Quakers, go back hundreds of years; others arise from missionary activities. APHEDA, by contrast, comes from the period opened up in the late 1970s by the victory of the Indochinese, Iranian, Nicaraguan, and Grenadian revolutions, while many of its larger international counterparts arose from the Second World War and the subsequent Cold War era (for instance, CARE, Oxfam, Plan International, and World Vision).

In the late 1980s APHEDA was able to gain substantial Australian government funding for "global education," because the unions offered reliable avenues to reach workplace audiences about development issues with the use of posters, articles in labor union newspapers, theater and musical groups, and modules delivered by the labor union trainers. Underlying the APHEDA approach was a belief in the dignity of labor and the right to work, and in international solidarity as opposed to charity and compassion. APHEDA could build on the member unions' specific identities and make bridges between Australian teachers and literacy programs, between journalists and training for democratic media, between nurses and women's health and traditional medicine programs, between metalworkers and village blacksmith training, between bank workers and microcredit projects, and between hotel workers and training for employment in the hospitality industry.

NEXUS

Unions in advanced capitalist countries don't spontaneously understand the complex humanitarian and development needs of countries such as Papua New Guinea, where waged workers are a small minority of the population, or Burma, where unions are banned. Unionization and workers' rights are only one part of the solution, and only one aspect—though essential—to developing democratic civil society.[5] Australian unions want workers in neighboring countries to be unionized in order to gain better wages and conditions as a means to defend job security for Australian workers. This understanding may not be shared with development NGOs, who rarely see the role of unions in winning decent wages, raising living standards, and expanding domestic markets as being central to national development strategies.

The other prevalent stance within unions is one of nonpolitical compassion: Australian unionists are most likely to respond by sponsoring a child through World Vision, though unaware of its evangelical objectives; by wanting to volunteer overseas; or by sending toys, computers, and clothes, without fully understanding or exploring the dynamics causing impoverishment or the actual needs or capacities of "recipient" organizations.

APHEDA was one of the strongest proponents of women in development strategies, and most training projects have focused on poor urban or rural women. Yet APHEDA has been reluctant to "advance" to the official "gender and development" agenda.

Initially the Australian government aid agency (now AusAID) granted funds for projects with minimal bureaucratic procedures. By the early 1990s accountability failures in the government and commercial aid sectors created more burdensome and intricate bureaucratic processes for the medium and small NGOs, to the exclusion of any understanding of the context and impact of development projects. Managerialism was triumphant. There was also an ideological shift by the Australian government back to charity models, and a corresponding retreat to neocolonialism in the NGO sector.

From the mid-1990s we struggled with the normalization of APHEDA aid programs: the democratic transition in South Africa, Eritrean independence, the peace process in Palestine, the UN process in Cambodia, the Matignon Accords in Kanaky, and the decreasing isolation of Vietnam. APHEDA projects were no longer on the cutting edge of struggles against imperialism, and the organization found itself facing an identity crisis— just one generalist development agency among many in Australia.

RESISTING GLOBALIZATION

In the last decade emphasis turned to work in partnership with labor unions on gender equality, literacy, cooperatives, HIV, and occupational and environmental health. These partnerships recognized labor unions as leading organizations in civil society and as uniquely placed to advance health and education agendas among working people. Only recently has APHEDA directly supported labor union training in Cambodia, East Timor, and Indonesia, under pressure from Australian unions, which see workers' rights in neighboring countries as crucial to their own fate. Reflecting greater confidence in the workers' rights agenda, and stronger ownership by its constituency and by the elected leaders of the ACTU, APHEDA began using the name Union Aid Abroad in 2000. This pride in our union base flies in the face of the political environment in Australia.

Following the election of a Conservative national government in 1996, there were attacks on progressive international aid agencies as part of the overall agenda of reversing women's, indigenous peoples', and workers' rights, and of handing over health and social security to the most conservative Christian churches. Australian governments have traditionally supported the military-political alliance with the United States, but none more so than those elected since 1996.

Overseas aid has been slowly dipping further below the OECD average, but the real deterioration is seen in the *quality* of aid, which has increasingly been defined in terms of "advancing Australia's national interest" and expanding free-market access.[6] Over 90 percent of the Australian official aid budget of AUS$1.7 million is "spent in Australia," with most of it contracted to a small group of development consultancy companies known as Australian Managing Contractors. Rates of profit-taking from the aid budget may not be publicly known, since details of major contracts are "commercial in confidence," but they are believed to be over 50 percent in some key instances.

The reelection of the Howard government in 2001 on an engineered tide of xenophobia, anti-refugee hysteria, and racism has thrown the future of the smaller and more creative and radical Australian NGOs into doubt. It has also caused the leadership of ACFOA to retreat from criticizing government funding or foreign policy. Open, competitive NGO funding windows will be replaced with a small number of longer-term "partnership" bilateral agreements with leading international development agencies. For Union Aid Abroad-APHEDA, the majority of project funding in most years has been derived from AusAID grants, yet core funding was from the unions. The main exception to "dependence" on government funding was the extraordinary mobilization of Australian workers to support the East Timorese struggle.

It is not simply the Australian political environment that has changed. More recent times have seen a return to conflict, including in those

countries where APHEDA has programs: Palestine, East Timor, Zimbabwe, Bougainville, and Solomons.

In this context, mandated to educate Australian workers on globalization issues, APHEDA finds itself often more partisan than other international development NGOs in Australia, and sometimes more circumspect.
APHEDA has never claimed to be apolitical and has always maintained
advocacy and activist campaigns, not only on mainstream development
issues such as landmines, but also on child labor, on Burma, and on independence struggles in Southeast Asia, the Pacific, Africa, and the Middle
East. While some major aid agencies in Australia argue against a human
rights–based approach, we seek to advance a distinctive workers' rights
and anti-colonial agenda within that framework.

Sometimes our allegiance to the labor movement hinders or delays
our speaking out. Traditionally, the Australian labor movement, which
championed Indonesian independence from the Dutch in 1948, and which
has provided several postwar Australian prime ministers, has been reluctant to challenge the territorial integrity of Indonesia. So there is a limit
to how far APHEDA-Union Aid Abroad, as an NGO chartered by all
factions of the labor unions, can go in advocating on behalf of Achinese
or Papuan independence. Strong relations with Vietnamese unions also
make close analysis of political rights in Vietnam unlikely.

While participating in the broad anti-globalization movement, and in
anti-WTO actions, as a labor union organization we find differences with
Oxfam, for example, on the fair trade agenda, particularly in relation to
strategies to defend specific workers' rights. As a labor union organization, APHEDA is also aware of the suspicion held by labor unions internationally of NGOs as not being democratically accountable through clear
mandates from memberships. In many cases development NGOs need
only market themselves to donors and report to appointed boards. Further, there is a history of hostility to unions by even progressive international NGOs. Many oppose union membership by their own metropoli-
tan or local field staff.[7] In Australia, of approximately seventeen hundred
staff of international development agencies, less than 15 percent are members of the Australian Services Union, and few agencies have legal agreements with the union. Those NGOs that support human rights–based
approaches to development often downplay the right to organize when it
comes to the industrial arena. Other NGOs, like CARE, which implement health projects among workers with support from employers, reject
working with unions, even in countries such as Vietnam, where unions are
by no means subversive of government. Labor unions are also suspicious

of NGOs that "service" or "educate" workers, substituting themselves for, or speaking in place of, emerging democratic unions, such as in Indonesia.

LABOR UNION–NGO ALLIANCES

Despite these suspicions, at the congress of the International Confederation of Free Trade Unions (ICFTU) in Durban in April 2000, a series of resolutions repositioned the world labor movement for the struggles of the new century, calling for labor unions to find ways to "organize the unorganized," such as informal-sector workers, and to build alliances with NGOs and civil society around shared values of human rights.

Not by accident, a key Durban congress resolution was on HIV and how labor unions should respond, including fighting for affordable treatments for workers in low-income countries and communities. Union Aid Abroad has supported HIV education with the Congress of South Africa Trade Unions since 1991 and now benefits from the exemplary lessons of the Treatment Action Campaign, which pioneered post-apartheid mass action with an alliance of churches, labor unions, NGOs, the medical sector, people with HIV, and community-based organizations.

As a labor union NGO, Union Aid Abroad is located in the middle of a challenging intersection. As a development agency, we have work experience with migrant workers and refugees, oppressed minorities, rural and urban poor, particularly women, and with advocacy alliances around key global solidarity campaigns. As labor unionists, we value the political and organizational heritage and lessons learned from workers' struggles in Australia and internationally.

SURVIVAL

In mid-2002, Union Aid Abroad came under attack from a conservative think tank in Melbourne, the Institute of Public Affairs, as one of a series of agencies critiqued by a spectral "NGO Watch." Specifically, Union Aid Abroad was accused of channeling Australian funds to strikers and separatists in Indonesia and of supporting Palestinian independence. This accusation was repeated in Jakarta newspapers and, after the Bali bombing, fueled the contradictory accusations in the Australian media that NGOs, such as Union Aid Abroad, were both provoking Indonesian retaliation and partnering terrorist movements.

Additionally, and surprisingly, the Institute of Public Affairs asserted that the "union movement itself does not bring unique skills" to implementing development projects (D'Cruz 2002). In reality, we are in a very privileged position in being able to source, for example, from health, journalists', and education unions, technical advisers for long-term in-country collaboration to transform pedagogy, agriculture, media, and primary health-care approaches.

Union Aid Abroad remains a medium-sized Australian aid agency, with around fifty projects in fifteen countries. It is one of the few larger agencies in Australia that is not affiliated to an international development alliance, such as Save the Children, UNICEF, World Vision, or Caritas. Until 2004 significant Australian government funds still flowed for particular projects, but the likelihood is after that, only union-donated funds will be available. The organization therefore faces decisions about its independence, alliances, direction, and sustainability. Without the "buy in" of Australian government funding, Union Aid Abroad, along with other Australian aid agencies, will be free to initiate smaller-scale but more ground-breaking projects in line with the demands of international workers' solidarity.

NOTES

[1] Based on "Flashback: Sabra and Shatila Massacres," available online at the bbc.co.uk website (accessed December 1, 2003).

[2] Since the late 1980s Olfat Mahmoud has been director of the Women's Humanitarian Organisation, which provides a range of services in the Burj el-Barajneh camp in southern Beirut. APHEDA has provided support to that organization since its inception.

[3] Bob Hawke, a former leader of the Australian Council of Trade Unions, was prime minister from 1983 to 1991.

[4] APHEDA's first major project brought nurses from the Palestinian camps to be trained in Australia.

[5] Unions have been the spearhead of winning democratic rights and democratic transformations in countries as diverse as Australia, South Africa, South Korea, Poland, and Zimbabwe.

[6] An example is the new AusAID strategy for Vietnam, which eliminates previous NGO projects in health and education in the poorest provinces, and defines the main aim as influencing Vietnamese public policy to facilitate accelerated foreign investment.

[7] One of the most notorious examples for over a decade has been Greenpeace in North America.

Part 3

Workers in the Informal and *Maquila* Economies

Eleven

Organizing Home-based Workers in the Global Economy

An Action-research Approach

RUTH PEARSON

In 1996 the ILO adopted a Convention on Homework that requires ratifying states to "adopt, implement and periodically review a national policy on homework" aimed at providing "equality of treatment between homework and other wage earners" (ILO 1996a). This convention, deeply contested by governments and employers' organizations over many years, for the first time recognized the rights of home-based workers as being on a par with other workers, even though most homeworkers lack a direct employment contract and do not work at the premises of those who are responsible for hiring their labor (Prugl 1999).

This was the result of many years of mobilization and organizing by and on behalf of home-based workers in different parts of the world. The focus on the ILO convention was based on the argument that homework, rather than being a remnant of previous modes of production that would disappear with modernization and industrialization, had spread through all economies of the world. It was also a conscious strategy to give voice and visibility to an important group of workers who remain unseen and unheard by policymakers and labor organizers.

But only two countries to date—Finland and Ireland—have ratified the Convention on Homework. This is not the place to enter into the many reasons why that may be so (for instance, its relatively low priority, the tripartite structure of the ILO, the focus on formal-sector employment by governments as well as international organizations, and the difficulty of monitoring and implementing such a convention given the invisibility of much home-based work). In addition, the interests and priorities of home-based workers, an estimated 80 percent of whom are female, have not been at the forefront of political or labor organizations outside specific networks—mostly of women workers, and mostly outside the international union structure.

At the beginning of the twenty-first century, however, the urgency of organizing home-based workers as one of the major constituents of informal employment has become more pressing. The process of globalization is characterized by deregulation, outsourcing, and the fragmentation of international supply chains. This means that corporations supplying Northern markets—such as Gap or Nike—no longer have to invest and produce directly in cheap labor platforms in order to achieve competitive levels of cost and quality. While much of this kind of branded production is subcontracted to locally owned factories, much production in consumer sectors that serve domestic markets is located in informal factories and workshops. Both types of subcontractors regularly or occasionally further subcontract stages or parts of the production process—such as assembling metal springs for factories making cars or plastic components for those making baby pacifiers—to home-based workers operating in their own private space.

This practice of outwork in many ways resembles what historians have identified as "proto-industrialization" in nineteenth-century Europe, when production of consumer goods was outsourced to family-based workshops. But while many commentators confidently expected that modernization and internationalization of trade and production would lead to the extension of factory production throughout the world, the current reality is different. Although some developing countries have industrialized in a manner that, at least until recently, has meant that the bulk of employment has been located within the formal regulated economy, in many such countries the informal economy continues to be the site of livelihood production for most of the population. Even countries such as Chile and Argentina—which in previous eras appeared to be achieving labor market structures that resembled those of the industrialized countries—have witnessed an "informalization" of the economy as factories have closed, public-sector employers have cut back, real wages have fallen, and ever more households have come to rely on what they can sell in the informal unregulated economy. In the formerly centrally planned economies of Eastern Europe, the transition to a privatized market economy has taken place over a comparatively short period, much of it accompanied by civil unrest and war. And in poorer countries such as Bolivia or Burkino Faso, where formal-sector employment never achieved a significant share of the (nonagricultural) labor force, poor urban and rural households increasingly resort to a range of informal activities in order to make a living.

Home-based work of various sorts appears to have increased with informalization. This is partly because, in the context of increasing competition and the need for flexibility, homeworkers are a flexible, dispensable, and cheap labor force whose invisibility makes it hard for them to demand higher wages, job security, or improvements in working conditions. Also, households worldwide have experienced constant pressure to increase their access to cash. Economic reform and structural adjustment policies in many developing countries have imposed direct charges (user fees) for essential services such as health and education, thus opening up cash-based markets for many elements of such services. On top of that, rural households all over the world have also faced declining returns for agrarian activities and have been put under pressure to diversify their income-earning activities. Moreover, in regions that have endured transitions from centrally planned to market economies—in China no less so than in Eastern Europe and the former Soviet Union—households that previously depended on secure employment in state-owned or managed enterprises and institutions are now having to explore multiple strategies to earn sufficient income to ensure their own survival.

It is difficult to find reliable evidence of the spread and extent of home-based work, however, not just because it is invisible but also because it gets lost in the general discussion of the informal economy. Much of the analysis on informal employment tends to present an undifferentiated picture of the kinds of activities falling within its compass, failing to distinguish between home-based work and other informal-sector activities, which include self-employment (including in own-account and family businesses), paid work in informal enterprises, unpaid work in family businesses, casual labor (where the worker has no fixed employer), and subcontracted work in informal workshops or businesses, which may be linked to both formal and informal enterprises. In an urban context this includes street vendors, domestic servants, and artisans; in rural areas it includes fishers, tenant farmers, and collectors of forest produce (Gallin 2001, 537). But not all these categories fall within the definition of home-based workers.

As with other aspects of the informal economy, earnings from home-based work are also underestimated, partly because of under-reporting but also because most home-based workers have multiple jobs, and census and other surveys tend to report only the primary occupation of the household or individual.

In light of these trends, the need for organization and representation of home-based workers is stronger than ever. Moreover, given the slow pace at which the ILO convention is being ratified, it is clear that international standards alone will not address the demands and aspirations of such workers. They need to be backed up with organization, though it is fair to note that the very existence of the convention is a major focus in many countries for extending the protection of homeworkers in national legislation.

Experience in the 1980s and 1990s has also indicated that organizing homeworkers is not a simple task that can be carried out along the lines of traditional labor union organization. The fact that most home-based workers are women; that they are often not perceived either by themselves or by others as workers; that they have no regular employment contract, wage agreement, or regular working hours; that their work is invisible to others in the community and to policymakers and government agencies; and that they are not considered entitled to non-wage benefits—such as health insurance and unemployment benefits—all makes organizing home-based workers an extremely complex task. In addition, given the wide variety of home-based work—and the very different political and economic contexts with which home-based workers have to contend—it is clear that, although organization is a common objective, the kinds of organizations that are possible, appropriate, or effective will differ according to circumstance.

This essay describes an action-research project that has the multiple objectives of mapping the range of home-based work in different countries, investigating the ways in which such work is embodied in local or international production chains, and developing a methodology that will facilitate the establishment of sustainable organizations of home-based workers.[1] It focuses mainly on Latin America and Eastern Europe, though the project is also active in India and has begun to explore the possibilities of extending to China.

WHO IS A HOMEWORKER
AND WHO IS A MICROENTREPRENEUR?

The terms *homeworker* or *home-based worker* cover a wide range of activities, though the former has tended to be used in Western countries, where homework is contrasted with the transition to factory production after the Industrial Revolution. In developing countries the broader term *home-based workers* tends to be used in recognition of the fact that the term *home* is not necessarily consistent with a private domestic space, and that women often work around or outside their home or travel to and from home in pursuit of different activities. This is particularly the case in activities related to agriculture or food processing. Recent literature and debates on the subject tend to make a distinction between "dependent" or "subcontracted" workers and "own-account workers," with the latter, according to one perspective, looking very much like "microentrepreneurs" (Prugl and Tinker 1997).

The Mapping Home-based Work (MHW) project uses the working definition that "home-based work is done in or around the home for a cash income" (Tate 2002). The established distinction between subcontracted or dependent homeworkers (who are paid by piece rate) and own-account workers (who operate without a direct supplier, contractor, or employer) is acknowledged, though it is nevertheless problematic. Key characteristics of subcontracted homeworkers—who can also be conceptualized as disguised wage workers—include payment by piece rate and lack of control over deadlines, designs, products, and raw materials. Own-account workers are by definition self-employed—seeking to design and create products that will find a market in order to provide a cash income for their households.

However, as our research indicates, the two groups share characteristics. First, both subcontracted and own-account home-based workers tend to achieve relatively poor earnings from this work. Most are engaged in multiple occupations—known as income patching—so that very often both of these kinds of home-based work are only one of many income-generating activities within a portfolio that may also include employment in informal sweatshops or in formal factories or offices. For example, the Women Working Worldwide report on a workshop held in October 2001 in Mumbai (Bombay) states that the workshop was "attended by 59 women workers. The majority were homeworkers but eight of the participants worked either in factories with 20 or more workers or in smaller sweatshops"; some of the homeworkers had previously worked in such units (WWW 2002, 30). Similarly, research by project partners in Brazil and Mexico indicates that many home-based workers are current or former factory workers, particularly in the garment sector. On the other hand, in various Eastern European countries many home-based workers retain either employment or welfare payments or pensions from

the public sector using the income from homework as one of many income-generating activities in a diverse portfolio.

The prevalence of multiple occupations is one of the explanations for
the under-reporting of women's employment in the informal sector
(Charmes 2000). Recent statistical analysis reveals that the real contribution of women's work to household income far outstrips the level of
employment recorded, indicating that it is multiple-earning strategies that
contribute to household survival in economies dominated by informal
employment. Statistical analysis also reveals a wide range of earnings
and income levels among households and individuals engaged in informal-sector activities. This diversity is found in both subcontracted dependent homeworkers and own-account home-based workers.

Some subcontracted home-based workers are engaged in processing
products that form part of a global value chain, meaning that the product
to which they contribute—usually involving labor-intensive finishing
work, like making trainer laces, sewing in labels, or assembling gold
chains—is part of an export industry. Others are engaged in processing
or assembling articles that are part of a chain of production organized for
the domestic market—for example, the manufacture of *argubattis* (in-
cense sticks), *bidis* (hand-rolled cigarettes), or leaf plates in India. Production is very often for both export and local markets, and part of the
differentiation within the sector may relate to whether the product is sold
internationally. In some cases home-based production for international
markets is long established (see Mies 1982 and Risseeuw 1988 for accounts of lace-making in Northern India and *coir* (jute) rope production
in Sri Lanka). But our research also indicates new kinds of export activity, such as the processing of seaweed in southern Chile for the manufacture of cosmetics in Japan and the United States.

As stated above, own-account workers are by definition self-employed.
They are usually responsible for collecting and assembling their own
raw materials, designing and manufacturing the products, and finding
and selling to particular markets. However, although some own-account
homeworkers may achieve the autonomy and control over production
and marketing that this definition implies, others only appear to be autonomous. Many own-account workers in fact supply a restricted range
of "middle men," for instance, Bulgarian knitters who supply traders who
then export their products over the border to Greece. Many own-account
homeworkers who produce handcrafts and handmade garments, using
raw materials they purchase or grow themselves, are also dependent in

the sense that they have no direct access or independent status in the market. While domestic markets face severe competition from cheap imports, buyers can set prices and quantities in an arbitrary manner, leaving homeworkers with little control over the flow of their work or the rewards for their production. Like subcontracted workers, they are another form of dependent workers rather than representing the autonomous home-based business that the term *microentrepreneur* suggests.

Whatever the differences, a major shared characteristic of both groups of home-based workers who are the focus of the MHW project is that they lack the opportunity or capacity to accumulate, that is, to invest in capital or machinery and grow into a profitable (or autonomous) business. This reinforces the argument of Prugl and Tinker (1997) that the distinction between dependent workers and microentrepreneurs is not a useful starting point for understanding or organizing homeworkers. More useful is the analysis of Grown and Sebstad (1989), who distinguish between the economic status of households involved in entrepreneurial activities in terms of the significance of home-based production for their economic prospects. Many households—including the bulk of those in the groups with which the MHW project is working—fall into the survival category, where very low-paid home-based work provides minimal cash income for daily reproduction. This kind of home-based work requires little or no machinery or access to utilities; it may be carried out on the basis of gathering natural products such as jute for rope, seaweed for cosmetics production, forest products for leaf plates, or bamboo for handcrafts.

Others undertaking home-based production—such as women in Bolivia who make sweaters, carpets, and handcrafts, or who produce food for casual sale in streets or markets, or who assemble leather footwear for international companies in low-income suburbs of Santiago, or who are manually assembling gold chains in Peru—often intermingle such activities with seasonal agricultural work. Many of these households have restricted access to earning money; their home-based work does not cover all the family's requirements, and so it often has to be combined with (mainly seasonal) agricultural activities or food processing, whether for sale or for consumption. These households are dependent on a narrow range of activities—which may be intermittent, seasonal, and poorly paid—and their home-based work reflects this; they operate at the bottom end of the market (for woven bags or knitted ponchos, for example); it is difficult for them to find markets to achieve a steady surplus over the cash cost of their inputs, never mind covering the cost of their labor time. They have little or no business experience and find it nearly impossible to achieve access to a market beyond their very local communities.

Grown and Sebstad (1989) also delineate households that are able to achieve some kind of security either through fairly well-remunerated activities in the informal economy or by having a number of wage-earning individuals. Households with access to a range of income-earning opportunities, including different kinds of home-based work, are more likely to achieve some kind of stability. This is the strategy adopted in many cases by households trying to maintain living standards that have been threatened by rapid economic transition—such as the decline of state enterprise and employment in Eastern Europe and the concomitant increasing reliance on private enterprise. Certainly, surveys undertaken for the project indicate that although the majority of home-based workers identified in Serbia and Bulgaria are not the sole or major income earners for their households, their contribution is crucial to the well-being and security of their families.

At the other end of the scale are households that are in a position to achieve "growth" on the basis of their informal income-generating activities. These are households or individuals who have access to working or investment capital, who have secure markets, and who can operate with a healthy return on the basis of enhanced labor productivity. These are often the enterprises that either show high rewards or indeed are able to employ other workers, such as the many informal sweatshops in the Brazilian town of Novo Friburgo, which produce underwear for the domestic and regional market.

The distinction between home-based workers and microentrepreneurs is not just a matter of semantics. Historically, policy approaches to homeworkers have been based on providing entitlements to social protection and non-wage benefits enjoyed by formally employed workers. By contrast, policy toward microenterprise has focused on the provision of credit for working capital and technical assistance with marketing, financial management, and production. However, as this and other research demonstrates, own-account homeworkers, while requiring better access to markets and microcredit, also need health insurance, health and safety protection, and pension provision. To lump them in the general category of enterprises, however small, is to lose sight of the precariousness of the work they carry out in order to ensure the survival or security of their families.

WHO ARE THE HOME-BASED WORKERS
INVOLVED IN THE MAPPING PROJECT?

The distinction made above helps to clarify the focus of the MHW project. The project works with homeworkers who generally fall into the categories of survival or security, or at some point between the two. Moreover, there is considerable variation both within and between regions. In Bolivia, for instance, many rural home-based workers are engaged in income-diversification strategies, often in conjunction with other household members, with very low returns for their labor. In urban households home-based workers are more likely to be working as dependent homeworkers, though many engage in a range of home-based work, such as producing handcrafts and so forth.

In Brazil the three sites of the project's activities reflect the different situations of home-based workers in that country. In urban Novo Friburgo the home-based workers with whom the project is engaged are mainly in households where previously one or more adults worked in a formal-sector job. Home-based production has often been a response to the breadwinner being made redundant; in these circumstances many men get drawn into tasks supporting home-based production. According to the general understanding of the term, these homeworkers would be categorized as dependent or subcontracted, which is indeed the case. However, if we use the more complex stratification classification, we could argue that these households are using home-based work to respond to changes in the economic environment that has threatened the security of households previously reliant on the formal sector. In Paciencia, however, a low-income "new" settlement on the outskirts of Rio de Janeiro, women have few alternatives to home-based work owing to the lack of employment opportunities in the formal sector; home-based work—assembling bracelets for sale on the international market through a complex chain of intermediaries—can be seen as an intermediate activity between subcontracted and own-account work. Participation in home-based work can also be seen as a strategy to achieve some income stability in the face of increasing male unemployment and the collapse of the contribution of male wage earners.

The third case study area in Brazil is quite different. Rocinha is a large *favela* in the south of Rio de Janeiro. This is a population with all the characteristics of social exclusion, including high levels of criminality and drug trafficking. Women within this community, particularly older women or women with small children, are unable to work outside the community and need to find income-generating occupations to support themselves and their dependents. Many of these women are engaged in a struggle for survival; in the absence of more lucrative subcontracted home-work, they have resorted to producing—either cooperatively or individually—consumption items such as handmade soap for sale locally, and their earnings are by definition limited by the low price of their products on the market.

The situation in Eastern Europe is also complex. The nature of the transition from centrally planned to market economies is such that many individuals previously employed in public offices or enterprises are now engaged in home-based work. People in these households may retain a public-sector post—but one that offers insufficient wages to cover the increasing cost of household survival. Or they may have been retrenched from such positions but still be entitled to a minimum pension or unemployment insurance. Homeworkers in Eastern Europe, especially those from the majority populations in different countries, tend to fall into this category, and there are many examples of home-based workers who have professional or technical qualifications. But such is the nature of labor market disruption that the previous activities can no longer provide for household reproduction—hence the clear strategy of working, often as own-account home-based workers, to develop new markets and new sources of income in order to reach a modicum of security for the family.

Some of these home-based workers are engaged in the manufacture of products such as traditional handcrafts. In previous eras the distribution and marketing of these products would have been supported by extensive state structures. By the start of the twenty-first century, however, these structures have disappeared and producers are left to secure raw materials and find markets as best they can. Some groups have experienced considerable deterioration in their standards of living. For Russian women settled in Lithuania, for example, the jobs in public-sector enterprises—the power stations or the hospitals—that previously employed them and their husbands are no longer available. Although previously a privileged group, they are now unable to realize any of their accumulated assets—by selling their houses, for example—and have no option but to resort to trying to commercialize products or services produced at home. In other countries too there are many professional women—teachers, doctors, computer programmers—who have either been retrenched or whose wages are so inadequate that they have been forced into home-based work to complement their main occupation. In addition to producing goods for sale, there has also been a rapid increase in home-based services including hairdressing and electrical and car repairs.

But in Eastern Europe there are also home-based workers who fall into the poorest survival category. They are very often migrant or minority women; for instance, Kosovar and Roma women in Serbia or Polish women in Lithuania tend to be excluded from the more lucrative markets and are an even more invisible group trying to secure a living outside the mainstream economy. In addition, the process of informalization that has been a feature of economic transition in Eastern Europe has meant that "there is a growing tendency of leaving factories and working at homes," and the production of garments for export relies on poorly qualified, mostly female labor (Bulgarian Gender Research Foundation 2001, 6–7).

The demand for subcontracted homeworkers in some Eastern European countries is boosted by the opportunity to avoid quota restrictions on exports from elsewhere. For instance, Turkish clothing companies find it profitable to source in Bulgaria and Romania; and Greek traders operating in Bulgaria are also supplying the Greek market for hand-knitted sweaters through home-based production around the city of Rousse in the northeast of the country. This work goes mainly to skilled homeworkers, but it is neither visible nor protected by national legislation. Many home-based workers producing handcrafts, including traditional embroidery have years of experience, but the national structures that previously ensured a market for their output have disappeared, leaving this group with no protection and little experience or skill in accessing markets or finding new buyers.

HOW THE MHW PROJECT WORKS

The design of the MHW project was based on the experience of researchers and organizers working with home-based organizations. The general aim is to improve the lives of home-based workers, ultimately by using the action-research approach to build sustainable and relevant organizations in different locations. The project stresses that general guidelines need to be adapted according to the specific trends in the local and national economy and the reasons why home-based work might be on the increase at this particular time. The project's methodology is to collect information about home-based work in a particular location; to work with home-based workers to analyze their situation, and to identify problems and priorities for action; and to devise plans for advancing strategies for change.

The project uses both horizontal and vertical mapping. Horizontal mapping refers to the process of discovering the nature and range of home-based work and the demographic and socioeconomic characteristics of those involved—a process described by Latin American researchers as "unveiling" home-based work. Horizontal mapping focuses on discovering the number and identity of home-based workers; their family situation; and the sectors, processes, and types of work in which they are involved. It probes the conditions of work supply; payment; and the different kinds of employment, subcontracting, and marketing arrangements to which they are subject. It is also concerned to identify formal and informal organizations with which home-based workers could liaise in order to explore alternative employment, training, and marketing possibilities, and to build up alliances for campaigning.

Vertical mapping is concerned with tracing the subcontracting or marketing chains with which different home-based workers are involved. These chains may be global—as many researchers have described in connection with the international garment industry (see McCormick and Schmitz 2002)—or national, confined to production and trade within a particular country. In some cases the chains may be very local—going no further than the nearest village or low-income housing settlement. In addition, there are chains that are characterized not just by geographical reach but also by institutional connection—fair trade marketing for international NGOs or production and supply for faith-based or diasporic networks. Vertical mapping is a central part of the project's approach because the isolation and exclusion of many home-based workers mean that they are often unaware of how their work fits into a global pattern or complex production chain. Unlike many academic approaches to vertical mapping, the MHW project includes an emphasis on organizational mapping—to identify potential allies from labor unions, consumer campaigns, NGOs, alternative trading organizations, government offices, and so on—and on case studies where vertical mapping has been used as a central part of successful organizational strategies. A clear differentiation is also made between the kinds of vertical chains and the different contractual relations under which they work, with separate sections for subcontracted and own-account workers. Although there is a great deal of academic literature on value chains (also referred to as producer chains and *filières*), the project aims to support organizers and groups to carry out vertical mapping from the bottom up, without requiring specialized academic training (see Barrientos 2002). In addition, it explores the extent to which uncovering the vertical chains can be the basis for the application of voluntary corporate codes of conduct to improve the work situation of home-based workers (see Brill 2002).

In both horizontal and vertical mapping the MHW project starts from the premise that homeworkers are the main stakeholders and an important source of information. The project has produced a pack for each kind of mapping, and these and other key documents have been translated into the languages used by local groups. The vertical-mapping pack takes groups through an analysis of the approach and provides suggested guidelines and tools (questionnaires, survey forms, etc.) to use in the action-research process. Both processes adopt an action-research approach, which is based on the involvement of home-based workers as subjects, not objects, of information gathering. This requires, where possible, the active involvement of homeworkers in the different stages of the research—from identifying home-based workers and organizing group meetings and training, to participating in seminars and meetings, entering into dialogue with government and international organizations, and deciding on organizational structures and campaigning priorities. The project envisions a two-way education process to learn about home-based workers' lives as well as to inform them about their rights and the importance of their economic role as workers around the world. In the Latin American participating countries, in particular, there has been significant emphasis on the development of local capacity and leadership as an essential component of the long-term sustainability of organizations initiated by the project.

ACTION-RESEARCH AND ORGANIZING

The characteristics of this action-research approach to organizing home-based workers in different countries have meant that the organizational structures and links established reflect the situation on the ground. In some countries, where there is a preponderance of own-account workers aiming at supplementing and stabilizing household income, we have collaborated with organizations already working to promote women's economic empowerment. Our experience in Latin America has been that the organizations acting as coordinators of the mapping project tend to be those with experience of working with formal-sector (factory) workers such as Ana Clara in Chile or Factor X in Mexico. Like Adithi in India, these organizations provide services and facilities such as training and have diverse experience with different groups of low-income women. In Bolivia the team is made up of activists from the Central de Mujeres with strong links to a union of informal workers. In other cases, such as Brazil and Thailand, the coordination has been undertaken by academic departments that have a commitment to community-based work.

In Eastern Europe the range of organizations with which the project has initiated its work reflects the diverse nature of home-based workers in the region as well as the recent political past, the survival (or not) of previously existing organizations, and the multiplicity of new organizations emerging to respond to the new economic circumstances. In Serbia, for example, the cooperating partners include the Association of Business Women in Belgrade, Vizija (Vision), a women's NGO aimed at supporting urban unemployed women; the Centre for Human Rights and Democracy; and the Women's Multi-ethnic Group in Seleus, the first rural women's NGO in the country. In Bulgaria the initial partner is the Bulgaria-European Partnership Association, a recently established NGO dedicated to the promotion of social, economic, and labor rights in both the formal and the informal economy. Recent work has also begun with labor unions and other non-state organizations.

The range of organizations involved contributes to the development of sustainable organizational structures that will respond to the wide-ranging concerns of home-based workers in the modern global economy. Some are linked with labor unions and modeled on traditional labor union approaches; SEWA (the Self-Employed Women's Association) itself is registered as a labor union and began as an offshoot of the Textile Labour Association.

The process of building homeworkers' organizations has also been varied. Founded in 1992, Ana Clara, an NGO describing itself as an "organisation and training centre for women workers," has strong links with the Chilean labor union movement. It focuses to a large extent on the training of women to take up leadership roles wherever they are active. It has established a number of small organizations in different *barrios*, five of which have formally registered as labor unions, which could form the network of labor unions for home-based worker and/or producer and marketing cooperatives. In Mexico the work has focused on an organization initially established in 1998 to work on labor rights with *maquila* workers in Tijuana. As subcontracting has grown in the border areas, Factor X has worked with home-based workers where women are engaged in a range of activities including garment finishing for the factories, handcrafts, snack foods, and household articles. In Bolivia initial contacts with the labor union committee and community organizations provided the basis for tracking and gathering home-based workers. In La Paz, El Alto, and Cochabamba, as well as with rural producers of Tiquina around Lake Titicaca, the project has begun to establish groups that aim to work with local labor unions and NGOs.

Brazil presents an interesting example of how different actors can contribute to organizing homeworkers. The coordination is carried out by an academic in the (community-oriented) social work department, and organizing in the different localities is being carried out through formal labor unions, community-based organizations, and cooperatives. Each structure presents its own possibilities and challenges. Each requires long-term, painstaking efforts to set up the nuclei of sustainable organizations that can carry the organizing strategies into the future.

ISSUES FACING HOME-BASED WORKERS

One of the reasons why organizing home-based workers is so complex is that the combination of their different contexts and the wide range of kinds of work and contractual and marketing relationships means that each group or subgroup finds different issues important.

All home-based workers face the problems of insecure orders and incomes, with a major preoccupation concerning their powerlessness in the face of subcontractors who delay and even withhold payments. However, the issue of invisibility—the cornerstone of the international campaign—presents its own complexities. In both Brazil and Mexico many home-based workers were reluctant to become involved in the research for various reasons. One factor was the fear of aggression from intermediaries on whom they rely for work, or fear that the subcontractors might take their business elsewhere. Others—as is the case in Eastern Europe— did not want to draw the attention of the fiscal authorities or health and safety regulators. These home-based workers are caught in a time of transition where the system of social protection and state purchasing and marketing is gone, but the regulatory framework remains a disincentive; professionals in Bulgaria, for example, have to pay an annual license fee to conduct any self-employed business, which can be a major disincentive to registration and so diminishes their visibility. Other workers expressed distrust of organizations because of earlier activities of religious sects; in other situations women did not want to get involved with political parties or labor unions, in which they had little confidence.

In many situations it is the invisibility of vertical production chains that obscures the perception of home-based work not only as a major contributor to the household budget but also to the regional or national economy.

Where home-based workers have been willing to organize, their priority ranking is also quite varied. Own-account workers need access to markets, advertising and promotion, technical assistance, and provision of training and credit. Subcontracted workers are most concerned about prompt and fair payment for work done, ending abuses (like accusing the worker of short-changing the supplier), and arbitrary changes in piecework rates (in some cases rates are different for men and women).

In many instances home-based workers were concerned with legal entitlements for pension and health care where these were extensively offered to workers in the formal sector; women whose husbands had access to social protection and insurance complained that not being able to access these through their own work reduced them to the status of a child or a destitute person. This has been a particular issue in Chile, which is undergoing a major reform of the public health system—reform that has largely ignored the existence and the entitlements of home-based workers.

But very often women home-based workers have little knowledge of legal or labor rights in their own country, and the organizations have to undertake substantive exercises in popular education and literacy before the bulk of their potential membership is able to make informed judgments about the priorities for campaigning and organizing.

CONCLUSIONS

In recent years the centrality of the informal sector and its increasing role in global protection has been recognized by at least some parts of the international labor union movement following the initiatives of the ILO on Decent Work and the Informal Economy (ILO/TUIS 1999). Dan Gallin observes that "the deconstruction of the formal sector through outsourcing and subcontracting . . . has led to a decline of labor union organization in most countries in the world," so that "the stabilization of what remains of the labor union movement in the formal sector now depends on the organization of the informal sector" (Gallin 2001, 536).

It is clear that the current concern of the labor unions for the organization of informal sector workers in general, and of home-based workers in particular, stems from the international lobbying and organizing of networks such as HomeNet International and, more recently, WIEGO (Women in Informal Employment Globalizing and Organizing).[2] For instance, the Home-based Worker Concern Society in Nepal reported that, since the Asian Regional Workshop on Home-based Workers in Ahmedabad, the participants from the Nepal Trade Union Congress and the General Federation of Nepali Trade Unions were aware of the need to organize this sector, given the widespread existence of home-based work in a range of sectors. Subsequently, the Nepal Trade Union Congress began to identify the presence and problems of home-based workers, especially women in given areas of Nepal. In 2001 a new society, the Home-based Worker Concern Society of Nepal, was registered—with the goals of organizing, initiating awareness activities, lobbying with labor unions as well as government, and networking (Pokhrel 2002).

This organization, which has been incorporated into the MHW project, is working particularly with homeworkers, mostly female, who are engaged in production of beaded necklaces, machine and hand-knitted woolen garments, and carpet weaving.

But labor unions need to proceed with caution in the matter of organizing home-based workers. What the MHW project indicates very clearly is that this is a slow process that is dogged by the lack of awareness about and visibility of many home-based activities in different areas, the hostility of policymakers who assume that homework is not significant and will disappear, and the historical lack of political and industrial agency on the part of this mostly female, highly marginalized, and isolated work force. It is hoped that the experience of the mapping project, together with the development of a participatory methodology designed both to explore the situation of home-based workers and to provide the opportunity and capacity for homeworkers to build their own organizations, will prove useful for the extensive challenges of constructing appropriate organizations and exploring feasible policy approaches that will benefit this long-overlooked section of the global work force.

ACKNOWLEDGMENTS

The author is research adviser for the MHW project, which is supported by DFID. The article greatly benefits from information, analysis, and advice from the project director, Jane Tate, as well as from a range of project reports and documents. The responsibility for errors, omissions, and inaccuracies remain my own.

NOTES

[1] This is a three-year project supported by DFID aimed at (1) strengthening the capacity of grassroots organizations through a program of action-research and (2) strengthening the capacity of the international organization in training and advocacy. The project is managed by Homeworkers WorldWide, the UK-based center of the international HomeNet network of home-based workers.

[2] WIEGO is an international network comprising labor unions, international development agencies, and organizations of women workers, including HomeNet and StreetNet (the international networks of homeworkers' and streetworkers' organizations), and SEWA (which has been organizing informal-sector workers since the 1970s). WIEGO has a number of programs to promote the interests of women in the informal economy. For further information, see the wiego.org website.

Twelve

Never the Twain Shall Meet?

*Women's Organizations and Labor Unions
in the* Maquila *Industry in Central America*

MARINA PRIETO AND CAROLINA QUINTEROS

THE *MAQUILA* INDUSTRY IN CENTRAL AMERICA

Relations between labor unions and NGOs are complicated and problematic the world over, though in some places more so than in others.
One context in which the complex dynamics of this relationship are most
clearly seen is in the so-called free trade zones in Central America, where
garment and textile manufacturing for the export market has undergone
rapid expansion in the last decade. This is largely due to the proliferation
of the *maquila* (assembly plant) industry, which all Central American
countries have promoted fairly successfully. National governments have
concentrated on attracting foreign investment through tax concessions,
and the *maquilas* are the easiest plants to install. These factories make
products for multinationals such as Gap, Liz Claiborne, Levi's, and Sears,
among others.

In terms of how many people the *maquila* industry employs, by 1999
there were at least 325,000 such jobs in Central America, of which between 65 and 95 percent (depending on the country) were held by women.
These women are on average twenty-three years of age and most are
unmarried (between 55 and 70 percent), although many have family
responsibilities (up to three-quarters of them are lone mothers).[1] Their
working conditions are disturbingly poor: long work shifts, low salaries, inadequate infrastructure in terms of safety and hygiene. There

are constant complaints about mistreatment by management, production goals that are too high, excessive control over the workers (for instance, no free access to the lavatory), frequent overtime hours (which are often obligatory and not properly compensated), discrimination against pregnant women, and sexual harassment. Freedom of association is almost a taboo subject for the workers in these factories. It is hardly surprising, then, that discontent and mobilization against working conditions should arise.

Central America has not generally been characterized by the presence of strong labor representatives who can engage and negotiate with the state. But it would be wrong to interpret any such shortcomings in terms of union action as passivity. On the contrary, there have been many examples of working women and men resisting their conditions of employment, and the *maquilas* are no exception. Despite the fact that labor organizers have faced severe repression in the *maquila* industry, each Central American country has also witnessed efforts to organize and strengthen groups who can represent workers' demands and intercede on their behalf.

Today, there are two principal approaches to pro-worker action in Central America: campaigns structured around defending labor rights by recourse to national mechanisms, or campaigns that adopt transnational strategies. The former rely on internal policies and procedures—legal claims through the courts and corresponding ministries, negotiation among national bodies (private enterprise, union, and nonunion organizations), negotiation within the company framework, or settling directly with the company. The transnational approach operates by placing pressure on the most vulnerable points at the top end of the production chain in which a given factory is located: the brand's corporate image. Such pressure essentially bypasses the state, seeking instead to use the global market itself as a means to convince consumers to force transnational companies to accept their share of responsibility for establishing decent working conditions. In this way, codes of conduct become tools for struggle and for action to reclaim established rights. These codes of conduct are understood here as documents that establish a company's values and intended performance on matters relating to how it operates in the area of labor rights.

Within any given Central American country those involved in these kinds of action may or may not be labor unions (Quinteros 1999, 2000). The unions have traditionally dominated the field of labor relations, but women's organizations are also emerging on the scene, a development that has led to problems of coexistence with the unions. These conflicts seriously undermine the chances of successful collaboration on labor issues in Central America, but the problem has scarcely been addressed from an analytical perspective. This essay is based on the experience and reflection of the authors, who have themselves participated in the events unfolding in Central America in recent years; the material on which the article is based comes from the authors' own observations, interviews, and fieldwork, in addition to secondary sources.

The essay concentrates on the importance of the relationship between labor unions and women's organizations, both of which are very active in the region. Given the nature of the conflict between the two types of organization, is it possible that they might one day both cooperate with and complement each other? More important, the main challenge for the entire labor movement is how to build inclusionary and strong national and international networks of solidarity in such a way as to make joint campaigns more effective. This is the underlying question we address here. We hope that this essay will offer some initial input into what will undoubtedly be a topic of future discussion and so contribute to a better understanding of some of the key actors on the Central American labor scene and of the relations between unions and women's organizations. The essay concentrates primarily on women's organizations that are involved in labor issues and uses gender analysis as a conceptual tool in order to understand the relationships among these organizations, the unions, and *maquila* workers. We argue that it is possible, though it will not be easy, to collaborate and coordinate efforts for the good of women workers in the Central American *maquila* industry.

PLAYERS INVOLVED IN LABOR ISSUES

Labor Unions and Their Weaknesses

Traditionally, labor issues have been a field reserved for—and jealously guarded by—labor unions. This is based on the view that unions are the authentic representatives of the working class, the institution par excellence that molds one of the forces of industrial society and working people. However, unions do not automatically embody these forces. Labor unions are shaped by the structures of the society to which they belong, constrained by the prevailing political system, and influenced by their own specific contexts as well as by their interactions with other actors within a wider setting. When these factors coincide in a way that favors the forming of labor unions, strong and autonomous organizations can emerge and become influential protagonists in the political arena.

Latin American labor unions have not experienced such a fortunate scenario, least of all in Central America. If the events of recent years have weakened what seemed to be the strongest unions in the region, the possibilities for unions to organize in new economic sectors such as the *maquila* are further reduced. In the garment-manufacturing industry, for instance, unions are almost nonexistent. With the exception of Honduras, labor union members account for less than 0.5 percent of workers in the *maquila* sector (Cordero 1999). Even more disturbing, again with the exception of Honduras, there appear to be no collective contracts with the *maquila* in any Central American country. Freedom of association would seem, in practice, to be a right that does not extend to the *maquila* workers in Central America. Under such conditions, it is almost impossible to unionize workers.[2] Attempts to do so have led to the sacking of workers in almost every case. Moreover, those who lose their jobs for having attempted to organize a union forgo the chance for any new work in the *maquila;* their names are put on so-called black lists (ILO 1996b; Cordero 1999). Nonetheless, beyond the repression of unions and the weaknesses of their local branches—often split along political lines—it is important to recognize that the absence of unions in the *maquila* is also due to the lack of appropriate strategies for organizing this new "proletariat."

A Response: The Emergence of Nonunion Actors

The difficult situation facing labor unions in Central America at the time when the *maquila* came onto the scene, in addition to a new proletariat made up basically of young women, explains in part why nonunion organizations are now actively involved in defending workers' rights in this sector. The emergence of these nonunion organizations has made it more likely that labor campaigns could be successful. Even more interesting, in our view, these organizations are shaping a new context for workers' struggles in Central America. Several women's organizations are now dealing with labor issues and working to defend workers' rights, especially in the *maquila*, where many of the problems concern not only labor and union rights but also questions of human dignity, given that allegations of physical mistreatment and sexual harassment are not rare in this setting.

There was a marked rise in NGO activity worldwide during the 1980s. This expansion corresponds both to the gaps and inefficiencies of the state in trying to satisfy social demands and to the attempt to fill the vacuum left by the weaknesses of traditional social movements. However, the growing presence of NGOs in activities that go beyond their original technical function is also a symptom of the weakness of civil society and of the so-called democratic deficit, which have resulted in both the inability of special-interest groups to organize and consolidate, and the failure of governments to satisfy citizens' needs (Sojo 1998).

Seen in this light, NGOs could be an alternative way for civil society to organize, bringing together various interests, making demands on the state, and, in the case of the *maquila*, also taking on the private sector. The activities of such NGOs, including women's groups, represent an effort to maintain the workers' capacity to act in their own interests at a time when labor unions cannot respond to their needs and in any case lack the political space to do so.

Women's Organizations

As we have said, women's organizations have begun to work directly to defend labor rights and have developed alternative ways to organize workers in the Central American *maquila*. Stressing the question of rights, they have focused on issues that do not form part of conventional labor demands: maternity rights, sexual harassment, child labor, the empowerment of women within their organizations, and the double working day, among others. For these organizations the *maquila* workers represent a new proletariat whose needs are best addressed by groups who can take into account not only the general problems facing all industrial workers but also the issues of gender. Two of the Central American women's organizations most active in this area are the Honduran Women's Collective (CODEMUH) and the María Elena Cuadra (MEC) women's movement in Nicaragua. Both form part of the Central American Network of Women in Solidarity with the *Maquila* Workers, which also includes women's organizations from other countries in the region.

CODEMUH began in 1989 as a grassroots feminist organization working in areas such as reproductive health, sexual and domestic violence, and self-esteem. Its founders come from peasant and labor union organizations who became committed to creating an autonomous feminist organization. CODEMUH's interest in labor matters began in 1992, when the founders extended their activities to the areas of San Pedro Sula and

Choloma, the major industrial bases in Honduras, and began to work with women in the *maquila*. Initially, they focused on encouraging women to organize so that CODEMUH could offer training in areas such as labor rights, reproductive rights, reproductive health, domestic violence, and so forth. When workers began to come forward with work-related claims, CODEMUH started providing legal assistance. Gradually, the organization began to get involved in various regional initiatives on the situation of women workers and was part of an effort to establish a code of ethics for the *maquila* in Honduras, which it lobbied the government to sign. However, the exclusive focus on labor issues and on creating new mechanisms for defending the rights of women workers started in 1997, when CODEMUH participated in the Independent Monitoring Team of Honduras, which began to operate in the Kimi factory. Subsequently, CODEMUH became involved with local labor networks as well as human rights and faith-based organizations that were also adopting approaches to labor activism (such as independent monitoring) that corresponded in turn to new campaigning strategies on the global chain of garment production. CODEMUH has always promoted women's rights and maintains its identity as a feminist organization.

MEC was founded in 1994 as an organization of women who had a marked (though not exclusive) interest in women's labor issues; several of its founders had worked in this area in the Sandinista Workers' Central union. The organization initially focused on women in the *maquila*, particularly in the free trade zone of Las Mercedes in Managua. Its principal activities were training workers about labor rights and accompanying them in resolving individual cases, especially claims for the payment of benefits or for reinstatement in the case of arbitrary dismissals and of women sacked while they were pregnant. Little by little its involvement went beyond such individual cases and MEC began to propose new government policies for the protection of workers, modifications in the Law on Free Trade Zones, reforms to the Labor Code, and the adoption of a code of ethics. This code, signed in 1998 by the Labor Ministry and some *maquila* owners, subsequently became a binding Ministerial Agreement.

At the same time, MEC expanded its activities into areas not necessarily related to the *maquila* and became a decentralized structure with a number of regional offices. Nonetheless, the work in the *maquila* remains MEC's main activity, and it has built up a solid national and even international reputation in this area. The work continues to cover assistance and accompaniment in taking forward individual claims, lobbying

the government to enact reforms to the labor law, and training and organizing work with *maquila* workers.

MEC has not intervened in collective claims or been involved in
transnational campaigns. It focuses mainly on making demands of the
Nicaraguan government rather than on the chains of global production
(which are, by definition, transnational). By contrast, CODEMUH has
intervened on issues such as the right to form labor unions and has participated in initiatives involving organizations not based in Central
America, believing that the global chains of garment manufacturing fall
within the scope of its work.

Despite their difference in focus, MEC and CODEMUH are both reshaping the way that workers can press their claims, responding to the
needs of a working class that is very different from the industrial workers
that have traditionally influenced the unions' agenda. The preference for
collaborating with women workers, albeit not to the exclusion of men,
has brought new labor demands to the fore. This, in turn, has created a
need for new ways of organizing and representing workers' interests, all
of them quite unlike the typical labor union approach.

These women's organizations claim that their work takes place in areas
that the labor unions cannot reach. As one member of CODEMUH puts it:

> The new actors are playing roles that previously belonged to
> the unions, but that the unions did not take on. For example,
> the issue of child labor was not taken up by the trade unions
> but by NGOs working on human rights issues. Perhaps now
> it is not so obvious that there are minors working in the
> *maquila,* but in those days [the early 1990s] it was scandal-
> ous. There were girls of thirteen and fourteen years of age in
> terrible situations. What else could we do?

Today, then, labor unions are no longer the only organizations demanding respect for labor laws and defending the rights of working people.

RELATIONSHIPS BETWEEN NGOS AND LABOR UNIONS

Many labor union representatives question the fact that women's organizations are participating in the field of labor demands. The unions challenge the legitimacy of women's organizations in representing women

workers. They believe that the only representatives of the working class are the labor unions and will therefore belittle any other initiatives, especially if they do not lead to the formation of unions (Compa 2000, 12). Referring to its relationship with MEC, one member of the Sandinista Worker's Central said:

> We have suggested that MEC should collaborate in the process of creating unions. They are doing some good things— they have promoted the rule of law, labor rights, and gender issues. That is good, but they have not been able to work for strengthening the unions. Perhaps they think that if they focused on organizing unions, they would lose their social base. We believe that they should think just the opposite.

Other critiques of nonunion organizations that are involved in labor matters vary from arguing that they are unstable because they depend on external funding and because their leadership is not elected by members, to more extreme claims that they lack experience, have hidden agendas, or are sectarian.

Women's organizations insist that they became involved in defending and promoting labor rights because labor unions were unable to attend to the needs of women workers in the *maquila*. They maintain that as long as unions do not change the way in which they organize and begin to view the problems in a different way, their organizing efforts in the *maquila* will not be successful, because women workers face not only the same problems as male workers but also have very specific problems such as sexual harassment, lack of maternity protection, and so on. A representative of one women's organization commented that "there are many women who wish to organize, but when they go to the labor unions, there is no response to their demands."

Women's organizations say that they do not oppose labor unions, but that they want to ensure that women can be the protagonists in their own struggles and that women workers can gradually be in a position to assess labor union structures from their own perspective. Their focus is on empowering women workers to organize themselves in whatever way they consider appropriate. As one member of CODEMUH put it: "The workers have the right to organize in whatever way they want. The important thing for women's organizations is training first and then formal organization." Nonetheless, she disagreed with organizing women in order that they then join traditional unions, especially given the current lack of collaboration and coordination between themselves and the unions. She also maintained that the methods and tactics of traditional unions are not effective, because the frequent result of union action is that people lose their jobs. As another worker, organized in MEC, stated, "It is very rare that anything good comes from striking." Yet another member of a women's organization commented, "It is unfortunate that the unions in Central America are so weak, but this is why organizations like MEC, MAM [the Mélida Amaya Movement in El Salvador], and CODEMUH have to take the initiative in improving working conditions in the factories."

Since the 1990s women's organizations have attempted to approach some of the labor unions but without significant results to date. They believe that it is possible to coordinate with the unions, but that they must find ways to handle the relationship so that the alliance is effective for women workers and based on mutual understanding and respect.

DEEPENING THE RELATIONSHIP BETWEEN ORGANIZATIONS AND UNIONS

Given their different perspectives, it is not surprising that the relationship between labor unions and women's organizations is so complex. The differences between their respective positions result from the way they relate to power, which, although it may not be clearly visible in the debates, is what underlies the conflicting discourses. We need to look more deeply at this if we are to understand the fundamental causes of these differences—and we need to apply a gender analysis to this task (Bickham Méndez and Köpke 2001).

From a gender perspective, women and men occupy very different places in the labor market. Women tend to have jobs that are worse paid, less valued, and entail more difficult working conditions than do men. Nor does having paid work exempt women from their reproductive responsibilities. They therefore face a double working day: the productive shift they perform in the labor market and the reproductive role they carry out in the home with their families. This reality is frequently ignored and attention is seldom paid to women's demands regarding maternity protection and the family responsibilities of working people.

Over and above this, women have been rendered invisible in the history of economics and politics, although this is gradually beginning to change through pressure from individual women and women's groups.

Women's organizations like MEC and CODEMUH are dedicated to ensuring that the voices of women workers are not left out and that their efforts do not remain invisible. At the same time, women's organizations regard reproductive work as important as the job in the factory and adopt a holistic focus based on the recognition that women's needs in relation to their work cannot be separated from their needs as individuals, as women, and as mothers (Prieto, Hadjipateras, and Turner 2002).

Unions have not been wholly successful in their strategies for recruiting women and are frequently criticized for their lack of consideration to matters such as the double working day and women's family responsibilities. In addition, and despite some limited progress—mainly in unions in the North and in international confederations (Cunnison 2002; Munro 2001)—there is an almost total absence of women in positions of power in unions worldwide; one explanation for this appears to be male resistance. Many women who formerly belonged to labor unions and are now active in women's organizations have recounted their experiences within the unions:

> Suddenly the men closed the space that the women had succeeded in opening. For example, the leadership of a federation withdrew the funds from the projects for women and designated them for mixed-sex projects. Moreover, in many cases the women's projects were subject to the authorization of male leadership. (Bickham Méndez and Köpke 2001)

From their perspective, unions believe that they represent the basic contradictions of contemporary capitalist society and are the legitimate representatives of the interests of workers (understood to be men). Unions are organizations within which the exercise of power has always been essentially masculine, not only in terms of the gender profile of their rank-and-file members and leadership, but also in terms of the ways in which power is handled. Women's organizations see themselves as part of another type of movement, one in which people establish shared interests not in relation to work but in terms of identity (ethnicity, gender, nationality, and so on) and in response to global issues such as the environment and human rights. In other words, women's organizations link into all those issues that used to be considered subjective or private matters or simply a question of demographics. These new social movements do not envisage the establishment of any particular political regime; rather, their utopian visions are about gender equity, a proper relationship with the natural environment, and the universal adoption of basic human rights (Garretón 1998).

Another major difference in the way that labor unions and women's organizations function is in relation to their attitude to power. Women's organizations and those born out of the feminist movement, for example, are characterized by informal organizational structures and a strong distrust of authoritarianism.

NEVER THE TWAIN SHALL MEET?

The different approaches to labor activism in Central America have fueled debates about who legitimately represents of working people. This essay has presented some of the main issues that have been the subject of discussion since the late 1990s.

Although the tone of the debate differs from one country to another, women's organizations tend to favor coexistence with the unions based on mutual acceptance and respect. Both types of organization have their limitations and weak points, but they share the common objective of improving working conditions in the *maquila*.

Women's organizations are helping to make visible the needs of an emerging proletariat in the *maquila,* and they focus directly on empowering women workers. Meanwhile, the unions draw strength from their own historic struggles and have a legal mandate to negotiate on behalf of working people. The two types of organization occupy parallel spaces and have no need to compete with each other. In principle, it is possible to coordinate in a way that plays to the strengths of both the labor unions and the women's organizations, learning from and complementing one another to the benefit of working men and women. But the basis for such coordination must be that of mutual recognition and respect, something that as yet is still wanting.

—*This article was translated from Spanish by Mary McCann.*

NOTES

[1] The statistical information is based on fieldwork undertaken by various organizations and, in particular, by Cordero (1999), Carrillo (1999), and Naranjo Porras (2000).

[2] In the case of Costa Rica the importance of *solidarista* organizations (management-sponsored alternatives to labor unions) must be taken into account. In 1999 there were 1,981 such organizations with a total of 211,038 affiliates. By contrast, there were 662 registered labor unions. Certainly, *solidarista* organizations appear to be favored by the *maquila* owners and represent a serious threat to the Costa Rican union movement.

Thirteen

Beyond the Barriers

New Forms
of Labor Internationalism

ANGELA HALE

Concern about working conditions in a global supply chain has brought unions and NGOs in the North to the same table. Collaborative initiatives include campaigns such as the European-wide Clean Clothes Campaign (CCC) and ethical trade forums like the UK Ethical Trade Initiative. Relationships have not always been easy. Unions and NGOs have different ways of working, and there has been lack of sensitivity on both sides. What we see emerging, however, are new forms of labor internationalism that can respond in effective ways to the threat globalized production poses to workers' rights.

Workers themselves are struggling with problems of how to organize and voice their grievances within the context of international supply chains. In many workplaces fully functioning labor unionism is simply not possible. The problems are particularly apparent in the labor-intensive industries that supply the world market with consumer goods, such as garments and fresh produce. In the absence of effective labor unions, NGOs have often been important not only as a source of local support but also as a channel to international networks. Where labor unions do exist, there have sometimes been tensions similar to those in the North but there are also many examples of collaboration. In both the South and the North, the reality is that when people from labor unions and NGOs work together on particular disputes or campaigns, their differences tend to disappear.

NGO INVOLVEMENT WITH WORKERS:
FILLING THE GAP

NGOs have been particularly important in situations of labor union repression, which can range from assassination to periodic harassment. Bogus unions may be established that serve the interests of employers and create disillusionment among workers. In such cases, it has often been easier for support to workers to be provided under the cover of a religious or human rights agenda. For example, under the Suharto regime in Indonesia, only one labor union federation was permitted, and it was largely controlled by the state and the military. However, human rights organizations were allowed to operate, and they provided not only immediate support for workers but also the basis for the development of democratic labor unionism once this became legally possible. Many of Indonesia's new labor unions have developed out of these NGOs.

Crucial support has also been provided by NGOs in particular contexts where labor union organization is difficult. In many export processing zones, unions are legally allowed, but the reality is that their presence is blocked. Governments deem it necessary to prevent any signs of labor unrest in order to encourage inward investment, and so even when labor unions are legal their activities are highly constrained. Many of the workers in export processing zones are young women who live together in boarding houses. Rather than seeking to join labor unions, they have developed their own ways of organizing. In many cases they are supported by small NGOs, often initially associated with a religious organization. In Sri Lanka, for instance, a number of women's organizations—such as the Women's Center, Da Bindu, and We in the Zone—have centers just outside the zones that have provided a basis for organizing. Again, it is such groups that provided the groundwork for the establishment of the new Free Trade Zone Trade Union once the legal situation changed in December 1999 to allow this.

While many NGOs are facilitating the development of labor unionism, there is also pressure from NGOs to change the nature of labor union organizing. The way in which the global economy is developing makes traditional forms of workplace organizing more difficult. Workers in globalized industries—such as garments—are in widely dispersed workplaces, with their ultimate employer on the other side of the world. In any case labor unions have never adequately represented workers outside main production units, the majority of whom are women. NGOs mainly initiated and run by women have emerged to fill this gap. They have often encouraged workers to develop their own associations or labor unions but with the home or community rather than the workplace itself as the focal point of organizing.

For example, Ana Clara in Chile, which is organizing homeworkers in garments and footwear sectors in Santiago and Concepción, has brought workers together and encouraged them to form unions, four of which are now registered. Ana Clara is a member of HomeNet, the transnational network of homeworking organizations, and so it is also able to provide local homeworker unions with links to global organizing. Similarly, the Korean Women Workers' Organisation United has initiated a new Women's Trade Union to meet the needs of the growing number of women workers who are in casual, unregulated employment. They too encourage new forms of organizing at a local level while maintaining links into a number of international networks such as Women Working Worldwide (WWW) and the Committee for Asian Women, based in Thailand.

The important thing about these new organizations is not whether they are called NGOs or labor unions, but rather their willingness to address the real needs of workers and to accept different ways of organizing from the standard labor union model. An openness to new ways of working makes it possible for NGOs and labor unions to form alliances that greatly strengthen the workers' movement. The problems faced by such alliances are less about how to bring unions and NGOs together than about how to deal with the power of corrupt unions or the involvement of bogus NGOs. For example, in Kenya, Workers' Rights Alert has formed as a loose alliance of NGOs and democratic labor unions with a common concern about the erosion of workers' rights in globalized production. The alliance has built campaigning links with organizations in Europe such as the Centro Nuovo Modello di Sviluppo and WWW. The effectiveness of such alliances is demonstrated by their success in establishing union rights on Del Monte plantations and their recent achievement in bringing flower-farm employers to the table in a new Stakeholder Initiative.

WWW AND ITS CODES OF CONDUCT PROJECT: AN EXAMPLE IN PARTNERSHIP

All WWW's own programs have involved both labor unions and NGOs. WWW works with a network of women workers' organizations and other organizations that have a strong gender component. The focus is on supporting workers in industries that supply the world market with consumer goods such as garments. The organizations involved include autonomous women's organizations, such as Karomjibi Nari in Bangladesh and the Women Workers' Organization in Pakistan, and also women's programs within labor unions, such as the National Federation of Labor in the Philippines. When representatives of these organizations meet together in project workshops, there are no differences or tensions between representatives of NGOs and labor unions. All are equally committed to the rights of women workers and to the principles of genuine labor unionism.

WWW's recent educational and consultation project on company codes of conduct is an example of this way of working. The project involved organizations working with garment workers in seven Asian countries. The results demonstrate the unity in approach to labor unionism among all the organizations involved, whether NGOs or labor unions. By the time the final report was issued, they had all reached a similar position on the relationship between codes of conduct and labor union organizing. All saw company codes of conduct that did not include the right to organize as either a waste of time or counterproductive. Also, all saw the development of genuine labor unionism as more important than the establishment of company codes. Some felt that codes could only be useful to workers if they were already able to organize in unions. However, some felt that organizing around codes could contribute to the development of labor unions, and in fact this actually happened in one or two cases during the course of the program (in Indonesia and Pakistan). These differences were not related to whether the representative came from an NGO or a union, but rather to the different political context in which the representative is trying to work. All agreed that educating workers about the existence of company codes helped them to be aware of their rights and gave them greater confidence in trying to organize and voice their demands.

Another clear finding of the WWW codes program was the value that workers' organizations placed on consumer-based NGOs. Workers were not previously aware that NGOs in the North were campaigning on their behalf, but once they realized it, they immediately saw their value and called for stronger worker-consumer links. The development of consumer campaigning has added another dimension to the workers' struggle. Many Northern labor unionists were unprepared for this, and sometimes campaigners have caused ill feeling by failing to understand or consult with the relevant labor union structures. However, once the initial tensions have been overcome, the value of collaborative action is generally recognized. As far as workers in the South are concerned, WWW's experience is that when their own demands form the starting point, there are no real tensions about whether support is being provided by labor unions or by NGOs.

OTHER EXAMPLES OF LABOR UNION– NGO COLLABORATION

Examples of successful labor union–NGO collaboration at an international level can be seen in the CCC, a Europe-wide network of NGOs and labor unions campaigning in support of workers' rights in the globalized garment industry. The focal point is in the Netherlands, but all member countries have a national platform and initiate their own programs. Although key players are mainly NGOs, the national platforms in Belgium, France, Germany, the Netherlands, and Sweden all include strong labor union representation. Collaboration takes place not only on campaigning and solidarity action but also on debates about effective mechanisms for the implementation of codes of conduct and other protective measures.

The UK platform of the CCC is the Labour Behind the Label, which WWW has helped to coordinate as a network since 1995. While it began as an alliance of NGOs, membership now includes all the labor unions that organize UK garment workers. With minimal resources the network has provided valuable support to workers' struggles through the recognition that all organizations have a specific role to play and different target audiences. While organizations have continued to run their own separate campaigns, decisions have also been made to focus jointly on particular issues or events and to support one another's initiatives. Collaborative action has included a Euro 2000 football campaign and the targeting of particular companies such as Gap and Disney with street demonstrations and postcards from consumers. It has also included letter writing in support of urgent appeals from workers' organizations and the hosting of workers' representatives from producing countries. In 2001 the focus was on a living wage, an initiative that incorporated the UK labor union and homeworker campaigns for the implementation of the minimum wage for all garment workers.

CONCLUSION

What can be seen in all these developments is the emergence of new forms of organizing in response to the globalization of production chains. The most successful initiatives involve not only labor unions and NGOs, but also organizations in both the North and the South. The CCC, for instance, is a Northern-based initiative but works in close alliance with workers' organizations in the South, not only consulting them on campaigning issues but also providing direct support to workers in factories supplying European retailers. This usually takes place in response to particular disputes, the majority of which concern the demand for labor union recognition. Meanwhile, the Workers' Rights Alert in Kenya is a Southern-based initiative that succeeded in bringing collective rights to Del Monte pineapple plantations because of links with an Italian NGO. What matters in these alliances is not so much whether an organization is a labor union or an NGO, but whether it is genuinely working in support of workers, listening to their demands, and representing their needs.

Part 4

Workplace Codes of Conduct

Fourteen

Who Should Code Your Conduct?

Labor Union and NGO Differences in the Fight for Workers' Rights

RAINER BRAUN AND JUDY GEARHART

The plight of workers in developing countries has become a hot issue over the last decade, thanks to a highly successful campaigning streak by labor unions and NGO advocacy groups. Their campaign successes have led corporations, labor unions, and NGOs to search for ways to improve working conditions internationally through various cooperative efforts. Yet the switch from a campaigning to a solutions phase has created unexpected tensions between labor unions and NGOs—they have become "wary allies" (Compa 2001). These tensions risk impeding the current political momentum behind the labor rights debate.

Corporate codes of conduct, along with the creation of systems to monitor corporate accountability, is one area where NGOs and labor unions encounter differences. Their disagreements range over several questions, from major discrepancies over what constitutes a living wage to the technical aspects of monitoring and strategic questions about the specific obligations of local producers, brand-name companies, and retailers. In some cases tension has turned into outright suspicion over who should monitor workplace conditions on an ongoing basis. This specific controversy has the potential to turn the NGO–labor union relationship from one characterized by complementarity to one based more on competition.

There is still no consensus—either within each group or between the two groups—about the purpose of codes of conducts and their implementation, but it is worth identifying basic trends in the perspectives that NGOs and labor unions each bring to shaping them. Although both groups share the same goal—to ensure the human rights of workers in a globalized economy—they disagree over how best to achieve this goal. This conflict is rooted in a fundamental misconception about the intent of codes of conduct. It is our view that codes of conduct ought to be understood as preliminary tools in a global campaign to alter the power relationship between capital and labor, and not as an isolated effort to improve working conditions in selected factories. As such, codes of conduct function as a wedge intended to open up political space by empowering workers, which will bring about social change. Codes of conduct as an instrument by themselves should not be seen as sufficient for bringing about social change, no matter how sophisticated their technical implementation becomes.

Employing a human rights perspective, we argue that there is a *conceptual* difference between labor unions and NGOs, and human rights NGOs in particular, regarding codes of conduct.[1] Each group seeks to influence power—both economic and political—but through different strategies. This chapter briefly sums up how labor unions and NGOs came together to advocate labor rights and promote codes of conduct, before discussing their institutional differences and their respective approaches to human rights. We believe that the similarities of intent between labor unions and NGOs far outweigh their strategic differences, and therefore that better collaboration between the two is both possible and desirable.

LABOR RIGHTS ADVOCACY STRIKES BACK

Labor rights in developing countries, in the past a fringe topic at best, have caught public attention. Bringing the plight of workers abroad into public awareness has been successful due in large part to a concerted effort by labor unions and human rights NGOs. Issues such as child labor, unfair wages, and inhumane working conditions have come to the attention of a wide audience in industrialized countries.

The public is highly receptive to stories about labor abuse. These accounts remind us of the realities of a globalized production structure, where not only goods but even the manufacturing and service processes that create them can be transferred at a whim. The existence of locations with drastically lower standards implies the threat that similarly low standards will be necessary at home to remain competitive. This is why globalization is increasingly viewed as a race to the bottom, where achievement of social protection will be sacrificed on the altar of international competitiveness—even in industrialized countries. As Dani Rodrik cautions, "Social disintegration is not a spectator sport—those on the sidelines also get splashed with mud from the field" (Rodrik 1997, 7). The fight against sweatshops, therefore, is not a remote issue but one that hits close to home.

Labor rights advocates understood this dynamic early on and made exploitative working conditions one of the ignition points in the globalization debate. Today, the fight against sweatshops is supported by a broad coalition of groups, including consumer activists, development organizations, and students. They coalesce around growing movements like the European-wide Clean Clothes Campaign (CCC) and the US student movement United Students against Sweatshops.

International labor rights campaigns increased significantly during the late 1980s, when some of the negative social side effects of neoliberal development policies became more apparent. Outward-oriented development policies invited transnational corporations (TNCs) to outsource an increasing share of their manufacturing processes to developing countries. In turn, dramatic reductions in transportation and communication costs, as well as a profitability crisis (Harrison and Bluestone 1988), induced companies to relocate some of their low-skill manufacturing processes to places with large, untapped labor resources and low levels of social and environmental regulation. While labor market flexibility and export-led growth did generate massive employment in developing countries, this success story often came at the price of exploitative working conditions.[2]

The presence of TNCs in developing countries (or at least the presence of some of their production) led labor rights campaigners to shift their advocacy away from governments to corporations. In the apparel sector, labor unions had tried to pin the label of responsibility for sweatshop conditions on retailers and brand-name companies for decades, as they have the most clout in clothing manufacture (Glickman 1997). The presence of brand-name manufacturing in developing countries, which yielded first-world levels of profits under third-world levels of industrial relations, gave US labor unions a target and a justification for activism abroad.[3]

Human rights NGOs taking on corporations is a much younger—and somewhat unexpected—phenomenon. Having focused on civil and political rights for decades, human rights NGOs began to address economic, social, and cultural rights seriously only after the Cold War. They joined social justice and development groups in debates that looked more closely at the economic and social structures that often underlie violations of human rights in developing countries. Meanwhile, the package of neoliberal policies promoted by the Washington Consensus led governments of developing countries to downsize substantially in the 1990s. As a result, human rights groups came to realize that their public-sector advocacy resembled barking up a bonsai tree, particularly with regard to economic, social, and political rights, which involve a government's aggressive action in providing services to vulnerable groups. As governmental power shrank, the power and reach of global corporations increased, and NGOs started to look at the relationship between TNCs and human rights. The focus on TNCs brought human rights NGOs more fully into the field of labor rights and, with the subsequent development of workplace codes and external monitoring systems, more formal coalitions emerged.

Human rights and labor movements in the United States still largely run on parallel tracks. But together they have put down the groundwork for what has become a tremendous political momentum with staying power. Labor rights are now discussed vociferously in national and international forums. The campaign for a so-called social clause linking labor rights to trade agreements had been stalled for years, but the debate over sweatshops gave it new life. The idea of codes of conduct is inextricably linked to these debates, for better or worse. Codes of conduct are being discussed by the EU and the US Congress, which have even made funds available to explore the potentialities of workplace codes. Although their levels of implementation and commitment still vary tremendously, codes of conduct have almost become required currency among international buyers and export producers in industries such as apparel.[4]

CODES OF CONDUCT

The first major victory in holding TNCs accountable for human rights came when Levi's published its code of conduct, *Global Sourcing and Operating Guidelines,* in 1991.[5] This code of conduct is generally considered to be the first time that a corporation acknowledged direct responsibility for the welfare of workers anywhere in its production chain, whether they were employed by Levi's or its legally independent subcontractors.

Public pressure fueled by this success forced most major apparel companies and other brand-conscious industries to follow Levi's example by publishing their own codes of conduct.[6]

In preparation for soccer's 1994 World Cup, the International Confederation of Free Trade Unions (ICFTU) succeeded in establishing the FIFA (Fédération Internationale de Football Association) code, an international code of conduct for better working conditions in the production of soccer balls. This code widened the debate by showing that poor working conditions are an industry-wide phenomenon and not a problem limited to individual companies.

Another major stepping stone—one that turned public awareness into a political opening—was the 1996 scandal involving US television celebrity Kathy Lee Gifford, under whose name Wal-Mart produced a clothing label that prided itself on charitable giving to needy children in New York City. Labor activists of the National Labor Committee exposed child labor and other labor rights violations at suppliers' factories in Honduras. Gifford acknowledged these problems after investigating them herself and helped initiate the White House Apparel Task Force under the leadership of Secretary of Labor Robert Reich, in order to curb labor rights abuses in developing countries. The task force comprised representatives from corporations, labor unions, and NGOs. Labor unions and NGOs certainly welcomed this newfound and mostly unforeseen political attention. Unfortunately, this coalition soon ended when labor union members and one of the NGOs left because of differences over the issue of a living wage. Similarly, various national and international multi-stakeholder initiatives have been born out of the need to create systems of monitoring corporate accountability, to give the voluntary codes some teeth.

Initially, labor unions demanded codes of conduct from TNCs to gain a written commitment of responsible corporate citizenship. Codes of conduct were negotiated with brand headquarters to secure corporate commitments to certain principles that could be used as a reference in future plant-based negotiations, but not with the purpose of setting up a monitoring system. Codes of conduct became full-fledged tools for corporate policy and risk management only when human rights NGOs got involved.

Today we can identify at least four major multi-stakeholder initiatives turning codes of conduct from statements of goodwill into policies of commitment: the Fair Labor Association (FLA), which replaced the White House Task Force; Social Accountability International (SAI), which developed and governs the auditing standard SA8000 for social responsibility (see SAI 2001); the Fair Wear Foundation, founded by the CCC, a European network of campaign groups; and the UK-based, research-focused Ethical Trading Initiative (ETI) (see ETI 1998). Multistakeholder initiatives bring together businesses and NGOs that focus on social justice, human rights, and/or consumer activism in creating systems of corporate overview. Labor union participation in these initiatives varies from direct involvement (CCC, ETI, SAI) to tacit tolerance (FLA).

In general, the systems created by these multi-stakeholder initiatives intend to hold TNCs accountable to a set of basic labor and human rights standards. The strongest codes are based on the provisions of the Universal Declaration of Human Rights, the Convention on the Rights of the Child, and the Declaration on Fundamental Principles and Rights at Work of the ILO, which entails international labor rights conventions that address freedom of association and collective bargaining, forced labor, child labor, and discrimination. The idea of deferring to the principles of the ILO conventions came from the 1994 FIFA code, which served as the reference text of the CCC, ETI, and SAI codes. The reference to ILO conventions is important in our discussion because of the central role that the right to freedom of association plays within the ILO.[7]

Multi-stakeholder initiatives translate the stipulations of these norms into a catalogue of observable minimum requirements that can be audited by external monitoring agents, such as management system auditors, NGOs, or independent consultants. The company—whether a brand-name TNC or a one-shop manufacturer—subjects itself voluntarily to the standards and to being monitored for compliance with them.[8] If the standards are violated, the initiatives can eventually withdraw their seal of approval or renounce the violator publicly, which threatens to harm the company's reputation or damage its hard-won competitive advantage as a responsible employer.[9]

The discourse on codes of conduct has become enormous over the last five years, and most of the criticism has been directed at corporations.[10] TNCs are accused of trying to evade public-sector scrutiny by promoting self-regulation. Other criticism focuses on the limited reach that codes have, because they largely address workplaces in brand-name manufacturing, which excludes the much larger generic and domestic sectors. Another argument against codes is the technical difficulty of monitoring hundreds of thousands of workplaces on an ongoing basis across national borders and across industries. Perhaps the most important challenge is that all the initiatives are based in industrialized countries. All initiatives court stakeholders in developing countries, but most of these are still largely peripheral to actual policy setting.

These are serious problems, but our concern here is to look at the disagreements that have arisen between the labor unions and human rights NGOs that are involved in, or to some degree internal to, the creation and implementation of codes of conduct. Many of these groups, labor union as well as NGO, have their own concerns and internal disagreements about the above-mentioned issues. The following is intended to explain the differences between labor unions and NGOs and shed some light on why they still choose to engage each other.

SEEKING POWER: INTERESTS VERSUS IDEALS

Over the last two decades the number of NGOs has dramatically multiplied, joining the much older triumvirate of labor unions, faith-based organizations, and business associations as a fourth voice of civil society. For NGOs to be closely involved in industrial relations (largely as a result of the codes of conduct debate) is even more recent. Within a short time, labor unions have had to accept additional powerful voices, first in society in general, and now in its particular policy area. As a result, discussions over codes of conduct are profoundly different from previous negotiations between capital and labor. The shift from a two-sided dynamic (labor unions and business) to a three-sided one upsets previously tried strategies for negotiating and seeking consensus. With the third side as multidimensional as NGOs, acting on premises different from businesses and labor unions, it is difficult to predict how and what coalitions will emerge. NGO motivations—the impetus behind their social engagement—will affect the outcome of negotiations.

We can identify three characteristics differentiating human rights NGOs from labor unions: one *teleological*, one *structural*, and one *operational*. These characteristics result in a fundamental difference in the way the two groups relate to political power, which in turn determines how they attempt to bring about social change.

The *teleological* difference is that labor unions are driven by particular interests, whereas NGOs purport to be driven by ideals. Labor unions have a clearly defined interest behind their agency; they seek to increase their control over resources and decision making. They stand in a direct win-lose confrontation with businesses, and their negotiations result either in altered authority relations or in revenue shifted from owners to workers (Elliott and Freeman 2001).

The interest drive of businesses and labor unions can be traced back to the clearly identifiable property rights that both groups possess. Business controls capital, obviously, and it is interested in maximizing its returns, whether those returns go to shareholder dividends or to investments to increase competitiveness. Labor unions, in turn, represent their members' property rights over their own labor. Workers are equally interested in maximizing their returns, in the form of either higher wages or improved working conditions. A poor return on property will result in serious hardship for either, eventually meaning bankruptcy for the business or poverty for the workers.

Labor unions and businesses are appropriate negotiation partners because they speak the same interest-oriented language. Furthermore, both are interested in a company's welfare, because workers stand to gain more in a thriving company and are the hardest hit in cases of bankruptcy. In the past this mutual interest was mirrored to some degree when management benefited from the communication and dispute-channeling functions of labor unions. In times of full employment, for example, these functions reduced employment-related costs and helped increase productivity.[11] Nonetheless, this reciprocal-interest relationship was often asymmetrical, and in today's era of global competitive pressures the interest deck is clearly stacked in favor of TNCs.

In contrast to labor unions and businesses, human rights NGOs pursue ideals, without having any immediate material interests other than institutional self-preservation.[12] NGOs are not bound by interests based on material consideration, which gives them tremendous freedom to support norms for the sake of their content rather than their returns. Their set of ideals is prescribed by a catalogue of human rights that addresses the responsibilities of states toward their citizens. The NGO counterpart for discussing these ideals is therefore the state, just as much as businesses and labor unions are the appropriate counterparts for discussing their respective interests. NGOs have used their power of persuasion very effectively with the world's governments over the last decade, as they played a crucial role in getting many of them to sign the International Treaty to Ban Landmines and to create the International Criminal Court (Korey 1999).

Talking about ideals is difficult, however, in discussions with interest-driven corporations. NGOs cannot exercise any direct power over corporations because they do not hold any stakes against them.[13] They can coerce business only through legislative efforts, a process in which NGOs face a formidable counter force in the corporate lobbying machine. Once NGOs engage in negotiations with businesses, they can try to influence corporate policies by reasoning and advising. But they lack the means to reprimand corporations in any real sense, because they have no access to their property rights. In corporate accountability NGOs can *argue* for change; labor unions strive to *force* it. This is one of the strengths of framework agreements, in which labor unions with influence at corporate headquarters hold TNCs accountable for their international conduct.

The second difference between labor unions and NGOs is *structural*: labor unions have members; human rights NGOs usually do not.[14] Labor unions are held accountable by their members. For the sake of their constituencies, who need and expect tangible and immediate results, labor unions generally operate in a context of political bargaining and compromise. Thus, labor unions are *forced* to bargain because of their members' expectations, and they are *enabled* to bargain because of the power they hold over their counterpart—they have the potential to reduce the return on the business's property. Their strength in numbers gives labor unions not only a stake over corporate interests but also over the public interest. Their potential to strike and to affect electoral outcomes gives them political power, which governments recognize.

NGOs, in contrast, do not represent members, which means they cannot easily invite feedback about their strategies from a large constituency. The freedom to follow ideals instead of interests coupled with a representational "free agency" results in political non-accountability. NGOs are primarily held accountable by their need to build a reputation in order to survive. For human rights NGOs, that reputation is based on upholding norms that are nonnegotiable and non-tradable, since the realization of one right may not be compromised for the sake of another. If anything, an NGO might find itself under competitive pressure with other NGOs whose integrity might attract better publicity and eventually better possibilities for funding. This welcome and necessary competition minimizes (but does not dissolve) the likelihood of NGOs being coopted or deceived by interest groups.

Finally, the *operational* difference between NGOs and labor unions lies in the way they each approach politics in order to reach their objectives. NGOs seek to analyze, advise, or influence policymakers' thinking without directly engaging in politics. The key objective of human rights in general is to mitigate the power relationship between a government and its citizens. Human rights NGOs consider their mandate to be to monitor the power bearer acutely without becoming a political alternative themselves. The less compromised an NGO is with the prevailing power structure, the more weight its judgment carries. That is why organizations such as Amnesty International and Human Rights Watch will not accept funding from governments or political parties.

Whereas human rights NGOs need to remain political outsiders, labor unions want to be political insiders. Representational organizations are invariably political, and labor unions are very clear about their intention to get involved in politics. This is manifested in voter mobilization, candidate endorsements, campaign donations, and in the frequent elections of labor unionists into office. Many center-left parties worldwide trace their origins back to labor movements, and some of them still carry that heritage proudly in their names. Government recognition and the open embrace of politics on the part of labor unions result in a close relationship between labor unions and the state. In different shapes and forms, labor unions are constituent elements of public governance structures. Governments, for example, set up and finance labor union programs (such as AFL-CIO Solidarity Centers in the United States and Hans-Böckler-Stiftung in Germany), ensure labor appointments in academia, or give labor unions access to international governmental organizations, such as the ILO or the OECD. One of the most interesting cases of cooperation between labor and government is the ILO, where labor unions along with employer representatives are constituent members of the organization, jointly shaping international law.

The relationship between labor unions and the state in non-totalitarian systems is not inherently conflictual but rather symbiotic. The labor union movement helped to build the modern welfare state, is an active participant in it, and therefore has a sense of ownership in it (Gallin 2000c).[15] In another example, the foreign policy of US labor became at times so closely allied with governmental power that labor unions found themselves defending US interests rather than those of workers in developing countries (Sims 1992). Today, though, much of the social contract that existed after the Second World War between labor unions and the state is eroding.

CODES OF CONDUCT AND HUMAN RIGHTS

The debate over codes of conduct is firmly rooted in the human rights discourse. This makes perfect sense, since we are dealing with a complex array of social arrangements in a wide range of cultural settings all over the world. A common denominator is needed that allows us to make the same demands at all workplaces everywhere. Thanks to the norm-setting work of the ILO and the inclusion of economic, social, and cultural rights in the International Bill of Human Rights, we have available a body of relevant universal norms. These rights apply across political systems, cultural preferences, and development stages. This is not to say that the development stage of an economy is of no importance. The degree of development will alter the overall level of benefits that workers can attain, but it will not change the validity of their human rights. The rights to organize, to be treated without discrimination, and not to be forced to work do not depend on the level of development. Child labor might be considered an exception, because the outright banning of all child labor in developing countries can run counter to the "best interest" principle for the child's welfare. The ILO acknowledged this by passing the Worst Forms of Child Labour Convention (No. 182), with developing countries specifically in mind.

In general, the strongest codes of conduct are based on universally recognized human rights, and this philosophical parentage is openly acknowledged (SAI 1997; SAI 2001; ETI 1998; CCC 1998).[16] The big challenge is to make human rights operational in the context of voluntary commitments. We can identify two paths along which human rights may be promoted: the *regulatory* and the *participatory* approaches. These approaches find their parallels in the discussion of codes of conduct, and they help us understand the differences between NGOs and labor unions.

The *regulatory* approach is to realize human rights through improved legislation and better enforcement. Traditionally, this approach has focused on state accountability alone, because only states wield the power to legislate and regulate. On the multilateral level the state accepts its responsibility for human rights by signing an international human rights treaty, changing its domestic legislation to comply with international law, and enforcing the law in the spirit of human rights. In the follow-up process the state itself reports on its progress, to which other states can react by making recommendations or voicing their concern. While this machinery enables us to talk about human rights in a meaningful way, it has not been particularly successful at turning the promise of human rights into reality, because each state individually still has the major responsibility for doing that. And unfortunately, protecting human rights does not rank high with many governments.

To realize the promises of human rights, we turn to a collateral dimension. The *participatory* approach goes in the opposite direction from the regulatory approach: up from the bottom. Here the idea of human rights is that it is the justification by which people can claim their entitlements vis-à-vis the state. Claiming rights from below then becomes a political process in which those with little power use human rights as the path for advancing their cause. Concretely, the participatory approach to human rights concentrates on the importance of turning people who are excluded from making decisions on any matter that affects their lives into active contributors to the political process. This understanding of human rights can range from micropolitics (at the family level) to macropolitics (at the state level). Participation then becomes the flip side of political empowerment, because participation can be meaningful only if it is backed by the power to veto or substantially to alter outcomes. Participation in public affairs is a human right in and of itself (UDHR, Art. 21,1; ICCPR, Art. 25). The regulatory and the participatory approaches are complementary. Ideally, each will beget the other.

In the end, what concerns us here is how human rights can be employed for social change in the workplace. Labor unions and NGOs work toward this change, and both agree on the importance of enforceable regulations as well as the participation of workers in corporate decision making. Where they differ is on how this change should come about.

In the regulatory approach, change is realized because the organization that holds power (traditionally the state) has acknowledged the importance of human rights and is willing to uphold them. In other words, power restricts itself mostly out of enlightened self-interest.[17] In the context of states, this is done for the sake of better international relations, which may result in more stability or peace. In the context of corporations, which hold power in employment relationships, compliance with human rights may be sought for better public relations or higher productivity, both of which increase returns. This top-down approach, benevolent as it may sound, carries a significant danger. If people are not truly aware of their human rights, if social change is granted to them rather than achieved, advances in human rights through regulation can be fairly easily withdrawn without creating much opposition. The entity that grants human rights controls them. The prospect of corporations "granting" human rights in their production chain without a countervailing force is therefore bound to raise labor union eyebrows.

With the distinction between the two approaches in mind, we can identify the different strategies that NGOs and labor unions take. Labor unions naturally consider the participatory element of human rights to be the most important. Therefore, their approach to codes of conduct focuses on the need to establish worker representation first, from which other improvements in the workplace will follow—in the order and by a magnitude influenced by workers. Codes of conduct thus serve labor unions in a larger political debate of social justice. For labor unions, the value of codes of conduct depends on their potential for building a political movement that helps open up space for organizing workers. Once sufficient numbers are organized, workers' demands can be brought from the factory to the nation, affecting labor and social protection legislation.

Human rights NGOs tend to consider the participation of disempowered and vulnerable groups as important, but their lack of membership and coercion mechanisms largely confine NGOs to the regulatory approach. Taking different routes to the same destination, however, does not explain why the two movers are sometimes in each other's way. The problem seems to be that NGOs and labor unions weigh the rights at stake differently. For labor unions, the rights to freedom of association and collective bargaining are tantamount to all other labor rights; once collective power is established in the workplace, all other changes will flow from there. The freedom to organize is in no way a guarantee that workers will actually decide in favor of a union. But without freedom of association first, labor unions consider all other advances somewhat meaningless. Labor unions define their role primarily by the power they are able to generate. Promoting human rights is a way that may help them gain that power, which in turn will be necessary to secure respect for human rights in the long term. Besides, advances in working conditions that are achieved without the efforts of a union are a disincentive for workers to join a chapter.

NGOs are in full support of the right to freedom of association, but they do not rank it above other rights. First, free labor unions are restricted by law in a number of countries that attract much low-skill manufacturing, most notably China and Vietnam. Second, even in countries with a more favorable union environment, organizing is often prohibited in the so-called export processing or special economic zones (Bangladesh), where most manufacturing for TNCs takes place. To wait for labor unions to establish a foothold in these factories before labor rights improve seems negligent, if change can be brought about in other ways. Finally, labor unions come in a large variety of shapes and sizes, and the presence of a so-called yellow union (one that sides with management rather than the workers) does not, in the view of NGOs, do much to further human rights in either the regulatory or the participatory way. Even "good" labor unions have come under attack for neglecting workers who are hard to organize. Apparel manufacturing, for example, is characterized by high staff turnover, volatile workloads, and easily relocated production facilities, all of which make organizing a risky gamble for resource-strapped labor unions. Engaging in codes of conduct has thus given NGOs the opportunity to push for the rights of workers that in their eyes are neglected by labor unions, especially women and children.

DEBATING CODES OF CONDUCT

The differences between labor unions and NGOs over codes of conduct have come to the fore on several topics, with the debates over a living wage clause and the role of NGOs in monitoring working conditions having been among the most divisive. These examples illustrate the rift between the two groups. An agreement on these questions would mean a major advance in helping to improve labor rights.

Living Wage

The living wage is contentious for several reasons, most of all because there is no agreement as to what exactly constitutes a living wage in any given place. The principal norm setter for labor rights, the ILO, has shied away from defining a living wage or an international minimum wage. The ILO defers to member states to set their own wage standards.

Labor unions consider that a living wage clause is a crucial component in the negotiations over codes of conduct, perhaps to the point of its being the second-most-important stipulation, after freedom of association. The reason for this lies in the economics of the sweatshop. Piore (1990) explains that bad working conditions exist as a result of a particular business strategy (the sweatshop) rather than as a result of moral ignorance on behalf of employers or society at large. Accordingly, in order to eliminate the abuses, one has to get rid of this business model, which is not concerned with productivity. Management is keen on reducing labor costs in sweatshops, because low capital costs (total and per piece) act as a disincentive to employers to focus on increasing productivity. The nature of the sweatshop strategy accounts for the labor violations we see in many low-skill industries, such as low wages, child labor (whose productivity tends to be low), and health and safety problems (such as crowding workers in order to minimize rent).

Labor violations in a sweatshop can be traced back to employers who see no reason to increase productivity. Once employers are pushed toward productivity, they have to become interested in the organization of the shop floor, and their compliance with particular regulations becomes a marginal adjustment. In other words, as long as labor is cheap, employers do not care about working conditions. The way to raise standards has to be to change the business strategy underlying bad working conditions rather than looking at violations as isolated social problems.

The living-wage clause will raise wage levels, if even only slightly, and therefore it is a major step in forcing productivity onto the employers' agenda. For labor unions, the commitment to a living wage is crucial, its definition (or definability) being secondary. The living-wage clause guarantees labor unions that wages have to be discussed. The absence of such a clause raises the suspicion that as long as better regulatory systems for other violations are in place, wages may continue to be defined by the logic of labor supply and demand alone, which in low-skill industries in developing countries is a losing battle for labor unions. Disagreement over a living wage clause was serious enough to be a major reason for the US apparel workers' union UNITE to leave the White House Apparel Task Force (Gereffi, García-Johnson, and Sasser 2001).

The living-wage clause appears to many TNCs to be a commitment they might never be able to fulfill. They saw it as a public-relations disaster waiting to happen, since promising a living wage and failing to deliver it would expose them to much criticism. Human rights NGOs, in turn, were more concerned with whether the codes could be implemented immediately. Since a living wage could not be defined, NGOs consider its exclusion to be permissible in order to make progress on the realization of other rights. From a regulatory perspective this makes sense, since regulation demands precisely defined indicators and benchmarks, and the absence of clear definitions leads to arbitrary enforcement.

Monitoring and Verification

Even more tension exists on the question of who ought to do the ongoing monitoring of workplaces. Monitoring implies frequent presence on the shop floor, and for labor unions the only desirable presence is that of a union. Labor unions see themselves as the only adequate monitors of labor conditions. Outsiders with professional credentials (whether for-profit or nonprofit) may come into factories to verify data presented by unions and management, but their role should steer clear of intervening in the immediate labor relations. Labor unions have developed unparalleled expertise in monitoring, and they fear that outsiders without the necessary knowledge of industrial relations will be easily coopted by management (see Compa 2001 and Chapter 16 in this volume). Governmental labor inspectors—outsiders with knowledge of industrial relations—are already being coopted by management in many countries, and there are no guarantees that NGOs will be immune to the same influence.

Labor unions see an ongoing presence by NGOs as a threat to their exclusive legitimacy to represent workers. In view of the fact that NGOs do not have members, we consider this concern to be justified. Monitoring does not automatically equal intervention, but it is a slippery slope from observing grievances to counseling the parties involved. Labor unions may welcome outsiders to help arbitrate between labor unions and management, but never between workers and management.

In contrast, many NGOs claim that their monitoring is essential, because too many shop floors in the world of low-skill manufacturing are inaccessible to free labor unions. Thanks to their campaigning successes, NGOs are now gaining access to factories that are all but closed to labor unions. The argument in favor of NGO monitoring is that it is better than no monitoring at all or than monitoring by for-profit auditors. This may be true, but to realize human rights fully, workers need to do the monitoring themselves, and the presence of NGO monitors may provide a disincentive for workers to organize. An NGO presence might be a victory in the short run, but in the long run it could pose serious threats to the idea of worker empowerment unless handled carefully. Whether in setting international policy or in monitoring locally, NGOs therefore need to set high priority on freedom of association and collective bargaining rights if they want to continue cooperating with labor unions.

There are some examples of NGOs that are able to walk the line between monitoring and maintaining constructive collaboration with labor unions on the ground. In Guatemala, the Commission for the Verification of Codes of Conduct, for example, makes a point of maintaining constant contact with local labor unions to keep them informed, build trust, and keep their own monitors well informed of labor union concerns. It helps that the commission's president is a former labor unionist. Finding groups like the Commission for the Verification of Codes of

Conduct will continue to be a challenge, however, especially since the number of human rights NGOs focusing on labor rights and having good relations (developed over time) with local labor unions are few. Building a network of these organizations will take time. It will also require an effort on the part of the labor unions' leadership (as well as patience and understanding) to guide the growing number of NGOs now focusing on labor rights. And given that the majority of people working in export processing zones today are women, many of these emerging NGOs are likely to be led by feminists—many of whom may not have fond recollections of past attempts to collaborate with male-dominated labor unions.

CONCLUSION

In sum, better working conditions in developing countries will not come about easily. Many approaches will be necessary to promote workers' rights, and tried and tested methods of the past will need to be reexamined. As Alan Howard has observed, "Workers and their unions in the apparel industry are now undergoing a historic adjustment of their strategic vision" (1997). The push for codes of conduct and monitoring systems to ensure their observance has to be seen as one approach in a larger structural battle over the future of industrial relations in a globalized economy.

Human rights NGOs have claimed a stake in this process. This development is welcome, but the role of NGOs in the world of labor needs to be put into context. Our previous characterization of labor unions and human rights NGOs is exaggerated. In reality, both groups are so heterogeneous and their ways of working so diverse that neither could be identified as a bloc. Nevertheless, a better understanding of the constraints under which each operates may guide us as to which specific role each should play in promoting workers' rights. Codes of conduct are characterized by the *absence* of government and take place in the context of a stark power bias in favor of TNCs. Because human rights NGOs have a relative lack of negotiating power and representational legitimacy, they should take on a *supportive* role vis-à-vis labor unions.

So far, much of the debate over codes of conduct tends to focus on getting their regulatory aspects exactly right. Indeed, this is what NGOs do best: continuously strive to analyze or develop the best possible policy proposal. This is not to say that the intense debate and extensive research about how best to improve workplace conditions is wasted. It has, in fact, helped promote the concept of responsible management, particularly in developing countries. And ever more governmental and intergovernmental bodies are beginning look more seriously at how they can build on the current trend in voluntary codes of conduct to reinforce the role of government in ensuring labor rights. TNCs further encourage this debate as well. They are, after all, looking for the best product on the market. As a result of these debates, codes of conduct and monitoring systems are improving continuously.

In many respects, however, discussions and disagreements over regulatory details are clouding the original purpose of codes of conduct: to secure a firm commitment from companies at local and international levels to respect workers' rights. Such rights do not just *include* the right to participate in decision making; they should *begin* with it. If, as we argue, human rights are primarily about empowerment, then workers and their representatives need to be at the core of any strategy to defend their rights. Therefore, for codes of conduct to be believable as a human rights instrument, labor unions need to be at the center of their development and implementation. Without their active participation, codes of conduct run the danger of becoming tools for corporate interests rather than workers' interests.

NOTES

[1] We focus on human rights NGOs because (1) human rights groups have shaped the debate on codes of conduct, and (2) social justice groups have also adopted a human rights approach in the context of codes of conduct.

[2] For a comprehensive account of how export processing plays out in a country such as Guatemala, see Petersen (1992).

[3] The US labor union movement, through the AFL-CIO, had long been active abroad, but not to campaign against US corporations.

[4] The apparel industry features prominently in this essay because the largest part of Northern activism for labor rights in developing countries has focused on apparel production.

[5] An account of the early history of codes of conduct can be found in Varley (1998).

[6] For an overview of corporate codes of conduct in the apparel industry, see US Department of Labor (1996).

[7] By virtue of ILO membership alone, member states acknowledge the rights to freedom of association and collective bargaining, even without adopting the respective conventions. For an introduction to the right to freedom of associa-

tion as a human right in general and as a core concept in the ILO in particular, see Leary (1996).

[8] The questions of which TNCs get involved and why they submit to voluntary codes are beyond the scope of this article.

[9] For more information about the codes and monitoring systems, see the Maquila Solidarity Network's "Codes Update," available online at the maquilasolidarity.org website.

[10] A vast list of references on corporate responsibility, including many websites, is provided in NGLS/UNRISD (2002).

[11] The tensions between the simultaneously mutual and conflicting interests of capital and labor are reflected in the different "industrial relation cultures" of cooperation in continental Europe and the more confrontational approach in the United States and the UK.

[12] Institutional self-preservation certainly is an interest, but it is only feebly linked to property rights, since NGOs do not own their organizations. NGOs cannot be sold or rented out. Their only immediate material interest, then, is that of pleasing their donors. But donors are not likely to part with their property to preserve an organization; they do so in order to further issues.

[13] One alternative to exercising power over corporations is through shareholder resolutions, which are purposely directed mostly at property rights. The shareholder approach (advocacy through ownership) holds some potential, but it is premised on owning rather large amounts of capital, to which only a few endowed NGOs have access.

[14] The notable exception is Amnesty International, perhaps the most widely known human rights NGO, which has a large membership base. However, the immediate beneficiaries of Amnesty International's policies are not its members but political prisoners.

[15] Dan Gallin argues that the labor movement actually spawned much of the civil society activism that has paved the way for NGOs since the Second World War. The labor movement founded many NGOs with the goal of changing society from various angles (socially, culturally, politically) and later withdrew from this widespread approach once labor became an entrenched force in the modern welfare state (Gallin 2000c).

[16] The FLA does not refer to international human rights instruments or organizations in its code. The presence of prominent human rights NGOs within the FLA, however, supports the impression that its intent follows the same spirit as that of the other initiatives.

[17] The state may also adopt human rights treaties because of political pressure from its citizens, who clamor for them. In such cases the participatory approach to human rights would have scored a tremendous success.

Fifteen

Sweating It Out

NGO Campaigns and Labor Union Empowerment

RONNIE D. LIPSCHUTZ

A critical set of issues arising from contemporary globalization is the organizational, social, economic, and environmental externalities that accompany production chains that cross national borders (Lipschutz 2002).[1] While globalization is much discussed in terms of the mobility of capital and production, the disruptive effect it can have on labor conditions and social organization is just as important, if not more so. Such effects include low wages, substandard working conditions, forced overtime, child labor, and lack of the right of free association (union organizing). I argue that these effects constitute *externalities*, following the terminology of neoclassical and resource economics (Pearce and Turner 1990), because workers are forced to bear their costs while producers benefit from not having to pay for higher standards. The classical example is a factory owner who gets free use of the air and water as waste dumps and does not bear any of the costs of pollution.

These externalities are a consequence of major changes in the contemporary capitalist system of production, trade, sale, and consumption associated with globalization. In historical terms, the present phase of capitalist expansion and development is only the latest in a centuries-old process of worldwide economic integration, and these effects are neither new nor unique. In combination with the rapid growth of international trade, consumption, and communication, however, we are seeing the broadest and deepest impact yet on social, political, and economic organization and practices. In effect, through export of manufacturing operations, the corporations of industrialized states are re-creating many of the deplorable working and operating conditions characteristic of the worst periods of the Industrial Age of the nineteenth and twentieth centuries.

To date, these externalities have not been extensively addressed either within the existing international system of regulatory conventions and regimes or by states themselves, where regulatory power is presumed to be vested. In recognition of the widespread failure of both states and corporations to address such effects and associated conditions, NGOs have begun to design and implement systems of rules intended to influence corporations and to bring to an end an international "race to the bottom." Capital has responded with what has come to be called the corporate social responsibility movement. As a result, transnational social regulation is increasingly the product of private (as opposed to public) interventions into the areas of global trade, corporate behavior, and consumer preferences (Haufler 2001; Pearson and Seyfang 2001).[2]

The campaigns and projects I discuss in this essay are directed primarily at US apparel companies and their subcontracting factories abroad. They are attempts to regulate the negative social impacts for labor associated with production of apparel in developing countries for US and European markets. Such campaigns take several forms, including consumer education and boycotts, inducement of corporate "good behavior" through codes of conduct, auditing and monitoring working conditions in factories subcontracting for particular firms, and establishing unions in specific plants. It is often thought that these campaigns have a significant impact on labor conditions and empower labor unions, but it is not clear either theoretically or empirically whether this is in fact the case. Indeed, there are good reasons to believe that such campaigns and codes, if successful on their own terms, only serve to entrench more deeply the arrangements that first gave rise to the conditions they are intended to remedy.

Drawing on fieldwork and interviews undertaken in Southeast Asia during the summer of 2001, I contend that what matters as much as improvements to life on the factory floor are "spillover" effects, whose force extends beyond factory walls into the broader society of the host country. I question whether consumer action alone can create the conditions in which workers will be free to exercise their rights as guaranteed by both domestic laws and ILO conventions. I argue here that reliance on market devices necessarily falls far short of aiding efforts on the ground to improve on a broader (political) scale the status of workers, unions, and local communities and to bring them more autonomy.

I begin with a general discussion of the conditions that have led to the imposition of so many externalities on workers in Eastern Europe and developing countries. I then turn to a description of the various types of campaigns intended to address these effects. In the third part of the essay I report on the findings and conclusions of my research in Southeast Asia. Finally, I conclude by pointing out that what is needed is greater interaction between civil society and labor unions globally. For the moment, the basis for effective labor law lies within states, and activism must focus on improving legal, political, and social conditions for workers in the host countries, rather than on trying to affect corporate behavior chiefly through consumer pressure.

AFFLUENCE AND EFFLUENTS: GLOBALIZATION, EXTERNALITIES, AND THE STATE

As noted above, a major cause of contemporary social dislocation for host country labor can be found in recent changes in patterns of production, trade, and sale of commodities, manufactured goods, and knowledge associated with globalization in its contemporary material form. The organization of production has become much more complex, with raw materials, commodities, semi-processed materials, parts, and finished goods moving among locales and plants in different countries according to both the interstate or interregional and the intra-firm logic of comparative advantage (Gereffi 2002).

Clothing companies in an industrialized state whose goods are produced under subcontract in low-wage states enjoy a positive externality in the cost differential they realize from sourcing offshore (the costs to the workers involved are evidently of only limited interest; see, for example, Klein 2000). Workers, lacking bargaining power in a highly competitive global system, yield up some part of the value of their labor beyond what would be the case were they organized. While low wages are generally rationalized through the concept of comparative advantage and relative factor costs, it could be argued that such advantage should not undercut the necessity for labor to receive a living wage. The extent to which workers are underpaid relative to their income requirements— a level that is contested and challenged—results in an unjustified and possibly inefficient benefit to both producers and consumers.

Imposing externalities is not an inevitable requirement of the reorganization of production and capitalism; rather, it results from a deliberate decision by both capital and states to downplay such impact and to disregard the embedded and largely obscured capital accumulation and transfers that result. The reasons are not difficult to surmise: holders of capital and power tend to benefit from these capital transfers and have little interest in sharing profits or control with labor. Most governments seek foreign investment and pay their main attention to the demands of capital, except in situations in which labor appears to threaten political stability. Indeed, given the rise in attention to "shareholder value" and the exigencies of intra-corporate competition, corporations would be foolish, on their own, to use their profits to pay for the costs of these externalities.[3]

What, specifically, has changed? During much of the twentieth century finished goods in the cloth and clothing industries were manufactured in factories owned and operated by the companies whose name appeared on those products. While many workers could not afford, even then, to purchase the clothing, they were eventually able to organize for improved working conditions and better wages. But the competitive nature and thin profit margins in the clothing industry motivated the companies continually to seek ways of reducing production costs. Some of these methods were made illegal (child labor, piecework rates, ignoring minimum wage levels); others were not (automation, relocation, open shops). The claims made by capital have been that, even so, costs were too high and labor too expensive and too vigorous a force. The first response by companies was to move production to locations with lower wages and unregulated labor standards; the second was to dispense with production entirely.

Nowadays, many industrialized-country apparel companies neither own nor operate any factories of their own; their role is limited to designing, ordering, wholesaling, and retailing. Instead of producing, they subcontract with specific plants—often owned by companies based in Japan, South Korea, and Taiwan but operating in host developing countries, such as Indonesia, Mexico, the Philippines, and Thailand—a practice generally known as outsourcing. Indeed, the assembly of articles of clothing may take place in several different countries, each one chosen for its particular cost advantage. Spreading out the apparel production chain represents, in part, an effort to spread risk by externalizing it onto others. As Edna Bonacich and Richard Appelbaum point out in their work on apparel production in the Los Angeles area:

> Much of the industry is driven by fashion, and sales of fashionable garments are highly volatile. The production of apparel is

generally a risky business, which discourages heavy capital investment and limits the availability of capital for firms that want to expand or upgrade. The riskiness is augmented by time. Fashion can change quickly. Apparel manufacturers want to be sure that any demand is fully met, but must be wary of overproducing garments that may fall out of fashion. The industry needs to be especially sensitive to changes in consumer taste, to respond quickly to these shifts, and to cease production in a timely manner. (Bonacich and Appelbaum 2000, 9–10)

It is in this light—the changing landscape of the global economy and industrial production as well as the volatility of demand for fashion—that the position of large US and European apparel corporations and their subcontractors should be seen.

The regulatory standards that individual corporations face vary greatly among countries and production sites, even though many states have ratified most, if not all, of the relevant basic ILO conventions. The owners of the factories where clothing is made are obliged, of course, to observe the laws of the jurisdiction in which they operate. At the same time, however, no one is legally required to exceed the minimums that those laws establish, and if they can get away with violating those laws, there is no compelling reason not to ignore them. The absence of monitoring and enforcement of those laws by governments, the tendency of responsible agencies to turn a blind eye to violations of the law, and a general lack of political support for labor rights make violations a normal, even necessary, part of "doing business" in a competitive global economy.

Such notional constraints on practices as may exist in host countries are further weakened by the practice of outsourcing and subcontracting. If apparel corporations do not own the factories with which they subcontract, they need not demand or require that their subcontractors observe the relevant regulations, although they may, as part of an agreement with the subcontractor, require that certain rules, or codes of conduct, be followed (Fung, O'Rourke, and Sabel 2001). But even these are weak constraints inasmuch as codes of conduct and corporate behavior are not very binding; from one day to the next subcontractors may post or remove codes of conduct, according to the mandates of whatever company has ordered a specific production run.

One result of weak standards and minimal enforcement is the revival and globalization of the sweatshop model of manufacturing. The term is used to cover a broad range of operations and working conditions, ranging from those in small establishments to those in large plants. The US General Accounting Office has defined a sweatshop as "an employer that violates more than one federal or state labor law governing minimum wage and overtime, child labor, industrial homework, occupational safety and health, workers' compensation, or industry registration" (GAO 1994, 1). This definition applies to operations anywhere—in the United States as well as in developing countries; developing country status is not a prerequisite for their existence. As Bonacich and Appelbaum (2000) have shown, sweatshops are as much a function of the industrial structure as they are of general economic development. To a significant degree their existence is a result less of inadequate regulation or weak enforcement and more of corporate desire to wring maximum profit out of the deal.

JUST DO IT:
THE NEW INTERNATIONAL DIVISION
OF REGULATORY LABOR

While concerns about the social and organizational externalities generated by globalization and under-regulated market activities have been most visible in the demonstrations and protests in Seattle, Boston, Washington, Geneva, Prague, and elsewhere, these are only the tip of the new global regulatory iceberg. As states have shed their responsibilities in the area of protecting labor, some are being taken up by other organizations and institutions, a growing number of which are private or semi-public, organized by activists in civil society, corporate organizations, and business associations (Cascio, Woodside, and Mitchell 1996; Cutler, Haufler, and Porters 1998; Haufler 2001). These are for the most part developing outside the framework of already-existing international bodies—the UN, WTO, IMF, ILO, and various human rights conventions (Lipschutz 2002). These regulatory projects, initiated by various groups, organizations, associations, coalitions, and corporations, and operating under the rubric of global civil society (Lipschutz with Mayer 1996), represent an effort to reestablish authority over self-regulating markets (Polanyi 2001). Private and semi-public regulation are nothing new, even at the transnational level, but there is reason to think that we are seeing something of a resurgence, and certainly an expansion, in privatizing international regulation (Cutler, Haufler, and Porters 1998). In a sense, these arrangements constitute a new international division of regulatory labor (see Table 15–1).

It is into regulatory gaps in the apparel industry that campaigners such as those in the anti-sweatshop movement have stepped. In organizations campaigning with respect to the apparel industries in both the United States and Europe, the movement has gained growing visibility and support in its efforts to shame, cajole, bully, or entice apparel companies into paying more attention to the conditions in their subcontractors' factories (Lipschutz 2002). The primary means by which this is accomplished is not, however, through enforcing existing laws in the host country or promulgating new ones. Instead, the incentive rests almost wholly on implied effect on a company's market share and its profits. By threatening to reduce market share through their influence on consumer preferences, such organizations are relying increasingly on economic means to achieve political ends. Activist campaigns can thus have an effect, but for the most part, *only on the targeted corporation and its subcontractors.* Extending such social improvements to other companies and labor sectors within host countries is neither inevitable nor, it would appear, even likely. In other words, efforts that do not address the political context within which violations of labor and other social regulations are taking place—that is, within specific state jurisdictions—are likely to have only a limited effect and therefore only a weak influence on societies. I return to this point below.

These campaigns involve three forms of market-oriented activity. First, some campaigns encourage consumers to boycott specific companies in order to cut down on their sales and to embarrass company executives by publicizing human rights violations in subcontracting plants. Second, some campaigns seek to develop certification programs whereby apparel produced under acceptable conditions may be labeled to this effect. Finally, some campaigns urge companies to adopt and implement corporate codes of conduct, which stipulate a set of minimum working conditions that must be met in their own and their subcontractors' factories (see O'Rourke 2000; Fung, O'Rourke, and Sabel 2001). Each of these methods has advantages and drawbacks, but they all rely on market pressure rather than political pressures for their effectiveness.

For the moment, the clean clothes movement has two broad segments. On the one hand, organizations such as the Fair Labor Association (FLA), an effort originally co-sponsored by capital and the US government during Bill Clinton's presidency with the participation of a few nongovernmental

Table 15–1. Some Current Global Social Regulation Movements and Campaigns

Issue area	Selected organizations and coalitions
AIDS/HIV	Global Strategies for HIV Prevention
Anti-big dams	International Rivers Network; World Commission on Large Dams
Anti-GMO	Campaign to Ban Genetically Engineered Foods; Genetic ID
Child soldiers	Coalition to Stop the Use of Child Soldiers
Climate	Climate Action Network
Corporate accountability	As You Sow; Business for Social Responsibility
Diamonds	Fatal Transactions International Diamond Campaign
Forestry	Forest Stewardship Council; Forest Products Certification
Indigenous rights	Survival International; International Indian Treaty Council
Labor	Campaign for Labor Rights; Maquiladora Health and Safety Network
Land mines	International Campaign to Ban Land Mines
Organic food	Organic Consumers Organisation; IFOAM; Pure Food Campaign
Small arms trade	International Action Network on Small Arms
Species diversity	TRAFFIC; Conservation International
Tobacco	International Tobacco Control Network; Tobacco-Free Initiative
Toxics	WWF Global Toxics Initiative; Center for Ethics and Toxics
Trade monitoring	Global Trade Watch; Ethical Trading Initiative
Women's rights	Amnesty International Campaign for Women's Human Rights

See Table 15–2 for groups and initiatives in the apparel industry groups, and the Global Business Responsibility Resource Center seek to foster corporate good behavior and to implement codes of conduct in manufacturing plants. On the other hand, activist, pro-worker organizations such as Sweatshop Watch in the United States and the Clean Clothes Campaign (CCC) in Europe attempt to use consumer boycotts and education to force companies to improve working conditions in factories. Groups in both sectors have also developed certification programs, whereby companies and factories are inspected, monitored, and given clean bills of health (when deserved), and logos, which can be affixed to products (see Table 15–2).

To what degree do these projects of global civil society, largely applied in specific plants, serve to change the fundamental political environment for labor in host countries? A number of further questions may be raised in this regard. If labor conditions are improved in one factory, what is the impact on other corporation operations, within and outside specific countries? If conditions for labor are improved in factories subcontracting for one apparel company, does this lead to improvement in the factories subcontracting for others? (Sometimes, of course, one factory produces for more than one company.) If labor conditions are improved in the apparel sector of a given country, do they improve in its other industrial sectors? And, most important, do selective improvements in some factories enhance the overall power of labor in relation to state and capital? That is, do market-based activist campaigns that are intended to impose global social regulation on transnational capital induce national governments to regulate the very markets in which social externalities of concern have emerged in the first place?

Under activist pressure, apparel corporations may be seeking to impose codes of conduct on subcontractors in developing countries. These corporations may be providing a variety of incentives to improve labor conditions in specific factories. They may even be paying wages above the legal minimum requirement and providing space in which workers can organize (Connor 2001). This is all well and good, but it is no more than would be expected of any enlightened business. But is there evidence to date that activist campaigns and corporate actions have resulted in major regulatory responses by states, or have the states taken a stance toward labor that is more supportive, especially in terms of the right of free association?

For the purpose of this discussion, I call this effect—the general sector-wide and countrywide upward ratcheting of labor rights as a result of improvements in some factories—social and political spillover. If such

Table 15–2. Organizations Engaged in Regulatory Initiatives in the Apparel Industry

Group	Type
Academics Studying Nike	Activist
AFL-CIO	Labor union
As You Sow	Activist
Business for Social Responsibility	Private
Campaign for Labor Rights	Activist
Clean Clothes Campaign	Activist
Corporate Watch	Activist
COVERCO	Activist
Ernst & Young	Private
Ethical Trading Initiative	Semi-private
Fair Labor Association	Semi-private
FairWear (Australia)	Activist
Global Alliance for Workers and Communities	Corporate
Global Exchange	Activist
ICFTU	Labor union
ILO	UN agency
International Organization for Standardization	Semi-public
Lawyers Committee for Human Rights	Activist
Maquila Solidarity Network (Canada)	Activist
National Labour Committee	Activist
National Mobilisation against Sweatshops	Activist
NikeWatch	Activist
Press for Change Nikeworkers.org	Activist-labor
PricewaterhouseCoopers	Private
Social Accountability International	Activist
Sweatshop Watch	Activist
UNITE	Labor union
United Students Against Sweatshops	Activist
US Department of Labor	Govt. agency
Verite	Semi-private
Workers' Rights Consortium	Activist
World Trade Organization	UN agency
Worldwide Responsible Apparel Production	Private

Many groups have websites on the Internet. For current information, check these sites.

spillover is taking place, it should become visible in host countries as a result of (1) reforms instituted in specific factories; (2) emulation by other factories and enterprises not affiliated with contracting transnational apparel companies; (3) increased respect for workers by state and capital; and (4) growing public and private support for the right to unionize inside the factory, across the apparel sector, and throughout industry in general. If there is no obvious spillover, or if evidence suggests that state and capital continue to disregard labor laws and even violate them (by, for example, sending police into factories where strikes are taking place), it is reasonable to conclude that the campaigns and corporate reforms have not as yet had a significant domestic social and political impact in the country as a whole.

The more likely result is some combination of these two outcomes, in which workers have organized independent unions in some factories, and some sectors are being organized more broadly, yet to which there continues to be resistance by both state and capital. Given that it took well over half a century in most industrialized states for the state to recognize workers' right to unionize, it should not be surprising that unionization and upward ratcheting of labor standards might so far remain limited. If the evidence is that campaigns and codes are having spillover effects within and across countries, it suggests that market-based approaches to the institutionalization of labor rights are effective in accomplishing broad political change. Conversely, if evidence of spillover is weak or lacking, applying market methods for political ends may not be effective. In the final section of this chapter, I explore the implications of this second proposition for market-based activism.

Consider, for example, the effect of activist campaigns on the Nike Corporation. At least a dozen civic action campaigns under way are aimed at the Nike Corporation (Connor 2001). All are meant to improve health and safety conditions, provide minimum wages in Nike's six hundred or so subcontractor factories scattered around the world, and set an example for other apparel companies. These campaigns have generated considerable public attention (although it is not clear that they have affected the company's financial performance), and Nike has responded energetically, concerned about its market share, its competitiveness, and its image. The company has adopted codes of conduct, contracted out audits of its subcontractors' factories, and permitted independent monitors either to accompany auditors or to conduct their own inspections. It has joined the FLA and co-established the Workers' and Communities' Association, as well as taken a number of other steps to improve workers' conditions and its own reputation. And while significant problems apparently remain in many, if not all, of its subcontractors' operations, the amount of ratcheting upward of conditions within the Nike subsystem of global apparel production has been considerable.

Nike's response to pressure by activists shows that it continues to be sensitive to public disapproval. What is less clear is whether these campaigns have actually had the desired effect on the company's profits, which might indicate changes in consumer behavior. In May 1998 the value of Nike's stock dropped almost 27 percent, perhaps due to a decline in sales growth as a result of bad publicity (although this cannot be confirmed) or, more likely, as an effect of the 1998 Asian financial crisis. The company's financial statements do not give a clear indication, although a small decline in revenues and income can be attributed to that crisis. Revenues from the United States have leveled out since a large increase between 1996 and 1997. While this might indicate some changes in consumer preference, the data do not provide compelling evidence one way or the other. Moreover, the positive media attention Nike has generated by its efforts—this despite the CEO being attacked in 2000 by a student campaign at the University of Oregon and the company subsequently withdrawing a sizeable donation to that university—and the relative paucity of hard data from more than a handful of plants seem to have reassured consumers that the company is addressing the problems.

But what have been the political effects of these campaigns? Nike offers improved conditions and higher wages to the workers in its subcontractors' factories, but both workers and consumers remain fully integrated into the overarching pattern of consumption that constitutes contemporary globalization and makes those workers and consumers subject to it. Campaigns against other apparel companies have had similar results. In the host societies as a whole there has been little in the way of political reform, stronger state regulation, or greater exercise of labor's right to unionize. The structures might have received a paint job, so to speak, but underneath, they are still the same old structures. In other words, amid all these efforts, almost no attention has been paid to the conditions that led to the demand for social regulation in the first place, to wit, that Northern capital makes substantial profits on the backs of relatively powerless, badly paid, mostly female workers. It is the very fact that labor is badly paid and powerless that makes the host countries so attractive in the first place—and has led to the reappearance of sweatshops in Los Angeles and New York (see Bonacich and Appelbaum 2000).

HAS ANYONE BEEN DOING IT?

Information is notably lacking about how effective the workplace codes of conduct are and what effect activist campaigns have had on host countries, although inspections of individual factories suggest some limited improvements (see, for example, O'Rourke 2000; Connor 2001). During July and August 2001, a graduate student and I traveled to four Asian countries—People's Republic of China (Hong Kong), Indonesia, the Philippines, and Thailand—to document private and public efforts in Southeast Asia to develop, introduce, and enforce transnational regulations designed to curtail the harmful social, economic, and environmental externalities that are commonly linked to globalization. We conducted thirty-nine interviews with representatives of government ministries, international organizations, labor unions, and local and transnational NGOs (although not all of these were related to the apparel industry). These interviews were, for the most part, unstructured and open ended, although organized around a set of specific questions. Most of the interviews were an hour in length.

We have drawn a number of conclusions from our fieldwork.

Concerning Corporate Codes of Conduct in the Factory

- Their principal influence is symbolic; they provide an opening for mobilization by helping persuade workers that future improvements are possible.
- Occasionally they are used as a bargaining tool in labor negotiations, inducing concessions by management fearful of outsiders becoming involved.
- They support worker resolve, especially in cases where a company openly fails to honor its publicized pledges and workers believe that the force of conscience can be used to their advantage.
- They are not, however, a barrier to corruption, which remains a major problem, especially in the context of widespread bribery and nepotism, and the notoriously poor monitoring of violations.
- Under conditions of high unemployment, they potentially threaten the jobs of low-paid workers; improved labor standards mean little to those who are faced with the loss of their only source of income.

Concerning the Nature and Extent of Spillover Effects

- In theory, when international conventions are ratified, signatory countries are required to respect them, but in practice, these endorsements carry little weight.
- The wider labor force and community remain unaffected by changes to specific workplace rules, inasmuch as their limited force does not extend beyond the walls of the local factory.
- In contravention of ILO conventions, union rights are sometimes heavily restricted by government authorities; efforts to organize unions are frequently met with resistance, while legal protests in state-run industries may be halted violently by police.
- Contempt remains pervasive for the domestic rule of law, as state authorities ignore existing regulations and worker grievances are summarily dismissed.
- The potential for social unrest in conditions of rising unemployment encourages states to set high priority on creating jobs, with quantity viewed as more important than quality.

Concerning Relations between Transnational NGOs and Local Labor Unions

- Caretaking interventions do not help raise the consciousness of workers or demonstrate the merits of self-leadership; in the interests of long-term change, greater emphasis must be placed on empowerment.
- Inasmuch as a preoccupation with conditions in the workplace can lead to neglect of critical issues such as education, health, and safety outside the factory, unions want NGO training and assistance to foster an overall improvement in workers' quality of life.
- NGOs too often view labor unions only as mediators, whereas they are a promising source of strength for workers whose greatest weaknesses are lack of a unified voice and limited organization.
- While many transnational NGOs are deeply skeptical of international conventions whose enforcement lies in the hands of particular states, the unions themselves believe that the future of effective labor regulation is to be found at the national level.
- National unions frequently ignore the distributive inequalities that are linked to globalization (and justifiably condemned by NGOs), because their particular mandates and delimited constituencies blind them to the regional nature of their struggles. Groups of exploited

workers in neighboring countries, who are potential allies in the fight for social, political, and economic rights, are often working at cross purposes. They view one another as competitors in a zero-sum game in which the unfavorable terms—as decided upon by major corporations—are wholly nonnegotiable.

Our meetings and interviews gave us only limited evidence of spillover. Local awareness is that, notwithstanding transnational campaigns and activism, the basis for effective labor law lies *within* states. Therefore, NGO activism should focus on improving legal, political, and social conditions for workers in the host countries rather than trying to affect the behavior of transnational corporations through consumer pressure and corporate good behavior. Despite the pressures of international economic competition, the fight for workers' rights is always a political one, and what is required is greater interaction among global civil society, *national* labor unions, and *national* politics. Indications are that this is beginning to happen, especially as unions in the North come to realize that their survival depends not on protectionism but on alliances with workers in the South.

WHAT ARE WE TO DO?

The effects of global campaigns by civil society are both controversial and uncertain. Some critics argue that social regulatory standards are a cultural feature of specific societies and should not be subject to global harmonization. Some economists point out that labor regulation would reduce the economic attractiveness of host countries, undermine their comparative advantage in low-cost labor, and increase unemployment. Some corporations resent being ordered around by consumers. But even supporters of these campaigns find much to be desired in the consequences of the pressures civil society places on apparel companies. Many subcontractors have begun to set up model factories, in which the work environment and wages are quite attractive, and to which visitors can be taken, while just down the road other factories operate under appalling conditions.

Of course, if one company implements its code of conduct in, for example, Vietnam, and that leads all other apparel factories in the country to adopt the code, and the Vietnam government monitors and enforces the code, and manufacturers choose not to relocate to places with weaker regulation, some degree of social regulation will have been accomplished. Nonetheless, it remains difficult for consumers always to purchase ethically, corporate good behavior is limited in what it can accomplish, and actual enforcement of labor law remains largely within the purview of national governments, which want little to do with social activism. Such conclusions suggest that the state remains central in reducing and eliminating social externalities, for only the state has the power, legitimacy, and authority to regulate market activities.

Here we face the basic challenge: will it be possible to re-empower the state and reduce the influence of capital? It would appear that efforts to foster global social regulation through market mechanisms are likely to lead only to limited success. Markets are not politics, and the decision to limit the freedom of capital to do what it wants is a political decision. The hegemony of neoliberal beliefs and practices has led to a situation in which no one has a clear idea of how to institute global social regulation through politics, and many have begun to abjure politics. Instead, market-based approaches are seen as being easier, less costly, and less offensive to capital. But it is clear that without politics—and this means domestic political activism—capital will always have the upper hand. Globalization may be inevitable; that does not mean giving the juggernaut free rein to run roughshod over people.

ACKNOWLEDGMENTS

David Newstone and Angela McCracken provided invaluable assistance in fieldwork and research for this chapter. Funding for the project was provided by the Institute for Labor and Employment of the University of California, the Nonprofit Sector Research Fund of the Aspen Institute, the Pacific Basin Research Fund of Sokka University—America, and the Social Sciences Division of the University of California, Santa Cruz.

NOTES

[1] Throughout this chapter I use the term *globalization* to denote material, ideological, and cognitive processes. Globalization is *material* in the sense that it involves the movement of capital, technology, goods, and (to a limited degree) labor to areas with high returns on investment, without regard for the social or political effect on either the communities and people to which it moves or to those left behind. Globalization is *ideological* in the sense that such movement

is rationalized and naturalized in the name of efficiency, competition, and profit. And globalization is *cognitive* in the sense that it fosters social innovation and reorganization in existing institutions, composed of real people, without regard for the consequences. In all three respects, although globalization opens numerous political opportunities for social movements and other forms of political organization and action, a frequent result is disruption of existing forms of beliefs, values, behavior, and social relations.

[2] *Regulation* is meant to cover not only formal laws and codes but also customary rules ("soft law"), norms, and practices within and across societies.

[3] Recent revelations of corporate malfeasance and corruption in the United States serve to illustrate the structural incentives to maximize both the reality and the appearance of accumulation whenever possible. There is little reason to think that capital has much interest in sharing its super-profits with labor.

Sixteen

Labor Unions, NGOs, and Corporate Codes of Conduct

LANCE COMPA

A "THIRD WAY" APPROACH TO LABOR RIGHTS?

Corporate codes of conduct on workers' rights and labor standards hold out a "third way" to promote labor rights in the global economy. Advocates argue that codes of conduct can harness the market power of informed consumers to halt abuses against workers in developing countries. Many supporters see such codes as a civil society alternative to "first way" government regulation or "second way" labor union organizing and collective bargaining to protect workers' rights.

Governments cannot possibly inspect every workplace and catch every lawbreaker, or so goes the conventional argument. And labor unions face a worldwide crisis of organizing and bargaining, especially in sweatshop industries. Codes of conduct offer a new option through private-sector self-regulation using civil society vigilance. And like cereal boxes on a supermarket aisle, a daunting variety of workers' rights codes of conduct has entered the public policy marketplace since 1999—the Fair Labor Association (FLA), the Workers' Rights Consortium (WRC), Social Accountability 8000 (SAI), the Ethical Trading Initiative (ETI), the Clean Clothes Campaign (CCC), and many more.

This article was first published in *International Union Rights* 8, no. 3:5–7, and has been reproduced with kind permission. A shorter version appeared in *The American Prospect* 12, no. 12, under the title "Wary Allies."

These "stakeholder" codes involve a combination of company officials, labor unionists, human rights activists, religious leaders, consumer and community organizations, and other social forces. They succeed an earlier generation of company codes of conduct issued by Levi's, Reebok, Nike, Gap, and others, which collapsed because of the inherent lack of credibility in corporate self-regulation.

But like "third way" politics generally, with its talk of putting a human face on free-market efficiencies, the substance behind the rhetoric on this new generation of corporate codes of conduct is open to question. Are consumer awareness and potential reaction enough to punish those who violate workers' rights or to reward those who respect them? Can private policing, even by the best-intentioned NGOs, really protect workers' rights and raise labor standards in a sustained way? Perhaps most challenging, will a rush to corporate codes of conduct undermine effective labor-law enforcement by governmental authorities and undermine workers' power in labor unions?

The proliferation of corporate codes of conduct generates both opportunities for alliance and sources of tension between labor unions and NGOs that deal with workers' rights in the global economy. Alliance, because labor unions and NGOs share a common desire to halt abusive behavior by multinational companies and a broader goal of checking corporate power in the global economy. Tension, because unions and NGOs have differing institutional interests, different analyses of problems and potential solutions, and different ways of thinking and talking about social justice in the global economy.

ALLIANCES ...

The potential for alliances between unions and NGOs is strongest when they both target the most virulent forms of exploitation, like child labor, gender discrimination, unsafe working conditions, and the firing, jailing, or killing of union organizers in factories in developing countries. A global supply chain of subsidiaries, contractors, subcontractors, and sub-subcontractors has taken shape in export processing zones around the world. Employers in these enclaves exploit cheap, abundant, and usually female labor in what is often called a global assembly line.

Many of these factories serve household-name companies, whose strongest marketing tool is their image, often conveyed by a logo, a slogan, or a famous spokesperson. But a company's image can also become its

Achilles' heel if consumers are made aware of abusive practices in factories that produce the goods they purchase. In the United States, labor unions and NGOs have collaborated in consumer awareness campaigns targeting Nike, Gap, Wal-Mart, Disney, Liz Claiborne, and other well-known firms, as well as personalities like TV star Kathie Lee Gifford (with a big splash) and basketball star Michael Jordan (with barely a ripple).

UNITE, the US apparel workers' union, first joined the International Labor Rights Fund, the Lawyers' Committee for Human Rights, the Consumer Federation of America, and other US-based NGOs along with Nike, Reebok, Levi Strauss, Liz Claiborne, and other firms in an effort sponsored by the Clinton administration and then Labor Secretary Robert Reich called the Apparel Industry Partnership. But UNITE pulled out of the partnership's FLA when union officials thought the NGOs were cutting what they considered a bad deal behind their back—a deal with allegedly weak language and poor enforcement measures.

While they left the FLA, UNITE and other union officials still joined officials from Toys "R" Us, Avon Products, and the Dole Food Company in the SA8000 program, which cheerfully proclaims that "being socially responsible is as easy as 1, 2, 3: adopt high standards, implement your policy, and measure your performance."

European labor union, NGO, and corporate spokespersons make up Europe's ETI and CCC campaigns. Students initiated the WRC linking labor unions, firms, and universities in a code of conduct requiring disclosure of factories making goods bearing universities' names. Social "labeling" and product-specific codes for soccer balls, toys, coffee, carpets, and so on have also taken shape, usually with labor union, NGO, and enterprise involvement.

Some labor unions are incorporating NGO concerns into their own advocacy programs in a move toward a "social unionism" that moves beyond purely bread-and-butter business unionism. Likewise, NGOs are becoming increasingly sensitized to labor concerns. But shared goals, strategies, and tasks do not erase differences. The new movement for corporate codes of conduct has also generated tensions between unions and NGOs that must be addressed squarely.

. . . AND TENSIONS

Some labor unionists believe in a "separate but cordial" relationship with NGOs so as not to dilute labor's goals with those of other groups. Others are more open to coalitions, but think unions should have a "first among equals" role because they are the more universal, representative, membership-based organizations, while NGOs are all over the lot in terms of membership accountability.

NGOs question leadership claims by the labor movement. They prefer a more horizontal "one among equals" arrangement for coalition work. Many NGOs see themselves as the focus of a new emphasis on civil society in international discourse that should give them equal status with labor union movements. And they point out that union formation is notably lacking among informal-sector workers, women workers, and export-oriented factories where the effects of globalization are most pernicious and where NGOs are most active.

But with stable organizations and dues-paying members, unions have a ready answer to the question—who do you represent? One can quibble over delegate elections versus direct elections of union leaders, but as elected leaders their capacity to speak for their members is accepted. The situation for NGOs is far more complex. No single organization speaks authoritatively for the NGO community. NGOs are troubled by the question "who elected you?"—a query sometimes put by labor unionists. Some NGOs have a membership base and elect board members and officials, but many more are answerable only to a board of directors. And in contrast to regular union dues, NGO sources of funding are often sporadic and crisis driven, and thus NGOs often tailor their projects to those that funders will support.

Elements of class antipathies also come into play. Many NGOs are composed mainly of middle- and upper-class intellectuals and professionals with a lingering perception of labor unions as a special-interest group devoted to protecting their own members' jobs and wages at the expense of the larger society. In turn, unionists, including labor's own intellectuals, are often suspicious of "do-gooders" in non-labor groups who presume to tell the labor movement what it ought to be doing without ever having passed through the crucible of an organizing campaign, hard-nosed collective bargaining, or even a strike in order to understand what workers are up against.

Even the term *NGO* is unhelpfully vague. While it usually implies the "side of the angels," NGOs range across a wide spectrum of funding sources, membership involvement, and willingness to confront corporate power. *Civil society* is another concept that evokes images of earnest, engaged citizens, when in reality it includes an infinity of left, center, right, and fringe groups that may or may not live up to the ideals imputed to the term.

In the end, the legitimacy of NGOs rests on the quality of their work and on their effectiveness as advocates. Many have achieved well-deserved respect and authority among governments and within society precisely because of the quality of their research, reporting, and advocacy. Still, many labor unionists believe that while NGOs may rightly take the lead on issues like landmines, torture, genocide, the international criminal court, and other human rights concerns, labor should lead on workers' rights in the global trading system.

HIDDEN AGENDA, NORTHERN AGENDA

Each of the new stakeholder codes of conduct—the FLA and SA8000—holds itself out as a model, jealously promoting its mission and criticizing, openly or implicitly, efforts under rival codes. In addition, most unions continue to see strong laws effectively enforced, self-organization, and collective bargaining as the best ways to advance workers' interests. For them, the "third way" of corporate codes of conduct should be seen not as an alternative but rather as a supplement to labor law enforcement and collective bargaining.

Many labor unionists suspect that behind the new enthusiasm for codes of conduct and related monitoring plans is an agenda aimed at replacing altogether the bargaining and representational role of labor unions and their impact on the political arena. Some see the real goal of corporate backers of codes of conduct as the destruction of strong, class-based workers' organizations that can organize and bargain and back up their demands with the power to strike. Replacing them would be scattered, small, resource-starved NGO monitors whose only clout would lie in ad hoc public relations campaigns of which consumers will soon grow tired.

Workers, unions, and NGOs in many developing countries have additional criticisms. For many of them, the movement for codes of conduct is a peculiarly Northern phenomenon. Some Northern advocates have been embarrassed by reports that codes of conduct long in the making at home took years to be translated into the languages of workers in developing countries covered by the codes. And even if they have been translated, some codes have been rarely disseminated to workers at large.

The FLA and SA8000 have been fashioned and refined in Washington DC and New York, not in Tegucigalpa and Jakarta. The ETI and CCC are driven from London and Amsterdam, not from São Paulo and Nairobi.

The WRC had to scramble to mend fences when claims of extensive consultation with developing country NGOs amounted, under examination, to just a few phone calls and email exchanges.

Many Northern advocates adamantly oppose a monitoring role for international accounting firms or other corporate-oriented social auditors. Some in the South oppose monitoring even by Northern-based NGOs or unions, insisting that only indigenous, locally based NGOs and unions should monitor codes of conduct. But some of the early monitoring experiences using this model only reinforced tensions between unions and NGOs. It turns out that problems of experience, knowledge, legitimacy, capacity, resources, stability, hidden agendas, turf rivalries, and others marking NGOs in the North afflict NGOs in developing countries, too.

MONITORING CHALLENGE

Two mid-1990s cases, widely known among activists, illustrate labor-NGO tensions and the less-than-ideal effects of "indigenous" monitoring. They involved the Mandarin apparel factory (Gap supplier) in El Salvador and the Kimi factory (a source for many large US retail companies) in Honduras. At first, when workers supporting unionization were fired, US unions and NGOs launched publicity campaigns in the United States that helped get many workers' jobs back. These efforts also led to improvements in some of the worst working conditions, such as forced pregnancy testing, denial of washroom privileges, and poor ventilation.

But follow-up monitoring activity by local NGOs sparked suspicions that the NGOs were supplanting the unions' role as worker representatives by discussing wages and working conditions with factory managers. Union leaders were also worried that having NGOs apply codes of conduct exempted government labor inspectors from enforcing national labor laws.

At Mandarin, the original union was challenged by a new, larger rival that it viewed as a company-sponsored ploy using codes of conduct as a cover. Mark Anner, an American living in El Salvador who was trusted by everyone (he was nearly killed in a death-squad bombing of a union office several years earlier), became a de facto mediator working to disentangle proper roles for unions and NGOs at the factory before the monitoring program could get traction.[1]

At Kimi a respected medical doctor with many years of experience fighting military abuses in Honduras investigated workers' complaints about wage violations and unfair treatment by supervisors. On paper, this reflected the monitoring model most often promoted by NGO advocates in the North: a local human rights activist who speaks the language and is trusted by workers, and not someone from a remotely based NGO or a corporate accounting firm. First-world NGOs eagerly awaited the chance to launch a new pressure campaign based on findings by a "model" monitoring mechanism. But this human rights leader had no experience in collective bargaining or in workplace issues. He emerged from a meeting with management agreeing that workers had to increase productivity and work more diligently before wages could be improved and before supervisors could ease their discipline. Management overwhelmed him with arguments that labor unionists are used to hearing and refuting, but which were new and plausible to him. The union at Kimi then focused on the collective agreement and on enforcing Honduran labor laws, not the code of conduct the company had agreed to follow. The Kimi factory closed in 2000.

CIRCULAR FIRING SQUAD

Even within the NGO community there are disputes about the adequacy of codes of conduct and polemics that sometimes resemble a circular firing squad. Thus, for example, NGOs involved in the FLA split over that mechanism's monitoring system and its approach to living-wage and country-eligibility requirements. Denouncing the FLA and the NGOs that are still part of it has become a standard agenda item for other NGOs, even when many of them are involved in alternative schemes (like SA8000 or the ETI) that are not fundamentally different or when they themselves are accused by yet other NGOs of selling out to corporate power. Reminiscent of left-sectarian politics, charges fly that the FLA is dominated by corporations; that SA8000 is a marketing ploy; that the ETI and the CCC are reporting systems with no enforcement; or that the WRC is a "gotcha" scheme with no plan for engaging producers in a systematic change of behavior. At the end of this chain of denunciation are NGOs that stake out an absolute no-compromise position. They see their role as keeping the heat on corporations through public exposure and denunciation rather than through negotiation for better codes of conduct, since any negotiation requires some measure of compromise with the hated corporate adversary.

FINDING A BALANCE

In many ways these disputes about what is a reasonable compromise and what is a sell out reflect similar disputes about labor clauses in trade agreements: whether to compromise on side agreements or other instruments that may not contain every goal, or to denounce any compromise as a sell out if it fails to achieve every goal. But at this still early stage of experimentation with new labor-NGO alliances, more patience and less vitriol are in order. None of the codes or monitoring systems has been fully implemented. At this stage, allowing for a variety of experiments and approaches to see what works and what doesn't, without falling into mutual recriminations, is a more fruitful approach for a labor-NGO alliance than denouncing some perceived weakness in one anothers' language or monitoring procedures.

To advance workers' rights in the global economy requires strong regulation and enforcement at both the national and the international level. Domestic labor law reform is key. So is an expanded role for the ILO, as well as new linkages of labor rights to trade agreements. Trade sanctions against abusive countries and firms are an important tool. Workers' rights also rely on strong labor unions that can organize, bargain, and strike effectively.

Given the weak presence of unions in the global assembly line and the rapid-response capabilities of many NGOs, especially when compared with union bureaucracies, codes of conduct are a valuable asset. The challenge is to find the right balance of national and international legal mechanisms, labor union power, and codes of conduct. The institutional tensions and differences examined here complicate efforts by unions and NGOs to work together for social justice in the global economy. But problems should not block progress. The two communities still have more in common with each other than either does with corporations, governments, or international organizations that see free trade and free-flowing capital as the solution to low labor standards. At the same time, unions and NGOs need to be clear-eyed about their differences and their proper roles as they navigate the opportunities and challenges that lie ahead.

NOTE

[1] Mark Anner is also a contributor, with Peter Evans, to this volume (see Chapter 3).

Seventeen

Workplace Codes as Tools for Workers

NEIL KEARNEY AND JUDY GEARHART

THE STRUGGLE TO ORGANIZE

Free Association Repressed

María Lesbia López will never forget her introduction to labor unionism. Two days after the registration of the Choi Shin union she had fought to establish in Guatemala, this frail sixteen year old was kidnapped as she stepped down from the bus on her way home. Dragged toward a waiting car, known to belong to her employer, she was threatened at gunpoint. María Lesbia had only been exercising her rights (enshrined in the Universal Declaration of Human Rights, in ILO conventions, and in numerous treaties) to freedom of association, to organize in a labor union, and to bargain with her employer. But in reality these rights are severely violated around the world. Nowhere is this more evident than in the textile, clothing, and leather industries.

Freedom of association is defined as a fundamental human right. ILO Convention No. 87, "Freedom of Association and Protection of the Right to Organize," is referred to directly by both the International Covenant on Civil and Political Rights (ICCPR, III, 8, 3) as well as the International Covenant on Economic, Social, and Cultural Rights (ICESCR, III, 22, 3). Nevertheless, International Textile, Garment and Leather Workers' Federation (ITGLWF)[1] affiliates report that cases like María Lesbia López's are common—if not worse.[2] As eighteen-year-old Carmen Rosario left the launch meeting of the union she had helped form in the Dominican Republic, for example, she was attacked by thugs who were

249

armed with nail-studded baseball bats; they broke her arm. In Lesotho two women were killed when management hired police to terrorize garment workers after they formed a union. This kind of repression is not limited to developing countries. In the United States, when workers at Brylane, part of the French multinational Pinault-Printemps-Redoute, began to organize to try to improve working conditions in Indiana, the company embarked on an anti-union campaign, before eventually reorganizing the union over a year later in January 2003.[3]

Still other cases are beyond the reach of ITGLWF affiliates. In China, when workers in a silk factory began to organize, Cao Maobing, the mild-mannered engineer delegated to raise the issues with management, was arrested and detained in a psychiatric hospital, where he was held for seven months before his release in July 2001.[4] In Burma, workers who try to form independent labor unions are subject to "intimidation and surveillance by the police and the military intelligence service."[5]

Exploitation Unchecked

Not only are workers overtly discouraged from organizing, but exploitation is often extreme in the textile, clothing, and leather sectors where profit margins are frequently small and competition fierce. Three recent reports from ITGLWF affiliates illustrate this pattern:

- In Central America sixteen-hour workdays, six to seven days a week, are common. Workers are often beaten when they make mistakes. Humiliation is constant. Workers who upset a supervisor may be forced to stand on their machine, stand outside in the sun for hours, or clean the factory toilets.
- In Cambodia young workers have died at their sewing machines from a combination of exhaustion and malnutrition—not surprising, given the long hours they work and the inadequacy of their wages.
- In Bangladesh a woman garment worker described her normal day. Rising at 4 a.m., she works for two hours on household chores, then walks for an hour to the garment factory, where she works until 10 or 11 p.m. After another hour's walk home, she spends another two hours on housework, after which she lies down at 2 a.m. to sleep—for two hours. When she began work in the garment factory she was well, but now she is sick, she said.

Women make up 70–80 percent of this work force. Many are very young. Many have been recruited in rural areas. All are vulnerable to exploitation. This exploitation is spurred by the intense competition in a globalized economy in which the textile, garment, and leather sectors of 160 countries are producing for export into only about thirty markets. It happens because governments are unable or unwilling to enforce their own labor legislation.[6] It happens because employers are increasingly transnational corporations (TNCs), often with a base in Korea or Taiwan or operating through local intermediaries (buyers), and with no respect for either the country in which they operate or the workers they employ.

Such exploitation is happening despite the existence of more than 180 ILO conventions, the ILO Tripartite Declaration concerning Multinational Companies and Social Policy, the OECD Guidelines for Multinational Companies, and some ten thousand codes of conduct, including companies' own codes, multi-company codes, and multi-stakeholder codes, all intended to protect workers' rights. And such exploitation is bound to continue as long as workers are denied the right to organize and engage in collective bargaining.

Overcoming the Challenges

To change this situation, workers, their unions, and other advocates are pursuing a combination of strategies designed to

- change the responsibilities of TNCs vis-à-vis their suppliers (particularly those in developing countries) and the overall rules of the game, requiring retailers to take more responsibility for labor conditions in their suppliers' facilities;[7]
- improve local employers' thinking and practices toward their employees, encouraging them to invest in their work force and to assume their legal responsibilities;
- strengthen the enforcement by national governments of labor laws and other protections for workers;
- build solidarity by enlisting the support of local and international labor unions and NGOs to encourage and enable workers to organize; and
- organize more labor union members and build the capacity among union members to analyze their situation and devise multi-layered strategies for advancing their rights.

Voluntary workplace codes of conduct are just one of the many tools that can be used to help advance these strategies. Since their advent in the early 1990s, codes of conduct have quickly become the primary tool for interested TNCs to commit themselves to a set of ethical principles and international labor standards and to convey those to their suppliers. The extent of this responsibility still varies considerably from company to company. While some TNCs seek less regulation, others have begun to suggest that national government regulation be enlisted and possibly even augmented.[8]

Multi-stakeholder codes like the Social Accountability 8000 (SA8000) standard (a system that defines a set of auditable standards and an independent auditing process for the protection of workers' rights) are intended to set a high bar for workplace codes and the independent verification of companies' compliance. SA8000 also seeks to provide incentives directly to local producers—regardless of TNC demands—by providing factory-based certification once the producer reaches a minimum level of compliance. A growing number of factories has acquired such certification, either at their clients' request or to demonstrate a competitive advantage and attract new clients.

CODES OF CONDUCT AS A TOOL FOR WORKERS

Codes as a Negotiating Tool

The advantage of workplace codes is that they focus on direct employer-employee relations and that—provided employers make a public commitment—workers can use the code as a negotiating tool. One such code is the SA8000, a standard developed in the late 1990s and overseen by the nonprofit organization Social Accountability International (SAI) for a safe and decent workplace. Workers should find two characteristics of SA8000 particularly useful. First, the content of the standard is comprehensive and self-reinforcing, including both freedom of association and collective bargaining, which are further reinforced by the basic-needs wage clause and clear limits on working hours (in accordance with ILO conventions or national law, whichever is strongest). These elements are at the core of any collective bargaining process, and one helps serve as a check on the others.

Second, SA8000 certification requires management to make a clear, public statement about the company's level of compliance. It obliges the company to say more than simply "we're working on making improvements." This public announcement also provides workers with a clearly defined set of expectations, which they can challenge if necessary. Some are concerned that certification is merely a public-relations wash, but without certification workers have no handle to grasp when they need to claim their rights. Although complaints have sometimes resulted in a factory deciding to forgo certification rather than make changes, workers' representatives are still testing the complaints process.[9]

One positive example of how this can work is the case of a Del Monte farm in Kenya that supplies Coop Italia, the largest supermarket chain in Italy. Because Coop's purchasing department is certified to SA8000, it was engaged to pressure Del Monte to reform according to the "control of suppliers" clause in SA8000. With Coop's help and the collaboration of Kenyan and Italian NGOs, auditing firms, and the local union, the farm management in Kenya worked to address the complaints of the local union and to improve working conditions for its employees.[10] Subsequently, the farm was certified as having achieved compliance with SA8000.

Codes as a Tool for Training Workers

Codes can also serve as a practical basis for training in workers' rights. The original Fédération Internationale de Football Association (FIFA) code developed by the International Confederation of Free Trade Unions (ICFTU), the Union Network International, and the ITGLWF was based on the main ILO conventions. Subsequent codes, such as those published by the Ethical Trading Initiative (ETI), the Clean Clothes Campaign (CCC), and SAI initiatives, have further honed this human rights language into practical terms of rights and responsibilities in the context of employer-employee relations. The direct language of codes cuts through the level of abstraction that comes with human rights, which are defined in terms of states' obligations but which are often (especially in the case of labor rights) violated by non-state actors.

By drawing directly on international human rights norms, codes can help reinforce workers' sense of entitlement. When such codes are used in worker training, they can help impart a broader understanding of human rights as well. This is important because in the long run it is not about the workplace code in x,y, or z company, but about workers everywhere understanding their rights—and claiming them.

CODES OF CONDUCT AND WORKERS' RIGHTS: A TRAINING PROGRAM

Program Development

In 2000 SAI and the ITGLWF initiated a training program designed to help workers understand how they can use workplace codes of conduct to their benefit. The program uses SA8000 as a study model, but the main purpose is to develop a program that reinforces existing efforts by workers to organize and educate themselves.

Like many workplace codes, the SA8000 standard requires management to ensure that workers understand the content of the standard and to enable them to participate in reviewing management's compliance. It is difficult to define, however, what minimum level of understanding auditors should expect workers to have. Several companies using SA8000 have reported difficulties in training workers. Meanwhile, more companies are demanding training for workers. SAI also received requests for more training from workers' representatives present at regional consultations conducted between 1998 and 2000 in Brazil, Hungary, and the Philippines.[11]

However, SAI was reluctant to provide this training directly, because this is not usually the role of an accreditation agency, nor is it SAI's original area of expertise. Such training needs to be closely coordinated with local—preferably workers'—organizations. Worker training that is not adequately guided by local, independent labor unions runs the risk of creating competitive organizations. Such competitors, particularly if they emerge as a byproduct of a voluntary workplace code, may be easily construed as obstructive tactics used by the employers to avoid unionization. The deliberate creation of such competing organizations violates ILO Convention No. 87 and, by extension, the SA8000 standard.

As workplace codes of conduct have rapidly spread throughout the apparel and footwear industries, the ITGLWF and its affiliates around the world have worked to influence the debate and to keep members up to date. In 1999 the ITGLWF conducted a workshop on codes in Central America. In 2000 workers in the Philippines started developing training modules around codes of conduct. Meanwhile, affiliates in several countries were seeking more training to continue building on the study-circle learning process (explained below), which the ITGLWF had helped them initiate. In response, the ITGLWF proposed a worker training model, for which SAI secured the initial funding.

Program Methods

The current training program was designed to build on and advance the use of worker study circles and develop a worker training curriculum that puts workplace codes in the context of globalization and the framework of international human rights.

Study circles are informal discussion groups that often take place in the plant or the neighborhood. Originally developed in Sweden, study circles are an important empowerment tool. Workers learn about a particular set of issues and are provided with some basic illustrative materials. Those workers then serve as study-circle leaders and meet in small groups of about ten to analyze further the issues outlined in the handout materials and to discuss related concerns of the workers. The materials are designed to facilitate discussion and group analysis. Study-circle meetings require almost no infrastructure, and educational materials are kept simple. In Bangladesh, for example, one worker learned to read through a study circle and eventually became a leader within the labor union. In many cases workers who began activity in their labor union as study-circle leaders have gone on to lead their unions.

In selecting the countries, priority was given to those where there was extensive export manufacturing, where the ITGLWF had already trained study-circle leaders, and where workers had used the study circles with some success. The twelve countries identified include six in Asia: Bangladesh, India, Indonesia, Pakistan, the Philippines, and Thailand; three in Africa: Ghana, Lesotho, and Mauritius; and three in Latin America: Chile, Ecuador, and Honduras. Indonesia and Mauritius were selected solely on the first criterion.

The program is designed in three phases: first, ITGLWF and SAI staff train twenty-five to thirty study-circle leaders in each country; second, the study-circle leaders convene two study circles (about ten workers in each circle), each meeting three times. In the course of three two-hour meetings, workers analyze (1) trends in the global production chain and the related pressures that come to bear on their lives at work and at home, (2) international human rights norms and workplace codes of conduct based on those norms, and (3) how they can use these codes to claim their rights.

In developing the curriculum, SAI and ITGLWF staff conducted a test run of the course in the Philippines, where ITGLWF affiliates had already developed training modules around workplace codes. The training course of study-circle leaders was extended to allow for evaluation of the modules and comments on them, and a trial study circle was convened with ITGLWF and SAI staff observing and incorporating changes accordingly. Interesting feedback from the Philippine workers included a request to lengthen the training session for study-circle leaders, a preference that training materials not contain cartoons, and considerable interest in learning about workers' rights directly from texts on international human rights norms.

WHAT MADE THIS PARTNERSHIP FEASIBLE?

Institutional Fit

The project fit well with the goals of each of the institutions involved. The ITGLWF saw the project as a way to (1) continue building on and reinforcing its study-circle infrastructure; (2) inform workers about trends in their industry, such as the proliferation of workplace codes in apparel and footwear industries; and (3) help workers take advantage of those trends. SAI's interest in the project emanated from an institutional commitment to (1) provide workers with information about how they could use the SA8000 standard to their benefit; (2) seek to incorporate workers' concerns and interests into future developments of SAI's work; and (3) reach out more directly to groups in developing countries. The project has also enabled SAI and ITGLWF staff to visit factories (including those with SA8000 certification); to meet with local NGOs, labor union representatives, and government officials; and to learn firsthand about workers' perspectives on codes.

Prior Collaboration

The rigorous content of the SA8000 standard reflects the input that the ITGLWF was able to make in its development. Because the ITGLWF was well represented on the SA8000 advisory board, it felt comfortable with SAI's commitment to make the SA8000 standard a tool that would advance the interests of workers.

Prioritizing Workers' Needs

Given SAI's multi-stakeholder mandate, labor union representatives on its advisory board provide a critical link to grassroots workers' organizations. Because SAI seeks both to work on international policy and to remain directly connected in the field, being able to gain input directly from workers' organizations is essential for it to be able to develop practical policy recommendations.

Recognizing this, SAI followed the ITGLWF's leadership on this project, taking primary responsibility for fundraising and program administration. The countries chosen did not necessarily correspond to places where there was a high demand for SA8000. SAI was not seeking to develop worker training in response to business demand but in response to workers' needs. As business demand grows for such training, however, SAI and the ITGLWF are evaluating potential expansion of the program and exploring ways to establish a role for labor union representatives in places where there is no union. A final evaluation phase with representatives of study-circle leaders from each country is planned and will serve to inform future worker training programs, as demand grows.

CONCLUSION

In the struggle for workers' rights many strategies are needed—at local, national, and international levels. But it is critical that workers themselves help shape those strategies. To that end, workers' representatives must seek to influence all aspects of the labor rights debate. Although the rule of law and government regulation may be the preferred means for ensuring labor rights, complementary strategies such as voluntary workplace codes can provide a handle for workers to demand their rights and may help move the broader debate in the desired direction.

It is critical, however, that such codes include elements that are useful in various organizing strategies. Thus, codes that are firmly rooted in the principles of ILO conventions and other human rights norms prove useful for educating and empowering workers. These codes can help reinforce workers' understanding of their entitlements, as embodied in those rights. And in the end, the long-term goal of empowering workers needs to focus not on the code itself but on promoting human rights.

NGOs can help develop programs that lay the framework for worker action, but when an organization is focused on policy recommendations, such as developing a system for locking in corporate commitment to a workplace code, it is an ongoing challenge to work also from the bottom up. For codes to work, top management at the factory must be committed to them—and often the buyer's headquarters as well. This top-down approach risks losing sight of the core goal of empowering workers. By engaging directly in efforts to translate such policy recommendations into something useful for workers on the factory floor, NGOs can gain the most important perspective. And by remaining engaged and continually seeking to inform and influence the thinking on such codes and monitoring systems, labor unions can keep workers' interests on the table.

NOTES

[1] The ITGLWF is the international trade secretariat for labor unions around the world in the textile, garment, and leather industries; its affiliates have more than ten million members.

[2] ITGLWF complaint submitted to US contact point for OECD Guidelines for Multinational Enterprises, March 6, 2002. A collective agreement was signed July 9, 2003.

[3] AFL-CIO complaint submitted to Wesley Scholz, US contact point for OECD Guidelines for Multinational Enterprises, July 2, 2002.

[4] BBC News Online, "Workers Demand Leader's Release," December 17, 2000; and *China Labour Bulletin*, "Independent Trade Unionist Cao Maobing Released," July 19, 2001, available online at www.china-labour.org.hk (accessed December 8, 2003).

[5] Bureau of International Labor Affairs, *Report on Labor Practices in Burma* (Washington, DC: US Department of Labor, 1998, updated 2000). Available online at www.dol.gov (accessed December 8, 2003).

[6] For example, a few years ago half the members of the Bangladesh Cabinet were also garment factory owners, thus creating a distinct disincentive for policing the sector.

[7] Global marketing and production have made it both extremely difficult for local producers to penetrate international markets independently and generally unprofitable for TNCs to remain loyal to their suppliers.

[8] Saying that this project has taught Gap the limit of its own influence, Elliot Schrage, senior vice-president for global affairs at Gap, told *The New York Times*: "We can't be the whole solution. The solution has to be labor laws that are adequate, respected and enforced. One of the problems in El Salvador is that that was not happening and is not happening." Quoted in Leslie Kaufman and David Gonzalez, "Labor Standards Clash with Local Reality," *The New York Times*, April 24, 2001.

[9] For reports on complaint resolutions, see SAI's website at www.sa-intl.org.

[10] Kenya Human Rights Commission (KHRC), *Exposing the Soft Belly of the Multinational Beast: The Struggle for Workers' Rights at Del Monte* (Nairobi, Kenya: KHRC, 2002).

[11] For reports on these and on other workshops, see the SAI website at www.sa-intl.org.

Part 5

Case Studies

Eighteen

United We Stand

Labor Unions and Human Rights NGOs
in the Democratization Process in Nigeria

E. REMI AIYEDE

Civil society continues to loom large in the discourse on democratic transitions in an era that has been described as the third wave of democratization. According to the popular optimistic view, civil society acts as a catalyst for mobilizing a transition from dictatorship to democratic rule. It is also critical to consolidating and deepening democracy, once an electoral democracy has been established. However, this optimism about the potential of civil society organizations to catalyze and advance democracy has been challenged recently. This challenge stems from the modest record of achievements in institutionalizing democratic processes in several of the countries making the transition to democratic rule (Zakaria 1997; Encarnación 2000).

How the actions of civil society advance democratization processes or promote the health of established democracies remains a subject of debate (see Newton 2001). This debate centers on the theory of social capital, which Larry Diamond describes as providing a powerful understanding of the missing link between the vibrancy of associational life and its various impacts on democratic deepening (Diamond 1999, 226–27). In his view the strength of the theory of social capital is in Robert Putnam's narrower conception of the civic community, which includes only associations that are structured horizontally around ties that are more or less mutual, cooperative, symmetrical, and trusting (Putnam 1993). This conception recognizes that there could also be an "uncivic community" (consisting of organizations with hierarchical and unaccountable internal leadership) within civil society, which is nevertheless active in democratization struggles and in the pursuit of democratic reforms in a larger political system. Given this appreciation of the range of organizations within a pro-democracy movement, it has been widely assumed that when such a movement is dominated by organizations that are not civic but rather are characterized by asymmetrical patterns of exchange, patron-client relations, and scant horizontal ties among the general membership, cooperation becomes difficult. This is because in such situations building broad fronts, not only for sustained opposition to dictatorship but also for the organizations to coalesce into forms that can meet the challenges of consolidating democracy, is likely to be harder.

However, this explanation of the disjunction between a vibrant associational life and limited "civic-ness," even in a context of serious pressure for democratization, may be less helpful in explaining concrete experiences in transitioning countries where democratic struggles typically involve a complex process of interaction among several organizations: local NGOs, labor unions, opposition parties or organizations, and international donor agencies.

For instance, what is the role of social capital in mediating the interactions among differing organizations that must nonetheless cooperate and work together to achieve the broad goals of democratization in the long term and the short term? Organizations that constitute the pro-democracy movement may well have differing levels of internal democracy, different leadership styles, different visions and practices, distinct organizational structures, and varying levels of trust among members. In situations where electoral democracy has been achieved, to what extent does the necessary networking and cooperation, with all its ups and downs, help to promote internal democratic practice in the less democratic organizations and thus increase the chances of building social capital and the subsequent consolidation of democracy?

In exploring these questions, this essay examines the interactions between labor unions and NGOs in the struggle against military dictatorship in Nigeria. It begins by reviewing the labor movement's involvement in politics, which was complicated by the development agenda of the 1960s and 1970s, and its subsequent victimization in the economic crisis of the 1980s and 1990s. It traces the context of the emergence and evolution of the human rights NGOs that spearheaded the pro-democracy movement in Nigeria. It then explores the internal dynamics of the alliances between these organizations to analyze how horizontal relationships have fared in exchanges within civil society. It argues that sustained political struggle throws up issues of participation, accountability, and egalitarianism that in turn promote social capital within civil society.

LABOR AND POLITICAL CHANGE IN NIGERIA

The labor movement in Nigeria emerged in opposition to the excesses that characterized Nigerian politics from independence until the 1980s. During this period the movement articulated the aspirations of the broad masses of society and mobilized public sentiments against the abuses of the ruling elite, whether military or civilian. Labor mobilized the public around nationalist causes and lambasted the widening gap between the affluence of politicians and the poverty of the majority of Nigerians. It raised questions concerning access to education, health, and other welfare services. It challenged authoritarian tendencies, exemplified by the call in the 1960s to create a national government in which official opposition would be abolished, by the preventive detention act of the 1960s, and by the general repression by the military in the 1980s.[1]

This was in spite of the labor movement's weaknesses, which included internal fragmentations caused by ideological differences, disagreements over international affiliation and strategy, personality clashes and individual ambitions, conflict over the use of union funds, disagreement over forms of collective political participation, and opportunism (Ananaba 1969; Yesufu 1984; Barchiesi 1996).

Given this record, there have been efforts to explain the achievements of the movement and to understand its relevance and potential in the political liberation movement of the 1980s and 1990s. For example, the effectiveness of labor has been attributed to its nature as a social movement and to its capacity as a vehicle for social mobilization. Also, a crisis in the state is often said to manifest itself as a crisis in labor relations, not so much because of the existence of a relatively large mass of formal-sector labor as because of organized labor's relatively long political experience beginning in the nationalist struggle for independence and its immense ability to articulate and mobilize popular forces to confront the ruling elite (Adesina 1994, esp. chap. 5; Bangura and Beckman 1993). This implies that the labor movement owes its prominence less to its internal democratic structure or its technical capacity than to its ability to mobilize as a vehicle to create space for democratic debate and contestation, or even constrain the state, especially when the leadership is urged on by pressures from below. Indeed, labor's strength lies in its unity, for moments of effective challenge to the state have often been moments when the labor centers unite in ad hoc committees and collectively pursue specific actions in order to make particular demands of the state. That said, a series of independent efforts by the various central labor organizations in Nigeria to coalesce into a single labor center have failed.

By the late 1980s, however, labor's preeminence had dwindled remarkably, as its organizational weaknesses, reinforced by the state's prolonged and sustained effort to subordinate and cow the movement, eventually threw it into disarray. How did this occur?

In the 1960s and 1970s the instruments, mechanisms, and processes of labor control were defined by corporatist principles permeated by a statist ideology of developmentalism, in which the fostering of peripheral capitalism was presented as development and any obstacle put in the way of capitalist accumulation was considered sectarian and illegitimate. Jimi Adesina (1995, 8) notes that the state's role in the accumulation process was felt at three levels in labor relations: (1) the increased use of statutes (especially military decrees) to control and restrain labor union actions; (2) the use of judicial processes to the same ends; and (3) the use of the coercive machinery of the state against the labor movement. The decrees increased the power of the state to intervene in labor relations and the labor process. The state was empowered to (and actually did) define labor unions and labor unionism as well as determine who could participate in and/or lead unions. The state prohibited unions in certain sectors by defining them as essential services not amenable to the disruptive activities of a unionized work force. The state not only regulated the internal administration of labor unions but freely proscribed them. It barred some union leaders from labor union activities and detained many of them without trial for indefinite periods. Extensive powers of oversight over unions were not only vested in the office of the Registrar of Trade Unions, but the state unilaterally restructured labor unions and inserted the "no work, no pay" rule in the statute book (Otobo 1988; Ohiorhenuan 1989; Adesina 1994; Adesina 1995).

The government's restructuring of the movement between 1975 and 1978 saw more than a thousand small unions, forty-two industrial unions, fifteen senior staff associations, and four professional associations reorganized into a central labor body. For the first time in Nigerian history, only one central labor organization was permitted to exist. Subsequently, the Nigeria Labour Congress became prominent within the polity as a federated organization and found a strong voice in the policy arena. But bureaucratic unity, achieved through the instruments of the state, foreclosed organic unity. Bureaucratization and elaborate hierarchical structures also removed control of the unions from the rank and file.

The economic crisis of the 1980s forced a change in the existing relations between the state and the Nigeria Labour Congress. If the 1960s and the 1970s were characterized by excessive state intervention in order to establish a corporatist framework to fit a statist accumulation program, the 1980s and 1990s were characterized by the virtual pushing out of unions from the policy arena. This period marked the collapse of corporatism into containment and exclusion, made possible by the reduction in the numerical strength of unions and the subsequent erosion of their financial base under structural adjustment, when retrenchments were common. Unions, especially the Nigeria Labour Congress, began to rely on government patronage for funding. This, more than anything else, weakened union organizational unity and independence and thereby the influence and power of union leadership. Massive redundancies and retrenchments in the public and the private sectors rendered union activism difficult, risky, and costly at both the shop floor and the central levels.

During this period the government used income policies to impose and sustain wage freezes (especially between 1982 and 1988). Decrees and presidential orders further strengthened the hand of the state, its agencies, and its agents to regulate unionism and determine the internal organization and structure of unions, their international affiliation, and the activities of individual union leaders and workers. These decrees and orders empowered state agents to detain individuals without trial for up to six months. The powers of the National Industrial Court and the Industrial Arbitration Panel were strengthened to enable them to be used to harass and deal with workers. Workers and union leaders were routinely arrested, detained, and intimidated. Labor unions were proscribed. A further restructuring of the labor unions in 1996 under General Sani Abacha redefined the role of union membership in order to weaken the influence of full-time union employees—who have always been the bulwarks of labor unions.[2] Union leaders were also coopted to weaken labor opposition to state action and policies.

There were, however, moves within the labor movement to counter these control measures. Union strategies included militancy, that is, the use of strikes to disrupt established procedures both within firms and in society more broadly. Labor unions organized to shore up solidarity and marshal resources to support collective action. Workers also drummed up external and public support for their cause in their many confrontations with the state; and they made scapegoats of particular representatives of government in an effort to secure advantage.

To be sure, the Nigerian labor movement was too weak to carry out an effective and coherent response to the challenges to its autonomy and effectiveness outlined above. Owing to the inability of unions to ensure that their members could survive the economic recession, the rank and file were not inclined to subordinate their immediate personal aspirations or interests to common rules and collective decisions. The reasons for this failure are to be found not only in the scale of the challenges that confronted the labor movement or the treachery and opportunism of some labor union leaders alone, but also in the ambivalent nature of the labor union as an institution. On the one hand, collective organization is the means through which workers create social power that is far greater than the sum of that which they possess as individuals, for unity and coordination replace competition and division (Hyman 1975, 194). On the other hand, collective organization is an instrument for disciplining workers and putting them under systematic control.

In Nigeria, through interventions in the leadership succession processes the Nigeria Labour Congress and other strategic unions came increasingly under the control of the state, especially in the period of economic reforms in the late 1980s. Personal economic pressures rendered labor union leaders easy targets of cooptation by the state. Unionists connived with state agents to subvert democratic processes within the labor movement. By the 1990s the movement had become militarized even in its internal dealings.

Thus, by the time the democratization struggle began to gather momentum in Nigeria, the labor movement had been badly battered. Besieged by state agents, enmeshed in ongoing internal conflicts, and converted into an instrument of capital accumulation, the labor movement became incapable of protecting its members. Unlike its counterparts in Poland and Zambia, it was unable to play a leading role in the fight for democracy. The government had sacked the leadership of the Nigeria Labour Congress in 1994 and appointed sole administrators to run its affairs.[3] Consequently, the entire movement was thrown into disarray. The pro-democracy elements within the movement had to fight for organizational rights and for autonomy from the state. After the capture of the Nigeria Labour Congress by the government, this struggle for the expansion of internal democratic space was undertaken by individual unionists, with their organizations where possible, in alliance with other civil society groups with similar aspirations. Very prominent were the twenty-two progressive labor organizations led by the unions in the oil industry, which had to forge alliances with human rights groups to play a significant role in the democratization struggle in the heat of the annulment of the June 12, 1993, presidential elections (Momoh 1996). These alliances became mutually reinforcing and provided an outlet for formidable resistance to military dictatorship.

AUTHORITARIAN RULE
AND HUMAN RIGHTS ADVOCATES

Nigeria has had the experience of radical lawyers standing up in defense of activists who were unduly detained or arrested without trial. Over the years some of these lawyers, such as Gani Fawehinmi and Femi Falana, became an alternative voice to a largely conservative bar association. Such lawyers became household names as they staunchly defended student activists, labor leaders, and other social critics who were arbitrarily jailed by various military governments. These lawyers, and other prominent social commentators like Tai Solarin, pursued this activist role at grave personal costs, as they were often victims of state repression, intimidation, and harassment.

With the economy in crisis, the Nigerian state was unable to meet the financial demands of the many programs with which it had sought to subordinate non-state centers of power while maintaining some measure of legitimacy. As a result, it became even more unaccountable, despotic, corrupt, and authoritarian. The state was increasingly driven to rely on the use of force to ensure compliance. The spate of unlawful and arbitrary arrests created a feeling of siege within the polity, thereby activating civil society into organizing to counter the assault on civil and political rights, freedom, and civic values.

The Civil Liberties Organisation (CLO) was established in 1987 by a small number of lawyers after receiving complaints from people who had been victims of abuses of state power. Even as the CLO gained visibility, state repression increased. As many activists, including labor unionists and the radical lawyers mentioned above, were clamped in detention, their friends and other concerned individuals began to establish organizations to pressure the government for their release. These organizations constituted the nucleus of the human rights NGOs that were eventually to lead the pro-democracy movement in Nigeria. A classic example is the Committee for the Defence of Human Rights (CDHR), which emerged from the original structure used to campaign for the release of Dr. Beko Ransome-Kuti and Femi Aborishade in the late 1980s (Enemuo and Momoh 1999).

These human rights NGOs initially set out to promote respect for the rule of law and due process, to fight for the recognition of basic rights as proclaimed by the Universal Declaration of Human Rights and the African Charter on Human and Peoples' Rights, to reawaken people to their social and political rights, and to put pressure on the government to improve prison conditions. They turned to pro-democracy activism when the democratization process became overly regimented and the government became very arbitrary in its actions. Apparently, they soon realized that respect for the rule of law only makes sense when the state itself is not lawless and contemptuous of individual and group freedoms.

Human rights NGOs were able to raise public awareness about human rights abuses and soon became the major proponents of liberal democracy as a way to resolve socioeconomic problems. They issued critical press releases and statements on human rights abuses at the hands of government, publicized the poor state of prisons, and resorted to the law courts to challenge arbitrary government actions. The CLO and CDHR annual human rights reports portray in graphic detail (sometimes even with photographs) the gross abuses of human rights and the torture of detainees. As the activities of these organizations gained national recognition and international support, the military government of General Ibrahim Babangida began to worry. However, the organizations continued to multiply as more donor funds became available. Their ability to secure such funds, especially from international agencies, further reinforced their independence and capacity.[4] The leaders of these organizations were also skilled in and conversant with court procedures, and the courts became the battleground on which to challenge dictatorship.

In an attempt to render these pro-democracy organizations less effective, the state began to include an ouster clause in every draconian decree. Such a clause usually put any case arising from an action falling under that decree beyond the jurisdiction of a court of law. It also strove to discredit the movement by portraying it as being made up of agents of foreign interests. It harassed and detained some officials of these NGOs for varying lengths of time. This, coupled with the annulment of the June 12, 1993, presidential elections, called for a change of strategy. After the annulment, there was a palpable need for a more organized mass defiance of the government and a more combative and confrontational challenge to the state. The human rights organizations had to find a way of meeting this need, and, being largely urban based and mostly concentrated in Lagos, they faced a particular challenge. What was required was the uniting and mobilizing of efforts of workers, young people, and other popular forces committed to democratization in order to make an impact on an obstinate military regime. This imperative of uniting all shades of organizations interested in expanding the democratic space was realized through the formation of the Campaign for Democracy (CD), an umbrella body whose membership spread to include labor unions, professional organizations, and students' and women's organizations, among others.

SOCIAL CAPITAL AND THE ALLIANCE BETWEEN LABOR UNIONS AND HUMAN RIGHTS NGOS

Even before the annulment of the 1993 presidential elections, labor unions had started to work with other groups in civil society to pursue common objectives. Apart from workers "playing" leading roles in popular struggles because of their centrality in the production process, as well as their long history of political struggle, unions have freely aligned with other groups when they have perceived that such a concerted effort could constitute a potent force in the pursuit of certain demands (Bangura and Beckman 1993, 98). These alignments have put labor unionists in touch with radical elements and social critics within the Nigerian polity.

Human rights groups have provided legal assistance to union officials arrested or detained by state security agencies. Thus, many members and officials of labor unions became actively involved in human rights groups, sometimes simultaneously holding positions in pro-democracy and human rights organizations. Human rights organizations and labor unions held regular meetings to pursue common goals, and some unions actually became officially affiliated with the umbrella bodies of pro-democracy coalition groups such as the CD, United Action for Democracy, and the Joint Action Committee of Nigeria.

But these alliances remain mostly informal. Journalists, union leaders, and student and human rights activists are joined by their shared experience of state repression. In fact, most human rights groups draw their membership from the labor movement, professional associations, academic unions, and the student movement. The idea of a broad-based social movement of the salaried classes therefore became an objective reality in Nigeria. However, while the coalescing of people of such diverse backgrounds has served to enrich the pro-democracy movement, it has also raised serious problems that have impeded its success. In other words, although forging such alliances holds the promise of a revitalized civil society, it is not without its drawbacks.

Alliances in Nigeria have been formed to challenge oppression and undemocratic practices jointly, and to uphold the rule of law, public accountability, and the freedom and independence of civil organizations within the country's political landscape. While these alliances have enabled labor to bring wider social content to the struggle, labor unions themselves have been exposed to new issues. Importantly, liberal discourse has largely supplanted leftist slogans, which were the hallmark of the dominant group within the labor movement until 1988, when government intervention in the internal affairs of the movement gave rise to the emergence of Paschal Bafyau as president of the Nigeria Labour Congress. Social issues such as the right to collective bargaining as deriving from the right to freedom of association, child labor, and gender equality within the workplace became areas of concern for human rights NGOs. The unions not only adopted the language of rights, but some labor union activists—in concert with members of the human rights community—also established NGOs for the promotion of specifically labor-based rights, plugging into donor funds in order to do so. Prominent among these is the Centre for Workers' Rights, formed in 1994 to campaign against the crackdown on labor unions, and the Campaign for Independent Unionism.

Alliances between labor unions and human rights NGOs have thrown open questions of civic values within these organizations. Pressures for internal democracy had become visible before 1993, but they exploded when the movement became "war wary" in 1997 as the General Sani Abacha–led junta infiltrated the movement and strove to divide it. Newspapers became awash with personality conflicts, accusations of mismanagement of funds, patron-client relations and autocratic leadership styles, and issues of ethnicity. These issues also frequently came up in seminars and workshops, especially those devoted to the expansion of democratic space in Nigeria. Individuals and groups within the labor movement made a case for greater participation in decision making. They decried the patronizing behavior of the movement's leaders, and thus called attention to the impact that prolonged military rule had had on the character of civil society itself, especially of such long-standing organizations as the labor unions.

The question of militarization was raised not only in terms of the general tendency among the populace to resort to violence but also by the replication of military command behavior in the management of many labor unions and NGOs. Thus, democratic struggles have to address the question of internal democracy within pro-democracy organizations themselves as well as dealing with issues of developing constitutionally governed relations between such groups and the state. Pressures for internal democracy often straddled the process of struggles for the autonomy of civil society organizations and for organizational rights. These struggles and how they are resolved have consequences for the outcome of civil society pressures for the democratization of the larger political system of Nigeria.

The struggles for internal democracy and accountability have led some members of these organizations to break away in protest to form their own separate organizations. Accusations of financial recklessness and authoritarianism and their attendant conflicts have ensured that such umbrella bodies like the CD remain ad hoc. Although a united front would have provided greater strength, the pro-democracy movement has created several umbrella organizations without any one of them commanding sustained and universal support for any extended period of time.

To be sure, differences in organizational structure and processes sometimes stand in the way of sustained cooperation. Organizational solidarity and competition have also been major sources of disagreement. Union leaders can sometimes be sensitive about the phenomenal rise of human rights groups. They fear that these groups may take over the entire leadership terrain of popular struggles. These fears have generated quarrels over roles, and have therefore weakened alliances. However, donor agencies, wary of duplicated efforts among these organizations, have continued to promote and support networking among NGOs within the country.

Over the years many of the human rights organizations, including the CLO and the CDHR and umbrella bodies like the CD, have experienced democratic changes of leadership, largely as a result of internal pressures. Relatively newer umbrella organizations like the United Action for Democracy, the Transition Monitoring Group, and the Citizens' Forum for Constitutional Reform have adopted a more decentralized and flexible way of working, often headed by a convener.

CONCLUSION

Two conclusions are supported by this review of the cooperation between labor unions and human rights NGOs in Nigeria's democratization struggle. The first is that studies of democratic transition could benefit from an engagement with actual political struggles, focusing on the
transforming character of the process of struggle even at the organizational level. Structures that shape inequality and disempowerment also
contain within them the grains of resistance, of greater or lesser strength.
In the course of struggle, forms of egalitarianism and participation can
and do emerge (Harrison 2001, 394).

Second, the Nigerian situation shows that if struggles for democratization are accompanied by more specific struggles within the pro-
democracy movement to democratize its own decision-making processes,
this can mitigate otherwise hierarchically structured and asymmetrical
patterns of exchange among members.

In this sense liberal ideas and the principled demand for democratic
processes for managing public affairs in the larger political system can
be generated from within civil society itself (and especially within those
organizations that focus exclusively on human rights and democracy),
and in fact may lead to a movement for the expansion of internal democratic space. As such, democratic struggles promote the level of social
capital when an array of organizations are forced by the exigencies of
struggle to cooperate, network, and pool resources, because sooner or
later the marginalized within these organizations will begin to clamor
for, and achieve, a voice that properly corresponds to their roles in taking
forward the objectives of the organization.

ACKNOWLEDGMENTS

The author would like to thank Professor Adigun Agbaje of the Department of
Political Science at the University of Ibadan for his comments on an earlier draft
of this paper. The article has also benefited from participants' observations and
informal discussions, as well as from formal interviews with human rights activists and unionists.

NOTES

[1] After the attainment of full statehood in 1963, Prime Minister Alhaji Tafawa Balewa called for a national government that would have abolished official opposition in the federal legislature. Under the cabinet system of government that Nigeria was practicing at the time, it also implied a move toward a one-party state. The labor movement mobilized other groups in society to oppose that move.

[2] The government restructured the existing forty-one industrial unions into twenty-nine; the decree (Decree No. 4 of 1996) providing legal backing to this action ousted the jurisdiction of law courts in matters relating to the restructuring. The decree redefined the conditions for union merger and attempted to generate tension between appointed union officials and elected officers in order to create conflicts of authority within the labor movement. It also aimed to rob unions of the experience and skills of more permanent union staff at critical moments of negotiation.

[3] The government relinquished direct management of the Nigeria Labour Congress in 1998 as part of the transition process under General Abdulsalam Abubakar. Workers elected its current president and other executive officers. Since its re-democratization, the Nigeria Labour Congress has been very visible in the public policy arena and has initiated a pro-democracy coalition, the Civil Society Pro-democracy Network, to push the democratization process forward. This coalition seeks to promote civil society involvement in the political process through joint action and the formation of a political party. But the initiative has not been successful.

[4] Prominent donors that have funded the human rights work in Nigeria include the Government of Denmark, the Canadian International Development Agency, USAID, the Ford Foundation, and the Friedrich Ebert Foundation.

Nineteen

Combining Worker and User Interests in the Health Sector

Labor Unions and NGOs

JANE LETHBRIDGE

This chapter describes some of the relationships between labor unions and NGOs in relation to health policies and services. It first looks briefly at various changes that labor unions and NGOs have made in the past two decades. It then gives two case studies of labor unions and NGOs working together, in spite of having had to overcome antagonisms and conflicts. Finally, it identifies conditions that can lead the two sectors to work together, what successful collaboration can produce, and what prospects there are for future alliances.

CHANGING LABOR UNIONS

Labor unions have undergone changes in the last twenty years, many of which have weakened their position. The expansion of multinational companies and the privatization of public services have led to a decline in union membership in many countries. It has taken time for national unions to recognize that action has to span national boundaries if labor unions are to limit the power of multinational companies to move from country to country in their search for cheaper sources of labor (Gallin 2000a).

Labor unions are also becoming aware that they have to act in coordination with other organizations. In some countries labor unions are becoming involved in campaigns for human rights. A specific example of a labor union declaring its belief in the importance of working with other organizations is the case of Finland's Municipal Workers' and Employees' Union (KTV), which published a book entitled *Everything at Stake: Safeguarding Interests in a World without Frontiers* (Artto 2001). In the book's introduction the KTV president states: "Even the most powerful multinational enterprises and other elements of international capital are not immune to pressure. People around the world can influence these forces in many roles: as employees, as consumers and as public activists." He calls for the "renewal of international collective bargaining by the trade union movement," and he also emphasizes the common cause that developed and developing countries have in this struggle against global capital. One of the book's recommendations is: "The trade union movement will achieve the best results by engaging in broad cooperation with non-governmental organisations, experts and policy-makers—and, on an equal footing, also with employers." This is an important policy position for KTV, and it forms the basis for future campaigning with other organizations. KTV is now developing a campaign with NGOs to fight against the privatization of municipal services.

A continuing strength of the labor union movement is that it is the largest representative movement worldwide. However, one of the issues that labor unions, particularly in developing countries, must face is how to become more representative of the informal-employment sector, in which the majority of workers in most developing countries find themselves. Informal employment has expanded because of industrial restructuring, with the result that outsourcing and contracting are now worldwide phenomena. Established labor unions are now beginning to support people working in this sector (ILO 1999; WIEGO 1999).

CHANGING NGOS

NGOs have also changed extensively in the last two decades. This has been caused partly by changes in the role of the state and public sector as a result of neoliberal policies. Many NGOs were set up to work with specific communities or interest groups and to develop services that governments were either unable or unwilling to provide. NGOs have moved in two sometimes contradictory directions. Public services have decreased because government budgets are limited; certain NGOs have therefore taken up provision of some of these services, sometimes under public contract. This role is similar to that of the private sector, and in such cases NGOs may be actively participating in the neoliberal project. On the other hand, some NGOs that traditionally developed innovative services have decided that they will now campaign for the public sector to recognize the needs of specific groups. Jenny Pearce argues that NGOs can go in four possible directions in the future: (1) work within the neoliberal model and deliver services; (2) push for new systems of market regulation and for international policies that favor the poor; (3) support anti-globalization movements; or (4) focus on grassroots work (Pearce 2000). Whichever route is taken, the future of NGOs is being debated extensively.

These changes in the role of NGOs have been taking place in both developing and industrialized countries. Among national and international NGOs alike, advocacy and campaigning have expanded, with many NGOs using increasingly sophisticated techniques to promote their views. Their advocacy work has also led some NGOs to become involved in formulating policies, bringing criticism that they have lost their independence. In cases where such NGOs have been contracted to deliver public services, questions have been raised as to whether their religious or ideological ethos undermines the neutrality that public services should have.

As NGOs have become ever more successful in campaigning in the area of international policies, they have also been criticized for not being truly representative of the interests for which they speak and campaign. This is in contrast to labor unions and the labor union movement in general, which are indubitably representative.

COMING TOGETHER

A conference held in Thailand in 2001 set out to clarify some of the positions of labor unions and NGOs following the uneasy relations that had emerged during the 1990s.[1] The tensions between them had become more visible in the demonstrations at the WTO meeting in Seattle. The differences centered around the International Confederation of Free Trade Unions (ICFTU), other labor unions, and some NGOs that wanted to set up a working group on social standards at the WTO Millennium Round. Labor unions advocated establishing linkages between trade and labor standards within the WTO system. Many NGOs, especially those from the South, opposed this and wanted the approach to globalization to be more centered on development. This difference in orientation is indicative of some of the tensions that have developed in the past decade between labor unions and NGOs, the former often focusing on workers' rights while the latter emphasize the interests of other groups.

There is much to be gained if labor unions and NGOs work together effectively. For labor unions, NGOs may provide access to a wider economic and social agenda, one where labor issues are very often not the priority. For NGOs, labor unions represent a large number of workers to whom they are accountable—few NGOs have such well-organized constituencies. Both groups can contribute ideas about future policies, campaigning tactics, and strategies that have been developed from different perspectives.[2] This chapter shows that, with regard to health issues, relationships between labor unions and NGOs are influenced and often determined both by the interface between users and service providers and by wider social movements.

INTERFACE BETWEEN USER AND SERVICE PROVIDER

The relationship between users of health services and service providers in the health sector has changed in the last twenty to thirty years. In developed countries there has been growing awareness that involving patients in their own care can lead to better health (Gatellari, Butow, and Tattersall 2001). Traditionally, patients had to struggle to get information about their illnesses and treatments. Although many national government policies now acknowledge the importance of keeping patients involved in their treatment, actually doing so is more difficult. But it is slowly being recognized that patients need information and support in order to take part in influencing the services and treatment that they receive. Examples of groups that have fought for more information and more informed choices include people with chronic diseases, users of mental health services, women using maternity services, and most recently HIV/AIDS patients. Many NGOs have been set up to fight for the rights of these groups.

NGOs have also been established to support the right of people to accessible health care. In India, for example, the Center for Enquiry into Health and Allied Themes: The Research Centre for the Anusandhan Trust undertakes research and advocacy projects on sociopolitical aspects of health and "works to establish direct services and programmes to demonstrate how health services can be made accessible, equitably and ethically." It works with people's movements to improve health care through research, training, and program development. In the United States the

Health Consumer Alliance (HCA) is a nonprofit partnership of eight Health Consumer Centers and the Health Rights Hotline, all of which provide one-to-one legal assistance to poor people through representation, education, and advocacy. A recent evaluation found that since it was set up in 1997, the HCA has helped over forty-five thousand people from disadvantaged communities in California enroll in the medical services, gain access to them, and retain them. It provides educational and outreach services for disadvantaged people so that they can become aware of their health rights and of how to get legal advice to secure those rights. The HCA also advocates improvements in health services in general.

Changes in the user-service interface often threaten the power of health professionals. The growing ability of patients to gather information and to question and guide their own treatment means that health service providers must also change their approach.

The differences between industrialized and developing countries in relation to the involvement of patients in health services are still significant. The concept of the "health consumer" has been adopted in many developed countries, further supported by the private health-care sector. This implies, however, that there are health-care choices available for patients needing treatment, which is not always the case. It has led to wider acceptance of the right of patients to receive a certain quality of care. However, health consumerism or patient involvement is often seen as an individual process rather than part of a collective action.

NGOs have played an important role in developing models of participatory involvement, which involve consulting service users. "Consultation with users is a necessary counterpart to the exercise of influence—providers need some way of knowing how users want services organised" (Standing 1996, 12). Although many NGOs have contributed to setting up models of participation and consultation, their own practice is often open to question.

HIV/AIDS has changed relationships between users and service providers and may also have contributed to the formation of alliances between them. It presents such challenges to existing health services, especially in developing countries, that common causes can be identified.

WIDER SOCIAL MOVEMENTS

Health is not always the first issue that unites a range of civil society groups. Sometimes, however, wider social movements have resulted in struggles for health rights, bringing together labor unions, NGOs, community organizations, political parties, and others. In anti-globalization campaigns the connections made between the expansion of multinational companies and the privatization of public services have often led directly to the development of health campaigns.

To illustrate some of the dynamics of labor unions and NGOs working together on health, this chapter examines two case studies: the Malaysia Citizens' Health Initiative (CHI) and the 2002 South Africa Treatment Congress organized by the Treatment Action Campaign (TAC) and the Congress of South African Trade Unions (COSATU). These two case studies address the following questions:

- What led labor unions and NGOs to come together on health issues?
- How did the campaign or activity develop?
- Were there tensions between labor unions and NGOs?
- What were the results in terms of health policy and working relationships?

MALAYSIA CITIZENS' HEALTH INITIATIVE

Labor Unions and NGOs Coming Together

The CHI was launched in March 1998 as an "informal grouping of organizations and individuals seeking to promote greater community involvement in healthcare reforms, and more generally in matters of health policy." It is a loose grouping, not formally registered, of people who support the aims of the Citizens' Health Manifesto and are willing to work for "equitable, accessible, and sustainable healthcare of quality." It describes itself as a "people's think-tank on health matters, which combines policy research and analysis with action-oriented publicity and mobilization."[3]

The CHI has fifty-eight members, mainly NGOs, community and consumer organizations, and networks such as the Federation of Malaysian Consumer Organizations, but also several key health labor unions. Labor union members include the Malaysian Trades Union Congress (MTUC), the Malayan Nurses' Union, and the Estates Hospital Assistants Association of Malaysia. MTUC is well represented on the CHI committee, and the general secretaries of MTUC and of the Malayan Nurses' Union are both members. MTUC joined because the labor unions had decided to become more active in consumer issues, a decision prompted by their members' concerns about inflation, the increasing cost of living, and declining real wages. The Malayan Nurses' Union has also been a strong supporter of the CHI.[4]

How the Campaign Developed

MTUC played an important role in the campaign to stop hospital privatization, and the CHI marshaled intense public pressure on the government to stop the "corporatization" of state-run general hospitals.[5] The signature campaign began in late May 1999, when doctors at a state-run general hospital in the city of Ipoh circulated a letter to the health minister expressing concern over the privatization of general hospitals. Soon after, more than eighty doctors at the city's hospital had endorsed the letter. Another 80 doctors attending the Malaysian Medical Association's annual general meeting in Penang also added their signatures to the petition.

The Malaysian Medical Association, whose members represent 80 percent of Malaysia's doctors, called for a moratorium on the "corporatization" plans. The Malayan Nurses' Union and the Estates Hospital Assistants Association of Malaysia supported its demands.

After less than two weeks of mobilization, MTUC delivered ten thousand signatures from union members to the office of the minister of health demanding a "halt to the corporatization of public hospitals and a review of the privatization of ancillary support services" (Chee Khoon 2003). The Federal Land Development Authority Employees' Union played an important role in this action and also disseminated the concerns to rural areas. In August 1999 the CHI sent out a letter to all political parties spelling out its demands. A week later the cabinet decided that government hospitals would not be "corporatized." This was in the run-up to the November 1999 elections and the "victory," although well received by the Malaysian public, was also seen as a government preelection ploy.

Tensions between Labor Unions and NGOs in the Campaign

MTUC is a confederation of 230 affiliate unions, which include many private-sector unions, while the Congress of Unions of Employees in the Public and Civil Services (CUEPACS) is a confederation of public service unions. In recent years CUEPACS has pursued a policy of working with the government, which has limited its power to criticize it. This has led to a rift between MTUC and CUEPACS on many labor issues.

There have also been conflicts at times between the Federation of Malaysian Consumer Associations (FOMCA) and MTUC, in which the CHI has acted as mediator. FOMCA and MTUC had a widely publicized disagreement some years ago when MTUC announced plans to lead a consumer boycott of high-priced consumables. FOMCA felt this kind of action fell within its own remit. The two organizations argued in the national press about their "appropriate" arenas of activity. While this argument has subsided, mutual wariness lingers.

In 2002, however, relations between MTUC and FOMCA improved, with the CHI being instrumental in drawing the two organizations together. A recent success, achieved while the CHI's coordinator was acting as FOMCA's health-policy adviser, was getting the health minister to include MTUC in the ministerial subcommittee in charge of drawing up the fee schedule for the National Healthcare Financing Scheme reimbursement system.

Results in Relation to Health Policy and Working Relationships

The CHI acts as a de facto health-policy adviser to MTUC and its affiliates. MTUC has little capacity for research, and the CHI fills that gap, as it also does for FOMCA and other NGOs. In 2001–2002 the CHI worked closely with the General Staff Union of the University of Malaya to organize a national conference on health-care reforms and financing for labor unionists.

At the 2002 health minister's annual dialogue with NGOs, the coordinator of the CHI, Dr. Chan Chee Khoon, outlined a number of concerns about the new scheme. These included the "absence of organized labour at the health ministry subcommittee responsible for drawing up this schedule, despite the fact that the scheme will be largely funded by payroll contributions from employees (and employers, who are represented by the Malaysian Employers' Federation at the subcommittee)."[6] The health minister acknowledged this "oversight," and MTUC was invited to join the subcommittee. At the same meeting Dr. Chee Khoon also highlighted the difference in government attitude toward NGOs that are "doers" and those that are vocal and question policy issues. These two interventions show how the CHI has been able to assume a critical position toward the government in relation to both labor union and NGO issues.

The CHI operates logistically under the infrastructural umbrella of Aliran, the country's oldest human rights and social justice organization. FOMCA's president is also a founding member of the recently established Human Rights Commission of Malaysia. The commission has been criticized recently because it is perceived by some not to be defending civil liberties strongly enough. Chee Heng Leng, the CHI's co-founder, is a former political prisoner, and many other human rights groups, women's rights groups, and groups fighting for economic and social rights are among the CHI's staunchest supporters.

The CHI campaign came at a time when several other campaigns were being launched, for example, on women's rights, Indian Chinese community rights, and labor union rights. People were interested and willing to take part in these because it was a time of political "opening." This is a good example of how timing and context play a significant role in influencing the relationships between labor unions and NGOs.

Summing up the Malaysia CHI

The CHI, whose members include labor unions and NGOs, has become a campaigning and advocacy organization for both these groups. It has also developed its role as mediator between labor unions and NGOs, made possible in part by its being a separate organization. Previous conflicts between MTUC and FOMCA were about spheres of activity and areas of responsibility. If labor unions take on a wide campaigning role, NGOs may feel their own activities are being encroached upon. The CHI can be seen as a part of a wider movement for its members, set up at a time of political opening. This may be significant in the development of relationships between labor unions and NGOs.

SOUTH AFRICAN TREATMENT ACTION CAMPAIGN AND COSATU CONGRESS

Labor Unions and NGOs Coming Together

The increasing incidence of HIV/AIDS in South Africa has led labor unions and NGOs to develop alliances to campaign for improved services and recognition of the rights of people living with HIV/AIDS. This has happened at a time when many feel that government has not acted strongly enough to counter HIV/AIDS, either in recognizing the seriousness of the problem or in providing treatment and taking adequate preventive measures.

The high prevalence of HIV/AIDS in South Africa, where up to 30 percent of the adult population is HIV-positive, and the lack of adequate treatment are having a severe impact on South Africa's economic and social system, which will affect the country's development for many decades to come. Part of the response to this major crisis has been that labor unions and NGOs have come together. In political terms, the alliance between TAC and COSATU has been described as the "Alternative Alliance, with the potential to split the labor union federation away from the South African Communist Party and the ANC."[7]

The issue of HIV/AIDS concerns labor unions in several ways:

- members with HIV/AIDS need the right to treatment;
- members need to be provided with health education programs; and
- HIV/AIDS is a major health and safety issue in the workplace and in collective bargaining.

For these reasons the unions are taking part in wider campaigns to improve access to treatment, to challenge stigmatization, and to lobby the government.

NGOs are concerned with similar issues, but they have a community focus; that is, they

- represent people living with HIV/AIDS;
- campaign for improved access to treatment and preventive care;
- work with communities on health education and human rights issues; and
- campaign for better health care.

NGOs also take part in wider campaigns to overcome the stigma associated with HIV/AIDS and to pressure the government to act, although they do not necessarily believe that the government has the resources to extend its health services to people with AIDS. Labor unions and NGOs thus share several common issues: rights, treatment, prevention, and better general health care.

How the Campaign and Activity Developed

The South African government has been criticized for its failure to take appropriate action to combat AIDS, and especially for not providing access to medicines such as antiretrovirals. In November 2001 the government fought a case that TAC brought against it, which was trying to ensure that HIV-positive pregnant women had access to affordable antiretroviral treatment to reduce the risk of transmitting HIV to their babies.[8]

The government's failure to provide treatment is considered inexcusable because it had won a victory against thirty-nine pharmaceutical companies. These companies had sued the government because of a 1997 law that allowed generic drugs for HIV/AIDS to be produced and imported. Intense national and international pressure led the companies to drop their suit. However, the government did not take up the opportunity to produce the generic drugs or to develop a nationwide treatment program. As a result, the demand for affordable, accessible treatment became the focus. Previous conflicts between NGOs in balancing efforts concerning treatment and prevention have been overcome, and labor unions and NGOs have developed new forms of collaboration.

In June 2002 TAC and COSATU sponsored a three-day conference on HIV/AIDS to debate how to adopt and implement a national treatment plan. The conference discussed strategies for HIV prevention, better care management, and distribution of antiretroviral drugs in public hospitals. It brought together labor unions, AIDS activists, health workers, NGOs, religious groups, scientists, and business leaders. Delegates from Brazil and from many African countries were also present.

Over 750 delegates from both urban and rural areas attended the conference. The majority was from COSATU (two hundred people from nineteen affiliates) and TAC (three hundred people). Delegates also came from the Federation of Unions of South Africa, the National Council of Trade Unions, and the Hospital and Other Service Personnel Trade Union of South Africa, among others. Over three hundred delegates were from the labor sector. Eighty nurses from various labor unions participated (Hospital and Other Service Personnel Trade Union of South Africa, Democratic Nurses Organisation of South Africa, South Africa Democratic Nurses' Union, and the National Education, Health and Allied Workers' Union) as did thirty doctors from the Rural Doctors' Association and Junior Doctors' Association.

A wide range of civil groups and organizations also participated, including faith-based organizations, NGOs, the Board of Health Care Funders, the Council for Medical Schemes, political parties, and traditional healers. The NGOs included some that had previously been critical of TAC, such as the AIDS Consortium, AIDS Foundation of South Africa, Children's Rights Centre, AIDS Law Project, and Community Health Media Trust.

The delegates thus came from a broad range of labor unions and NGOs. Many NGOs had been critical both of each other and of TAC, the co-sponsor. As well as bringing together labor unions and NGOs, the congress drew many groups that had not worked together before and convinced them of the common interests that they shared and the importance of taking concerted action.

Congress participants broke into working groups or "commissions" to examine and make recommendations in the following areas:

- upgrading the capacity of nurses, doctors, and volunteers to treat HIV;
- improving information about prevention;
- defining the role of youth in the national treatment plan;
- treating sexually transmitted infections and opportunistic infections, especially among vulnerable groups such as women and children;
- piloting antiretroviral treatment and diagnostics in the public sector;
- cutting prices of medicine and diagnostics—investing in public health care; and
- supporting social campaigns to support the national treatment plan.

The recommendations of the working groups demonstrate a vision that brings together the interests of labor unions, NGOs, and the wider civil society. For instance, the recommendations of the commission discussing how to increase the capacity to treat HIV demonstrated most strongly the power that labor unions and NGOs can exert when they work together. The group was co-chaired by a member of COSATU and a member of TAC. It looked at the experiences of people providing health care and those receiving it. It found that although health professionals were committed to providing care, it was becoming increasingly difficult to deliver an adequate level of care. Reasons given included the shortage of nurses, the growing number of patients, an inadequate supply of medicines, lack of support to front-line professionals, and limited capacity to implement new policies put out by central and provincial governments.

This commission recognized that "providing quality care in the public health services depends on rebuilding relationships."[9] The relationships identified as needing to be rebuilt were between a wide range of professionals and agencies involved in providing care: between health professionals and public health and other welfare services; between public health services and communities and the private sector; between education and training institutions and public health providers; and between traditional healers and health professionals. By pointing out the need to rebuild relationships, the commission acknowledged that such relationships had deteriorated over the past decade. H. Schneider and J. Stein also mention the breakdown of trust among stakeholders in the health sector. They point out that before the 1994 election of the ANC government, there were "strong networks between NGOs, researchers, sympathetic health workers, an infrastructure of AIDS counselling and information centres . . . and anti-apartheid political groupings" (Schneider and Stein 2001, 723). By 1998 there had been conflicts and a breakdown of trust within government and between government and NGOs. This same commission also recognized that "there is a need for better conditions of services, higher salaries, and a better working environment (safety) for doctors and nurses to prevent the exit of people from the public health service. It was proposed that the nursing unions and staff associations should meet to set a figure for minimum salary and that this should be negotiated with the government."

There were also recommendations to support and strengthen professional nurses, public health doctors, volunteers, and community-based workers, who do much of the HIV prevention and care work, in recognition of the growing role that community workers play in the health sector. It may also explain the nature of some of the recommendations made by this group in that they recognized difficulties that health workers experience in trying to deliver services and made positive suggestions about how to resolve them.

Three of the commissions recommended training for health workers. The commission discussing voluntary testing and counseling found that current testing facilities and counseling were inadequate. To describe training needs in HIV/AIDS, this group used the phrase "treatment literacy," which it recommended for a broad range of groups, including health workers. The commission for youth recommended that health workers be trained in the needs of young people. Wider policies for school programs were also recommended: life-skills education, the use of condoms to prevent infection, and treatment literacy.

One of the major issues bringing together an alliance of NGOs and activists was the government's lethargic approach to treatment. Promoting a national strategy focused on prevention, the government was, at the time of writing, unwilling to address the need for treatment. The congress pointed out the positive results of a pilot project using highly active antiretroviral treatment: patients' health had improved, and so they were better able to look after themselves and their families as well as remain employed. The congress also recommended replacing the current social grant system, arguing that corporations should explore means of treating their employees.

Differences between Labor Unions and NGOs

Relations between labor unions and NGOs in the health sector in South Africa have not always been smooth. One of the issues that showed their different reactions to government policy was notification of HIV status. In 1999 the South African government planned to make AIDS a notifiable disease. NGOs strongly opposed this plan, because they believed it would damage people with HIV/AIDS due to the stigma and often even violence that infected people have experienced in South Africa. However, some political parties and COSATU supported the government plan to make notification mandatory. They argued that if high-profile politicians and labor union members made public their own HIV-positive status, people would be influenced to seek treatment and health education. NGOs thought that this was unlikely to happen, given that few public figures have publicly acknowledged being HIV-positive.

Results of Working Together

The TAC-COSATU Congress and its recommendations represent an important joint effort to address a major crisis in South Africa. The congress developed a common cause between users of health services and health workers, and it recognized the need for better services through support and training for health workers. Both groups agreed on the need to invest in improving services and rebuilding relationships. The need for treatment literacy among health workers and other individuals was also widely acknowledged. This is interesting because it suggests demystifying treatment, which has traditionally been part of professional power, and a willingness for a wide range of groups to be educated in the same issue.

The congress recommended that the government develop a "multifaceted approach to managing the HIV/AIDS epidemic." This is to complement the existing government strategic plan, which deals mainly with prevention. Prevention and treatment cannot be separated. The unwillingness of the government to provide treatment was one of the issues that brought the alliance between NGOs and COSATU into existence.

The congress recommended that the national treatment plan include and "synchronise a range of health interventions," but it also went much further, stating that "the HIV/AIDS epidemic is an economic, development and labour issue. The plan recognises the need to develop urgent plans to tackle social issues linked to the alleviation of the epidemic, such as social grants, children's rights, public education, school life-skills programmes, de-stigmatisation on HIV . . . further research into vaccines . . . and affordable health solutions."

Recognizing HIV/AIDS as an economic, development, and labor concern links it to health as a development and human rights issue, which has the power to unite labor unions and NGOs.

The congress was "adamant that working conditions in the public health sector, particularly for nurses, must be addressed. A plan will not succeed without greater investment in public health and [reduction of] the growing gap between the private and public health sectors."

The major criticism made of the TAC-COSATU conference was that the government was only minimally represented. Only two government officials attended, one of whom was the director of HIV/AIDS issues in the Ministry of Health and whose position is considered weak. However, the presence of a large number of delegates working together still made it a valuable event.

CONCLUSION

Spurs That Bring Labor Unions and NGOs Together

The two case studies outlined above illustrate that labor unions and NGOs can come together on specific health-sector issues and also on wider causes. In Malaysia proposed changes in the health sector brought about an alliance, which then evolved into a separate organization. In South Africa the impact of a public health issue on the country's entire society and economy, along with the government's failure to provide treatment, has led to the development of a broad alliance.

Anti-globalization campaigns have become an important instigator for labor unions and NGOs to work and campaign together. Campaigns opposing the privatization of health services have often developed from such anti-globalization work. For example, the German affiliate of the international movement ATTAC (Association for the Taxation of Financial Transactions for the Aid of Citizens) is developing an anti-privatization campaign entitled "Health Is Not a Commodity." The campaign has stemmed from anti-globalization campaigns and an awareness of the impact of the General Agreement on Trade in Services (GATS) as well as from current moves by the German government to privatize health services and social insurance funds. ATTAC and a group of German labor unions both see that the reduction of funds going to the public health sector and the privatization of hospitals are part of wider neoliberal policies and global pressures.

On September 14, 2002, in a day of joint action that was the culmination of six months of preparation, labor union youth and ATTAC members demonstrated against neoliberal policies. The campaign brought together the youth organizations of Ver.di (the German affiliate of Union Network International, the global labor union for commercial workers), the public-sector workers' union, the industrial metalworkers' union, and other industrial unions. The labor union youth organizations and ATTAC issued a joint statement to explain their day of action: "Our political and economic demands are the same. We stand together in favour of socially meaningful investments and against the proponents of neo-liberal ideologies." ATTAC has actively promoted labor union involvement in the health campaign. Separate campaigning organizations can also play an important role in bringing together labor unions and NGOs, often identifying common issues and making overtures to various other organizations.

Reproductive health rights have also become a focus for mobilizing labor union and NGO action. During the 1990s the Women's Network of Towns and Neighborhoods (Red de Mujeres de Villas y Barrios) in the Argentine province of Córdoba brought together women's and community organizations to resist and eventually overturn a provincial law that prevented public hospitals from providing family-planning services. The campaign "fought under the banner of the right to build citizenship, the right to choose as well as the right of access to resources that guarantee true choice" (Harcourt 1998, 11). The network worked with an alliance of health workers, NGOs, labor unions, and national women's movements such as the National Women's Network (Red Nacional de la Mujer). Their example is one of a successful alliance in which health workers, labor unions, and women's organizations joined to fight for reproductive health rights. This alliance can also be seen as part of the social changes taking place within Argentina during the 1990s, when NGOs were rapidly expanding as a result of a wider social movement that grew out of economic changes in the country.

The role of social movements in facilitating alliances between labor unions and NGOs is recognized. However, wider social movements do not always take up health issues in the first place. The Malaysia CHI was set up at a time when broad social changes were taking place and is located under the umbrella of a human rights organization. But the increasingly vocal role of health service users and their demands for improved health services can lead to wider alliances being developed. Reproductive health rights and HIV/AIDS are examples of how inadequacies in the provision of health services have brought labor unions and NGOs together.

Tensions between Labor Unions and NGOs

Tensions between labor unions and NGOs have sometimes developed because when one group decides to broaden its approach, the other perceives that as encroaching on its activities. In Malaysia, MTUC decided to mount a consumer boycott of expensive items because its members were being affected by inflation and the rising cost of living. But this led the Federation of Malaysian Consumer Associations to feel that MTUC was taking on issues that traditionally fell within its sphere of activity.

In South Africa tensions between labor unions and NGOs arose because of differences in interpreting government policy. Their different points of view about government policies or about formal structures are one of the main causes for these tensions. Labor unions have formal structures and systems of representation and have a role in formal negotiations. Their main concern has traditionally been the immediate jobs of their members, which NGOs may feel is short term in nature and not addressing longer-term service issues. Similarly, NGOs sometimes focus on the quality of services provided without acknowledging the position of health workers.

NGOs may also develop campaigns that are designed to raise awareness of government policies but without wanting to become part of the formal political process. However, the role of NGOs in the policymaking process at national and international levels is changing, and they are taking on strategies that will lead them to having a role in negotiations. The attempts by campaigning groups to negotiate within a system can cause tension both between labor unions and NGOs and among the labor unions and the NGOs themselves.

The Results of Collaboration between Labor Unions and NGOs

The most immediate types of activities are local, national, and international campaigns. The ATTAC health campaign organized days of action throughout Germany, for example, while reproductive health campaigns have been focused at all levels. In Córdoba, as we have seen, the focus was on changing provincial legislation.

Conferences are another potentially influential form of activity. They can be a way of bringing groups together and may develop alternative policies, which are important in presenting new policy responses to existing government policy. The South Africa Treatment Congress is one example of how a conference can cement an alliance.

Several anti-privatization campaigns in the health sector around the world have developed alternative policies. For instance, in Brazil, anti-privatization campaigns in the health sector developed proposals for improving the quality of health services. NGOs representing chronically ill patients were most active in these campaigns and brought a specific perspective to such proposals.

The long-term result of labor unions and NGOs working together can be defined more as that of developing a process than in terms of specific outcomes. In bringing labor unions and NGOs together, the CHI has given rise to a new organization that can mediate between these two groups and the government. It has conducted research that labor unions and NGOs can draw on and has developed policy recommendations that recognize the needs of both workers and activists.

Often the experience of collaboration can lead to greater understanding of different perspectives, which will benefit future campaigning of both groups. It also provides future allies and potential coalitions. Being part of a wider social movement can mean that health issues have a higher profile and are more widely recognized as being relevant to broader development issues.

In reproductive health and HIV/AIDS campaigns, labor unions and NGOs working together can help improve the understanding between the users and providers of health services. This may lead to better relationships, which will ultimately improve the quality of care. The recommendations of the congress in South Africa represent an important step in bringing health service workers and health service users together, though it is also important to recognize that the providers of public health services are also users of those same services.

Specifically, when they collaborate with each other, labor unions and NGOs can form stronger alliances that can challenge government policy as in the case of Malaysia. In South Africa the TAC-COSATU alliance may result in changing wider political alliances. Both outcomes will provide the basis for future action and policy developments. The testing point will be whether these alliances can continue to develop when the initial reason for coming together has been removed and circumstances have changed.

NOTES

[1] Unpublished reports of the Bangkok International Roundtable of Unions, Social Movements, and NGOs Conference entitled "Focus on the Global South and Freidrich-Ebert-Stiftung," Bangkok, March 11–13, 2001, and follow-up meeting, July 17–18, 2002.

[2] Conclusions of the follow-up meeting of the Bangkok International Roundtable of Unions, Social Movements, and NGOs, July 17–18, 2002.

[3] See the Malaysia Citizens' Health Initiative's website, www.prn.usm.my /chi.html.

[4] Dr. Chan Chee Khoon, CHI, personal communication, September 2002.

[5] For details about the campaign, see Anil Netto, "Malaysian People Power Wins Health Care Back-down," InterPress Service, *Asian Times,* August 24, 1999.

[6] Dr. Chan Chee Khoon, CHI, personal communication, September 2002.

[7] *Africa News,* June 28, 2002.

[8] Human Rights Watch news report, "South Africa: Stop Court Fight on AIDS Drugs," November 21, 2001. Available online at the www.hrw.org website.

[9] Details and quotations in this section are derived from reports and resolutions of the COSATU/TAC National HIV/AIDS Treatment Congress, 2002.

Twenty

More Than a Token Gesture

*NGOs and Labor Unions Campaigning
for a Common Cause*

JONATHAN ELLIS

A NEW CURRENCY FOR ASYLUM SEEKERS

With the passage of the 1999 Asylum and Immigration Act a new currency was approved for the support of asylum seekers in the UK. Despite widespread opposition from the refugee sector, this act introduced a system of asylum vouchers for all new asylum seekers from April 2000. Such vouchers were redeemable only at certain stores, expired after four weeks, and no change was given when the vouchers were used. For a vulnerable group in society, existing on around 70 percent of standard income support, this was an additional hardship to bear. Yet the government expressed its firm desire to implement this scheme, as it was a key flagship policy in its new approach to asylum.

Nonetheless, within eighteen months a new home secretary was announcing that asylum vouchers were to be scrapped. How had that turnaround occurred? And what impact had a fresh campaigning coalition consisting of development and refugee charities together with labor unions had on this volte-face in government asylum policy?

BRINGING TOGETHER A COALITION
AGAINST THE VOUCHER SCHEME

The opposition to vouchers had widened from the refugee sector just before the scheduled implementation of the scheme on April 1, 2000. A number of leading charities such as Oxfam GB announced that their shops would not be taking these vouchers. It was a hard call for such organizations, which knew that asylum seekers would benefit from being able to shop at their stores. For Oxfam GB's trading program and its UK Poverty Programme, it was in particular the "no change" ruling that was a step too far. Although Oxfam GB's refusal to participate in the scheme added to the existing opposition and gained widespread media coverage, it seemingly had no impact on the government. The scheme went into effect as planned, and, with a few notable exceptions such as Safeway, most of the major supermarkets took part.

Thus in April 2000 an embryonic campaign coalition had unconsciously been formed bringing the opposition of the refugee groups together with the charities running High Street shops. Oxfam GB realized that media coverage of its boycott alone would not shift government thinking and therefore decided to launch a popular campaign to show the level of public opposition to the scheme. It also realized that, despite being one of the largest campaigning charities in the UK, this campaign would need partners, especially in the refugee sector.

In June 2000 an initial Oxfam GB campaign action card designed for customers to hand in at their local supermarket was rapidly re-branded to include the Refugee Council logo. This partnership would remain a cornerstone throughout the campaign. It was a new partnership, and despite the potential for suspicion between the two NGOs, their mutual desire to defeat the voucher scheme and their recognition of the scale of the challenge helped them put any such fears aside.

In April, Bill Morris, general secretary of the Transport and General Workers' Union (TGWU), had written an article in the *Independent* newspaper expressing his concerns about the government asylum policy and in particular about the voucher scheme. Oxfam GB picked up on this article and subsequent speeches by Morris and asked the TGWU if it could use a quotation from these statements against vouchers on its action card. The TGWU agreed and the quotation was featured on the card. The establishment of such contact would prove to be important.

Yet by the summer of 2000, despite tens of thousands of cards having been distributed, the campaign did not seem to be making progress. Indeed, there was a discussion within Oxfam GB as to whether the effort had run out of steam and should come to an end. There was, however, an event on the horizon that might potentially raise the profile of the campaign. The Trades Union Congress was to meet in Glasgow in September, and there was already a tabled motion that included a reference to scrapping the voucher scheme.

Mindful of this opportunity, Oxfam GB and the Scottish Refugee Council arranged with the TGWU for Bill Morris to go shopping with an asylum seeker during the conference. This stunt generated substantial media interest and proved that the scheme was not working and was hurting people. It also showed Morris that he was right to oppose this scheme, and the account of his shopping visit formed a moving part of his speech to the conference. Later that day the motion was passed unanimously.

With the momentum achieved at the Trades Union Congress, the TGWU decided to move an emergency motion at the Labour Party conference at Brighton due to be held two weeks later. In the meantime the three organizations had shared their intelligence on the voucher scheme, and this allowed the TGWU to pull together a "dossier of disgrace" on the scheme; it was the first time that the impact of the scheme had been collated. The result of this collaboration was a statement by Labour's National Executive Committee recommending a review of the voucher scheme. It should be acknowledged here that not all NGOs regarded this development as an unqualified success; Oxfam GB and the Refugee Council, respecting the TGWU's judgment, publicly welcomed the review.

AN EARLY CAMPAIGN SUCCESS

Thus, within six months of the voucher scheme coming into operation, the government had been forced into agreeing to hold a review of this new measure to support asylum seekers. It was an early campaigning success for this novel alliance of the TGWU, the Refugee Council, and Oxfam GB. All three organizations were beginning to realize that, despite their differences, they all were bringing something invaluable to the campaign. The TGWU had political connections with the Labour Party, the Refugee Council had close contact with the experience of asylum seekers across the UK, and Oxfam GB brought the reassurance of a household name together with its campaigning resources.

After this success in obtaining a review, this NGO–labor union partnership continued as all three organizations realized that any submission would be much more effective if it was presented jointly. As a result of this decision, a joint report entitled *Token Gestures* was published in December 2000. It featured the findings of fifty organizations working with asylum seekers across the UK. Some of the key findings included that 98 percent of respondents felt that the voucher system was causing serious difficulties, and that respondents had been unable to buy essential items such as shoes, over-the-counter medicines, and baby milk in 96 percent of the cases. Discrimination caused by vouchers was another key finding: 70 percent of respondents reported cases where people had received poor treatment from shops accepting vouchers, and 62 percent had received complaints from asylum seekers about hostility from other shoppers when they used their vouchers. The findings also proved that the scheme was an administrative disaster, a fact that would continue to haunt government ministers. Hence vouchers were causing real problems to asylum seekers trying to live their lives and were encouraging discrimination. One young woman likened her experience of using vouchers to "getting a stamp saying that you don't belong."

Following the joint press launch of *Token Gestures*, substantial media coverage was obtained, and this report became the first and definitive account of the impact of vouchers on asylum seekers. In subsequent debates on the voucher scheme in Parliament the report was frequently cited. Undoubtedly, part of the report's credibility stemmed from the fact that it was owned by three highly regarded organizations from three different sectors.

KEEPING UP THE PRESSURE

Despite the momentum that was built up by the publication of this report and the fact that its findings were never challenged by the government, Home Office sources soon confirmed that the government was anxious to delay an announcement on the voucher review until after the general election, which was called in May for June 7, 2001.

The three organizations took a gamble and decided that it was worth waiting until after the election to rebuild pressure for change. A joint letter on World Refugee Day in June, published in the *Guardian* newspaper and signed also by the Local Government Association, the British Medical Association, and others, ensured that an early warning shot was fired. It also demonstrated that the campaign to abolish vouchers was still active.

A new ministerial team at the Home Office gave the campaign hope that change was possible. This hope increased when the new minister, Lord Rooker, admitted that vouchers were seen as stigmatizing. The next month a new action card was produced by Oxfam GB and the Refugee Council. It was based on the findings of the *Token Gestures* report, and fifty thousand cards were circulated across the country. The popular campaign was back on the streets.

Throughout the summer contradictory media stories claimed both that vouchers were to be scrapped and that they were to be maintained. Each time joint letters were printed in the press by the emerging coalition of Oxfam GB, the Refugee Council, and the TGWU reemphasizing the case for the abolition of vouchers. The summer also saw a major asylum campaign run by the Body Shop in seventy of its shops and in ten Oxfam GB shops. A petition against vouchers was signed by over six thousand people in this initiative.

The campaign coalition, now meeting on a regular basis, decided to go for broke on a decision being made at the Labour Party conference in September 2001. In the meantime, efforts were made to place articles in left-leaning journals such as *Tribune*, *Progress*, and *Red Pepper* in order to disseminate the findings of *Token Gestures* more widely to the labor movement.

At the party conference in Brighton the coalition handed out "product recall" cards to the delegates with the clear message that vouchers had to go. While the conference was in progress a major article by Bill Morris was published in the Sunday newspaper the *Observer* challenging the new home secretary to abolish vouchers. Pressure increased further by a TGWU emergency motion that topped the delegates' ballot. The fringe meeting among Amnesty International, Oxfam GB, and the Refugee Council with the TGWU attracted 120 delegates, despite the fact that it took place after the formal end of conference.

Home Secretary David Blunkett, MP, asked the conference to trust him, and a month later in the Commons he announced that vouchers were to be scrapped, meaning that a flagship of the government's asylum policy was to go. The government would now use the technology of new "smart cards" to provide cash to asylum seekers. This development allowed the government to avoid returning to benefits while still being able to drop the voucher scheme. Hence the government had a winnable solution, and it could be presented as not being a total retreat. From April 8, 2002, asylum seekers in the UK have been able to use cash in their daily shopping. The campaign objective had been achieved.

NGO–LABOR UNION COLLABORATION: SOME LESSONS

From an initial campaigning alliance between Oxfam GB and the Refugee Council, united in their desire to oppose vouchers, the two organizations worked increasingly closely with the TGWU. There had been no previous history of collaboration among these three organizations, and the experience therefore broke new ground for each.

For Oxfam GB, this was its first real campaign on a domestic issue in the UK. For the Refugee Council, the experience meant working on one of its key issues with organizations that were relatively new to this area of work. And for the TGWU, the campaign represented a new way of working with the NGO sector.

Yet the three were united by an explicit common purpose, an understanding of what each could offer to the campaign, and a realization that none of them could achieve success alone. Oxfam GB and the Refugee Council identified the outspoken comments of the TGWU on the voucher system and were increasingly keen to work with the TGWU on the campaign in order to develop a broader front. Over the following months Oxfam GB and the Refugee Council worked hard in a spirit of mutual respect to prove that the TGWU could trust them and to show that each organization had a fresh perspective to offer on the campaign.

What lessons can be drawn from this campaign for NGOs working with labor unions? First, when there is an area of common interest and a common goal, such a relationship is vital for a successful campaign as it involves new audiences and taps into fresh political influences. Both sectors are keen to promote campaigning for social change, encourage activists, and influence decision makers. But these things alone are not enough to build an effective relationship. There must be a clearly defined common goal.

NGOs need to realize that labor unions work differently and have different pressure points. No matter how close the alliance becomes, NGOs have to respect the fact that there will be occasions when labor unions will need to retreat and deal with internal or external issues in their own ways. NGOs have to respect that there will be some distance between them, and that this distance may grow or shrink, but they should not expect a completely transparent relationship at all times. Yet in respecting this sensitivity, there must be mutual confidence that all sides are working toward the same goal.

The NGOs must also be clear regarding the priorities of labor unions and how these are determined. They must be clear about where power lies and who can make a decision on whether a campaign is supported. This intelligence is vital before an NGO makes any kind of approach to a labor union. In the voucher campaign the public statements of the general secretary were the encouragement that Oxfam GB and the Refugee Council needed to approach the TGWU.

In respecting the differences between sectors, NGOs must realize that their new labor union partners, despite their enthusiasm, will not always feel able to support every campaign action and may feel the need to make their own contribution. For example, in the case of the voucher campaign the action cards did not carry the TGWU logo, but the research was jointly branded. Much of the media work was jointly undertaken by the Refugee Council and Oxfam GB, while the TGWU used its own networks; however, the press conference on the research was run by all three organizations. The clear message is that, even with an excellent relationship and a track record of cooperation, NGOs should not expect that their labor union partners will want to join or will feel comfortable about engaging in every proposed joint action.

During the voucher campaign the Refugee Council and Oxfam GB were pleased when the TGWU came on board, but they did not expect it to do so and were therefore relaxed when it chose not to engage. Both realized that the TGWU added real impact working in its own style. Any cooperation between NGOs and labor unions needs this flexible approach.

SHARED VISIONS, SHARED GOALS

Yet for all the lessons outlined above with the luxury of hindsight, the key point is that the campaign was not built on these lessons but on the enthusiasm of certain individuals in each organization who were committed to a shared goal and were willing to give working together a try for greater impact. In Oxfam GB's early campaign plans there was no statement of the need to work with a labor union, but there was a desire to build a wide coalition of groups showing the strength of opposition to vouchers. What drove the campaign and this NGO–labor union relationship was the unity of commitment to a clearly defined goal—the abolition of vouchers.

During the course of the campaign the debate was being conducted within a very hostile media environment. The voucher campaign was never going to change everyone's views on asylum, but it did expose a cruel and inept system that was funded through public taxes. The campaign also succeeded in raising the level of debate on how asylum seekers should be treated in the UK. And as the government begins another overhaul of the asylum system, this campaign should have proved that the public has no time for state-sponsored separation. We hope that this will be the legacy of the voucher campaign.

The campaign that started in early 2000 was fueled by a passionate view that asylum vouchers had no place in a civilized society. Over the next few months a loose campaign coalition emerged including organizations in both the NGO and the labor union sectors. On April 8, 2002, vouchers ceased to exist—a clear campaign success. The lesson here is not simply that NGOs must work with other organizations/sectors. The message is in fact much broader—that by working with others, united by a common goal, we really can challenge injustice and make a difference to people's lives.

Twenty-one

Trade Unions and Women's NGOs

Diverse Civil Society Organizations in Iran

ELAHEH ROSTAMI POVEY

Labor unions and women's NGOs in Iran are inherently countervailing centers of power in civil society with the potential to promote the struggle for democracy. However, their activities are limited because they operate in wholly different social spheres and are not engaged with each other. The labor unions, with their ninety-year history, have remained male-dominated organizations. Women's NGOs, an extension of the women's movement of the 1990s, are solely engaged with gender issues and do not concern themselves with the collective action efforts of women workers to enhance their working conditions.

My premise is that if civil society is conceptualized as an autonomous space between state and the market (Oommen 1996), this case study on Iran demonstrates that labor unions and women's NGOs, albeit in different ways, provide opportunities for fundamental social change as well as new sources of identity for individuals and groups (Whaites 2000). However, the creation of autonomous spheres of social activity for women has been undermined by a patriarchal social order and the multiple sites—the intertwining of civil society, state, religion, and family—through which social gender is constructed (Joseph 2000). Nevertheless, women's NGOs have been challenging institutional power, especially gender-specific access and influence, and have achieved substantive goals. They are recognized as a social group that shares common interests and legitimate claims on society. All the same, their segregated activities are limited. Hence, collaboration between labor unions and women's NGOs is crucial to the process of democratization.

This essay opens with a historical account of labor unions in Iran and examines the difficulties faced by women, their ingenuity, and their strategies within male-dominated labor unions. The aims are to discuss why "gendering" the labor union question is so critical and to identify possibilities for enhancing women's issues within labor unions. The following section draws on fieldwork carried out between 2000 and 2002 and illustrates the activities of women's NGOs since the 1990s. My aim is to explore the prospects and constraints they face. The concluding section raises the issue of possible collaboration between the two sectors. I argue that adopting strategies for transforming existing labor union structures as well as establishing linkages between them and women's NGOs may strengthen both institutions in their bargaining efforts. Furthermore, collaboration between the two institutions may create social solidarity and cohesion within formal workplaces as well as at various community levels. As a coalition, they could act as pressure groups to take gender issues forward as well as take steps toward the general democratization of institutions both within the state and in civil society.

LABOR UNIONS: TRADITIONAL CIVIL ASSOCIATIONS

The history of the Iranian labor movement and labor unions began in the early twentieth century. From 1912 to 1916 teachers, journalists, copper-smelting workers, and oil workers laid the foundations for the establishment of labor unions. In 1918 the printers' union succeeded in winning its demands after a two-week strike: an eight-hour working day, overtime pay, provision of medical care, and a ban on arbitrary dismissal. Between 1918 and 1922 bakery workers, textile workers, shoemakers, postal and telegraph workers, confectionery workers, and clerks also formed their own labor unions (Ladjevardi 1985, 1–28).

In this period the labor movement was associated with the communist movements in Iran and in Russia, and it was hostile to Britain, which owned the Anglo-Persian Oil Company and supported the autocratic governing regime in Iran. In 1922 the forty-seven thousand oil workers went on strike demanding a 100 percent wage increase. The strike was broken by British troops, and many strikers were arrested. Nevertheless, they managed to win a 75 percent wage increase (Ladjevardi 1985, 14).

In 1936, with the assistance of the ILO, a bill entitled "Regulations for Factories and Industrial Establishments" was approved. This bill guaranteed a minimum standard of safety, hygiene, and sick pay. For the first time women workers also won gender-specific demands such as maternity leave and the right of mothers to have paid time off to breast feed their babies during working hours (Ladjevardi 1985, 24). These rights formed part of the future labor law.

In 1944 the World Federation of Trade Unions and the ILO recognized the Iranian labor unions and invited them to their 1945 conference in Paris. The Iranian labor unions, by then numbering 276,150 members, organized strikes, factory occupations, and demonstrations in major industrial cities and won the forty-eight-hour week, paid holiday for Fridays (the weekend), and the right of workers to form unions. In 1951 the oil workers' strike led to the victory of Mossadegh's nationalist government and the nationalization of the oil industry. This period ended with the 1953 CIA-sponsored coup. The new autocratic monarchy imposed control over labor unions and other social movements (Ladjevardi 1985, 50–70, 233–54), replacing the term *trade unions* with *syndicates.* The number of syndicates, or factory-based unions, increased from 30 in the 1960s to about 519 in 1972. In many cases workers' representatives were affiliated to the state secret police, but many of the workers remained militant and conscious of the class-based nature of their economic demands. Despite the dictatorship, some strikes were successful and workers won the rights to national insurance, guaranteed sick pay, and retirement and unemployment benefits (Ladjevardi 1985, 240).

The failure of the dictatorial regime to deal with the economic and political crisis led to a growing revolutionary movement that finally led to a general strike, including the seventy-thousand-strong oil workers' strike, and the collapse of the monarchy in February 1979. During the revolution these strikes were organized by strike committees, which replaced the syndicates. After the revolution the strike committees provided the core of the leadership of the new *shoras* or workers' councils (Bayat 1987, 77–81; Poya 1987, 135–41).

In the early 1980s the Islamic *shoras* and Islamic associations replaced the independent *shoras*, but militancy and strikes continued. Of these strikes 90 percent were illegal, yet in 65 percent of all cases workers won their demands for pay increases, overtime pay, and benefits, and successfully fought against delayed wages (Bayat 1987, 100–141). Throughout the 1990s and up to 2002 a significant number of workers' protests against delayed and non-payment of wages, inadequate health and safety provision, and layoffs as the result of subcontracting took place.

From the mid-1990s a growing democracy movement radicalized the majority of the population. Many Islamists joined the growing reformist and democracy movement and argued for the democratization of different institutions. A number of activists in the Islamic *shoras* and associations argued that the term *Islamic* for workers' organizations could lead to the exclusion and alienation of some workers, and that this would weaken the *shoras*. They argued for the need for independent workers' organizations.

The history of labor unions in Iran demonstrates that they have not been homogeneous institutions; some have had grassroots support, and some have been agents of the state. Unions have survived long periods of authoritarianism, and at certain historical periods their actions have confirmed a profound reactivation of civil society. However, they remain male-dominated organizations, despite the facts that 36 percent of workers in the formal sector are women (30 percent of them in state enterprises and the remaining 6 percent in private enterprises) and that a large number of women work in the informal economy (Poya 1999, 94–98).

Prior to 1979 cultural restrictions affected women's mobility, and many families did not allow their daughters and other female relatives to join syndicates. But during and after the 1979 revolution, women became active *shora* members. In 1979 I was engaged in field research on women's employment. Many women employed in pharmaceutical industries, food industries, and textile industries were involved in the *shoras*. They were struggling to set up workplace nurseries, literacy classes for women workers, and better health and safety conditions. During this period, women's activities raised gender consciousness. For the first time these women were engaged in labor union activities *as women*. This was significant in a number of ways: the *shoras* were under attack, and male and female workers alike were struggling to save them. But male workers were against female representation, believing that women should leave these activities to men. For their part, women believed that they should be represented in the *shoras* as women workers, because they had specific demands. This experience was extremely important to them at a later stage. In the early 1990s a woman was elected as the leader of the hairdressers' *shora* for the first time in Iranian history (Poya 1999, 125–30).

Since the 1990s a growing women's movement has led to the broader discussion of women's issues. The women's media boldly pioneered a challenge to traditional Islamic laws and regulations in relation to marriage, divorce, custody of children, and inheritance. In 1998 the Women Journalists' Trade Association (union) was established (Rostami Povey 2001, 44–71). In 2002 its newspaper, *Women's Voice,* discussed gender wage differentials among media workers, women's long hours of work, their absence at the management level, and the impact of the closure of the media in 2000–2002 on women's employment (Farhadpour 2002). Following this, the Women Publishers' Trade Association, the Women Teachers' Trade Association, the Women Nurses' Trade Association, and the Women Lawyers' Trade Association were also established.

Studies on gender and labor unions in Iran demonstrate that women in the country have been and continue to be involved in labor unions, syndicates, *shoras,* and professional associations. But they remain a minority and have little voice in decision-making processes. There has been a continuing resistance by male labor unionists to women's participation in unions, and while in most *shoras* women serve as treasurers, their participation is limited when important decisions are taken.

As I have argued elsewhere (Poya 1999, 83–93), notions of masculinity and femininity locate women in unskilled and low-paid jobs; this, in turn, affects their earning power and working conditions. They pay higher taxes and receive lower bonuses and other entitlements. There are a large number of unpaid—and even paid—women workers in the agricultural and the informal sectors whose issues are not addressed by the male-dominated labor unions. If more women were involved in labor unions, and could participate at the leadership levels and have a say in decision making, then the conditions of working women in Iran would improve significantly.

The establishment of women's trade associations beginning in the late 1990s demonstrates that Iranian women workers find it difficult to create the conditions in which men and women can develop their democratic rights within the same space. In their own way, then, these women are challenging the male-dominated labor unions. This may lead to the formation of more women's labor unions, or it may enable women workers to force male-dominated institutions to recognize female membership in labor unions. In the meantime, as I will discuss in the next section, some women's NGOs are acting as support groups for women outside the formal workplace. These groups are not substituting for labor unions, and they do not organize women as workers. Nevertheless, despite the limited nature of their activities, they have transformed themselves into alternative civil society organizations.

WOMEN'S NGOS:
ALTERNATIVE CIVIL SOCIETY ORGANIZATIONS

The massive expansion of the Iranian NGO sector since the 1990s can be seen as a consequence of the New Policy Agenda, which regards markets as the most efficient mechanism for development, states as facilitators, and NGOs as service-providing agencies. In this context NGOs are seen as appropriate vehicles for democratization and the strengthening of civil society (Eade 2000).

In 1968 there were 377 NGOs in Iran (IRIPRSIM 1999). By 1999 there were 4,000 registered NGOs (IRIPCIB 2000), and many more that were not registered. In 1976–77 there were 13 women's NGOs in Iran; by 2001–2 that number rose to 137 (CNWN 2000). There was also a large number of women's cooperatives, mainly in rural areas, which were linked to women's NGOs (UNDP 2000).

This rise in the number of women's NGOs should also be seen as an extension of the women's movement in the 1990s, when women's issues became an integral part of the politics of the Islamic state and society. Four crucial factors led to the creation of the women's movement: (1) women's massive participation in the 1978–79 revolution; (2) women's collective actions in the mosques to produce food communally and to provide medical aid for the soldiers during the Iran-Iraq war (1980–88); (3) the imposition of *hejab* (Islamic dress code) and sex segregation, which ironically opened up opportunities for many religious women to participate in political life; and (4) the growing contradictions between the Islamic state and other institutions, which led to the gradual development of a feminist consciousness. Despite structural limitations on the social activities in which they could engage, women of different classes and different levels of religiosity and secularity have been able to challenge the social construction of gender through the women's movement and women's NGOs. Women in Iran are far from being either homogeneous or victims of the process of Islamization, an impression which has too often colored studies on women in Iran and other Muslim societies (Poya 1999; Rostami Povey 2001).

As will be discussed below, some women's NGOs are working with women in urban and rural areas in sectors that are difficult to organize. Through networking, provision of resources, and income-generating activities they are acting in a range of circumstances and for differing purposes.

Feminist writers have long criticized the inclusion of gender issues in development agendas unless these challenge women's subordination (Elson 1992; Jackson and Pearson 1998; Mayoux 1998). But the experience of Iran demonstrates that women's NGOs are in fact challenging women's subordination by confronting the state and other patriarchal institutions (family, community, tradition, and religion). Moreover, they have made some gains by broadening their activities to include attempts at advocacy or policy influence.

My premise is that if labor unions and the wider society's cultural restrictions deny women the space to articulate their own specific needs, these women's NGOs have created a space of their own, within which some women can develop negotiating and leadership skills. The detailed analysis of women's activities highlights the slow yet steady change in gender consciousness, self-confidence, and self-determination. Although their activities are limited and they are not involved in formal workplace collective activities, women's NGOs have provided opportunities for women's empowerment and are paving the way for the establishment of alternative civil society organizations.

WOMEN'S NGO ACTIVITIES IN URBAN AREAS

Networking

There are a number of women's NGOs networking in Iran, including the Communication Network of Women's NGOs, the Women's NGOs' Network, and the Zaynab Kobra Foundation. They attempt to provide information to women's NGOs and make connections between NGOs and national and international institutions. There is also the Centre for Women's Participation, a governmental organization that offers a support system for women's NGOs, provides funds, and makes connections among NGOs, governmental organizations, and international institutions. These networking organizations have a maternalistic and top-down approach and could be criticized for promoting their own agenda rather than those that are in the interests of the community.

However, some of my interviewees were in favor of these organizations. For example, the women's NGOs representing religious minorities (Zoroastrian, Jewish, and Armenian) found networking positive, as it created opportunities for them to raise their gender/ethnicity demands, which are culturally and religiously specific. One important form of discrimination against minorities, under the Islamic state, is the *Dieh* (blood money law). According to Article 881 and Articles 10 and 59 of civil law, one-twelfth of the *Dieh* is applied to religious minorities. This means that if a member of a religious minority accidentally kills a Muslim, that person has to pay the full *Dieh* to the person's family. But if a Muslim accidentally kills a member of a religious minority, the Muslim only pays one-twelfth of *Dieh* to the family of the dead person. According to this law the blood money of all women is half of that of men, a provision that discriminates particularly against women from religious minorities. Throughout the 1990s the minority women's NGOs, together with other women's NGOs and governmental organizations, campaigned for the reform of this law and succeeded in changing it in favor of minorities in August 2002. Following this victory, women's NGOs in collaboration with women's lawyers and female members of *Majles* (Parliament) are pressing for the same blood money for men and women. This is a major challenge by women across ethnic and religious identities to traditional Islamic laws in Iran.

Another issue specific to gender/ethnicity, especially for Zoroastrian and Jewish women, is that of divorce, which is all but impossible in both religions. There are women in both communities who are exposed to domestic violence. They take their cases to court and are granted the right to be divorced. But their respective religions do not allow this. In the words of Hassidim, the leading member of the Iranian Jewish Women's NGO:

> We have argued that we are first Iranian and second Jewish. Therefore, as citizens of this country, we should be able to get divorced and enjoy *Mahr* [bride price] and *Ojratolmesl* [the monetary equivalent of a woman's contribution to her family throughout the life of the marriage] as Muslim women do. We are pressing our members of parliament to fight for us. . . . But we are more optimistic that we can pressure the state and other institutions through women's NGO networks. As women we understand each other's pain.

Networking between some women's NGOs and governmental organizations has established the basis for organizing women across religious and ethnic boundaries. This alliance, in turn, has allowed them to act collectively to pressure the state and other patriarchal institutions to change laws and regulations in their favor. These activities are also a great step toward the general democratization of institutions both within the state and in civil society.

Provision of Resources to the Marginalized Sections of Society

Disabled people constitute about 10 percent of the Iranian population; most of them are living in poverty. The Ladies' Charitable Society provides care for disabled people over sixteen years of age in the south of Tehran. This institution is one of the oldest NGOs in Iran and has been mobilizing women voluntary workers since 1972. In 2001–2 the organization created two thousand voluntary and one thousand paid jobs for women. Most of the people the society cares for are women. The main reason for this is the fact that in most cases husbands are older than their wives. Women look after men when they become old or develop disabilities. Men do not reciprocate. Ehteram Malakoti Nejad, a prominent member of this NGO, explained: "We have a number of cases where disabled women are left alone because the husbands married younger and healthier women. Therefore, our institution, which is run by women, serves more women than men, because women need more care."

Female Suicide, Addiction, and Street Children

Fatemeh Farhangkhah is an active member of the Society for the Protection of Socially Disadvantaged Individuals. The alarming rise in the number of victims of addiction, homelessness, and suicide since the mid-1990s persuaded her to work in this field. She organizes lectures and seminars in various working-class areas of Tehran where these social problems are most acute. She believes that "access to information is empowering. It enables families to overcome their isolation and understand that these issues are social problems [that] can be eradicated."

According to Farhangkhah, the largest number of female suicides has occurred in Ilam (one of the poorest regions of Iran) and Esfehan (one of the most traditional cities in the country). If we see suicide, especially when the victims set fire to themselves, as a form of social protest and a rejection of the status quo, why have these incidents occurred in such regions? Farhangkhah explains that "forced and arranged marriages are common causes of suicide among women in these regions. These are in many ways traditional and religious women but they are rejecting forced and arranged marriages."

The number of young girls who run away from home is also increasing. Some become sex workers, and others become street children. Several women's NGOs are concerned for their welfare and have pressured the state to take responsibility for street children and female sex workers. These NGOs offer a variety of services to street children, to disabled and older women, and to the victims of suicide and drugs, in ways that address the issues of women's subordination. They also campaign to raise women's voices at the level of state and other patriarchal institutions.

Policy Influence

Between 1979 and the early 1990s the Islamization of state and other institutions stripped women of the right to be judges, and the law gave men the exclusive right to obtain a divorce and have custody of the children. In the early 1990s, as a result of pressure from below and through the efforts of women lawyers and women members of Parliament, a number of reforms were made. Women were allowed to be research judges or investigative judges, and reforms were made in laws regarding marriage, divorce, and custody of children. Under the reformed law a woman has the right to ask for a divorce, refuse the husband the right to marry another woman, and have custody of her children (Poya 1999, 98–103). However, many women under pressure from patriarchal gender relations do not benefit from this reform. Shirin Ebadi, a lawyer and an active member of the Society for the Protection of the Rights of Children, explains:

> Under pressure from men and the family, many women do not exercise their rights to custody of children. Under these circumstances, men re-marry and the children from the previous marriage could suffer as a result of domestic violence. In one particular case a child died, so our NGO organized a memorial in the local mosque and asked the local people to attend the memorial and bring flowers to [honor] the memory of the child. We explained that the child's life could have been saved if she [had not been] taken away from her mother. We argued that the law should be reformed further to give custody of the children to the suitable parent. We asked our audience to leave the flowers in the mosque if they agreed with such a reform. As everyone left, we found the floor of the mosque covered with flowers.

Community support for reform of the traditional laws and regulations in favor of women, combined with the efforts of women lawyers and women's NGOs, made it possible for Leila Davar, a woman judge, to start working on the bench of the State Retribution Organisation in Esfehan in February 2003, after twenty-four years. This is an important victory for women in Iran. If more women work as judges, there will be more reforms to family laws and regulations from which women, men, and children alike will benefit.

Noushin Ahmadi Khorasani is a leading member of the Women's Cultural Centre. The aim of this NGO is also to press for reform of traditional laws through women's participation. On international women's day they organize postcard campaigns demanding legislative reform. She explains: "For many ordinary women, the thought of writing to the members of the Parliament and the judiciary is a daunting experience. This way thousands of cards were sent to the authorities, raising many women's voices protesting against laws which are oppressive to women."

Thus, in terms of policy influence over social welfare and gender equity, women's rights advocates have made an impact through campaigning and taking gender issues to a wider public in a way that has made them worthy of attention.

Strategies to Help Women's Access to Employment and Income Generation

In urban areas many women's NGOs are involved in helping women gain access to employment and income-generating activities. In order to assess the impact of their work, I asked a number of women NGO activists how they integrate gender analysis in practice.

Marzieh Seddighi of the Women Work Creators' Centre has concentrated on providing information for the growing number of female university graduates who are seeking employment in an increasingly competitive job market. Since the 1990s the percentage of women in higher education has exceeded that of men. As she put it:

> Historically men, even [if] poorer, . . . have more access to information, money, and finances. Women don't have these opportunities. We therefore set up a committee consisting of bank managers, financial advisers, and women NGO activists to help women gain access to employment or income generation. We also organize workshops for women who are

interested in entering business and trade, and we provide them with information and knowledge about how to acquire loan and financial assistance.

Fatemeh Shabani, who heads up an NGO called Female Enterprise, is involved in similar activities:

> The authorities and officials who are the decision makers are usually men, and they do not cooperate with women to facilitate their activities. Despite these difficulties, I have witnessed many women who have entered this profession with an empty hand and have succeeded through hard work. I have also seen some men who have entered this profession with many opportunities at their disposal and have failed. Women have learned that they can fail, but they can stand up on their feet and start again. Women experience managerial skills on a day-to-day basis by feeding the family, getting the hole in the ceiling fixed, helping children with their homework. Women use these skills, which are the key to their success.

Mahbobeh Abbasgholizadeh of the Association of Women Writers and Journalists has been involved in income-generating activities and policy influence. In 2000 a large number of newspapers and magazines were closed down. Her aim became to support and facilitate the work of unemployed female media workers. "I did not give them money," she says. "I organized projects and exhibitions and suggested to them to work for these projects and exhibitions. I provided them with computers and cameras. Once they completed the projects and the exhibitions, they benefited intellectually and financially." Through her activities she has also raised the issue of women's right to work and the undemocratic nature of the closure of newspapers and journals.

Khadijeh Moghadam is a leading member of the Women's Society against Environmental Pollution. She works with women-headed households in the poorer areas in the south of Tehran, combining income-generating activities with consciousness-raising discussion groups about environmental issues. She has provided women with sewing machines and other materials to produce pencil cases, school bags, and carrier bags. As she explained:

> These women regularly visit their local schools and their neighbors and discuss with them the environmental consequences

of using plastics. They try to convince school children and their parents to replace the plastic items with cloth materials. This way, besides raising awareness on environmental issues, they sell their products and earn a living.

The strategies and policies of these women's NGOs for increasing women's access to employment and ways of generating an income highlight the multiple pressures that women are facing in the household, family, and community. They also show how, through establishing organizations and alliances, women can achieve their goals.

WOMEN'S NGO ACTIVITIES IN RURAL AREAS

Income-generating Activities through Women's Clubs and Cooperatives

In rural areas most projects are run by governmental organizations and NGOs, several of which are sponsored by international bodies. One such example is the women's clubs set up by the Ministries of Agriculture and Reconstruction Crusade with the help of the Food and Agriculture Organization of the United Nations. These clubs have provided opportunities for women to have access to information, training, and income-generating work. Parvin Maroofi, from the Institute for Research, Consultation and Marketing of Women's Products, summarizes the benefits of such activities:

> Many women through these clubs were able to earn from growing fresh flowers, vegetables, and herbs. These projects not only provided these young women with income, [but] they were able to work communally, which gave them an identity separate from individual young women waiting to be married.

Maroofi was also actively involved with the Rural Women's Cooperatives. In the spring of 2002 I visited the Noavaran Women's Handcraft Cooperative in Garmsar, in northeast Iran. Sodabeh Golvari, a member of the cooperative, reported that

> the cooperatives have provided opportunities for women to sell their products in the national markets by organizing

exhibitions. The involvement of women in producing for the
market has increased the income of the family. This has created more harmony in the family rather than conflict. In the
past, men went to the market and sold the products of women.
Now they look after the home and children while women go
to towns and cities to exhibit their products and to sell them.

Women's involvement in clubs and cooperatives has been widely debated. For instance, Mayoux's study of a number of cooperatives in India highlights the exploitative nature of these cooperatives (1995). It is
important to recognize that these case studies from Iran constitute only a
small percentage of rural women's involvement. For example, at the time
of this research (2001–2) there were 100 rural women's cooperatives
officially registered (UNDP 2000), and 2,000 female development workers. These are significant numbers, if we assume that these projects are
empowering women, but they need to be set against the fact that there are
60,000 rural villages and some 11,421,320 rural women. There is no
question, therefore, that overcoming the massive and diverse nature of
the poverty, oppression, and subordination of women requires fundamental structural change. Nevertheless, the creation of women's rural
clubs and cooperatives has, in some communities, changed traditional
values that were biased against women.

Income Generation and Sustaining Tribal Life
through Participatory Approaches

Through participatory approaches, income generation, and female participation the Hableh Rood project, known as the Management of Land
and Water, aims to protect the environment in northeast Iran. A number
of organizations are involved in this project as advisory and fundraising
bodies and as facilitators. These include the UNDP, the Ministry of Agriculture, the Ministry of Reconstruction Crusade, and Tehran Mehr Foundation, a women's NGO.

Jaleh Shadi Talab, a sociologist and writer on women's issues as well
as a former adviser to the project, explains how the already existing traditional women's informal organizations made the participatory approach
successful:

Women regularly get together on Thursday evenings to collectively perform a religious duty, that is, to read *Doaye*

Komail [a form of praying], which is considered to bring luck to the community. This is also a social gathering for many women; they eat food and drink tea together and discuss their issues and share their problems with each other.

For some weeks Jaleh participated in these gatherings and raised the issue of income generation. Finally, the women welcomed the idea and decided to set up the Rural Women's Bank so that they can take out low-interest loans in order to set up small businesses for themselves.

In some communities, men, women, and the clergy objected to the involvement of women in development projects, in particular to women and men working in a non-segregated way. Fatemeh Mafi, the director of education and a participant in this project from the Ministry of Reconstruction Crusade, explained:

> Our strategy was to deal with cultural issues with women's and men's cooperation. In some areas we gradually managed to get more and more women involved in the project. In other areas, men, women, and the clergy resisted. Therefore, we pulled out because we believed that we could not force them to do what they did not want to do.

Mansoureh Khalily, a leading member of Mehr Foundation, has also been involved with these projects. The foundation provides funds and resources for women to be able to work according to their skills and abilities. She told me:

> Khorshid Khanom escaped from her violent husband and came to our organization for help. I asked her to describe her skills. She said that she could bake bread. We provided her with an oven. She now provides bread for the whole village and has not allowed her violent husband to return home.

Catherine Razavi, executive director of the Centre for Sustainable Development, has been involved since 1979 with different projects using participatory approaches in rural areas and among tribal communities. The prospect of water and food insecurity is very real, with grave implications for tribal communities. To sustain rural and tribal life Razavi has involved local women in the design and the construction of a prototype solar water heater and solar box cookers. She says:

Local women have been practicing solar energy in their own
traditional way for centuries. For example, dried herbs, vegetables, and fruit are all prepared by leaving them in the sun.
Women can, therefore, relate to this technology and are modi-
fying their local recipes to fit with the solar box cooker.

Participatory discourses, methods, and practices have been criticized by
many academics and practitioners (Cooke and Kothari 2001; Porter and
Judd 1999). The Iranian case studies demonstrate that these women's
NGOs have succeeded to a limited extent in incorporating homeworkers
into formal wage labor. Such a strategy has assisted women to get away
from the home and the isolation of homework. In some tribal areas
women's NGOs have successfully engaged women in sustaining tribal
and rural livelihoods through local knowledge. As mentioned above, this
is the result of these women's NGOs being an extension of the women's
movement in Iran, and at the center of their policy and practice is the
goal of challenging women's subordination.

CONCLUSION

Women's NGOs and labor unions in Iran are diverse civil society organizations operating in two separate spheres. The labor unions have remained
male-dominated organizations, and women's NGOs have remained to-
tally detached from union activities.

If democratic impulses are generated by strengthening civil society,
then the labor unions must address the issue of patriarchal gender relations, while women's NGOs must also recognize their limitations and
learn that they cannot win their civil and democratic rights unless they
are part of a broader struggle for democratization.

Women's involvement in labor unions is crucial. For ninety years labor unions in Iran have defended the rights of the workers and successfully pressed for reform of the labor laws in favor of the workers. Despite
authoritarian regimes they have made important qualitative shifts in the
relationship between civil society and the state. However, as industrial
workers, unpaid workers, low-paid workers, homeworkers, NGO workers, Muslims, Armenians, Jews, or Zoroastrians, women carry multiple
identities. Hence, their involvement in women's NGOs is also necessary
in order to deal with the whole spectrum of their interests.

The case studies presented in this paper illustrate that women's NGOs are working in sectors that are difficult to organize, though they do not organize women as workers and are not engaged with collective actions to enhance their working conditions. However, in a number of ways they have had more impact than the labor unions, for example, policy influence on social welfare; paving the way for women in rural areas to have access to marketing their goods and earning a wage; and engaging women in sustaining rural and tribal livelihoods. They have been able to do this through raising gender issues at the level of state and other institutions in both the rural and the urban sectors. Therefore, women's involvement in women's NGOs as well as in labor unions would create the basis for improved working conditions of all women in formal and informal enterprises as well as enhancing their position in the wider society.

Families and male workers alike depend on women's work both in the home and outside. Male labor unionists have nothing to lose and everything to gain by supporting legislation to improve women's conditions within the formal workplaces, which will change gender ideology both inside and outside these sites. A major challenge, therefore, is to integrate the diverse activities of women's NGOs with labor union activities so that both institutions are mutually strengthened.

A process of social change is underway in Iran. There is an important opportunity here for labor unions and women's NGOs to move beyond their separate spheres. Through mutual cooperation these organizations—both effective civil society organizations in their own right—can address the economic as well as the social and political demands of women and men in Iran.

ACKNOWLEDGMENTS

I am grateful to Ziba Mir-Hosseini, Ruth Pearson, Tara Povey, John Rose, and Deborah Eade for reading earlier drafts of this paper and making valuable suggestions and corrections. I am also indebted to Mahbobeh Abbasgholizadeh and Catherine Razavi for the many discussions that I had with them in Iran from 1999 to 2002 and for their introduction to different NGO specialists and women cooperative workers.

Twenty-two

"The Sword of Justice"

*South Pacific Labor Unions and NGOs
during a Decade of Lost Development*

Satendra Prasad and Darryn Snell

Labor unions are often typified as having "two faces" (Flanders 1970, 15). First and primarily, they have focused their energies on improving the position of their members through representation, bargaining, and collective determination. Their other role, however, goes beyond this, encompassing broader objectives such as the promotion of democracy, human rights, social justice, and social policies that support disadvantaged groups and unorganized workers. These roles are not mutually exclusive and coexist as union objectives at any one time. The balance between these two features has, however, changed dramatically since the 1980s. Unions have come to be perceived as conservative institutions, concerned primarily with defending the relative advantages of a minority of the working population. The more unions have become focused on narrowly defined "bread-and-butter" workplace issues, the more they have lost sight of their larger role. How to revive and redefine their role as "sword of justice" is one of the key challenges presently confronting labor unions (Hyman 2000, 1).

This chapter develops an understanding of the "sword of justice"–type challenges that characterized labor union responses during a decade of "lost development" in the Fiji Islands, Papua New Guinea (PNG), and the Solomon Islands (UNDP 1999). It examines labor unions' efforts to preserve and advance workers' rights in an environment in which they were required to play a major role in responding to broad development challenges relating to democratic accountability, conflict, and peace building. Experiences in the South Pacific demonstrate that new alliances have been evolving to deal with these broader development challenges. Unions and NGOs are beginning to work more cohesively, albeit slowly. This essay throws light on some of these developments and presents tentative conclusions about their prospects.

BACKGROUND

Labor unionism has long roots in the three countries, although its study has suffered from years of neglect (Prasad and Hince 2001). The failures of labor unions in the Pacific are well documented. These failures are attributed to a range of factors that include legal restrictions on labor unionism, restrictive political climates (especially during the years of military rule in Fiji), the narrow base of formal-sector employment, institutional weaknesses, and the failure to represent those engaged in the large agrarian and informal sectors of the economy (Prasad and Snell 2002; Hess 1992; Prasad and Hince 2001). These researchers also highlight some of the successes of labor unions—although these are rather limited. Overall, the evidence points to a generalized picture of labor union failures. Starting from already weak organizational bases, labor unions in PNG, the Fiji Islands, and the Solomon Islands have suffered further from a harsh economic climate induced by the twin factors of domestic political instability and structural adjustment reforms over the past decade.

Fiji attained its independence in 1970, followed by PNG in 1975, and the Solomon Islands in 1979; with independence each country adopted new political structures and processes. These often collided with traditional social and political institutions, leading to heightened political instability within the first decade of independence. Their economic fortunes also began to falter around that time. Microeconomic reforms that each country was forced to adopt in the 1980s induced far-reaching change. New vulnerabilities emerged in national labor markets as they were deregulated. The degradation of employment rights and the expansion of employment in semi-formal and small-enterprise sectors made it even more difficult to sustain or expand the base of representation and collective bargaining.

By the end of the 1980s labor unions were forced to respond to multiple challenges resulting from sweeping adjustment reforms. At the same time, political instability in the three countries forced labor unions to focus their attention on broader issues related to democracy and human rights. Paradoxically, political crises and economic reforms have drawn out creative responses from labor unions. Labor unions in Fiji, PNG, and the Solomon Islands have attempted to evolve new strategies for working on concerns important to them. These have involved the development of new networks and new forms of engagement through efforts to nurture alliances with other groups in society and focus collective energies not only on the workplace but also on broader objectives. Labor unions' efforts to work in nontraditional ways suggest that they are capable of creative responses. The case studies presented here illustrate that the story of union responses and strategies is one of despair and hope at the same time.

PAPUA NEW GUINEA

Background

PNG has a population of 5.1 million and a population growth rate of 2.7 percent; 17 percent of its population resides in urban regions, where a large, long-term-unemployed underclass has developed. Approximately 38 percent of the population subsists below the national poverty line. PNG nationals have a life expectancy at birth of fifty-eight years and an adult illiteracy rate of 35 percent. Its GDP was US$3.8 million in 2000, of which 44 percent came from mining and agriculture. The formal-sector employment base remains narrow, with fewer than 0.3 million people earning wages and salaries in this sector (ADB 2002). The largest proportion of the population is involved in subsistence, semi-formal, and informal sectors of the economy. Most formal employment remains in the public sector—the government employed just under sixty thousand people in 2000 (Prasad and Snell 2002, 19–20). PNG's minerals and petroleum sector remains the most dynamic of the economy, contributing approximately 18 percent of GDP and over 80 percent of export revenues, and employing around five thousand people on average between 1999 and 2002. The economic base of the export economy remains narrow, and efforts to develop other sectors have been constrained by the absence of foreign investment and an uncertain policy environment.

For PNG, the lost decade of the 1990s was characterized by persistent economic decline. This forced the government to adopt structural adjustment programs that were driven by the Asian Development Bank (ADB) and Australia, PNG's largest aid donor. The first set of major reforms was introduced in 1992 and included the devaluation and flotation of the Kina (the national currency), a freeze on wages, and cutbacks in public spending. But public opposition to these reforms, as well as efforts by the Chan government to source soft loans from Taiwan and other countries in order to bypass the conditionalities imposed through structural adjustment loans, led to a deepening of the country's economic crisis. Further structural adjustment reforms occurred after the 1997 elections, which brought the Skate government to power. Prime Minister Skate worked to repair relations with multilateral agencies by deepening neoliberal reforms and improving oversight of public-sector cutbacks. This included a commitment to retrench seven thousand public employees, the abolition of central wage determination, and a commitment to proceed with major privatization programs. Widespread opposition to these reforms indirectly resulted in the fall of the Skate government in 1998.

Relations with multilateral agencies improved rapidly when Sir Mekere Morauta became prime minister of a coalition government in 1999. Sir Mekere, a former merchant banker and Reserve Bank governor, committed his government more fully to broad privatization and radical public-sector restructuring. These policies triggered widespread opposition from a cross-section of civil society organizations, labor unions, and the military. This opposition contributed to the eventual collapse of support for the reforms and to the fall of the coalition government, leading to a fresh round of elections in 2002. Political violence, voter intimidation, and ballot irregularities marred the June 2002 elections. It was not until August 4, 2002 that Sir Michael Somare, the former opposition leader and PNG's first prime minister after independence, was confirmed as the country's new prime minister.

Overall, the lost decade in PNG was characterized by severe economic crisis and the failure to achieve sustainable economic development. Economic reforms during this period served to deepen political instability, as illustrated in the 2002 general elections, and harmed PNG's development prospects. These factors define the background within which PNG labor unions and civil society groups have operated.

Labor Unions

In PNG, labor unions emerged in the last decade of Australian colonial rule. However, poor leadership and a stagnant base of private-sector employment acted as constraints to their rapid development. After independence in 1975, the PNG Teachers' Association, Public Employees' Association, and Waterside Workers' Union emerged as autonomous labor unions. Many unions that formed in the 1960s and early 1970s had folded by the time PNG achieved its independence. After independence, unions enjoyed greater success in the mining sector, which was largely controlled by multinationals. Nationally, most of the active private-sector unions are affiliated to the Papua New Guinea Trade Unions' Congress (PNGTUC), which is affiliated to the International Confederation of Free Trade Unions (ICFTU). A number of larger unions, however, remain unaffiliated to the PNGTUC, including the powerful Public Employees' Association and the Teachers' Association. Over the past few years the PNGTUC has been modestly successful in promoting a series of union amalgamations to create more viable foundations for the labor unions.

Labor union strategies in PNG in recent years have largely been a mixed set of responses to the sweeping structural adjustment reforms that have followed years of poor governance, inadequate public-sector management, and internal political crisis (ADB 2002; Prasad and Snell 2002). Union responses and strategies need to be understood by reference to the fact that they are weakly established. With an estimated overall union density of less than 10 percent in 1999, unions have been less capable of responding to the challenges of economic reform than have their counterparts in Fiji, as will be discussed below.

One of the first victims of structural adjustment was tripartite partnership in PNG. Tripartism was reasonably well established in PNG until the reforms commenced. The PNGTUC's inclusion in the formulation of labor and social policy through this mechanism helped to overcome its size and representation deficits. But labor and social policies have generally become subservient to the broader objectives of macroeconomic reform and public-sector reform, a process that has further marginalized the labor and employment segments of the government machinery. Because of this, the PNGTUC's participation in social security programs has declined. Serious mismanagement and heavy losses in the National Provident Fund followed, leading to its almost total collapse in 1999. The management and operation of the fund has subsequently come to be placed more directly within the prime ministerial and finance offices. This has served to alienate labor unions even further.

Since then, PNG unions have been battling, seldom with much success, against the "excesses" of public-sector reform. In 2000 the PNG

Communications Workers' Union took industrial action to oppose privatization in the communications sector. But the strike fizzled when the government agreed to compensation claims under pre-privatization terms and paid both the union and employer contributions to the National Provident Fund. This strike paved the way for short-term concession bargaining in the public sector, and a period of intense disputes followed. Broadcasting workers took similar action in 2001, leading to an improved retrenchment package with a lower taxation rate. Nurses, teachers, and doctors were able to use industrial action to win real wage increases and significant improvements in working conditions in 1998 and 1999, delivering a blow to the targets for cuts in public spending that were part of the austerity measures at the time. This demonstrated the efficacy of traditional styles of union activism in the public sector, something that had been absent for a long time. These strikes by doctors, teachers, and nurses thus had the effect of rejuvenating labor union activism, especially in the public sector. They also served to raise public awareness about structural adjustment and economic reforms more generally.

Public anger and discontent against the ADB and IMF reforms boiled over in 2001 when the national student union body, with the support of public-sector labor unions, took to the streets in protest. Sadly, these protests led to the death by police action of four student activists. Several weeks of unrest followed in the capital, Port Moresby. These protests demonstrated that broad social alliances could be created and their energies harnessed to promote worker rights. The violent turn of events, however, quickly dampened enthusiasm and energy and reflected negatively on the labor union genesis of the protests. In this instance it was clear that inadequate attention had been paid to organization and sustainability concerns for the social alliance.

The activities of multinational companies operating in PNG's mining industry have been another area where workers have successfully developed alliances with civil society organizations. Unions have been less successful than community, environmental, and other grassroots organizations in exposing social justice and environmental concerns in this industry. But this has not been for want of trying. On the island of Bougainville an informal alliance between workers in the copper mines and landowning, environmental, and community groups formed in the early 1980s. These coalitions often took combined action against unfair employment, environmental, and mining royalty issues. Sporadic protests boiled over and crystallized into demands by some groups for the independence of Bougainville after the perceived failure of the PNG central government to pressure the multinationals into making concessions.

Partly in recognition of its failures both in the workplace and more broadly, PNG's labor unions took a gigantic leap in 2002 when they supported the formation of the PNG Labour Party. Barely a month after its formation, it fielded eighty-two candidates in the 2002 general elections. Although it failed to win any seats, the Labour Party has captured the interest of many workers, students, and other groups who feel disenchanted by the reforms of the past decade. In a country where political processes are dominated by regionalism, tribalism, and a "big men" type of politics that are sources of political fissure and political and national fragmentation, a labor union–supported party has the potential to offer a politics that is less affected by such factionalism, more focused on the real problems of development, and capable of articulating alternative development policies. How labor unions and community organizations develop in the future may largely determine the future success of this political party. But it does provide a useful substitute for the overall failure of the traditional type of labor unionism in PNG.

THE FIJI ISLANDS

Background

Fiji has a population of 0.82 million, of which less than 48 percent lives in urban regions. Some 53 percent of the population is composed of indigenous Fijians, roughly 44 percent are Indo-Fijians, and the rest come from other communities (Prasad, Dakuvula, and Snell 2002, 4). It has a 0.9 percent rate of population growth, mainly because of high emigration levels, especially among the non-ethnic Fijian segments of the population. Fiji has an adult illiteracy rate below 10 percent and a life expectancy at birth of 69 years (UNDP 2002).

Fiji's economic decline set in around 1987, when the military staged a coup against the Fiji Labour Party (FLP)–led coalition government. A subsequent period of military rule and heightened ethnic chauvinism undermined stability and confidence. In 1997 the principal political parties and ethnic group leaders in this multiethnic society agreed to a multiracial and democratic constitution. Elections under this constitution led to the formation of an FLP-led multiparty government in 1999. Like its 1987 predecessor, this government was forcibly removed from power in

May 2000 by ethnic Fijian nationalists supported by some military officers. General elections did not take place until May 2001. These elections brought to power the nationalist United Fiji Party (SDL) under Prime Minister Qarase. The FLP, however, performed well, winning the second largest number of seats. Despite constitutional provisions for multiparty government, the SDL-led government has refused to involve the FLP in government. Fiji continues to be torn by ethnic tensions, and its constitutional provisions for government are still not observed.

The net result of the political crisis is that Fiji remains locked in a low-investment and low-growth trap, which only adds to heightened inter-ethnic group tensions. Two military coups in 1987 led to a sharp 12 percent economic contraction in that year, followed by a further 6 percent contraction in 1989. Modest recovery occurred between 1997 and 1999. However, Fiji again entered a severe downward spiral as its economy shrank by 6 percent following the military takeover of the Parliament in 2000. The economy declined by a further 4 percent in 2001. Between 1986 and 2001 Fiji has experienced a deterioration in all human development indicators—its position on the UNDP Human Development Index fell from 44 in 1986 to 72 in 2001 (UNDP 2002). Between May 2000 and December 2001, over 350 businesses ceased operation and the export-processing enterprises lost about 35 percent of their work force. The proportion of households below the national poverty line has more than doubled in this short period (Prasad and Snell 2001). While Fiji's structural adjustment reforms were broadly similar to PNG's, they were different in one key respect. Reforms in Fiji included a raft of measures to rein in organized labor, especially given the fact that this provided an important electoral base for the FLP. It is clear that Fiji will continue to face broad development challenges in the medium term as it confronts the twin problems associated with ethnic tension and bad governance. This backdrop broadly defines the parameters within which labor union and civil society alliances have been forged. (For more information on Fiji, see Pacific Islands Forum 2003.)

Labor Unionism

Fiji has a long history of labor unionism. Indentured workers recruited from India to work on the sugar plantations organized themselves sporadically at the turn of the twentieth century and laid the foundations for powerful industrial unions. Labor unionism expanded considerably in the 1960s as Fiji progressed toward independence. In the post-independence era Fiji developed a vibrant pluralist system of industrial relations. By the early 1980s, unionization rates reached nearly 50 percent, with most major unions affiliated to the Fiji Trade Union Congress (FTUC).

Significantly, the FTUC sponsored the formation of the FLP in 1985. The FLP formed government twice, first in 1987 and then in 1999, only to be forcefully removed from office both times. Its electoral success has largely been the consequence of one key labor union development: the FTUC's commitment to support the expansion of labor unionism beyond the narrow wage and salaried employment base in the formal cash economy. The formation of the FLP was preceded by the formation of the National Farmers' Union in 1982, through which smallholder peasant farmers in the sugar sector were organized. The union was able to engage in negotiations with the government and the Fiji Sugar Corporation to win real gains for farmers. This provided an agrarian base for the FLP.

Although the FLP has twice been removed from power in its short history, it has also won real concessions. In 1997 and 1998 it fought for and ensured that Fiji would have not only a democratic constitution but one that entrenched labor union rights as its core feature. Through the constitution it also gained further concessions for workers in the public sector, including their right to appeal against personnel decisions through an independent commission. In this manner the FLP has been able to advance workers' rights even when the workplace has become more hostile. Clearly, the sustainability of a labor-type party in Fiji has been premised on the extension of labor unionism into the agrarian sectors of the economy.

The 1987 military coups delivered a crushing blow to the leadership and the grassroots membership of the FLP. Its organizational base collapsed under the weight of restrictions on civil and political rights. To open up democratic spaces labor unions needed to flex their muscles. Working with NGOs, churches, and community organizations, the FTUC marshaled broad support for international labor union sanctions. The FTUC not only engaged with other domestic actors but also nurtured new alliances with nonunion groups such as progressive human rights organizations in the international arena. These support networks were deployed to pressure their labor unions internationally to exert pressure upon the military government by frustrating the shipment of goods and flights to Fiji. In response, the military regime assured an ICFTU mission that the rights of labor unions would be protected in Fiji.

However, after having provided such assurances, the military government sought to use economic reforms to curtail labor unions. Harsh anti-union legislation in the guise of structural adjustment policies was thus introduced in 1992. This included the imposition of up to fourteen-year jail sentences for unionists convicted of promoting illegal industrial action. The FTUC engaged with NGOs in Fiji and internationally to oppose these reforms. It supported broad-based industrial action in the sugar sector and threatened a national strike and disruptions to Fiji's trade. Through this campaign Fiji's labor unions managed to ensure that the most controversial aspects of the labor reforms were shelved.

These lessons were to prove useful when the FLP-led government was taken hostage in 2000. In order to pressure for the release of the government, the FTUC's initial instincts were to take national and international labor union action. But it had learned important lessons from 1987. When labor unions undertook such large campaigns on their own, they were more easily isolated. From early in the 2000 crisis, labor built alliances with NGOs, including the Citizens' Constitutional Forum, the Fiji Women's Crisis Centre, the Fiji Women's Rights Movement, as well as churches and other religious organizations. This initiative crystallized into the NGO Coalition on Human Rights. The FTUC took the next step in calling for punitive trade disruptions and secured the support of members of the coalition, which also included the Fiji Employers' Federation and many of Fiji's commerce chambers. This initiative, called the Fiji Blues Campaign, went far in ensuring that the constitution was upheld and that fresh elections were held in 2001. The success of the FTUC is traced to its willingness to work with civil society organizations in an alliance based on equal partnership rather than labor dominance. Although problems remain with respect to the constitutionality of the SDL government, Fiji's labor unions played a pivotal role in ensuring that the return to democracy was rapid rather than gradual, as had been the case after the coups of 1987.

This new way of working also bore positive results at the workplace level. In the aviation industry, reforms to the public sector have tried to remove the presence of the Fiji Public Service Association (FPSA) through the introduction of individual contracts of employment. The victory of the FLP in 1999 put this reform agenda in the aviation industry specifically, and in the public sector more generally, on hold. However, soon after the overthrow of the FLP-led government this agenda was firmly reinstated. In the aviation industry the FPSA got shut out by a new reform-minded management. The FPSA's efforts to use the courts to reassert its collective agreement was frustrated by a management that simply ignored the courts' directives. The lessons from the FTUC's recent campaigns were not lost on the FPSA. It educated landowners on whose lands the airports were situated and local communities about collective and individual contracts of employment and social protection. It developed partnerships with human rights NGOs. Having marshaled broad support, the FPSA sought international solidarity from Australian unions to disrupt tourism and trade. In June 2000, some sixteen months after the unions were locked out, the government finally agreed to recognize the collective agreement. This type of workplace engagement to maintain representation rights was unprecedented. But both the broader approach adopted by the FTUC and the micro approach adopted by the FPSA demonstrate that unions are capable of reengaging in creative and nontraditional ways.

Despite these successes Fiji's labor unions are on the defensive on several fronts. First, their membership and resources have crumbled under the combined weight of economic downturn and the loss of jobs following the upheavals of 1987 and 2000. Labor market reforms made it far more difficult for unions to take industrial action. The withdrawal of "check off" provisions also squeezed the lifeline of the centrally organized unions, leading to a 12 percent decline in union density between 1986 and 2000 (Prasad and Snell 2001). Union representation in newly "corporatized" sectors has declined significantly. In the higher wage manufacturing sectors, unions have been essentially decimated. In the public sector, bargaining with central public-sector unions has come to a virtual halt. This situation is compounded by the concerted move by the SDL-led government to further fragment labor unions along racial lines. Such challenges dissipate union energies and exert pressure on progressive labor union leaders. Because many union members experience a heightened sense of vulnerability, they want their unions to "play by the rules." Poor communication, hierarchical decision-making structures within unions, and the pressures from patriarchal-traditionalist social structures also affect labor unions. All these factors constrain the development of new labor union and NGO networks and, paradoxically, stress the need for labor unions to engage with government and society in newer ways. Fiji's labor unions need to manage this transformation skillfully if they are not to be torn apart by these contradictions.

SOLOMON ISLANDS

Background

The Solomon Islands has a GDP per capita of US$1,648 and was ranked 121 on the UNDP Human Development Index in 2000. It has a population of over 400,000, growing at a rate of 3.2 percent a year; 42 percent of that population is under fifteen years of age. Life expectancy at birth is sixty-eight years. The Solomon Islands had an adult literacy rate of 77 percent in 2000 (UNDP 2002).

Only 12 percent of the economically active population is engaged in the cash economy, with just over thirty-four thousand people employed in the formal sector (and the government accounts for 32 percent of those jobs). Despite the continued significance of the public sector, the private sector grew at a healthy rate of 5 percent throughout most of the 1990s (Prasad and Snell 2001). Foreign investment activity expanded into timber, fisheries, mining, and other strategic export industries during this period. However, the Asian financial crisis in 1997 took a heavy toll, as investments collapsed and national debt spiraled. In response, the country was forced to adopt painful structural adjustment reforms, which included a significant devaluation of the currency in 1997, public-service restructuring, privatization, and a freeze on public-sector wages.

Like PNG and Fiji, the Solomon Islands is a culturally diverse society. Diversity and inequality between Malaitans and Guadalcanalese have been sources of conflict and political unrest since independence. The job losses and harsh economic reforms of the late 1990s accentuated these ethnic tensions. Ethnic leaders on the mainland of Guadalcanal accused settlers from the island of Malaita of taking jobs and opportunities away from the Malaitan people. In June 2000 these simmering tensions boiled over and led to the removal of Prime Minister Ulufa'alu and the takeover of government by the Malaitan Eagle Force.

In October 2000 an internationally mediated initiative led to the Townsville Peace Accord, which had the support of both warring groups, the Malaitan Eagle Force and the Isatabu Freedom Movement (UNDP/ILO/University of Queensland 2000). This laid the basis for political rehabilitation and the establishment of a broad-based interim government, under the leadership of Manasseh Sogavare, with a commitment to hold fresh elections in December 2001. This political crisis had a devastating impact on the economy, with the export of palm oil and fish collapsing by mid-2001 (Prasad and Snell 2001). Many foreign-owned companies stayed closed, and civil-servant salaries remained unpaid as the government struggled to address the financial crisis.

The 2001 general elections brought to power a new coalition government led by Sir Allan Kemakeza. Politically, this government is highly unstable and vulnerable to infighting. The government, which contains several key figures who came to power in the 2000 coup, has yet to prove popular with Solomon Islanders or the international community. The Australian and New Zealand governments, which contribute about US$21 million in aid annually, have insisted that further development funds will depend on the Kemakeza government implementing economic reforms and addressing law-and-order problems. By conservative estimates the country's economy contracted by 5 percent in 2002 and a further 2 percent in 2003 (Prasad and Snell 2002). Clearly, the Solomon Islands will continue to face acute and broad developmental constraints over the medium term.

Labor Unionism

Labor unionism in the Solomon Islands traces its roots to the establishment of the British Solomon Islands General Workers' Union under colonial rule. The emerging strength of this union led to its fragmentation by the colonial office into the Solomon Islands Building and General Workers' Union and the British Solomon Islands Plantation and Farmers' Association (Prasad and Hince 2001). During the transition to independence the Solomon Islands Building and General Workers' Union—the predecessor to the Solomon Islands National Union of Workers (SINUW)—played an active part in the decolonization struggle. Its key leaders, such as Bart Ulufa'alu and Joses Tuhanuku, would rise to important political positions in the post-colonial era.

For most of the 1980s and 1990s the Solomon Islands labor unions proved quite successful in organizing and maintaining a total union membership in the range of 60–70 percent of the wage and salaried work force. The establishment of the Solomon Islands Council of Trade Unions (SICTU) in 1986 helped to unify the labor union movement and strengthen its capacity to influence national policymaking. In the 1990s SINUW and the public-sector unions, with the support of the SICTU, made considerable progress in advancing workers' rights and improving the labor relations environment in the country.

In 1998, the Solomon Islands labor movement became more directly involved in national politics with the formation of the Solomon Islands

Labour Party (SILP). Politically, the SILP has found it difficult to win parliamentary seats, largely because it has not made sufficient inroads into the large subsistence sector of the economy in order to have the diversified support base needed to win elections. Nonetheless, the SILP has consistently won enough seats to become a minor, though significant, player in the assorted coalition politics of the country. The SILP joined two coalition governments, including the Solomon Islands Alliance for Change that was overthrown by the 2000 coup. The president of the SILP, Joses Tuhanuku, is currently serving as secretary to the leader of the opposition.

Overall, the Solomon Islands labor unions have been more successful than their PNG counterparts. However, their successes and gains in the workplace and at the national level have been virtually wiped out as a result of the armed ethnic conflict that broke out on Guadalcanal. Ever since, SINUW and powerful public-sector unions have again been forced to take rearguard action to defend jobs and working conditions in a severe economic climate. Sweeping cutbacks in the public sector have been taking place since 2000 as the government faces a financial meltdown. Meanwhile, the government continues to find it difficult to pay civil-servant salaries. Some teachers have not been paid for over a year and a half. The export-oriented industries, which the government depends on for tax revenue, are unwilling to start operations or to restore operations to their pre-conflict peaks. Investor confidence has not improved under the new government, and the government's failure to disarm militias has not helped the overall situation.

The future for the economy and for labor unions is bleak by any measure. The Solomon Islands labor union movement, however, has taken the initiative of joining other civil society organizations in an effort to restore peace and stability in the nation. The Solomon Islands Civil Society Network—a loosely formed group of organizations that includes the union movement, Chamber of Commerce, women's organizations, churches, and various NGOs—was established in early 2001. At the heart of the network's campaigns was a quick return to democratic rule and fresh elections following the 2000 coup. The network maintained pressure on the interim administration to behave responsibly through a number of public campaigns, including protests against the interim administration's granting of duty remissions to private companies and individuals closely connected to the government and attempts to change the Constitution and the Electoral Act. The Civil Society Network's use of peaceful demonstrations led to the successful defeat of two attempts by the interim government to delay federal elections. In the lead-up to the 2001 elections, the network worked to ensure that the electoral process was free and fair.

Since the 2001 elections the Civil Society Network has continued to campaign on a number of issues, including disarmament and the need for a responsible and credible government to assist in economic recovery. The Kemakeza government's failure to tackle law-and-order problems, a rising wave of crime, physical harassment, and rape were the themes of a set of formal meetings organized by the Civil Society Network in March 2002, which the government and police were invited to attend. The meetings illustrated just how far the Civil Society Network had come since its formation and the continued commitment of the various organizations involved in the network in the post-election period.

However, the government's decision in July 2003 to allow the deployment of Australian troops as a way to restore law and order in the troubled nation has generated tensions within the Civil Society Network. Many NGOs and labor unions have thrown their support behind foreign intervention and view it as the only viable option to restore peace and rebuild the nation. The National Unity Summit hosted by the National Peace Council and attended by a number of religious, community, and women's organizations in early July ended with unanimous support for foreign intervention. Other NGOs, however, have expressed grave concerns about the costs associated with increased foreign intervention in the governance of the country. Claims that the move represents a form of "re-colonization" by a few opposition politicians and NGOs, such as Transparency Solomon Islands, have contributed to polarization over the issue. This situation has placed SICTU, which was central to pre-independence struggles, in a difficult position. While it has received some pressure from organizations outside the labor union movement to resist the government's request for foreign military intervention, SICTU has witnessed the devastating effect that the instability has had on the organization, employees, and their members. SICTU, somewhat reluctantly, has therefore supported the government's effort to allow the deployment of troops from Australia, New Zealand, and other Pacific Island Forum countries. Whether such support will harm its relations with other NGOs or weaken the Civil Society Network remains to be seen. It is the hope of SICTU and other NGOs, rightly or wrongly, that such extreme measures will succeed where all other efforts to restore order have failed.

ORGANIZED LABOR:
OPTIONS, LIMITS, AND POSSIBILITIES

Throughout the past decade traditional forms of union action and representation have been found wanting. Unions in PNG, Fiji, and the Solomon Islands have been unable to reach out to a new generation of more casual employees in the formal sector and economically active people in the traditional sectors of the economy. Employment growth has been dismal in all these countries. In view of this, it is clear that new entrants to the labor market and those who lose employment in the formal sectors are likely to engage in economic activities in the informal, semi-formal, and subsistence sectors. Precarious forms of employment are more likely to exist in such sectors, where most of the parameters of "decent work" are largely irrelevant. In these sectors evidence indicates that labor unions have taken a back-seat role to grassroots community-based organizations (Prasad and Snell 2002). But taking a back seat does not mean that they have completely retreated. Unions are beginning to work with community organizations that can directly reach economically active groups.

Clearly, the traditional forms of union representation have a limited potential for success in all these challenged economies. Deregulation of the labor markets, as seen in these case studies, has eroded the membership base of labor unions. The emphasis on decollectivization through structural adjustment policies in the South Pacific has been especially strong. In such a hostile environment labor unions that have maintained a more exclusive workplace focus have less to show for themselves. Those that have been more willing to engage with broader issues and work in nontraditional ways have been more successful. Such unions have been willing to nurture broader alliances and share their privileges—such as monopoly representation on peak tripartite bodies—with other labor market actors (Jose 2002). But this transition is inherently difficult for labor unions, which still guard their "self-interest." Recent experiences that throw light on these dilemmas are assessed below.

Across all three countries labor unions have become far more vulnerable. They are on the defensive at the national level and in workplaces. To respond to this changed environment, labor unions need to use new strategies and ways of working. Their efforts to develop broad alliances are less likely to be successful if these are sporadic and merely responsive to new challenges. Alliances that involve actors such as women's groups or development and human rights NGOs need to pay attention to organizational and sustainability issues. "Successful participation in such alliances will reinvigorate labor unions . . . and will keep the question of social equity on the agenda of other social movements" (Stevis and Boswell 2000, 162).

It is clear that labor unions in these countries need to pay far greater attention to rebuilding industrial alliances among existing labor unions. Labor unions are often too fragmented and susceptible in the face of politically motivated labor market reforms. They need to learn from community organizations alternative strategies that can be deployed to pursue workplace or labor rights. It is also critical that unions secure an institutional presence in the vibrant informal and agrarian sectors of economic activity. Furthermore, unions clearly need to remain engaged with democratic rebuilding. They are one of the few organizations across these countries capable of maintaining a strong public watchdog role. They are also able to wield international attention and pressure when democratic institutions are threatened.

These suggestions are rooted in the practical experiences of PNG, Fiji, and the Solomon Islands. At this stage of development unions need to pay attention to both the "sword of justice" and their "self-interest" objectives. This requires new structures and alternative forms of engagement. How these will evolve remains to be seen.

CONCLUSION

Labor unions have had a difficult start in PNG, Fiji, and the Solomon Islands. In each of these countries, economic downturn, political and resource conflicts, and bad governance have extracted a heavy price from national development efforts. As a consequence, labor unions have been simultaneously challenged on two fronts. First, they have been forced to respond to harsh measures of stabilization and adjustment. Second, they have needed to play a far more important role in promoting good governance and democracy. Both these challenges have exposed unions, and their effectiveness, especially within the workplace, has declined. In this context labor unions find that they need new language and modalities for engagement. It is becoming increasingly apparent that the success or failure of labor unions in these countries is contingent on their relationships and partnerships with NGOs. Positive experiences have emerged, but much work remains to be done.

It is likely that unions will come out of this substantively transformed. The problem is that unions do not appear to possess concrete ideas about organizational forms, mechanisms for ensuring democratic accountability within social alliances, and procedures for formulating social pacts. These are matters that labor unions and NGOs will need to think through, and this project is equally worthy of promotion by social development partners. The past decade has been one of lost development. Labor unions have been able to do little to arrest this. Should alternative institutional forms and modalities of engagement crystalize and be sustainable, the present decade might be more hopeful.

Part VI

Resources

Twenty-three

Labor Unions and Development: An Annotated List of Selected Resources

CAROLINE KNOWLES WITH DEBORAH EADE

This selected resources list seeks to provide an introduction to the contemporary literature on labor unions and development and signposts to websites and organizations offering further information. In bringing together material from many different sources, we have aimed both to give a flavor of the range and type of organizations working in the fields of labor and development and to highlight resources of particular relevance to the key issues raised by contributors to this volume.

There is an extensive literature on NGOs and issues such as gender and diversity, empowerment and participation, and policy-related advocacy. Much of this literature is covered in the resources lists to earlier titles in this series, all of which are available free of charge at the www.developmentinpractice.org website. Far less familiar is the role of the labor movement in development, and relatively little has yet been written about the relationship between unions and development organizations. Writers tend to represent either one sector or the other, and despite many interests they share in common, the two perspectives are seldom brought together. Case studies about organizing the unorganized, anti-poverty campaigns, or discussions about globalization and the corporate sector—all profoundly relevant to development agencies and labor unions alike—tend to be presented from only one standpoint.

It is also clear that the buzz words now adopted by the multilateral agencies—*civil society organizations, transnational movements, corpo-*

rate social responsibility, anti-globalization campaigns—in fact focus largely on NGOs. Writings on these topics constantly repeat the clichéd litany of "new social movements" such as the environment lobby or the international women's movement, or specific success stories such as the anti-landmines campaign. This in itself is curious, given that so few development NGOs, including those that are household names, even existed before the Second World War. By contrast, many labor unions have been active in the international arena since the mid-nineteenth century. For instance, the 1891 International Labour Conference established frameworks for transnational cooperation, and the ILO was founded in 1919. Though this is now increasingly challenged, one obvious reason why "civil society" became almost synonymous with NGOs during the 1990s was that, within a neoliberal agenda of deregulation and anti-statism, NGOs became the development delivery channel or implementing body of choice for many donor agencies. This mutual dependence placed NGOs center stage as the "responsible" advocates and interlocutors of civil society, often displacing other more valid (and often more militant) representational bodies such as labor unions, religious congregations, and political parties. It is hoped that the resources listed here will help to redress this imbalance by drawing attention to the critical importance of labor unions within the spectrum of civil society organizations concerned with development and with the broader agenda of social and economic justice for all.

The core business of labor unions is to organize, press for fair terms and conditions of work, negotiate on behalf of the work force, provide services for members, network, and mobilize. Myriad websites containing up-to-date labor union news and information have replaced the activist newsletters, flyers, and magazines of old. Some are run by individual labor union organizations, and others act as information hubs (such as the Cyber Picket Line); they are a particularly useful way to find out about union activities worldwide.

Many of the large European and North American labor unions and global or regional union federations also raise funds from their members for aid and development work. There are far too many to describe each one individually, but some of the most important include AFCSME (www.afscme.org), AFL-CIO (www.afl-cio.org), and the United Electrical, Radio and Machine Workers of America (www.ueinternational.org) in the United States, the Deutsche Gewerkschaftsbund (www.dgb.de) in Germany; the Federatie Nederlandse Vakbeweging (www.fnv.nl) in the Netherlands; the Trade Unions Congress (www.tuc.org.uk) in the UK;

and many of the Scandinavian unions. Some of these have formed specialist development organizations such as Norwegian People's Aid (www.npaid.org), networks such as Solidar (www.solidar.org), and special union funds such as the Steelworkers' Humanity Fund, founded by the United Steelworkers of Canada, whose members donate 40 cents a week on the basis of which co-funding from the government is leveraged, currently running at a total of some CA$5 million annually.

Similarly, there are many NGOs with strong connections to, or affinities with, the labor movement. These include Amnesty International (www.amnesty.org.uk) and Human Rights Watch (www.hrw.org), which work closely with the labor movement on issues such as freedom of association and the right to organize and join labor unions, as well as the many NGOs and think tanks that research social and labor issues, such as the New Economics Foundation in the UK (www.neweconomics.org) and IBASE in Brazil (www.balancosocial.org.br). A growing number of organizations also undertake some kind of watchdog, monitoring, or campaigning role on the behavior of transnational corporations (TNCs), particularly in relation to labor standards. Space does not permit extensive exploration of these organizations, some of which are described by contributors to this volume, but well-known examples include the Clean Clothes Campaign (www.cleanclothes.org), Corpwatch (www.corpwatch.org), the Ethical Trading Initiative (www.ethicaltrade.org), and SA8000 (www.cepaa.org).

Apart from the labor unions and union-related organizations there are innumerable other agencies, governmental and nongovernmental, that fund initiatives to educate or organize workers in both the formal and informal economies. These include the UK government's Department for International Development (DFID), which recently carried out a survey of labor union activity in developing countries (see Spooner 2000) and is co-funding the educational website, Global Workplace, run by War on Want (see Chapter 9 herein).

The Internet has revolutionized bibliographic research and made it possible to find many of the documents listed here from the comfort of one's home or workplace. Readers who do not have such resources at their fingertips might contact one of the specialist libraries offering research services. Staff at the ILO library will answer queries, and the library of the German Foundation for International Development (www.dse.de) and the Friedrich Ebert Stiftung (www.fes.de) also offer enquiry services.

This selected resources list was compiled and annotated by Caroline Knowles, communications manager at the Institute of Development Studies at the University of Sussex and formerly reviews editor of *Development in Practice*, with Deborah Eade, editor of *Development in Practice.*

Every effort has been made to ensure that the URLs in this list are accurate and up to date. However, with the rapid changes that occur in the World Wide Web, it is inevitable that some pages or other resources will have been discontinued or moved, and some content modified or reorganized. The publisher recommends that readers who cannot find the sources or information they seek with the URLs listed below use one of the numerous search engines available on the Internet.

BOOKS

Addison, John T., and Claus Schnabel, eds. *International Handbook of Trade Unions.* Cheltenham: Edward Elgar Publishing, 2003.
A comprehensive review of the determinants of union membership, models of union behavior, the effects of union membership on wages, pay inequality, and firm performance, including specific chapters examining recent developments in the UK and the United States, and the prospects for Europeanization of collective bargaining. Also includes a review of union density in over one hundred nations.

Balakrishnan, Radhika, ed. *The Hidden Assembly Line: Gender Dynamics of Sub-contracted Work in a Global Economy.* Bloomfield CT: Kumarian Press, 2001.
Contributors explore the impact of economic globalization in terms of the dynamics and growth of subcontracted labor among women, including homeworkers. With chapters on India, Pakistan, Philippines, and Sri Lanka, the book seeks to put a human face on macroeconomic trends.

Barber, Mary, ed. *Mapping Trade Unions: British and International Trade Union Organisations.* London: Department for International Development, 1999.
A basic background on labor unions, listing and describing the main labor union organizations in the UK and their international activities (lobbying and development work) as well as their principal European and international counterparts.

Bendt, Heinz. *One World, One Voice, Solidarity: The International Trade Secretariats.* Bonn: Friedrich Ebert Stiftung, 1996.
A handbook and guide to the international trade secretariats (now called Global Union Federations), their history and origins, structure, activities, and programs. Contains useful background information about their relationships to one another and to the ICFTU and other international organizations. A detailed description of each organization is given (with contact details), and an overview section discusses issues and challenges for the future.

Boris, Eileen, and Elisabeth Prügl, eds. *Homeworkers in Global Perspective: Invisible No More*. London: Routledge, 1996.

Homeworkers are usually women and generally dispersed, which makes them more vulnerable to exploitation and thwarts traditional union organizing methods. Establishing networks among them requires a detailed knowledge of international production and supply chains, areas in which some international NGOs and unions have played a role.

Brecher, Jeremy, Tim Costello, and Brendan Smith. *Globalization from Below: The Power of Solidarity*. Cambridge, Mass.: South End Press, 2000.

The 1999 Battle of Seattle saw labor unionists, environmentalists, women's rights groups, and human rights advocates converging in a broad-based global protest movement. This book draws on previous experiences of social mobilization, particularly in the area of organized labor, in order to set out the pitfalls facing the movement and its potential to reshape global politics. See also Brecher and Costello's *Building Bridges: The Emerging Grassroots Coalition of Labor and Community* (New York: Monthly Review Press,1990).

Briskin, Linda, and Patricia McDermott, eds. *Women Challenging Unions: Feminism, Democracy and Militancy*. Toronto: University of Toronto Press, 1993.

While jobs in traditional areas of union membership have declined, there has been an increase in part-time, nonstandard work in small workplaces that are difficult to organize and also in practices such as outsourcing. More women are now in the work force, and more people are employed in sectors and conditions previously associated with women's work. Contributors argue that the gendered nature of economic restructuring requires unions to abandon traditional ideologies about women's work, embrace broader-based bargaining methods, and ensure that their own practices do not marginalize women.

Brown, Malcolm, ed. *Trade Unions and Community Action: Bridging the Gap*. Manchester: William Temple Foundation, 2000.

A collection of papers from a workshop organized by the William Temple Foundation and UK Trade Union Congress in which practitioners from labor unions and different branches of community action explored experiences and the potential of different organizing models. Case studies from the UK and the United States report on progress in a field where new thinking and initiatives are emerging, but where much remains to be done if those who are most exploited are to be empowered.

Castells, Manuel. *The Information Age*, Vol. 1, *The Rise of the Network Society*. Rev. ed. Oxford: Blackwell, 2000.

This classic text presents a systematic theory of the information society taking into account the social and economic effects of information technology on the contemporary world. The book examines the processes of globalization that have marginalized and excluded whole countries and peoples from information networks. It investigates the culture, institutions, and organizations of the network enterprise; explores the concomitant transformation of work and employment;

and suggests that these changes may not generate mass unemployment but rather the extreme flexibilization of work and individualization of labor. Volumes 2 and 3 are *The Power of Identity* (1997), which discusses social movements and transformational politics, and *The End of the Millennium* (1998), which examines globalization and the state.

Clark, John, ed. *Civic Engagement: Civil Society and Transnational Action.* London: Earthscan, 2003.
This book looks at what civil society organizations can achieve and the barriers they face when they participate in global networks. Case studies focus on the effectiveness of transnational action in terms of influencing government policies and public attitudes in a world of rapid structural and ideological change. Civil society organizations studied include NGOs, new forms of citizen mobilization, advocacy organizations, and global union federations.

Cohen, Robin, and Shirin M. Rai. *Global Social Movements.* London: Athlone Press, 2000.
The authors argue that the new global social movements, namely, the human rights, women's, environment, labor, religious, and peace movements, are altering earlier agendas for social change and political engagement. Chapters on the international labor movement suggest that its goals have become more modest and more achievable, and that many union activists recognize their similarities with other social movements. The authors conclude that political life is moving beyond the confines of the nation state to take on new global and cosmopolitan dimensions as part of an emerging global civil society.

Colgan, Fiona, and Sue Ledwith, eds. *Gender, Diversity and Trade Unions: International Perspectives.* London: Routledge, 2002.
This multi-disciplinary compilation drawn from an international team of academics and labor unionists examines the impact of women's activism and new social movement politics on labor unions. Contributors develop an international perspective on labor union gender democracy worldwide, while also identifying and assessing structural and cultural developments in labor unions in different countries as they respond to challenges to the traditional forms of unionism from increasingly diverse agendas.

Compa, Lance, and Stephen F. Diamond, eds. *Human Rights, Labor Rights, and International Trade.* Philadelphia: University of Pennsylvania Press, 1996.
Contributors provide a comprehensive view of labor rights in the international trade system and the options available to workers to protect their rights in a global economy through instruments including international human rights law, trade laws, free trade agreements, corporate codes of conduct, and the legislative framework of organizations such as the World Trade Organization and regional economic structures such as the European Union or the North American Free Trade Agreement. Authors seek to distinguish between union rights that are enshrined in human rights and claims that amount to defending certain privileges.

Craven, Matthew. *The International Covenant on Economic, Social and Cultural Rights: A Perspective on Its Development.* Oxford: Oxford Univ. Press, 1995.
Despite their formal recognition in a number of international instruments since 1945, the second generation of economic, social, and cultural rights have been marginalized. This is particularly apparent with respect to the International Covenant on Economic, Social, and Cultural Rights (ICESCR), which was intended to form part of the International Bill of Rights along with the International Covenant on Civil and Political Rights (ICCPR). This legal study examines the origins and development of the ICESCR and discusses particular aspects of the covenant, such as the nature of state obligations; the principle of nondiscrimination; and the rights to work, to join and form labor unions, to housing, and to food.

Curtin, Jennifer. *Women and Trade Unions: A Comparative Perspective.* Aldershot: Ashgate, 1999.
Examining how women labor unionists have sought to make union structures and policy agendas more inclusive of the interests of women workers, the author analyzes how far such a partnership has been developed between women and labor unions in Austria, Australia, Israel, and Sweden. She addresses questions such as the strategies pursued by women unionists in each country; the circumstances and issues around which women have employed class-based or gender-specific strategies in furthering the interests of women workers; the relevance of the history of women's inclusion and representation by labor unions to their choice of strategy; and the political and cultural environment within which labor unionism has operated.

Elkington, John. *Cannibals with Forks: The Triple Bottom Line of Twenty-first Century Business.* 2nd ed. Oxford: Capstone, 1999.
An exposition of the enlightened self-interest argument for corporate social responsibility, which holds that companies must be seen to address environmental and social concerns and not merely the financial bottom line to avoid the risk of damaging their public credibility. While the author highlights the role of NGOs as watchdogs (such as Greenpeace) or in monitoring codes of conduct, it is noteworthy that neither employees nor organized labor feature as core stakeholders within the "triple bottom line" approach.

Education International. *Education Is a Human Right: EI Barometer on Human and Trade Union Rights in the Education Sector.* Brussels: Education International, 1998.
The report provides statistical information about access to education in every country where EI has a member organization, the incidence of child labor, and the extent to which teachers and educators enjoy fundamental human rights and labor union rights. EI argues that improvements in each area require progress on all three fronts simultaneously.

Edwards, Michael, and John Gaventa, eds. *Global Citizen Action.* Boulder, Colo.: Lynne Rienner, 2001.
This volume examines the agendas encompassed within civil society and explores civil society's engagement with international institutions in relation to four areas:

a conceptual framework defining civil society; influencing the international financial institutions; examples of global campaigns (landmines, debt, free trade, children's rights, sustainable development, the environment, women's rights, urban issues); and lessons for advocacy networks and global citizen action. The focus is mainly on NGOs and global campaigns, though since labor unions are active in many of these areas some of the lessons apply.

Ewing, K. D., and Tom Sibley. *International Trade Union Rights for the New Millennium*. London: Institute of Employment Rights, 2000.
In 1996 the International Centre for Trade Union Rights embarked on a project to review international labor standards and to consider how they might be reformed and adapted. This book reports on the research setting out the case for universal labor standards and international labor union rights. It discusses the modernization of the conventions on freedom of association and the supervision and enforcement of standards. It contains the texts of the main ILO conventions in the Appendices.

Fairbrother, Peter, and Gerard Griffin, eds. *Changing Prospects for Trade Unionism*. London: Continuum, 2002.
After thirty years of national and international economic restructuring, often accompanied by major legislative reforms, the way forward for labor unions is unclear. Throughout the 1980s and into the 1990s union membership slumped in most industrialized economies, and unions lost their former prominence and their place in the polity. This book explores the background, current roles, and prospects of labor unions in six countries in order to determine whether they can reestablish their political salience, or whether there will be still further declines in union strength and power. See also Peter Fairbrother, *Trade Unions at the Crossroads* (London: Mansell, 2002), which focuses on case studies from the manufacturing, privatized utilities, and the public sector in the UK, and looks at the prospects for union renewal.

Fox, Jonathan A., and L. David Brown, eds. *The Struggle for Accountability: The World Bank, NGOs and Grassroots Movements*. Cambridge, Mass.: MIT Press, 1998.
This book analyzes reforms within the World Bank to adopt more rigorous environmental and social policies, and the subsequent conflicts over how and whether to apply them. The World Bank has become more accountable as the result of protest and public scrutiny, and the empowering effect of these on inside reformers. Transnational NGO networks are also becoming more accountable to their local partners, partly because grassroots movements are demanding this and partly in response to the World Bank's challenge to the legitimacy of its NGO critics. Although the book contains little on labor union–NGO alliances as such, the lessons it draws about advocacy work are relevant to both sectors.

Fyfe, Alec, and M. Jankanish. *Trade Unions and Child Labour: A Guide to Action*. Geneva: ILO, 1997.
The international labor union movement is crucial in the fight against child labor. Workers' organizations are ideally placed to discover and denounce abuses and to

advocate both for the right of children to adequate education and for adults to receive decent wages, thereby reducing the need for child labor in poor families. The authors show how unions can be involved in specific measures locally and nationally, and they describe the main UN agencies, instruments, and standards regulating child labor. Case studies present innovative approaches by workers' organizations to serve as examples of good practice and an inspiration for action.

Gallin, Dan. *Trade Unions and NGOs: A Necessary Partnership for Social Development*. Geneva: UNRISD, 2000.
A discussion paper on the role of labor unions and NGOs in relation to other actors in civil society (religious organizations, educational institutions, professional associations, and so on) in which the author argues that they are distinguished by having specific agendas for the improvement of society. The paper reviews the historical background, the record, and the potential for and constraints to cooperation. Drawing on examples of collaboration between NGOs and labor unions (especially in relation to human rights, women's rights, the informal economy, environmental issues, and corporate codes of conduct) the paper examines the conditions that must be met in order to strengthen such alliances.

Gunnell, Barbara, and David Timms, eds. *After Seattle: Globalisation and Its Discontents*. London: Catalyst, 2000.
The demonstrations leading to the collapse of the WTO talks in Seattle in December 1999 were among the first major public expressions of concern about contemporary economic globalization, particularly in relation to the environment and the rights of workers within a global trade regime. The chapter by John Edmonds, general secretary of the GMB, is entitled "An Agenda for the Labour Movement."

Harper, John, ed. *Trade Unions of the World*. 6th ed. London: John Harper Publishing, 2005.
John Harper provides a comprehensive directory of labor union organizations worldwide, with an introductory section for each country outlining the national political and economic context within which unions operate. This is followed by an overview of the history, structure, scale, and influence of the union movement, including information on ratification of ILO Convention No. 87 (Freedom of Association and Protection of the Right to Organise, 1948) and Convention No. 98 (Application of the Principles of the Right to Organise and to Bargain Collectively, 1949). A third section describes the various labor union centers and gives detailed information on affiliates in countries where the labor union movement is highly developed and industry-level unions are significant in social and political life. An appendix gives details of international and regional labor union organizations.

Hosmer Martens, Margaret, and Swasti Mitter. *Women in Trade Unions: Organising the Unorganised*. Geneva: ILO, 1994.
A collection of case studies from around the world on organizing women workers at national and local level in areas that are difficult to mobilize: small-scale enterprises, the informal economy, homework, domestic service, and export processing zones.

Hutchinson, Jane, and Andrew Brown, eds. *Organising Labour in Globalizing Asia.* London: Routledge, 2001.

This study of contemporary organizing capacities of workers in Asia with case studies from Bangladesh, China, India, Indonesia, Malaysia, the Philippines, and Thailand examines workers' responses to class relations through independent unions, NGOs, and (dis)organized struggles. While economic globalization is generally held to have negative consequences for labor organizing, some openings for local activism can arise from transnational production arrangements.

International Council on Human Rights Policy. *Beyond Voluntarism: Human Rights and the Developing International Legal Obligations of Companies.* Versoix: ICHRP, 2002.

The responsibility of private companies to respect human rights is now of major concern to companies as well as governments, multilateral agencies, NGOs, investors, and consumers. This report reviews the applicability and implementation of existing human rights laws in this context. Voluntary codes alone are regarded as ineffective while their proliferation is leading to contradictory or incoherent efforts. Campaigns that play to the self-interest of companies, ethical trading initiatives, consumer boycotts, and voluntary codes of conduct all have a role to play; but the authors stress the role of international law in ensuring that companies are accountable in relation to human rights.

International Labour Organization. *Freedom of Association: An Annotated Bibliography.* Geneva: ILO, 1999.

A trilingual (English, French, and Spanish), annotated bibliography prepared by the editorial staff of the *International Labour Review*, this practical reference book provides source information for officials, researchers, and activists promoting human rights and, in particular, protection of freedom of association and labor union rights. The bibliography covers the major sources of international law on the subject, with information on global and regional institutions and a fully referenced guide to supervisory bodies and procedures.

International Labour Organization. *World Labour Report 1997–8: Industrial Relations, Democracy and Social Stability.* Geneva: ILO, 1998.

This report focuses on the state of labor union membership and industrial relations worldwide with a statistical summary and overview of the main issues in the changing global economy. Separate chapters discuss current issues for labor unions; changes within labor unions; employers' organizations; new features of production and industrial relations; diverse institutions of social dialogue (collective bargaining, national agreements, legislation, and so forth); industrial relations and the informal sector; and future social dynamics.

Jenkins, Rhys, Ruth Pearson, and Gill Seyfang, eds. *Corporate Responsibility and Labour Rights: Codes of Conduct in the Global Economy.* London: Earthscan, 2002.

The proliferation of voluntary corporate codes of conduct since the early 1990s responds to a widespread retreat from state regulation of TNCs and a consequent emphasis on self-regulation in areas such as basic working conditions, environmental standards, and human rights. Academics, practitioners, NGO workers, and activists review such codes particularly in relation to labor rights and global value chains. The book also lists major websites relating to this aspect of global corporate activity.

Jose, A. V., ed. *Organized Labour in the 21ˢᵗ Century.* Geneva: International Institute for Labour Studies, 2002. Available from the ILO.
Growing out of a research project on the role of the labor union movement in contributing to dynamic social policy and equitable growth, this book focuses on the changing environment of labor and unions; labor union responses to these changes; and future perspectives for labor in society and in the global economy. The project included an electronic network linking labor unionists with academics and the ILO as well as comparative research into union responses and strategies. The book offers an overview of labor issues and lessons for developing countries followed by case studies on Chile, Ghana, India, Israel, Republic of Korea, Lithuania, Niger, South Africa, Sweden, and the United States.

Kabeer, Naila. *The Power to Choose: Bangladeshi Women and Labour Market Decisions in London and Dhaka.* London: Verso, 2000.
In Bangladesh, despite a history of female seclusion, women are now a prominent industrial labor force. By contrast, Bangladeshi women in the UK, a secular society with a long tradition of female employment, are largely concentrated in homeworking for the garment industry. Kabeer contrasts these work experiences to ask what constitutes "fair" competition in international trade. She concludes that international labor standards must take account of the forces of inclusion and exclusion *within* local labor markets.

Keck, Margaret E., and Kathryn Sikkink. *Activists beyond Borders: Advocacy Networks in International Politics.* Ithaca, N.Y.: Cornell Univ. Press, 1998.
Transnational activist networks have a long history, including the antislavery and women's suffrage campaigns. The authors sketch the dynamics of emergence, strategies, and impact of contemporary pressure groups on issues such as human rights, the environment, and violence against women—issues that are also relevant to international NGOs (and NGOs working internationally) and to the international labor movement.

Kester, Gérard, and Ousmane Oumarou Sibidé, eds. *Trade Unions and Sustainable Democracy in Africa.* Aldershot: Ashgate, 1997.
Contributors discuss the role labor unions have played in the establishment of political democracy and their potential in making democracy sustainable in this survey of labor unions and development in sub-Saharan Africa, drawing on ten case studies (from Benin, Burkina Faso, Cape Verde, Ghana, Mali, Mozambique, South Africa, Sudan, Tanzania, and Togo). Four issues—democracy, development, labor unions, and participation—are addressed in each study. The overall conclusion is that Africa needs a framework of sustainable democracy, but this will be established only if democracy has a visibly positive effect on development.

van der Linden, Marcel, ed. *The International Confederation of Free Trade Unions*. Berne: Peter Lang Publishing, 2000.

This first history of the ICFTU describes the development of its precursors (the International Secretariat of National Trade Union Centres, the International Federation of Trade Unions, and the World Federation of Trade Unions) and reconstructs the history of the ICFTU from its origins during the Cold War, through anti-colonial struggles, European unification, international campaigns against apartheid, and many other issues. A final chapter discusses the ICFTU's prospects in the twenty-first century.

McBride, Anne. *Gender Democracy in Trade Unions*. Aldershot: Ashgate, 2001.

In 1993 the UK's largest union, UNISON, decided to create a framework for empowering women. This book describes UNISON's strategies for reshaping labor union democracy and achieving gender democracy, illustrating the impact of these strategies on women's participation and representation in the union. Arguing that union structures need to be organized around principles of individual *and* group representation, McBride concludes that reformed structures are necessary to achieve equality between men and women but that they are not a sufficient condition for the empowerment of women.

McNally, David. *Another World Is Possible: Globalization and Anti-Capitalism*. Winnipeg: Arbeiter Ring Publishing, 2002.

The author traces the history of what he calls the anti-corporate globalization movement from 1994, along with the political and economic orders it seeks to resist. Drawing on the experience of radical movements of workers, peasants, and indigenous peoples in countries including Bolivia, Brazil, Indonesia, Korea, and Mexico, McNally proposes an alternative politics based on diversity and internationalism, one that moves beyond commodification and the market. See also David McNally, *Bodies of Meaning: Studies on Language, Labor, and Liberation* (Albany, N.Y.: State Univ. of New York Press, 2001).

Martin, Brendan. *In The Public Service*, London: Zed/PSI, 2002.

Transforming the quality and efficiency of public services is critical to both economic stability and social justice, but ideological and technocratic approaches are not delivering the improvements required. Martin argues for a more participatory approach to reform, involving both service users and public service employees in the process. Case studies include slum dwellers from Brazil's Porto Alegre explaining how a "participative budget" has encouraged local democracy; Swedish social service caretakers directing budget cuts without cutting jobs or services; and doctors in the Czech Republic saving their country's health services by a new approach to public-private partnership. While top-down reforms and business-school fads have largely failed, the new partnership model is rooted in true empowerment, reconciling efficient public spending, quality of service, and secure and satisfying public employment to the benefit of all. See also Brendan Martin, *In the Public Interest? Privatisation and Public Sector Reform* (London: Zed/PSI, 1993).

Meiksins Wood, Ellen, Peter Wood, and Michael Yates, eds. *Rising from the Ashes: Labor in the Age of "Global" Capital*. New York: Monthly Review Press, 1998. A collection of essays by progressive scholars, union leaders, and activists reflecting on the contemporary nature of labor organization and mobilization. Contributors discuss issues including the changing composition of the international working class, patterns of work under contemporary capitalism, the relationship of race and gender to class, the promise and limitations of recent eruptions of labor militancy, and the strategic options available to working people in an age of globalization. The book focuses on the United States but includes essays on Mexico, East Asia, and Europe.

Moody, Kim. *Workers in a Lean World: Unions in the International Economy*. New York: Verso, 1997. This book looks at the roots and structures of globalization, their impact on the working classes of different parts of the world, and recent responses to the "lean regime" in the workplace, the global jobs crisis, government-imposed austerity, and the general decline in the living standards of working people. The author calls for "social movement unionism," which goes beyond the "organizing" model of unionism to assert the centrality of union democracy as a source of power and broader social vision and also views outreach and alliance building as means of enhancing that power.

Munck, Ronaldo. *Globalisation and Labour: The New 'Great' Transformation*. London: Zed Books, 2002. The TNCs search for cheap labor on the global market is changing the world of work. Munck argues that the labor movement is increasingly transnational, with workers developing agendas and ways of organizing that transcend national boundaries. He suggests that the union movement could play a major role in regulating a global economic system now largely out of control, arguing that we may be witnessing what Karl Polanyi called "the great transformation," the implications of which profoundly affect workers, unions, and their TNC employers.

Munck, Ronaldo, and Peter Waterman, eds. *Labour Worldwide in the Era of Globalisation: Alternative Union Models in the New World Order*. Basingstoke: Macmillan, 1999. Arguing that the globalized nature of modern capitalism makes it necessary to reconsider the role of class and of the labor union as an organizational form, the editors believe that for labor to retrieve its political and a moral force, it must make alliances with the "new social movements," such as the women's, environment, or human rights movements. In chapters exploring labor organization in Brazil, India, Japan, North America, Pakistan, Russia, South Africa, and Western Europe, contributors call for a new "social unionism" that addresses civil society as a whole, recognizes new terrains and levels of struggle, and draws on the experience of new social movements. Transcending nations and national labor strategies, social unionism would require emancipatory action within as well as by the union movement. See also Peter Waterman, *Globalisation, Social Movements, and the New Internationalism* (Washington, D.C.: Continuum, 1998).

Munro, Anne. *Women, Work and Trade Unions*. London: Mansell, 1999.
This study focuses on working-class women, in particular catering and cleaning workers, and shows how the institutional bias within labor unions precludes the full representation of women's interests. Based on research carried out in two labor unions in the UK public health service, the author stresses the need to understand how women's work is structured in order to investigate the role of labor unions in challenging or reproducing gender-based inequalities.

Nissen, Bruce, ed. *Unions in a Globalized Environment: Changing Borders, Organizational Boundaries, and Social Roles*. Armonk, N.Y.: M. E. Sharpe, 2002.
Organized labor in the United States has suffered from the impact of TNCs, the establishment of new trade pacts, and the dismantling of certain import barriers. Nissen argues that to revitalize themselves and expand their role on a global stage, US unions must create ties with workers and unions internationally and also focus on recruiting immigrant workers at home. The resulting "social movement unionism" would be less focused on the market and more on social issues and rights. See also Bruce Nissen, *Which Direction for Organized Labor? Essays on Organizing, Outreach, and Internal Transformations* (Detroit: Wayne State Univ. Press, 1999); idem, *Unions and Workplace Reorganization* (Detroit: Wayne State Univ. Press, 1997); idem, *US Labor Relations 1945–1989: Accommodation and Conflict* (New York: Garland Publsihing, 1990), and Bruce Nissen, co-editor, *Theories of the Labor Movement* (Detroit: Wayne State Univ. Press, 1987).

O'Brien, Robert, ed. *Global Unions? Theory and Strategies of Organised Labour in the Global Political Economy*. London: Routledge, 2002.
Labor issues are now on the international agenda and unions have sought to influence policies of organizations such as the WTO, the IMF, the EU, and trade agreements in the Americas. The author introduces various theoretical approaches to understanding global union issues, and discusses labor responses to global challenges, constraints on labor internationalism, union responses in the South, labor and the architecture of international economic institutions, the global labor standards debate, and labor as a global social force. The book includes case studies on labor struggles in the United States; labor union training on globalization in the UK and Brazil; transformation in the international policies of US and Canadian unions; and labor and regional integration in the Americas, Europe, and the Asia-Pacific region.

O'Brien, Robert, Anne Marie Goetz, Jan Aart Scholte, and Marc Williams. *Contesting Global Governance: Multilateral Economic Institutions and Global Social Movements*. Cambridge: Cambridge Univ. Press, 2000.
Arguing that increasing engagement between international institutions and sectors of civil society is producing a new form of global governance, the authors investigate "complex multilateralism" in relation to the IMF, the World Bank, and the WTO, and three global social movements (environmental, labor, and women's movements). The book includes a comparative analysis of the institutional response to pressure from social movements, tracing institutional change, policy modification, and the tactics adopted by civil society organizations in trying to

influence the rules and practices governing trade, finance, and development regimes.

Oxfam GB. *Trading Away Our Rights: Women Working in Global Supply Chains.* Oxford: Oxfam GB, 2004.
Based on a twelve-country study, this campaign document highlights the impact of the flexibilization of labor on women workers worldwide. It argues that the export-oriented employment favored by the current model of economic globalization benefits the corporate sector at the expense of the employees at the bottom of the supply chain, particularly women, most of whom are poorly paid and enjoy little or no social protection or job security.

Reynolds, David B., ed. *Partnering for Change: Unions and Community Groups Build Coalitions for Economic Justice.* Armonk, N.Y.: M. E. Sharpe 2004.
Bringing together activists and intellectuals involved in alliances between labor unions and community-based initiatives in the United States, related, for instance, to the environment, religious groups, low-income organizations, local employers, and living-wage campaigns, this volume offers a broad overview of the potential and limitations of labor-community coalitions.

Rose, Kalima. *Where Women Are the Leaders: The SEWA Movement in India.* London: Zed Books, 1992.
SEWA, a forty-thousand-strong union of some of India's poorest women, has become both an example of a new development model and an inspiration to low-income women worldwide. This historic account traces SEWA's work from its initial organizing around basic wage and credit issues to its research and lobbying activities on development policy issues and its growing international influence on employment and resource strategy.

Rowbotham, Sheila, and Swasti Mitter, eds. *Dignity and Bread: New Forms of Economic Organising Among Poor Women in the Third World and the First.* London: Routledge, 1994.
An early account of the growth in casual female labor, analyzing how global economic change is affecting women internationally and focusing on their responses to these developments. Case studies from India, Malaysia, Mexico, the Philippines, Sri Lanka, Tanzania, and the UK give examples of women organizing in the cotton textile and garment industries, in free trade zones, and through the formation of national and international networks of self-employed women. Rowbotham's *Homeworkers Worldwide* (London: Merlin Press, 1993) describes how homeworkers' organizations and labor unions can work together.

Smith, Jackie, and Hank Johnson, eds. *Globalization and Resistance: Transnational Dimensions of Social Movements.* Lanham, Md.: Rowman and Littlefield, 2002.
This collection of theoretical essays and case studies explores how global economics and politics alter the way citizens engage in contentious political action. Chapters include analyses of transnational mobilization and networking in relation to globalization, national politics, local-global linkages, and specific events or projects, such as protests against World Bank projects in the Amazon or the

Battle of Seattle in December 1999. See also Jackie Smith, Charles Chatfield, and Ron Pagnucco, eds., *Transnational Social Movements and Global Politics: Solidarity beyond the State* (Syracuse, N.Y.: Syracuse Univ. Press, 1997).

Southall, Roger, ed. *Trade Unions and the New Industrialisation of the Third World.* London: Zed Books, 1998.
Focusing on issues confronting labor unions in the 1990s, in particular how the globalization of production and prolonged recession have undermined the bargaining power of labor, this book focuses on organized labor and industrialization in the Third World; industrial restructuring, repression, and labor union responses (with studies of labor unionism under military rule in Argentina and in Nigeria, in export processing zones in Sri Lanka, workers' councils in Iran, the "Japanization" of labor unions in Malaysia, and labor unions and human rights in Africa); and the prospects for labor internationalism (with chapters on US labor intervention in Latin America, the ILO and protection of labor union rights, nationalism as a labor union perspective, and a new communications model for working-class internationalism).

Spooner, Dave. *A View of Trade Unions as Part of Civil Society.* London: DFID, 2000.
A background paper prepared for the UK government on labor unions and NGOs in development, this work provides an overview of the different types of labor union organizations and the activities they have funded, particularly in the areas of human rights and freedom of association, and reviews the obstacles and conditions for successful collaboration between the two sectors.

Starr, Amory. *Naming the Enemy: Anti-corporate Social Movements Confront Globalisation.* London: Zed Books, 2001.
The "anti-globalist" opposition to TNCs and globalization comprises a wide range of organizations including NGOs and labor unions. The author defines three types of movement: those trying to constrain corporate power through democratic institutions and direct action, those attempting to create "globalization from below," and those seeking to create an alternative small-scale community "de-linked" from the global economy. Wider issues such as development, small businesses, human rights, labor, the environment, and democracy are also covered.

Thomas, Henk. *Trade Unions and Development.* Labour and Society Programme Discussion Paper DP/100/1999. Geneva: ILO, 1999.
This research paper was written for the International Institute for Labour Studies and reflects on the role of the labor movement in development processes and social transformation, particularly in developing countries. It explores a new methodology to analyze the labor union movement, recognizing that traditional industrial relations patterns no longer offer effective guidelines for policy design and action in many newly industrialized countries, and that as a major player within civil society, the labor movement is vital to sustainable development and participatory democracy. See also Henk Thomas, ed., *Globalisation and Third World Trade Unions: The Challenge of Rapid Economic Change* (London: Zed Books,

1995). Focusing on the crisis facing organized labor in the South in the mid-1990s, this includes case studies from Chile, Malaysia, Pakistan, Venezuela, Zambia, and Zimbabwe. The challenges include new TNC management methods, the growth of the informal economy, the widespread casualization of labor, and the increasing number of women workers who remain inadequately represented by labor unions.

Wets, Johan, ed. *Cultural Diversity in Trade Unions: A Challenge to Class Identity?* Aldershot: Ashgate, 2000.

With particular reference to European unions, the author examines how unions deal with regional differences and competing cultural identities, in particular those of migrant workers, and asks whether regional and cultural differences jeopardize working-class solidarity.

Wunnava, Phanindra V., ed. *The Changing Role of Unions: New Forms of Representation.* Armonk, N.Y.: M. E. Sharpe, 2004.

Leading labor economists analyze the future of labor unionism and conclude that new forms of representing and organizing workers need to be generated in order to replace traditional approaches, which are declining around the world. While not seeking to predict exact models for new employee institutions, contributors argue that working people may experience greater satisfaction from increased representational involvement and a broader community constituency.

JOURNALS

Economic and Industrial Democracy. Published quarterly by Sage on behalf of the Arbetslivsinstitutet (National Institute for Working Life), Sweden. Editors: Lars Magnusson and Jan Ottosson. ISSN: 0143–831X.

Explores the new labor market and work processes, organizational aspects regarding working life and its policy implications, and the interaction among political, technological, and economic factors and various aspects of labor markets and industrial relations. Topics of relevance include gender and equal opportunity, deregulation, and unemployment issues.

Gender, Work and Organization. Published quarterly by Blackwell. Editors: David Knights and Deborah Kerfoot. ISSN: 0968–6673.

Dedicated to the applied analysis of gender relations at work, the organization of gender, and the gendering of organizations, topics recently addressed include the concept of paid and unpaid work, "masculinities," sex work and prostitution, the economics of equal opportunities, and culture change in organizations.

Industrial Relations: Journal of Economy and Society. Published quarterly by Blackwell. Editors: David I. Lefvine and Daniel J. B. Mitchell. ISSN: 0019–8676.

Offering an international and multi-disciplinary perspective on developments in labor and employment, *IR* focuses on the implications of change for business, government, and workers. Issues covered include corporate restructuring and downsizing, the changing employment relationship in union and nonunion settings, high performance work systems, workplace demographics, and the impact of globalization on national labor markets.

International Labour Review. Published quarterly by the ILO in English, French (*Revue Internationale du Travail*, ISSN: 0378–5599), and Spanish (*Revista Internacional de Trabajo*, ISSN: 0378–5548). Editor-in-Chief: Ifthikhar Ahmed. ISSN: 0378–7780.

Publishing original research and analysis by economists, labor lawyers, and other experts on questions of labor and employment issues the *ILR* also includes short articles on emerging issues, and book reviews.

Journal of Industrial Relations. Published quarterly by Blackwell on behalf of the Industrial Relations Society of Australia. Editors: Rom Callus and Russell Lansbury. ISSN: 0022–1856.

Focusing on the way in which individuals, groups, organizations, and institutions shape the employment relationship, *JIR* addresses the economic, political, and social influences on the relative power of capital and labor and also the interactions among employers, workers, their collective organizations, and the state.

LABOUR, Capital and Society: a journal on the Third World/TRAVAIL, capital et societé: une revue sur le Tiers Monde. Published twice-yearly by the Centre for Developing-Area Studies, McGill University. Editor: Rosalind Boyd. ISSN: 0706–1706.

A bilingual journal on labor issues in Africa, Asia, Latin America, the Caribbean, and the Middle East exploring the social, economic, cultural, and political dimensions of development, labor struggles, and the conditions in which people live and work. Topics covered include women in the labor movement, child labor, labor unions, and unorganized labor protests.

Labour Education. Published quarterly in English, French (*Education Ouvrière*, ISSN: 0378–5572) and Spanish (*Educación Obrera*, ISSN: 0378–5564) by the ILO Bureau for Workers' Activities. Editor: Luc Demeret. ISSN: 0378–5467.

Issues of interest include vol. 90, no. 1 (1993) on women's participation in labor unions; vol. 116, no. 3 (1999) on labor unions in the informal sector; and vol. 121, no. 4 (2000) on what workers and labor unions should know about social protection.

Labor Studies Journal. Published quarterly by West Virginia Univ. Press for the United Association for Labor Education. Editors: Paul Jarley and Bruce Nissen. ISSN: 0160–449X (print), 1538–9758 (online).

Focuses on work, workers, labor organizations, labor studies, and worker education, and including reviews of print, audio-visual, and electronic materials. The *LSJ* is aimed at a general readership of union, university, and community-based labor educators as well as labor activists and scholars from across the social sciences and humanities.

Monthly Review. Published monthly by Monthly Review Press. Editors: Paul M. Sweezy, Harry Magdoff, John Bellamy Foster, and Robert W. McChesney. ISSN: 0027–0520.

Combining scholarship and activism, *MR* seeks to be accessible to workers and labor organizers as well as academics, taking an editorial stand against class, racial, and sexual exploitation and analyzing current realities, their historical roots, and the prospects for change.

New Technology, Work and Employment. Published three times a year by Blackwell. Editor: Christopher Baldry. ISSN 0268–1072.

Focusing on changing technological and organizational systems and processes, this multi-disciplinary journal seeks to promote debate that is rooted in the analysis of current practice. Recent topics include labor union renewal in the UK motor industry, participatory company management, technology and work patterns in the restaurant sector, and teleworking and media workers.

Work, Employment and Society. Published quarterly by the Cambridge Univ. Press for the British Sociological Association. Editor: Theo Nichols. ISSN: 0950–0170.

Analyzing all forms of work and their relation to wider social processes and structures and to quality of life, *WES* focuses on the labor process and changes in labor markets, industrial relations, and the gender and domestic divisions of labor. It supports contemporary, historical, and comparative studies and both qualitative and quantitative methodologies.

ORGANIZATIONS

Business Human Rights

A website that contains information from the UN and ILO, companies, human rights, development, labor, and environmental organizations, governments, academics, journalists, and so on. It serves as an online library to provide easy access (through links) to a wide range of materials and to promote informed discussion of important policy issues. The website contains an overview section (with general information about business and human rights), a section on getting started, and information about human rights across a wide range of business sectors.

www.business-humanrights.org

Catalyst Forum

Describing itself as a non-aligned organization of democratic socialists, Catalyst seeks to promote new, practical policies directed to the redistribution of power, wealth, and opportunity. It publishes policy papers and books across the whole span of social and public policy issues, including labor unions and the world of work.

www.catalystforum.org

CIVICUS: World Alliance for Citizen Participation
A global alliance of organizations committed to strengthening citizen action and civil society, CIVICUS believes that private action for the public good can take place both within the civil sphere and in combination with government or with business and that a healthy society needs an equitable relationship among these sectors. Publications include *Civil Society at the Millennium* (edited by Kumi Naidoo, 1999) and *Promoting Corporate Citizenship: Opportunities for Business and Civil Society Engagement* (Laurie Regelbrugge, 1999). Parts of the website are available in Spanish, French, and German.
www.civicus.org

Commonwealth Trade Union Council (CTUC)
The CTUC works in cooperation with other international labor union organizations and seeks to promote a democratic and prosperous Commonwealth in which international labor standards are observed. Main activities include providing education and training, improving collective bargaining practices, providing technical assistance for capacity building activities, collecting and disseminating information, defending and promoting labor union rights and labor standards, and activities to promote the participatory and leadership role of women.
www.commonwealthtuc.org

Congress of South African Trade Unions (COSATU)
Since its foundation in 1985, COSATU has been in the forefront of the struggle for democracy and workers' rights. It is based on five core principles: non-racism; paid-up membership; one industry, one union, one country, one federation; worker control; and international worker solidarity. The COSATU website contains a useful page of links (labor directories and union organizations worldwide) and a list of its publications.
www.cosatu.org.za

Cyber Picket Line
A web-based resource for the international labor union movement designed to assist direct communication among union activists around the world, to designate useful resources available on the web, and to enliven topics with humor and commentary. The centerpiece of the site is the *World Trade Union Directory*, with over two thousand links to international union organizations, national unions, local branches, and union resource sites in every continent. A section entitled "Trade Union Resources" gives access to the sort of information previously available only in union headquarters.
www.ca.ac.uk/socsci/union

Essential Information
A nonprofit organization that encourages citizens to become active in their communities, EI's information clearinghouse (the Multinational Resource Center) disseminates information to grassroots organizations in the United States and developing countries. Essential Information also publishes a range of books on multinational issues and *The Multinational Monitor*, which tracks corporate activity, especially in

the South, focusing on the export of hazardous substances, health and safety, labor
union issues, and the environment (published ten times a year).
    www.essential.org

Ethical Trading Initiative (ETI)
    An alliance of companies, NGOs, and labor union organizations committed to
    working together to identify and promote ethical trade, defined as good practice
    in the implementation of a code of conduct for good labor standards, including
    the monitoring and independent verification of the observance of code provisions
    as standards for ethical sourcing. Ethical business includes working toward the
    ending of child labor, forced labor, and sweatshops, looking at health and safety,
    labor conditions, and labor rights. Its website has information in various Euro-
    pean, African, and Asian languages.
        www.ethicaltrade.org

European Trade Union Confederation (ETUC)
    Established in 1973 the ETUC is a cross-sectoral organization that seeks to ad-
    vance the social agenda of its partner organizations in economic and social policy
    dialogue at the European level. Representing 60 million members in seventy-four
    national labor union confederations from thirty-four countries, its primary objec-
    tive is to safeguard and promote the rights of workers and labor unions, which it
    does through direct representation in various European institutions and advisory
    bodies and the cultivation of relations with employers. The European Trade Union
    Institute, the European Trade Union College, and the Trade Union Technical Bu-
    reau are all organized under the auspices of the ETUC. The European Trade Union
    Institute Documentation Centre houses a large collection of labor union publica-
    tions, answers research enquiries, and is open to external users by appointment.
        www.etuc.org

Fair Labor Association (FLA)
    A nonprofit alliance of multinational companies and NGOs that have agreed to
    the FLA Charter Agreement, the first industry-wide code of conduct and moni-
    toring system. This provides for an independent monitoring system to hold com-
    panies publicly accountable for their labor practices as well as those of their prin-
    cipal contractors and suppliers. The FLA accredits independent monitors, certifies
    that companies are in compliance with the code of conduct, and serves as a source
    of information for the public.
        www.fairlabor.org

Friedrich Ebert Stiftung (FES)
    Founded in 1925 as a political legacy of Germany's first democratically elected
    president, FES runs a major social and political education program within Ger-
    many through its four academies, workshops and conferences, and the provision
    of scholarships. About half of its annual budget is spent on international activities
    in over one hundred countries, focusing on support for labor unions, independent
    media structures, human rights work, democratization, and peace and coopera-
    tion. FES houses the largest specialized library and archives on the German and

international labor movement. Its journal, *International Politics and Society,* is published in English.

www.fes.de

Focus on the Global South

Based in Thailand, this policy-oriented research organization emphasizes a Southern perspective with a particular focus on the Asia-Pacific region. Its central purpose is to acknowledge innovative activities by grassroots civil society organizations, and to relate these to broader macro questions of state relations and the role of Northern NGOs in sustainable development. Focus takes a strong position in questioning the legitimacy of labor unions in helping the poorest workers.

www.focusweb.org

Global Alliance for Workers and Communities

An alliance of private, public, and nonprofit organizations to improve the lives, workplace experience, and communities of young workers in global manufacturing and service companies, the Global Alliance aims to help corporations respond to workers' needs and aspirations on a factory-by-factory basis. Its main goal is to build a sustainable assessment-and-development process and the infrastructure to ensure it lasts.

www.theglobalalliance.org

Global Labour Institute

A labor service organization established in 1997 in Geneva, the Global Labour Institute supports the efforts of the labor movement to deal with the globalization of the world economy. To this end it works to strengthen the links between labor unions and other civil society organizations in the defense of human and democratic rights.

www.global-labour.org

Global Unions

A news bulletin board jointly owned and managed by the group of global union federations (GUFs) associated with the ICFTU and other international labor union organizations, enabling members to publicize union news and campaigns (www.global-unions.org). The GUFs are Education International (www.ei-ie.org); the International Federation of Chemical, Energy, Mine and General Workers' Unions (www.icem.org); the International Federation of Building and Wood Workers (www.ifbww.org); the International Federation of Journalists (www.ifj.org); the International Metalworkers' Federation (www.imfmetal.org); the International Textile, Garment and Leather Workers' Federation (www.itglwf.org); the International Transport Workers' Federation (www.itf.org.uk); the International Union of Food, Agricultural, Hotel, Restaurant, Catering, Tobacco and Allied Workers' Associations (www.iuf.org); Public Services International (www.world-psi.org); and Union Network International (www.union-network.org). While all have some involvement in development issues, some GUFs have a more sustained relationship with development agencies, including NGOs. For example, EI, the largest of the GUFs, was a key member of the Education Now! campaign, and the ITGLWF is actively involved in the Ethical Trading Initiative and with organizations concerned with homeworkers, such as HomeNet.

The Global Workplace

A development education project among labor unions coordinated by the UK NGO War On Want and funded by DFID and the EU. The website illustrates the impact of globalization on workers' rights and labor union strategies to protect those rights. It also has links to campaigns being coordinated by WoW as well as urgent actions from unions worldwide, labor union education materials, links to WoW affiliates and overseas partners, and a page on women workers.
www.globalworkplace.org

HomeNet

An international network of organizations working with homeworkers to render them visible, fight for recognition of their rights, and campaign for improvements in their living and working conditions. HomeNet collects and disseminates information on homework, assists in obtaining technical assistance for homeworkers, and publishes a regular newsletter for homeworkers and their organizations.
www.homenetww.org.uk

Institute of Employment Rights

Launched in 1989 as a labor law think tank supported by the labor union movement, the institute exists to provide research, ideas, and detailed argument. The IER does not claim that legal remedies can offer ultimate solutions for political, economic, and social problems, but it recognizes that law plays a role in influencing the employment relationship both individually and collectively.
www.ier.org.uk

International Confederation of Free Trade Unions

Founded in 1949 as the result of a split within the World Federation of Trade Unions (WFTU), the ICFTU is by far the largest confederation of labor union centers, with 221 affiliated organizations from 148 countries and territories worldwide. Its primary activities include coordinating campaigns; representing the interests of its affiliates in international bodies and agencies; and providing research, education, training, and information services. The ICFTU is based in Brussels and maintains offices in Geneva, New York, and Washington D.C. Regional affiliates are the Asian and Pacific Regional Organisation in Singapore, the African Regional Organisation in Nairobi, and the Inter-American Regional Organisation of Workers in Caracas. Regular publications include the annual *Survey of Trade Union Rights*, which details over one hundred countries that violate basic labor union rights, and the monthly magazine *Trade Union World* (also available as *Le Monde Syndical* and *El mundo sindical*).
www.icftu.org

International Cooperative Alliance (ICA)

An international umbrella NGO for cooperatives worldwide, ICA's website provides information on the cooperative movement in sectors including agriculture, banking, credit, consumer, energy, fisheries, housing, insurance, workers, tourism, and healthcare. It also contains case studies, further resources, and information about ICA publications on cooperative and development issues.

www.coop.org

International Centre for Human Rights and Democratic Development (Rights and Democracy)

Founded in 1988 to encourage and support the universal values of human rights and the promotion of democratic institutions and practices worldwide, Rights and Democracy works with individuals, organizations, and governments to promote the human and democratic rights defined in the UN International Bill of Human Rights, including the right of workers to organize. Its bimonthly e-magazine *Libert@s* is also distributed in print twice yearly.

www.ichrdd.ca

International Federation of Workers' Education Associations (IFWEA)

A global federation of labor unions, NGOs, and political institutions active in workers' and labor union education, the IFWEA was founded in 1947 with the aim of promoting "free and voluntary educational work, according to the principles of solidarity and cooperation, justice and equality, democracy and freedom." It publishes a quarterly journal, *Workers' Education*, and the Red, White and Blue Pamphlet Series, which focuses on social and economic issues, political freedom and democracy, and various technical concerns of the workers' education movement. The IFWEA coordinates an innovative distance-learning project through International Study Circles on topics such as migrant workers in the global economy, women and the global food industry, and tackling TNCs.

www.ifwea.org

International Institute for Labour Studies (IILS)

Established in 1960 as an autonomous facility of the ILO to promote policy research and public discussion on emerging labor issues, IILS provides a global forum on social policy enabling governments, business, and labor to interact informally with the academic community and other opinion makers; international research programs and networks linking academics with business, labor, and government representatives to explore emerging policy issues and contribute to policy formulation; and educational programs to assist labor unions, employers' organizations, and labor administrations in developing their institutional capacities for research, analysis, and policy formulation in the economic and social fields.

www.ilo.org/public/english/bureau/inst

International Labour Organization (ILO)

The ILO is the UN specialized agency advocating social justice and universal human and labor rights. It formulates international labor standards in the form of conventions and recommendations setting minimum standards across the entire spectrum of work-related issues and supervises their application worldwide. The ILO also provides technical assistance in vocational training and rehabilitation and on issues such as employment policy, labor law and industrial relations, and occupational health and safety. It promotes the development of independent employers' and workers' organizations and provides training and advisory services. The ILO's unique tripartite structure comprises workers, employers, and national governments, and its business is conducted through three main organs: the International Labour Conference, the Governing Body, and the International Labour Office. ILO publications include technical manuals and reference works, training materials, the annual *World Labour Report*, two journals available in English, French, and Spanish (*International Labour Review* [ISSN: 0378–5548] and *Labour Education* ISSN: 0378–5564]), and the magazine *World of Work* (five times a year, ISSN: 1020–0010), which covers health and safety issues internationally.

www.ilo.org

ILO Bureau for Workers' Activities (ACTRAV)

ACTRAV focuses on activities to strengthen workers' organizations at the international, regional, and national levels. Its mandate is to strengthen representative, independent, and democratic labor unions worldwide, to enable them to play their role effectively in protecting workers' rights and interests and in providing effective services to their members, and to promote the ratification and implementation of ILO conventions. Specific programs include standards and fundamental principles and rights at work, employment, social protection, social dialogue, gender promotion, and decent work.

www.ilo.org/public/english/dialogue/actrav/

ILO Library

Located at the ILO headquarters in Geneva, the ILO Bureau of Library and Information Services is the world's leading library in the field of labor and labor issues. Its collections include books, periodicals, reports, journal articles, legislation and statistics covering labor relations, employment, child labor, social security, vocational training, women workers, working conditions, and all labor-related aspects of economics, social development, and technological change in countries around the world. Much of the catalogue is available online, and library staff will carry out bibliographical searches on request.

www.ilo.org/bibl

International Centre for Trade Union Rights (ICTUR)

ICTUR is a research and advocacy center established in 1987 to extend and strengthen the rights of labor unions in line with the major UN declarations and international agreements on human and labor rights. ICTUR publishes the quarterly journal *International Union Rights* (ISSN: 1018–5909), containing articles on specific countries and regions or taking up broader international issues concerning labor unions, freedom of association, and related rights. The most recent issue is available on the ICTUR website.

www.ictur.labournet.org

International Labor Rights Fund (ILRF)

An advocacy organization dedicated to achieving just and humane treatment for workers worldwide, ILRF promotes labor rights through public education and mobilization; research; litigation; legislation; and collaboration with labor, government, and business groups. Its books include *Workers in the Global Economy* (2000), *Trade's Hidden Cost* (John Cavanagh et al., 1988) and *Global Village versus Global Pillage: A One-World Strategy for Labor* (Jeremy Brecher and Tim Costello, 1991).

www.laborrights.org

Labour and Society International (LSI)

LSI works for human rights in the global workplace through advocacy, education, and research, in partnership with labor unions and civil society organizations in developing and transition economies. LSI's work includes helping unions to campaign for basic human and labor rights; develop labor union education programs, including tutor training and materials development; negotiate and campaign for improvements in health and safety; ensure that the concerns of women workers are reflected in unions' priorities; and recruit and work with unorganized workers. LSI coordinates *LabourStart*, a news bulletin produced by a worldwide network of 100 volunteer correspondents.

www.labourstart.org

LabourNet

A website containing news, information, and articles submitted by individual labor unionists and labor unions, LabourNet promotes computer communications as a medium for strengthening and building organized labor. Part of the Association for Progressive Communications, LabourNet organizations are now based in Austria, Canada, Germany, Japan, Korea, Spain, the UK, and the United States.

www.labournet.net

Labour Telematics Centre (LTC)

Established in 1993 to support and encourage labor unions and labor organizations in gaining access to and benefits from computer-based electronic communications and information technology (telematics), the LTC is also concerned with the impact of such technologies on the labor process, conditions of employment, and the nature of work itself. It provides technical consultancy, organizes seminars and conferences, publishes research and reports, and supports national unions in Africa, Asia, and Central and Eastern Europe to make better use of online communication.

www.labourtel.org.uk/Welcome.html

Maquila Solidarity Network (MSN)

Promoting solidarity with groups in Mexico, Central America, and Asia organizing in *maquila* factories and export processing zones to improve conditions and wages, the MSN works through corporate campaigns, government lobbying, popular education, and international links. Its campaign Exposing the Labour behind the Label exposes the "global sweatshop" behind everyday goods in order to make retailers and international companies accountable for the conditions under which their products are made and to increase consumer understanding of the issues.

www.maquilasolidarity.org

The National Labor Committee for Worker and Human Rights (NLC)

A human rights advocacy group dedicated to promoting and defending the rights of workers. Through its longstanding relationships with NGOs and human rights, labor, and religious organizations, primarily in Latin America, NLC seeks to put a human face on the global economy. The NLC educates and involves the public in action aimed at ending labor abuses, improving living conditions for workers and their families, promoting the concept of a living wage, and achieving true independent monitoring.

www.nlcnet.org

Norwegian People's Aid (NPA)

Founded in 1939 by the Norwegian labor movement, NPA is one of Norway's largest NGOs. Based upon the principles of solidarity, unity, human dignity, peace, and freedom, NPA is involved in more than four hundred projects in thirty countries. Its international activities include long-term development assistance, emergency assistance, mine-clearance and mine-awareness programs, and conflict prevention and resolution.

www.npaid.org

Public Services International Research Unit (PSIRU)

Set up in 1998 to carry out empirical research into privatization, public services, and globalization, PSIRU houses an extensive database on the economic, political, financial, social, and technical experience of privatizations of public services worldwide and tracks the involvement of specific TNCs in such processes. Many of its reports are published on its website.

www.psiru.org

Self-Employed Women's Association (SEWA)

An organization of self-employed women workers in the informal economy (in which women constitute 93 percent of the labor force in India), SEWA is a *sangam* or confluence of the labor movement, the cooperative movement, and the women's movement. Its main goals are to organize women workers for full employment and self-reliance.

www.sewa.org

Solidar

An alliance of NGOs, labor unions, and campaigning groups from fifteen countries with links to the social democratic and socialist parties and to the labor union movement, Solidar is active in the fields of development work, humanitarian and emergency assistance, social welfare policy, development education, policy formulation, lobbying, and mediation.

www.solidar.org

StreetNet

A global network of street sellers, activists, researchers, and others working to increase the profile and bargaining power of street vendors throughout the world, StreetNet seeks to mobilize support for an ILO convention on the rights of street

vendors and exchange information and ideas on critical issues facing street vendors and on practical organizing and advocacy strategies.

www.streetnet.org.za

Trade Union Advisory Committee (TUAC)

An interface among fifty-six national labor unions from the thirty OECD member
countries, TUAC aims to represent its affiliates in intergovernmental discussions,
such as the G7 economic summits and employment conferences, and to advance
the social agenda in economic policy debates. TUAC's recent work has focused
on structural adjustment and labor market policies, the impact of globalization on
employment, education and training, multinational enterprises, and OECD relations with nonmember countries, as well as the environment, sustainable development, and the globalization of information.

www.tuac.org

UNRISD

An autonomous agency within the UN system that carries out research, stimulates dialogue, and contributes to policy debates on the social dimensions of contemporary problems affecting development, UNRISD focuses on how development policies and processes of economic, social, and environmental change affect
different social groups. UNRISD publishes extensively, and its work in progress
is often available online.

www.unrisd.org

Women in Informal Employment: Globalizing and Organizing (WIEGO)

Established in 1997, WIEGO is a worldwide coalition (including SEWA, UNIFEM,
and Harvard University) concerned with improving the status of women in the
informal economy, which is where women workers, particularly the poorest, are
concentrated. Their work and the contribution it makes to the broader economy
remain largely invisible in official statistics and policies. WIEGO seeks to improve the status of the informal economy by compiling better statistics, conducting research, and developing programs and policies.

www.wiego.org

Women Working Worldwide (WWW)

An NGO working with a global network of women workers' organizations, WWW
supports the rights of women workers in an increasingly globalized economy in
which they are used as a source of cheap and flexible labor. The focus has been on
industries that have moved to the South, particularly the textile and garment and
electronics industries. WWW publishes a range of working papers and coordinates the Labour Behind the Label network, which campaigns for improved conditions in the international garment industry.

www.poptel.org.uk/women-ww/

World Bank Labor Markets Group

The website of the Labor Markets Group gives information about labor unions,
particularly in developing countries; the role of unions in economic and social

development; and cooperative initiatives between the World Bank and international labor unions.

www.worldbank.org/labormarkets.

World Confederation of Labour (WCL)

Founded as the International Federation of Christian Trade Unions in 1920, with a strong focus on Europe and Latin America, the WCL was reconstituted in 1968 and describes itself as being inspired by humanist, ethical, and moral values. With affiliates in 116 countries, WCL's regional structures are the Latin American Central Federation of Workers, the Brotherhood of Asian Trade Unionists, and the Democratic Organisation of African Workers' Trade Unions.

www.cmt-wcl.org

World Federation of Trade Unions (WFTU)

Established in 1945, the WFTU replaced the earlier International Trade Union Confederation, taking its inspiration from the defeat of fascism and prospect of decolonization and propelled by unions across Europe and the Soviet Union. During the Cold War the WFTU was essentially the labor union arm of the Eastern bloc, though also drawing strength from its affiliates in developing countries.

www.wftu.cz

Reference List

Every effort has been made to ensure that the URLs in this list are accurate and up to date. However, with the rapid changes that occur in the World Wide Web, it is inevitable that some pages or other resources will have been discontinued or moved, and some content modified or reorganized. The publisher recommends that readers who cannot find the sources or information they seek with the URLs listed below use one of the numerous search engines available on the Internet.

Action Canada Network. 1991. Minutes, 14th National Assembly. Unpublished report. Ottawa: Action Canada Network Assembly.

————. 1993. Minutes, 22nd National Assembly (verbatim). Unpublished report. Ottawa: Action Canada Network.

————. 1995. ACN/CLC Meeting. Unpublished report. Ottawa: Action Canada Network.

ADB (Asian Development Bank). 2002. *Papua New Guinea at a glance*. Manila: ADB.

Adesina, Jimi. 1994. *Labour in the explanation of an African crisis*. Dakar: CODESRIA Book Series.

————. 1995. State, industrial relations and accumulation regime in Nigeria: Reflections on issues of governance. *Ibadan Journal of the Social Sciences* 1, no. 1:1-26.

Alecio, Rolando. 1995. Uncovering the truth: Political violence and indigenous organizations, in *The new politics of survival: Grassroots movements in Central America*, edited by Minor Sinclair. New York: Monthly Review Press.

Americas Watch. 1989. *Honduras: Without the will*. Washington, D.C.: Americas Watch Committee.

Ananaba, Wogu. 1969. *The trade union movement in Nigeria*. Benin City: Ethiope Publishing.

Ancel, Judy. 2000. Response I: On building an international solidarity movement. *Labor Studies Journal* 25, no. 2:25-35.

Anderson, Sarah. 2001. Revelry in Quebec. *The Progressive* 65, no. 6:24-27.

Anner, Mark. 2001. The international trade union campaign for core labor standards in the WTO. *Working USA: The Journal of Labor and Society* 4, no. 5:45-63.

————. 2002. Defending labor rights across borders: Central American export-processing plants. In *Struggles for social rights in Latin America*, edited by Susan Eckstein and Timothy P. Wickham-Crowley. New York: Routledge.

AP (Associated Press). 1978. About 300 union locals "severely influenced" by organized crime. *International Herald Tribune* 25. April.

Ardón, Patricia. 1999. Post-war reconstruction in Central America: Lessons from El Salvador, Guatemala, and Nicaragua, Oxfam Working Papers. Oxford: Oxfam GB.

371

Arquilla, John, and David Ronfeldt. 2001. What next for networks and netwars? In *Networks and netwars: The future of terror, crime, and militancy,* edited by John Arquilla and David Ronfeldt. Santa Monica, Calif.: Rand.

Arrighi, Giovanni. 1990. Marxist century, American century: The making and remaking of the world labour movement. *New Left Review* 179, no. 1:29-63.

Artto, Juhano, ed. 2001. *Everything at stake: Safeguarding interest in a world without frontiers.* Helsinki: KTV.

Asia Pulse. 2000. *Nationwide Financial News,* September 12.

Bacharach, Samuel B., Peter A. Bamberger, and William J. Sonnenstuhl. 2001. *Mutual aid and union renewal: Cycles of logics of action.* Ithaca, N.Y.: Cornell Univ. ILR Press.

Bangura, Yusuf, and Bjorn Beckman. 1993. African workers and structural adjustment. In *The politics of structural adjustment in Nigeria,* edited by Adebayo Olukoshi. Ibadan: Heinemann.

Barchiesi, Franco. 1996. The social construction of labour in the struggle for democracy: The case of post-independence Nigeria. *Review of African Political Economy* 23, no. 69:349-70.

Barndt, Deborah. 1998. Personal interview with Sophia Huyer, November 30.

Barrientos, Stephanie. 2002. Mapping codes through the value chain: from researcher to detective. In *Corporate responsibility and labour rights: Codes of conduct in the global economy,* edited by Rhys Jenkins, Ruth Pearson, and Gill Seyfang. London: Earthscan.

Bashevkin, S. 1989. Free trade and feminism: The case of the National Action Committee on the Status of Women. *Canadian Public Policy* 15, no. 4:363-75.

Bayat, A. 1987. *Workers and revolution in Iran.* London: Zed Books.

Bickham Méndez, Jennifer and Ronald Köpke. 2001. *Mujeres y maquila: Respuestas a la globalización: Organizaciones de mujeres centroamericanas en medio de la competencia y cooperación transnacional en la industria maquilera.* 2nd ed. San Salvador: Ediciones Heinrich Böll.

Biekart, Kees. 1999. *The politics of civil society building: European private aid agencies and democratic transitions in Central America.* Utrecht: International Books and the Transnational Institute.

Bob, Clifford. 2002. Merchants of morality. *Foreign Policy* 129 (March/April): 36-45.

Bonacich, Edna, and Richard Appelbaum. 2000. *Behind the label—Inequality in the Los Angeles apparel industry.* Berkeley and Los Angeles: University of California Press.

Brill, Lucy. 2002. Can codes of conduct help home-based workers? In Jenkins et al. 2002.

Bronfenbrenner, Kate. 2001. Changing to organize. *The Nation* 3 (September 2001).

Bulgarian Gender Research Foundation. 2001. Social environment and standards and the work place in the garment industry: Results from a preliminary research for a Clean Clothes Campaign International Project. Sofia: BGRF.

Bullard, Nicola. 2000. The world's workers need solidarity, not sanctions. *Development* 43, no. 2:31-35.

Canada Summit. 1987. The Canada Summit. *Council of Canadians Newsletter.* 3-5.

Carew, Anthony. 1998. The American labor movement in Fizzland: the Free Trade Union Committee and the CIA. *Labor History* 39, no. 1:25-42.

Carr, Barry. 1996. Crossing borders: Labour internationalism in the era of NAFTA. In *Neoliberalism revisited: Economic restructuring and Mexico's political future,* edited by Gerardo Otero. Boulder, Colo.: Westview Press.

Carr, Shirley. 1986. CLC plans free-trade fight. *Globe and Mail* 12 September: A3.

Carrillo, Francia. 1999. *Estudio de identificación de necesidades de empresarios de la maquila en Costa Rica.* San José: ILO.

Cascio, Joseph, Gayle Woodside, and Philip Mitchell. 1996. *ISO 14000 guide: The new international environmental management standards.* New York: McGraw Hill.

Catalano, Ana María. 1999. The crisis of trade union representation: New forms of social integration and autonomy-construction. In *Labour worldwide in the era of globalization: Alternative union models in the new world order,* edited by Ronaldo Munck and Peter Waterman. New York: St. Martin's Press.

Cavanagh, John. 1997. The global resistance to sweatshops. In Ross 1997.

CCC (Clean Clothes Campaign). 1998. Codes, monitoring, and verification: Why the CCC is involved. Available online at the cleanclothes.org website (accessed September 10, 2002).

———. 2001. Clean Clothes Campaign International Meeting, Barcelona 2001. Unpublished report. Amsterdam: CCC.

Charmes, Jacques. 2000. Informal sector, poverty, and gender: A review of empirical evidence. Background paper for the *World Development Report 2001.* Mimeo C3ED. Versailles: University of Versailles.

Chee Khoon, Chan. 2003. The political economy of health care reforms in Malaysia. In *Restructuring health services: Changing contexts and comparative perspectives,* edited by K. Sen. London: Zed Books.

Clarke, Tony. 1999. Personal interviews with Sophia Huyer, July 7 and August 17.

CNWN. 2000. *[Communication network of women's NGOs in the Islamic Republic of Iran].* Published in Farsi. Iran: CNWN.

Cohen, Marjory. 1999. Telephone interview with Sophia Huyer, August 12.

Collier, David, and Ruth Berrins Collier. 1991. *Shaping the political arena: Critical junctures, the labor movement, and regime dynamics in Latin America.* Princeton, N.J.: Princeton Univ. Press.

Common Frontiers. 1991. Note from Common Frontiers Meeting. Unpublished report. Ottawa: Common Frontiers.

———. 1999. News from Quito Encuentro. Press release. October 13. Available online at the web.net website (accessed March 26, 2003).

Compa, Lance. 2000. NGO-labor union tensions on the ground. *Human Rights Dialogue* 4, no. 2:12-15.

———. 2001. Wary allies. *The American Prospect* 12, no. 12 (July): 8-9.

Connor, Tim. 2001. *Still waiting for Nike to do it.* San Francisco: Global Exchange.

———. 2002. We are not machines: Despite some small steps forward, poverty and fear still dominate the lives of Nike and Adidas workers in Indonesia. Unpublished report. Sydney: Clean Clothes Campaign, Global Exchange, Maquila Solidarity Network, Oxfam Canada, and Oxfam Community Aid Abroad. Available online.

Cook, Maria. 1997. Regional integration and transnational politics: Popular sector strategies in the NAFTA era. In *The new politics of inequality in Latin America: Rethinking participation and representation,* edited by D. Chalmers, C. Vilas, K. Roberts-Hite, S. Martin, K. Peister, and M. Segarra. New York: Oxford Univ. Press.

Cooke, Bill, and Uma Kothari, eds. 2001. *Participation: The new tyranny?* London: Zed Books.

Cordero, Allen. 1999. *Relaciones laborales y condiciones de trabajo en las ZPE y empresas maquiladores.* San José: ILO.

Cunnison, S. 2002. Gender, class and equal opportunities: A grass-roots case study from the trade union movement. *Journal of Gender Studies* 11, no. 2:167-81.

Cutler, A. Claire, Virginia Haufler, and Tony Porters, eds. 1998. *Private authority and international affairs*. Albany, N.Y.: State Univ. of New York Press.

D'Cruz, Don. 2002. Dangerous liaisons. *IPA Review* (Melbourne) (September).

De la Cueva, Héctor. 2000. Crisis y recomposición sindical internacional. *Nueva Sociedad* 166: 111-22.

Della Porta, Donatella, and Mario Diani. 1999. *Social movements: An introduction*. Oxford: Blackwell.

Diamond, Larry. 1999. *Developing democracy toward consolidation*. Baltimore, Md.: Johns Hopkins University Press.

Dillon, John. 1999. Personal interview with Sophia Huyer, January 7.

DiMaggio, Paul, and Walter Powell. 1991. The iron cage revisited: Institutional isomorphism and collective rationality. In *The New Institutionalism in Organizational Analysis*, edited by P. DiMaggio and W. Powell. Chicago, Ill.: University of Chicago Press.

Doern, Bruce, and Brian Tomlin. 1991. *Faith and fear: The free trade story*. Toronto: Stoddart.

Dreiling, Michael. 2001. *Solidarity and contention: The politics of security and sustainability in the NAFTA conflict*. New York: Garland.

Eade, Deborah, and Suzanne Williams. 1995. *The Oxfam handbook of development and relief*. 3 vols. Oxford: Oxfam GB.

Eade, Deborah, ed. 2000. *Development, NGOs, and civil society*. Oxford: Oxfam GB.

EAI (Enterprise for the Americas). 1992. Minutes of the EAI Working Group. Unpublished report. Ottawa: Common Frontiers.

Ehrenreich, Barbara. 2001. *Nickled and dimed: On (not) getting by in America*. New York: Henry Holt.

Elliot, Kimberly Ann, and Richard Freeman. 2001. White hats or Don Quixotes? Human rights vigilantes in the global economy. National Bureau of Economic Research Working Paper No. 8102. Cambridge, Mass.: NBER.

Elson, Diane. 1992. Gender issues in development strategies. In *Women 2000*. Vol. 1. New York: UN Division for the Advancement of Women.

Encarnación, O. G. 2000. Tocqueville's missionaries: Civil society, advocacy, and the promotion of democracy. *World Policy Journal* 17, no. 1:9-18.

Enemuo, Francis, and Abubakar Momoh. 1999. Civic associations. In *Nigeria: Politics of transition and governance, 1986-1996,* edited by Oyeleye Oyediran and Adigun Agbaje Dakar: CODESRIA.

ETI (Ethical Trading Initiative). 1998. The ETI base code. Available online at the ethicaltrade.org website (accessed September 10, 2002).

Evans, Peter. 2000. Fighting marginalization with transnational networks: Counter-hegemonic globalization. *Contemporary Sociology* 29, no. 1:230-41.

Farhadpour, L. 2002. Do women journalists need their own trade association? *[Sedaye Zan: The Journal of Women Journalists Trade Association]* 1. Published in Farsi.

Featherstone, Liza, and Doug Henwood. 2001. Clothes encounters: Activists and economists clash over sweatshops. *Lingua Franca* 11, no. 2. Available online at the uvm.edu website (accessed December 5, 2003).

Featherstone, Liza, and USAS. 2002. *Students against sweatshops*. New York: Verso.

Flanders, A. 1970. *Management and unions*. London: Faber.

Fletcher, Bill, and Richard W. Hurd. 2000. Is organizing enough? Race, gender, and union culture. *New Labor Forum* 6 (Spring/Summer): 59-70.

Frundt, Henry J. 2002. Central American unions in the era of globalization, *Latin American Research Review* 37, no. 3:7-53.

Fung, Archon, Dara O'Rourke, and Charles Sabel. 2001. Realizing labor standards—How transparency, competition, and sanctions could improve working conditions worldwide. *Boston Review* 26, no. 1:4-10.

Gallin, Dan. 2000a. *Trade unions and NGOs in social development: A necessary partnership*. Geneva: UNRISD.

———. 2000b. Civil society—a contested territory. Euro-WEA seminar on Workers' Education and Civil Society, Budapest, June 16-17.

———. 2000c. Trade unions and NGOs: A necessary partnership for social development. Civil Society and Social Movements Programme Paper No. 1. Geneva: UNRISD.

———. 2001. Propositions on trade unions and informal employment in times of globalisation. *Antipode* 33, no. 3:531-49.

———. 2002. Organising in the informal economy. *Labour Education* 127, no. 2:21-26.

GAO (General Accounting Office). 1994. *Garment industry—Efforts to address the prevalence and conditions of sweatshops*. GAO/HEHS-95-29. Washington, D.C.: GAO.

Garretón, Manuel Antonio. 1998. ¿En qué sociedad vivi(re)mos? *Estudios Sociales* 14, no. 1.

Gatellari, M., P. H. Butow, and M. H. N. Tattersall. 2001. Sharing decisions in cancer care. *Social Science and Medicine* 52:1865-78.

Gentile, Antonina. 2002. Transnational networking, INGOs and the domestic roots of transnational labor contention. Paper presented at the 98th American Political Science Association Annual Meeting, Boston, Mass., August 29–September 1.

Gereffi, Gary, Ronie García-Johnson, and Erika Sasser. 2001. The NGO-industrial complex. *Foreign Policy* 200 (July-August): 56-65.

———. 2002. The international competitiveness of Asian economies in the apparel commodity chain. Economics and Research Department Working Paper No. 5. Washington, D.C.: Asian Development Bank.

Gerlach, Luther. 2001. The structure of social movements: Environmental activism and its opponents. In Arquilla and Ronfeldt, *Networks and netwars*.

Glickman, Lawrence. 1997. *A living wage: American workers and the making of consumer society*. Ithaca, N.Y.: Cornell Univ. Press.

Gonick, Cy, and Jim Silver. 1989. Fighting free trade. *Canadian Dimension* (April-May): 6-14.

Gorz, André. 1999. *Reclaiming work: Beyond the wage-based society*. Cambridge: Polity Press.

Greenfield, Gerard. 1998. The ICFTU and the politics of compromise. In *Rising from the ashes? Labor in the age of "global" capitalism*, edited by Ellen Meiksins Wood et al. New York: Monthly Review Press.

Grown, K., and J. Sebstad. 1989. Towards a wider perspective on women's employment. *World Development* 17, no. 7:937-52.

Harcourt, Wendy. 1998. Rethinking difference and equality: Women and the politics of place. SID programme report. Rome: Society for International Development.

Harrison, Bennett, and Barry Bluestone. 1988. *The great U-turn: Corporate restructuring and the polarizing of America*. New York: Basic Books.

Harrison, Graham. 2001. Bringing political struggle back in: African politics, power and resistance. *Review of African Political Economy* 28, no. 89:387-402.

Hart, Michael. 1994. *Decision at midnight: Inside the Canada-US free-trade negotiations*. Vancouver: UBC Press.

Harvey, David. 1998. The geography of class power. In *The socialist register 1998: The Communist Manifesto now*, edited by Leo Panitch and Colin Leys. London: Merlin Press.

Haufler, Virginia. 2001. *Public role for the private sector—Industry self-regulation in a global economy*. Washington, D.C.: Carnegie Endowment for International Peace.

Hernández, Héctor. 1991. *Solidarismo y sindicalismo en Honduras*. Tegucigalpa: Federación Unitaria de Trabajadores de Honduras.

Hess, M. 1992. *Unions under economic development: Private sector unionism in Papua New Guinea*. Melbourne: Oxford Univ. Press.

Home Office. 2003. *Charities and not-for-profits: A modern legal framework*. London: Home Office.

Howard, Alan. 1997. Labour, history, and sweatshops in the new global economy. In Ross 1997.

Howlett, Dennis. 1996. People's movement coalitions: The politics of solidarity. In *From resistance to transformation: Coalition struggles in Canada, South Africa, the Philippines, and Mexico*, edited by Mary Boyd. Ottawa: Canada-Philippines Human Resources Development Progam.

Howse, Robert. 1999. The World Trade Organization and the protection of workers' rights. *Journal of Small and Emerging Business Law* 3, no. 1:131-72.

HSA (Hemispheric Social Alliance). N.d. Building a hemispheric social alliance in the Americas. Available online at the web.net website (accessed March 26, 2003).

———. 2003. The FTAA unveiled: A citizens' critique of the November 2002 draft of the Free Trade Area of the Americas. Available online (accessed March 26, 2003).

Huddleston, Trevor. 1956. *Naught for your comfort*. London: Collins.

Huyer, Sophia. 2000. What constitutes a social movement? The Action Canada Network and free trade opposition in Canada, 1983-1993. Unpublished dissertation. York Faculty of Environmental Studies, York University.

———. 2001. Networks for social knowledge: The anti-NAFTA challenge. In *Citizenship and participation in the information age*, edited by Manjunath Pendakur and Roma Harris. Toronto: Garamond Press.

Hyman, Richard. 1975. *Industrial relations: A Marxist introduction*. London: Macmillan.

———. 2000. An emerging agenda for trade unions? Available online at www.labournet.de (accessed September 18, 2002).

ICFTU. 2000. ICFTU Resolution XIII. Adopted at Congress, Durban. Available online at the icftu.org website (accessed October 12, 2002).

———. 2001. Report of the ICFTU Task Force on Informal and Unprotected Work meeting. Unpublished report. Brussels: ICFTU, September 25-26.

ILO (International Labour Organization). 1996a. *ILO convention on homework*. Geneva: ILO.

———. 1996b. *La situación sociolaboral en las zonas francas y empresas maquiladoras del Istmo Centroamericano y República Dominicana*. San José: ILO.

———. 1999. Trade unions and the informal sector: Finding their bearings. Nine country papers. *Labour Education* 3, no. 116.

ILO/TUIS (International Labour Organization/Trade Union Internationals). 1999. *Trade unions and the informal sector: Towards a comprehensive strategy*. Geneva: ILO/TUIS.

International Labour Conference. 2002. Report of the Committee on the Informal Economy. Available online at the ilo.org website (accessed November 8, 2002).

IRIPCIB (Islamic Republic of Iran Population Council Information Bank). 2000. *[NGOs and Iranian people's organisations]*. Published in Farsi. Tehran: IRIPCIB.

IRIPRSIM (Islamic Republic of Iran Political Research Studies of the Interior Ministry). 1999. *[The role and the place of NGOs in the national and international arenas]*. Published in Farsi. Tehran: IRIPRSIM.

ITF Congress. 2002. Motion 6: Organising workers in informal and unprotected work. London: ITF.

IUF. 2001. IUF and NGO group sign global agreement with the world's chocolate/cocoa industry to address child labour in cocoa growing. Petit-Lancy: IUF.

Jackson, Cecile, and Ruth Pearson. 1998. *Feminist vision of development: Gender analysis and policy*. London: Routledge.

Johnston, Paul. 2001. The emergence of transnational citizenship among Mexican immigrants in California. In *Citizenship today: Global perspectives and practices*, edited by T. Aleinikoff and D. Klusmeyer. New York: Sage.

———. 2003. Outflanking power, reframing unionism: The basic strike of 1999-2001. Available online at the newcitizen.org website (accessed December 5, 2003).

Jose, A. V., ed. 2002. *Organised labour in the 21st century*. Geneva: International Institute for Labour Studies.

Joseph, Suad. 2000. *Gender and citizenship in the Middle East*. Syracuse, N.Y.: Syracuse Univ. Press.

Justice, Dwight. 2002. Work, law, and the "informality concept." *Labour Education* 127. Geneva: ILO.

Keck, Margaret, and Kathryn Sikkink. 1998. *Activists beyond borders: Advocacy networks in international politics*. Ithaca, N.Y.: Cornell Univ. Press.

Klein, Naomi. 2000. *No logo—Taking aim at the brand bullies*. New York: Picador USA.

Knight, Graham, and Josh Greenberg. 2002. Promotionalism and subpolitics: Nike and its labor critics. *Management Communication Quarterly* 15, no. 4:541-70.

Korey, William. 1999. Nongovernmental organisations and human rights. *Ethics and International Affairs* 13:51-174.

Korzeniewicz, Roberto Patricio, and William C. Smith. 2000. Poverty, inequality, and growth in Latin America: Searching for the high road to globalization. *Latin American Research Review* 35, no. 3:7-54.

Labour Rights in China. 1999. No illusions, against the global cosmetic SA8000. Unpublished report. Hong Kong: Labour Rights in China.

Ladjevardi, H. 1985. *Labor unions and autocracy in Iran*. Syracuse, N.Y.: Syracuse Univ. Press.

Leary, Virginia. 1996. The paradox of workers' rights as human rights. In *Human rights, labor rights, and international trade*, edited by Lance Compa and Stephen Diamond. Philadelphia: University of Pennsylvania Press.

Levitsky, Steve, and Tony Lapp. 1992. Solidarismo and organised labor. *Hemisphere* 4, no. 2:26-30.

Lewington, J. 1986. Flag-wavers threaten to torpedo trade talks, hearing in U.S. is told. *Globe and Mail*, September 12.

Lipschutz, Ronnie D. 2002. Doing well by doing good? Transnational regulatory campaigns, social activism, and impacts on state sovereignty. In *Challenges to sovereignty: How governments respond*, edited by John Montgomery and Nathan Glazer. New Brunswick, N.J.: Transaction.

Lipschutz, Ronnie D., with Judith Mayer. 1996. *Global civil society and global environmental governance.* Albany, N.Y.: State Univ. of New York Press.

Lipsky, Michael. 1980. *Street-level bureaucracy: Dilemmas of the individual in public services.* New York: Sage.

Locmant, Cecilia. 2001. Informal economy: Trade unions need to recapture lost territory. *Free Union World.* May 5.

Marshall, Judith. 1997. Globalization from below: The trade union connections. In *Globalization, adult education and training: Impacts and issues,* edited by Shirley Walters. London: Zed Books.

———. 1998. Worker exchanges between Chilean and Canadian miners. *Canadian Dimension* (March-April): 37-39.

———. 1999. Personal interview with Sophia Huyer. August 10.

Martínez-Salazar, Egla. 1999. The "poisoning" of indigenous migrant women workers and children: From deadly colonialism to toxic globalization. In *Women working the NAFTA food chain: Women, food, and globalization,* edited by Deborah Barndt. Toronto: Second Story Press.

Marx, Anthony. 1992. *Lessons of struggle: South African internal opposition, 1960-1990.* Oxford: Oxford Univ. Press.

Mayoux, Linda. 1995. Alternative vision of utopian fantasy? Cooperation, empowerment, and women's cooperative development in India. *Journal of International Development* 7, no. 2:211-28.

———. 1998. Women's empowerment and micro-finance programmes: Approaches, evidence, and ways forward. DPP Working Paper 41. Milton Keynes: Open Univ.

McCormick, Dorothy, and Hubert Schmitz. 2002. *Manual for value chain research on homeworkers in the garment industry.* Brighton: IDS/WIEGO.

McCue, Helen. 2001. Cliff Dolan Memorial Award Address, NSW Parliament, December 5.

McNally, David. 1998. Globalization on trial: Crisis and class struggle in East Asia. In *Rising from the ashes? Labor in the age of "global" capitalism,* edited by Ellen Meiksins Wood et al. New York: Monthly Review Press.

Meza, Victor. 1982. *Honduras: la Evolución de la Crisis.* Tegucigalpa: Editorial Universitaria.

Mies, M. 1982. *The lace makers of Narsapur: Indian housewives produce for the world market.* London: Zed Press.

Momoh, Abubakar. 1996. Labour and democratisation: Honest brokerage or collusion? In *Corruption and democratisation in Nigeria,* edited by Alex Gboyega. Lagos: Agbo Areo Publishers for Friedrich Ebert Foundation.

Moody, Kim. 1988. *An injury to all: The decline of American unionism.* London: Verso.

Moreira Alves, Maria Helena. 1984. Grassroots organizations, trade unions, and the church: A challenge to the controlled *abertura* in Brazil. *Latin American Perspectives* 11, no. 1:73-102.

Munck, Ronaldo. 1999. Labour dilemmas and labour futures. In *Labour worldwide in the era of globalization: Alternative union models in the new world order,* edited by Ronaldo Munck and Peter Waterman. New York: St. Martin's Press.

Munro, A. 2001. A feminist trade union agenda? The continued significance of class, gender, and race. *Gender, Work, and Organisation* 8, no. 4:454-71.

Murillo, M. Victoria. 2001. Labour unions, democracy and economic liberalization in Latin America. Paper presented at the 2001 meeting of the Latin American Studies Association, Washington, D.C., September 6-8.

Naranjo Porras, A. V. 2000. *Participación sindical de las mujeres en Centroamérica.* San José: Aseprola.

Nash, Peggy. 1998. Personal interview with Sophia Huyer, September 21.

Newton, Kenneth. 2001. Trust, social capital, civil society and democracy. *International Political Science Review* 22, no. 2:201-14.

Ng, Roxana. 1998. Work restructuring and recolonizing third world women: An example from the garment industry in Toronto. *Canadian Woman Studies* 18, no. 1:21-25.

O'Brien, R., A. M. Goetz, J. A. Scholte, and M. Williams. 2000. *Contesting global governance: Multilateral economic institutions and global social movements.* Cambridge: Cambridge Univ. Press.

O'Rourke, Dara. 2000. *Monitoring the monitors: A critique of PricewaterhouseCoopers labor monitoring.* Independent report. Cambridge, Mass. Available online at http://nature.berkeley.edu/orourke (accessed at MIT website September 10, 2003).

Offe, Claus. 1985. Two logics of collective action. In *Disorganized capitalism: Contemporary transformations of work and politics*, edited by John Keane. Cambridge, Mass.: MIT Press.

Ohiorhenuan, John. 1989. *Capital and state in Nigeria.* New York: St. Martin's Press.

Oommen, T. K. 1996. State, civil society, and market in India: The context of mobilization. *Mobilization: An International Journal* 1, no. 2:191-202.

Oseguera de Ochoa, Margarita. 1987. *Honduras hoy: sociedad y crisis política.* Tegucigalpa: CEDOH and CRIES.

Otobo, Dafe. 1988. *State and industrial relations in Nigeria.* Lagos: Malthouse.

Pacific Islands Forum. 2003. Critical crossroads for governance in Fiji. Background Briefing Paper for Pacific Islands Forum, Aukland, New Zealand, August. Available online at the www.flp.org.fj website (accessed November 28, 2003).

Parker, Mike, and Martha Gruelle. 1999. *Democracy is power: Rebuilding unions from the bottom up.* Detroit: Labor Research and Education Project.

Pearce, David, and Kerry Turner. 1990. *Economics of natural resources and the environment.* Baltimore, Md.: Johns Hopkins Univ. Press.

Pearce, Jenny. 2000. Development, NGOs, and civil society: The debate and its future. In *Development, NGOs, and civil society*, edited by Deborah Eade. Oxford: Oxfam GB.

Pearson, Ruth, and Gill Seyfang. 2001. New hope or false dawn? Voluntary codes of conduct, labour regulation, and social policy in a globalizing world. *Global Social Policy* 1, no. 1:49-78.

Pérez Sáinz, Juan Pablo. 1999. *From the finca to the maquila: Labor and capitalist development in Central America.* Boulder, Colo.: Westview Press. English translation of *De la finca a la maquila: modernización capitalista y trabajo en Centroamérica.* San José, Costa Rica: FLACSO, 1996.

Petersen, Kurt. 1992. The maquiladora revolution in Guatemala. Occasional Paper Series 2. New Haven, CT: Orville H. Schell Jr. Center for International Human Rights, Yale Law School.

Piore, Michael. 1990. Labor standards and business strategies. In *Labor standards and development in the global economy*, edited by Stephen Herzenberg and Jorge Pérez-Löpez. Washington, D.C.: US Department of Labor, Bureau of International Labor Affairs.

Pokhrel, Pratima. 2002. Mapping programme proposal. London: Homeworkers WorldWide.

Polanyi, Karl. 2001. *The great transformation*. 2nd ed. Boston, Mass.: Beacon Press.

Porter, M., and E. Judd. 1999. *Feminists doing development: A practical critique*. London: Zed Books.

Posas, Mario. N.d.a. *Breve historia de las organizaciones sindicales de Honduras*. Tegucigalpa: Friedrich Ebert Stiftung.

———. N.d.b. *Breve historia de las organizaciones campesinas en Honduras*. Tegucigalpa: Friedrich Ebert Stiftung.

Powell, Walter. 1990. Neither market nor hierarchy: Network forms of organization. In *Research in Organizational Behavior*, edited by B. Staw and L. L. Cummings. Greenwich, CT: JAI Press.

Poya, M. 1987. Iran 1979. In *Revolutionary rehearsals*, edited by Colin Barker. London: Bookmarks.

———. 1999. *Women, work, and Islamism: Ideology and resistance in Iran*. London: Zed Books.

Prasad, Satendra, and Darryn Snell. 2001. Globalisation, economic crisis and the changing face of labour relations in Fiji Islands. Report prepared for the Fiji Trades Union Congress.

———. 2002. Globalization and workers' rights in the South Pacific: Case studies of Fiji Islands, Solomon Islands, Vanuatu, and Kiribati. Report. Suva: ILO.

Prasad, Satendra, Jone Dakuvula, and Darryn Snell. 2002. *Economic development, democracy and ethnic conflict in the Fiji Islands*. London: Minority Rights Group International.

Prasad, Satendra, and Kevin Hince. 2001. *Industrial relations in the South Pacific*. Suva: SSED Publications, University of the South Pacific.

Prieto, Marina, Angela Hadjipateras, and Jane Turner. 2002. The potential of codes as part of women's organisations' strategies for promoting the rights of women workers: A Central America perspective, in *Corporate Responsibility and Labour Rights: Codes of Conduct in the Global Economy*, edited by R. Jenkins et al. London: Earthscan.

Pro-Canada Network. 1990. *Experience in the movements: Synthesis*. Report of a Pro-Canada Network Workshop, Quebec, June 15.

Prugl, Elisabeth. 1999. *The global construction of gender—homebased work in the political economy of the twentieth century*. New York: Columbia Univ. Press.

Prugl, Elisabeth, and Irene Tinker. 1997. Microentrepreneurs and homeworkers: Convergent categories. *World Development* 29, no. 9:1471-82.

Putnam, Robert. 1993. *Making democracy work: Civic traditions in modern Italy*. Princeton, N.J.: Princeton Univ. Press.

Quinteros, Carolina. 1999. ¿Juntos otra vez? Los nuevos actores laborales en la maquila. *Realidad 71* (October): 587-601.

———. 2000. Acciones y actores sindicales, para causas sindicales: el caso del monitoreo independiente en Centroamérica. *Nueva Sociedad* 169 (September): 162-76.

Rebick, Judy. 1998. Personal interview with Sophia Huyer, December 8.

Risseeuw, Carla. 1988. *The fish don't talk about the water: Gender, transformation, and power among women in Sri Lanka*. Leiden: E. J. Brill.

Robinson, Ian. 1994. The Canadian Labor Movement Against "Free Trade": An assessment of strategies and outcomes. Paper presented at the conference entitled "Labor, Free Trade and Economic Integration in the Americas: National Labor Union Responses to a Transnational World," Durham, North Carolina, August 25-27.

Rodrik, Dani. 1997. *Has globalization gone too far?* Washington, D.C.: Institute for International Economics.

Rogers, David. 2002. Fast-track faces textile tie-up—industry group plans campaign to kill Buss trade-promotion bill. *Wall Street Journal*, April 23: A4.

Ross, Andrew, ed. 1997. *No sweat: Fashion, free trade, and the rights of garment workers*. London: Verso.

Rostami Povey, E. 2001. Feminist contestations of the institutional domains. *Feminist Review Collective* 69:44-72.

Rowlands, Jo. 2003. Beyond the comfort zone: Some issues, questions, and challenges in thinking about development approaches and methods, in *Development methods and approaches: Critical reflections*, edited by Deborah Eade. Oxford: Oxfam GB.

SAI (Social Accountability International). 1997. SA8000. Available online at the cepaa.org website (accessed December 8, 2003).

———. 2001. *Social accountability 8000*. New York: SAI.

Salomón, Leticia, comp. 1989. Honduras: Panorama y Perspectivas. Tegucigalpa: CEDOH and Depto. de Ciencias Sociales de la Universidad Autónoma de Honduras.

Salutin, Rick. 1989. *Waiting for democracy*. Markham, Ontario: Penguin Books.

Schadler, Holly. 1998. *The connection: Strategies for creating and operating 501(c)(3)s, 501(c)(4)s, and PACs*. Washington, D.C.: Alliance for Justice.

Schneider, H., and J. Stein. 2001. Implementing AIDS policy in post-apartheid South Africa. *Social Science and Medicine* 52:723-31.

Scipes, Kim. 2000. It's time to come clean: Open the AFL-CIO archives on international labour operations. *Labor Studies Journal* 25, no. 2:4-25.

Scott, Joan W. 2000. The "class" we have lost. *International Labor and Working-Class History* 57 (Spring): 69-75.

Seidman, Gay W. 2001. Response to Peter Evan's essay. *Critical Sociology* 1, no. 1:7-9.

Selser, Gregorio. 1983. *Honduras, república alquilada*. Mexico DF: Mex-Sur Editorial.

Seymour, Al, and Tony Wohlfarth. 1990. Memorandum to Bob White, Buzz Hargrove, Bob Nickerson, and Sam Gindin. Toronto: Canadian Auto Workers, October 17.

Silver, Jim. 1999. Ongoing e-mail correspondence with Sophia Huyer.

Sims, Beth. 1992. *Workers of the world undermined: American labor's role in U.S. foreign policy*. Boston: South End Press.

Smith, Jackie. 2001. Globalizing resistance: The battle of Seattle and the future of social movements. *Mobilization* 6, no. 1:1-19.

Smyth, Ines. 1999. A rose by any other name: Feminism in development NGOs, in *Gender works: Oxfam experiences in policy and practice*, edited by Fenella Porter, Ines Smyth, and Caroline Sweetman. Oxford: Oxfam GB.

Sojo, Carlos. 1998. *Reforma económica, estado y sociedad en Centroamérica*. San José: FLACSO.

Spooner, Dave. 2000. *A view of trade unions as part of civil society*. London: DFID.

Standing, Hilary. 1996. The user-service interface in child health provision in developing countries. Discussion paper prepared for the ODA Research Work Programme "Improved Care of Diseases of Childhood." London: ODA.

Stevis, Dimitris, and Terry Boswell. 2000. From national resistance to international labour politics. In *Globalization and the politics of resistance*, edited by B. Gills, 150-70. New York: Palgrave.

Swanger, Joanna B. 2003. Labor in the Americas: Surviving in a world of shifting boundaries, *Latin American Research Review* 38, no. 2:147-66.

Swartz, Donald, and Greg Albo. 1987. Why the campaign against free trade isn't working. *Canadian Dimension* (September): 23-27.

Swenarchuk, Michelle. 1999. Telephone interview with Sophia Huyer, January 15.

Tate, Jane. 2002. Defining home-based workers—who should be included? Discussion paper (draft). Leeds: Homeworkers Worldwide.

Thomas, Robert. 1985. *Citizenship, gender, and work: Social organization of industrial agriculture.* Berkeley and Los Angeles: University of California Press.

Thompson, James. 1967. *Organizations in Action.* New York: McGraw-Hill.

Thompson, Martha. 1996. Empowerment and survival: Humanitarian work in civil conflict (Part 1), *Development in Practice* 6, no. 4:324-33.

Thomson, Don, and Rodney Larson. 1978. *Where were you, brother? An account of trade union imperialism.* London: War on Want.

Traynor, Ken. 1999. Personal interview with Sophia Huyer, June 16.

Turk, Jim. 1999. Personal interview with Sophia Huyer, July 7.

UN-NGLS/UNRISD (United Nations Non-governmental Liaison Service/United Nations Research Institute for Social Development). 2002. *Voluntary approaches to corporate responsibility: Readings and a resource guide.* UN-NGLS Development Dossier. Geneva: NGLS.

UNDP. 1999. *South Pacific human development report 1999: Creating opportunities.* Suva: UNDP.

———. 2000. *Non-governmental organisations (NGOs) in the Islamic Republic of Iran: A situation analysis.* Technical Paper. Iran: UNDP.

———. 2002. *2002 human development report.* New York: UNDP.

UNDP/ILO/University of Queensland. 2000. *Experts' group meeting on the post-conflict situation in the Solomon Islands, report of proceedings.* Suva: UNDP.

US Department of Labor. 1996. *The apparel industry and codes of conduct: A solution to the international child labor problem?* Washington, D.C.: Bureau of International Labor Affairs, US Department of Labor.

Utting, Peter. 2000. Business responsibility for sustainable development. Occasional Paper 2. Geneva 2000. Geneva: UNRISD.

Utting, Peter. 2001. *Regulating business via multistakeholder initiatives: A preliminary assessment.* Geneva: UNRISD.

Varley, Pamela, ed. 1998. *The sweatshop quandary: Corporate responsibility on the global frontier.* Washington, D.C.: Investor Responsibility Research Center.

Voss, Kim, and Rachel Sherman. 2000. Breaking the iron law of oligarchy: Union revitalization in the America labor movement. *American Journal of Sociology* 106, no. 2:303-49.

War on Want. 2001. *The Global Workplace Manual.* Available online at the globalworkplace.org website (accessed December 8, 2003).

Waterman, Peter. 1993. Social movement unionism: A new union model for a new world order? *Review* 16, no. 3:245-78.

Wedin, Åke. 1991. *La "solidaridad" sindical internacional y sus víctimas: Tres estudios de caso latinoamericanos.* Göteborg: Instituto de Estudios Latinoamericanos de Estocolmo.

Weick, Karl E. 1976. Educational organizations as loosely coupled systems. *Administrative Science Quarterly* 21, no. 1:1-19.

Wells, Don. 1998a. Mexico mantra: Labour's new internationalism. *Our Times* 17, no. 6:20, 22-27.

———. 1998b. *Building transnational coordinative unionism*. Kingston: IRC Press.

———. 1998c. Building transnational coordinative unionism. In *Confronting change: Lean production in the North American auto industry*, edited by Steve Babson and Humberto Juárez Núñez. Detroit, MI: Wayne State Univ. Press.

Wells, Miriam. 1995. *Strawberry fields: Politics, class, and work in California agriculture*. Ithaca, N.Y.: Cornell Univ. Press.

Whaites, Alan. 2000. Let's get civil society straight: NGOs, the state, and political theory. In Eade, *Development, NGOs, and civil society*.

White, Bob. 1988. Lost opportunity: Letter to NDP officers and executive members. Unpublished report. Toronto: Canadian Auto Workers.

———. 1999. Telephone interview with Sophia Huyer, September 14.

WIEGO (Women in Informal Employment Globalizing and Organizing). 1999. Notes on trade unions and the informal sector for the discussions at the International Symposium on Trade Unions and the Informal Sector, Geneva, October 18-22, 1999. Cambridge, Mass.: WIEGO.

———. 2001. About WIEGO: Origins and mission. Cambridge, Mass.: WIEGO.

———. 2002. *A policy response to the informal economy*. Cambridge, Mass.: WIEGO.

Wills, Jane. 1998. Taking on the CosmoCorps? Experiments in transnational labor organization. *Economic Geography* 74, no. 2:111-30.

Wood, Ellen Meiksins. 1982. The politics of theory and the concept of class: E. P. Thompson and his critics. *Studies in Political Economy* 9 (Fall): 45-75.

World Bank. 2003. Unions and collective bargaining: Economic effects in a global environment. Available online at the worldbank.org website (accessed August 29, 2003).

WTO. 1999. *Trading into the future*. Geneva: WTO.

WWW (Women Working Worldwide). 2002. *Company codes of conduct and worker rights: Report of an education and consultation programme with garment workers in Asia*. Mimeo. Manchester: WWW.

Yesufu, T. M. 1984. *The dynamics of industrial relations: The Nigerian experience*. Ibadan: Ibadan Univ. Press.

Zakaria, Fareed. 1997. The rise of liberal democracy. *Foreign Affairs* 76, no. 6:28-45.

Zapata, Francisco. 1993. *Autonomía y subordinación en el sindicalismo latinamericano*. Mexico: El Colegio de México, Fideicomiso Historia de las Américas / Fondo de Cultura Económica.

About the Contributors

E. Remi Aiyede is a Fellow at the Development Policy Centre, an independent policy think tank in Nigeria, and teaches political science at the University of Ibadan, Nigeria.

Mark Anner is currently studying at Cornell University and has worked for many years as a union organizer in the United States and as an adviser to the labor movement in El Salvador.

Rainer Braun combines teaching on human rights and development at Columbia University's School of International and Public Affairs with studying at the Freie Universität Berlin. He previously worked in the New York office of the Friedrich Ebert Foundation.

Lance Compa is a Senior Lecturer at Cornell University's School of Industrial and Labor Relations, before which he was Director of Labor Law and Economic Research in the North American Free Trade Agreement (NAFTA) labor commission. An experienced labor union organizer and negotiator, he has practiced international labor law and published widely on labor and human rights issues.

Tim Connor is Coordinator of Oxfam Community Aid Abroad's NikeWatch Campaign.

Ken Davis is International Programs Manager for the Australian organization Union Aid Abroad (formerly known as APHEDA).

Deborah Eade began working in Mexico in 1982 and was Oxfam GB's Deputy Regional Representative for Mexico and Central America from 1984 to 1991. Editor of *Development in Practice*, she has been consultant to various official agencies and NGOs and has published extensively on international development and humanitarian issues.

Jonathan Ellis was Campaign Manager for Oxfam GB in 2000-2001 and led its campaign against asylum vouchers. He is currently Chief Executive of the Empty Homes Agency in the UK.

Peter Evans is Professor of Sociology at the University of California, Berkeley, and is currently researching the strategies being explored by labor movements in the United States, Europe, and the Global South in the face of global neoliberalism.

Judy Gearhart teaches at Colombia University's School of International and Public Affairs and is the Program Director of Social Accountability International (SAI), responsible for research and NGO and labor union outreach. She has worked on women's labor issues in Mexico and is author of the ILO study on child labor in Honduras, where she has also undertaken evaluations for UNICEF.

Angela Hale is Director of Women Working Worldwide (WWW), a UK-based NGO that works with organizations supporting women workers in industries such as garments, toys, and electronics. WWW also helps to coordinate Labour Behind the Label, a network of NGOs and labor unions that campaigns for the rights of workers in the international garment industry.

Sophia Huyer is a Consultant and Research Fellow in the Faculty of Environmental Studies at York University in Canada, and Director of WIGSAT, an international network that engages in and promotes policy research, advocacy, and networking in the areas of gender, science and technology, and new communications technologies.

Paul Johnston is a former union organizer for the United Farm Workers and Service Employees' International Union and previously taught sociology at Yale University. He is Director of the Citizenship Project in Salinas, California, and has a research affiliation with the University of California at Santa Cruz in the United States.

Neil Kearney is General Secretary of the International Textile, Garment, and Leather Workers' Federation (ITWGLF), which represents some nine million workers worldwide. He is also an adviser to Social Accountability International and serves on the board of directors of the Ethical Trading Initiative.

Caroline Knowles is Communications Manager at the Institute of Development Studies (IDS) at the University of Sussex. She previously worked at the Society for International Development in Rome and Transparency International in Berlin and was for many years the Reviews Editor of *Development in Practice*.

Alan Leather is Deputy Secretary General of Public Services International (PSI) and previously taught at Ruskin College, which is closely linked to the UK labor union movement. He has worked for Oxfam GB both in the UK and in India and served for several years in an advisory capacity on Oxfam GB's Asia Committee.

Jane Lethbridge is a Senior Research Fellow at the Public Services International Research Unit at the University of Greenwich in London and a health policy consultant with a particular focus on public health issues.

Ronnie D. Lipschutz is Professor of Politics at the University of California at Santa Cruz in the United States and has published extensively on global politics in the post–Cold War world.

Ruth Pearson has long been involved in research and advocacy on issues concerning women workers in the global economy. She is Professor of Development Studies at the University of Leeds in the UK and Director of its Institute for Politics and International Studies.

Elaheh Rostami Povey is a gender and NGO specialist and lectures at the School of Oriental and African Studies (SOAS) at the University of London. She has published widely on such issues in the UK and Iran, both in her own name and under the pen name Maryam Poya.

Satendra Prasad is Senior Lecturer in Industrial Relations at the University of the South Pacific in Fiji and Associate Professor in Management at Ritsumeikan Asia Pacific University in Japan.

Marina Prieto is an Associate Researcher with the New Academy of Business and a member of the London-based Central America Women's Network.

Carolina Quinteros is a sociologist with a longstanding involvement with unions and women's organizations in the *maquila* sector. She was, until 2002, Executive Director of the Independent Monitoring Group of El Salvador (GMIES).

Joseph Román is in the Politics Department at Carleton University in Canada.

Jackie Simpkins is the labor unions officer at the NGO War on Want in the UK, where she has worked since 1998. She was previously an agricultural researcher in Kenya.

Darryn Snell is Lecturer in Sociology in the School of Humanities, Communications, and Social Sciences at Monash University in Australia.

Dave Spooner is the International Programmes Officer of the Workers' Educational Association (England and Scotland) and has worked in Asia, Africa, and Europe. His recent focus has been on the informal economy.

Index

Also from Kumarian Press...

Development in Practice Readers

Development in Practice Readers draw thematically on articles from the acclaimed international journal *Development in Practice* published by Routledge, Taylor & Francis Group. Each DIPR title includes an annotated list of relevant resources, and the series presents cutting-edge contributions from practitioners, policymakers, scholars, and activists on important topics in development. The readers are ideal as introductions to current thinking on key topics in development for students, researchers, and practitioners.

Other Development in Practice Readers

Development and the Learning Organisation
Edited by Deborah Eade, Jethro Pettit, and Laura Roper

Development, Women, and War: Feminist Perspectives
Edited by Deborah Eade and Haleh Afshar

Development Methods and Approaches: Critical Reflections
Edited by Deborah Eade, Introduction by Jo Rowlands

Development and Advocacy
Edited by Deborah Eade, Introduction by Maria Teresa Diokno-Pascual

Development and Agroforestry: Scaling Up the Impacts of Research
Edited by Steven Franzel, Peter Cooper, Glenn Denning, and Deborah Eade

Development and Cities
Edited by David Westendorff and Deborah Eade

Other Books from Kumarian Press. . .

Creating a Better World: Interpreting Global Civil Society
Edited by Rupert Taylor

Globalization and Social Exclusion: A Transformationalist Perspective
Ronaldo Munck

Human Rights and Development
Peter Uvin

The Charity of Nations: Humanitarian Action in a Calculating World
Ian Smillie and Larry Minear

Visit Kumarian Press at **www.kpbooks.com** or
call **toll-free 800.289.2664** for a complete catalog.

 Kumarian Press, located in Bloomfield, Connecticut, is a forward-looking, scholarly press that promotes active international engagement and an awareness of global connectedness.